ISBN 978-0-282-76456-2
PIBN 10863886

1 MONTH OF
FREE
READING

at

www.ForgottenBooks.com

By purchasing this book you are eligible for one month membership to ForgottenBooks.com, giving you unlimited access to our entire collection of over 1,000,000 titles via our web site and mobile apps.

To claim your free month visit:
www.forgottenbooks.com/free863886

English
Français
Deutsche
Italiano
Español
Português

www.forgottenbooks.com

Mythology Photography **Fiction**
Fishing Christianity **Art** Cooking
Essays Buddhism Freemasonry
Medicine **Biology** Music **Ancient
Egypt** Evolution Carpentry Physics
Dance Geology **Mathematics** Fitness
Shakespeare **Folklore** Yoga Marketing
Confidence Immortality Biographies
Poetry **Psychology** Witchcraft
Electronics Chemistry History **Law**
Accounting **Philosophy** Anthropology
Alchemy Drama Quantum Mechanics
Atheism Sexual Health **Ancient History**
Entrepreneurship Languages Sport
Paleontology Needlework Islam
Metaphysics Investment Archaeology
Parenting Statistics Criminology
Motivational

PREFACE

In the course of preparing this account of the Western Rebellion I have received assistance from so many that it is impossible to mention each person by name, yet there are those whose exceptional kindness and help deserves recognition. Among these stand first my two esteemed friends, now gone from our midst, Dr. T. N. Brushfield, who suggested that I should write upon this subject, placing his notes at my service, and Dr. James Gairdner, who not only read and revised my manuscript, but would have written an introductory note had he been spared to us. His kindness to students and his readiness to help them from his vast store of information drawn from original documents makes his loss irreparable. Two others whose kindness I would have acknowledged have passed away, the Hon. Mark Rolle and Mr. W. E. Mugford. I am indebted to many who have helped me to discover and to decipher documents in the National collections, especially to Mr. E. Salisbury and Mr. S. C. Ratcliff of the Public Record Office. I desire to thank Mr. A. W. Pollard of the British Museum for his kind assistance ; Mr. A. Neale, for copies of the unique ballads of 1548, with permission to use them, and Mr. J. Hobson Matthews for the copy and translation of the Welsh Chronicle. To the authorities of the Inner Temple for allowing me to examine the transcript of the letters written to Lord Russell by the Government; to those of the Bodleian Library, especially the present librarian ; to those of Corpus Christi College, Oxford ;

and to the Archbishop of Canterbury, in connection with
" A Copye of a Letter; " to the Marquis of Salisbury
for allowing access to the manuscripts at Hatfield House,
and to his librarian, Mr. Gunton, for his help in copying
therefrom; to Sir John Kennaway, Bart., to Mr.
Thurstan Peter of Redruth, to the Rev. W. F. Surtees,
late vicar of Sampford Courtenay, to the Rev. W. Lewis
of St. Constantine; to Mr. Lloyd Parry, town clerk, and
Mr. W. H. Bowers of the Diocesan Registry, Exeter, I
offer my sincere thanks for the ready help given me.
Those whom I have not named will, I trust, consider
that my thanks are none the less sincere.

FRANCES ROSE-TROUP.

August, 1913.

CONTENTS

CHAPTER XI

RELIGIOUS FEELING IN EXETER

PAGE

The Cathedral Body. Heynes' election and his troubles. Religion of laymen in Exeter. Dusgate's examination and execution. Suppression of St. Nicholas's Priory. Bonyfant's treason. Hoker's opinion of citizens

CHAPTER XII

THE SIEGE OF EXETER. WITHIN THE CITY

Arundell's advance to Exeter. Appointment of officers. Number of besiegers. Russell supine. Mayor called upon to yield City. Proclamation of siege. Preparations against rebels. Attack and burning of gates. Mine and countermine. Divisions within city. Wolcot's proposed treachery. Taylor's riot

CHAPTER XIII

THE SIEGE OF EXETER. WITHOUT THE CITY

City encircled. Opponents imprisoned. Highways closed. Conduits cut. Attempts to capture city by stratagem. Threat to burn city by fireballs. Protest of Vicar of St. Thomas. Spies. Difficulties of attack. Control of army

CHAPTER XIV

THE ARTICLES OF THE REBELS

First set of Articles. The King's Message. Second set of Articles. Somerset's answer. Council's reply. Cranmer's answer. Udall's answer. Articles considered

CHAPTER XV

THE ROYAL FORCES

Russell at Mohun's Ottery. Demand for supplies. Council's reply. Mercenaries. Departure from Honiton. Loan from Exeter merchants. Government by proclamation. Supplies promised. Estimate of forces. Ottery St. Mary. Description of English soldiers. Plymouth. Soldiers hastened forward

CONTENTS

CONTENTS

APPENDICES

LIST OF ILLUSTRATIONS

LIST OF BOOKS QUOTED

Ames's Typographical Antiquities (Herbert)
Ascham's Epistles
Bale's Leland's New Year's Gift
Baring-Gould's Book of the West
Bateson's Letters of the Bishops
Batten's Henry VII. in Somerset (Somerset Archæol: Proc. XXV.)
Blake's Rebellion of Cornwall
Blomefield's Norfolk
Blunt's History of the Reformation
Brady's Episcopal Succession
Brewer's Henry VIII.
Brushfield's East Budleigh
Burnet's History of the Reformation
Cambridge Modern History, Vol. II.
Carew's Survey of Cornwall
Cecil Papers
Chanter's Barnstaple
Charldon's Sermon
Cheke's Hurt of Sedition
Collier's Ecclesiastical History
Conway Papers
Cooper's Epitome of Chronicles
Cotton & Woollacombe's Gleanings from Exeter Records
Crowley's Way to Wealth
Dasent's Edition of Privy Council Register
Davidson's Bibliotheca Devoniensis
Dixon's History of the Church of England
Ellacombe's Church Bells
Fabyan's Chronicle
Fish's Supplication of the Poor Commons
Fisher's Sermons

Forest's Grysilde the Seconde
Foxe's Acts and Monuments
Froude's History of England
Gairdner's English Church in XVIth Century
Gasquet's Henry VIII. and the English Monasteries
Gasquet and Bishop's Edward VI. and the Book of Common Prayer
Gay's Midland Revolt. (Trans. Roy. Hist. Soc. XVIII.)
Gilbert's (C.S.) Cornwall
Gilbert's (Davies) Cornwall
Giustiniani's Four Years at the Court of Henry VIII.
Godwin's Rerum Anglicanum
Grafton's Chronicles
Grafton's Proclamations
Hals's Cornwall
Harrison's Description of England
Hayward's Edward VI.
Herbert of Cherbury's Henry VIII.
Heylin's Ecclesia Restaurata
Hibbert's Dissolution of the Monasteries
Hoare's Modern Wilts
Hoker's History of Exeter
Holinshed's Chronicle
Homily against Rebellion
Hook's Archbishops
Hume's Spanish Chronicle
" Information and a Petition "
Izacke's Exeter
Jenkin's Exeter
Jenkin's Cranmer's Remains
Jewel's Defence
King Edward's Journal

Lamond's Commonweal
Latimer's Sermons
Leadam's Court of Requests
Leland's Itinerary
Lloyd's State Worthies
Lodge's Illustrations of British History
Lyson's Devon
Lyson's Cornwall
Maclean's Sir Peter Carew
Maclean's Trigg Minor
Matthew's St. Ives
Merriman's Cromwell
Morebath's Churchwarden's Accounts
Nichols's Edward VI.
Nichols's Illustrations of Manners
Norden's Speculi Britanniæ, Cornwall
Oliver's Bishops of Exeter
Oliver's Ecclesiastical Antiquities
Oliver's Monasticon Exoniensis
Pocock's Troubles connected with the Prayer Book
Political History of England, Vol. V. (Fisher)
Political History of England, Vol. VI. (Pollard)
Pollard's Cranmer
Pollard's Protector Somerset
Polwhele's Cornwall
Poynet's Politick Power
Prince's Worthies of Devon
Puttenham's Arte of English Poesie

Relation of the Island of England
Reynold's Ancient Diocese of Exeter
Reynold's Old Ways in Old Days
Ridley's Works
Risdon's Devonshire
Robbins's Launceston
Rogers's Six Centuries of Work and Wages
Roy's Satire
Rudder's Gloucestershire
Russell's Kett's Rebellion
Sandford's Genealogical History
Savine's English Monasteries
Selve's Correspondence Politique
Sleidan's Chronicle
Smith's English Gilds
Smith's Commonwealth
Spanish Chronicle, *see* Hume
Speed's Chronicle
Stowe's Chronicle
Strype's Cranmer
Strype's Ecclesiastical Memorials
Troubles at Frankfort
Tudor Proclamations
Tytler's Edward VI., &c.
Weever's Funeral Monuments
Westcote's Devonshire
Wilkin's Concilia
Wootton's Castle of Christians
Worth's Plymouth
Zurich Letters

THE
WESTERN REBELLION OF
1549

CHAPTER I

REBELLIONS

" Rebellion cometh often to passe, whenas menne be of diuerse opinions
concernynge their fayth and religion : for al be it that many other
matters make one to hate another, yet nothing is there that bredeth
so deadly hatred as diversities of minds touching religion."—CHRIS-
TOPHERSON, " Exhortation against Rebellion." 1554.

IT is too often assumed that the people of England
accepted Henry VIII.'s action in suppressing the
monasteries, and his alterations in Church government,
without demur. They are usually represented as readily
listening to the stories against the monks and watching
them driven from their homes without protest. The
impression left on the mind of the casual reader is that
the only objection to the destruction of the religious
establishments came from those who dwelt therein and
that these were properly punished for their evil conduct,
and that the innovations in religion were eagerly accepted
by all except certain priests, who were by them deprived
of their means of livelihood. The student of history
knows better, but, unless he is well informed, he does
not consider that many men resented the changes : he
looks upon the Pilgrimage of Grace as evidence of a
feeling confined to the northern counties, and, perhaps,

B

he thinks it was due to agrarian discontent which assumed a mask of religion.

Yet, if the Calendars of State Papers are examined, it will be evident that not only Lincolnshire and York-shire were up in arms, but that England, from one end to the other, was permeated with sedition. In the spring, after the Pilgrimage, no less than twenty-three different cases of sedition are mentioned : seditious preaching at Bristol ; seditious songs at Diss, Norfolk ; sedition in Wales, Salisbury, Oxford, Sussex, Devon, Kent, and Cornwall ; indeed, on all sides there was sedition which needed to be dealt with sternly to prevent it from spreading.

Had the Northern men succeeded in marching to London adherents would have flocked to their standard from all parts of the country. But history records Henry's treacherous methods to prevent their advance and his terrible vengeance.

Nor were plots and abortive risings confined to that year. In Somerset rebels were executed in April, 1536— that is, before the Pilgrimage,[1] and we find traces of risings in nearly every year down to the date of the Western Rebellion—one of some moment occurred in Yorkshire, resulting in the condemnation of sixty persons, including Sir John Nevil, which was followed immediately by the brutal execution of the aged Countess of Salisbury.

The legitimacy of armed remonstrance against a tyrant who acted in opposition to the welfare of the commonwealth was much argued at this period. Fore-most among the upholders of this doctrine was Reginald Pole, afterwards Cardinal. He firmly maintained the constitutional right of the English people to rise against their King when the country was ill-governed in order to compel him to change his ministers. If he refused

---

[1] In May, 1537, the following year, there was much ill-feeling against Mr. Horner—the original Jack Horner, probably—because he had executed certain Western men taken at " Nonye " (L. & P. XII. i. 1194).

to listen to the righteous complaints of his people they could depose him—only it was essential that both the commons and peers of the realm should combine to dictate to the king. This proposition had the authority of custom until comparatively recent times, and in the coronation ceremonies it was recognised by inference that the king ruled by the sufferance of the people. This was especially true of Henry VII., whose usurpation of the throne was legalised by the acceptance of the fact by the nation. Hence Pole argued that the insurrections caused by the high-handed proceedings in regard to the monasteries, his unjust execution of many of the nobility, and his oppressive taxation—all due to the advice of evil counsellors, low-born men, not of the nobility—were constitutionally justifiable, and that Henry should of right be deposed. Wherever the risings were but the motion of the common people they might be ignored, but as soon as representatives of the higher estate, either temporal or spiritual lords, joined them, then the movement became of importance, and legitimately claimed support ; they were even justified in seeking the assistance of foreign potentates to aid them in their righteous cause.

Viewed from this standpoint, the action of the Northern men assumed a legitimate aspect, and their success in fulfilling these constitutional requirements by obtaining such general support from the nobility renders the movement of greater moment than is usually admitted. Apart from its own importance in the history of England it has a particular interest as a precursor of the Western Rebellion, so no excuse is offered for a brief account of it, particularly as many of the ideas and even acts were imitated by the later insurgents.[1]

---

[1] The four writers who have dealt with this subject at some length are Froude, Gasquet, Dixon, and Fisher. While use has been made of the documents they quote much additional information has been gleaned from papers in the Public Record Office.

Early in the summer preceding the Pilgrimage, rumours were afloat concerning the discontent in the North, which was soon aggravated by the issue of three commissions by the Crown—one to collect the subsidy, another to carry out the suppression of the abbeys, and the third to examine into the efficiency of parish priests with power to eject them—" each of which would have tried the patience of the people if conducted with the greatest prudence and at the happiest opportunity." [1]

Rumour told of the sacrilegious use of sacred vessels and vestments ; that a payment must be made for every christening, wedding, and burial ; that one church only was to be allowed to remain for every seven or eight miles ; that jewels, crosses, etc., were to be removed, leaving but one chalice, and that of tin ; that a tax was to be levied on all unmarked cattle ; that all who ate pig, goose, or capon in his house must pay certain dues to the King; and that all the gold in the country must be taken to the Tower to be " touched." " Every element," writes Froude, " necessary for a great revolt was thus in motion."

At Hexham the Commissioners for the Dissolution encountered armed resistance from the monks of the Abbey, before which they retired. The Bishop of Lincoln's Chancellor roused the wrath of the priests of his diocese by his examination, while the people did " grudge and murmur " at the new opinions touching our Lady and Purgatory, or were shocked by the rumours of the removal of church goods ; both united in complaining of Cromwell, " the false traitor," Audeley and Rich, " the two false pen-clerks," and the heretic bishops, and demanded the removal of such plebeian counsellors from the King's entourage. But discreet priests warned the people not to meddle with the King's Highness, but to seek only the repression of heresies and the maintenance of the faith of Christ.

[1] Froude, III. p. 96.

Louth was a centre of discontent, so when a " singing-man " there suggested following the crosses in procession ere they were taken from them, the people eagerly followed his advice and promptly took steps to prevent their church jewels from being handed to the Bishops' Commissary, who was about to visit the town. The next day, when the Commissioner sent by Cromwell arrived, they set upon him, threatening to kill him. He only escaped by swearing to be true to God, the King and the Commonalty. Soon after he took this oath, the Bishop's Registrar got down at the Saracen's Head, where he was seized, deprived of his books, and hustled to the market-place, preceded by a man with a burning brand to start a bonfire of his books. A monk tried to help him rescue some of the most important papers, but was first made to read their contents; whenever the King's name was mentioned the people reverently bared their heads. The Registrar was at last forced to climb the market-cross and cast his books into the flames, to which were added all the English service-books, Testaments, etc. The Registrar barely escaped with his life.

Balked of this prey, the enraged crowd rushed to Leyborne Abbey, outside the town, which had been recently suppressed, where they captured the caretakers and placed them in the stocks. Report said that one had been hung and the other, covered with a bull's hide, had been baited to death ; but, in fact, they were put safe in prison to save them from the fury of the mob.

The Commons, now thoroughly roused, obliged all the gentlemen they met to join their cause under threats of hanging them at their own door-posts, while the priests were commanded to bring all their parishioners next day to a great meeting at Caistor. The men of Horn-castle followed the example of their neighbours, swearing in, among others, Sir William Sandys, whom they " harried forth by the arms," and Dr. Reynes, the

Bishop's Chancellor, whom they dragged from his sick-bed at Bolingbroke to Horncastle. When he arrived under escort, the people shouted, " Kill him ! kill him ! " dragging him from his horse, and, as he knelt, piteously begging his life, they beat him to death with their staves, then stripped him and distributed his money to the poor.

The Commissioners and Justices who were to meet at Caistor, hearing of these doings, and that ten thousand men were assembled from the surrounding district, retired discreetly and precipitately, leaving the insurgents to repeat in Caistor the scene enacted at the burning of the books at Louth.

The Commons were not without sympathisers among the gentry, while some joined them in order to convert the movement into a more orderly demonstration. The brothers Dymocke, one of whom was Sheriff, were readily accepted as leaders, and when they propounded certain articles, the crowd accepted them with acclamation.

These six articles complained of the dissolution of religious houses and the consequent destitution of the " pooralty of the realm " ; of restraints imposed on the transfer of property by the "statute of uses"; of the grant of the tenths and first-fruits of spiritual benefices to the King ; of the payment of the subsidy ; of the presence of Cromwell, Rich, and other such persons in the King's council, and of the promotion of the Arch-bishop and others who had " clearly subverted the faith of Christ." [1]

Meanwhile, some of the Commissioners who had gone to Caistor had been made prisoners, and were forced to write to the King that they had taken the oath to be

[1] L. & P. XI. 70, lvii. The Articles are given practically as above by Gasquet and vary little from those in L. & P. XI. 703, except that they are in a different order and conclude with " Think the beginning of all this trouble was the bishop of Lincoln." Froude gives another variant. It is curious to compare these demands with those of the Western insurgents.

true to him and to the Commons, and to ask for their captors' pardon, or else " we be never like to see your Grace or our own houses," adding that the Commons protested their loyalty to the King and would defend his person.[1]

Thomas Moigne, one of the Commissioners who escaped, tried to pacify the mob by explaining that the rumoured removal of Church goods was false, but failing, and fearing the worst, he ordered his servants to bring into the great hall all his harness. A neighbour's servant arrived while he was thus occupied, and soon spread the news of his preparations, with the result that he was captured.

The Commons, too, armed themselves with a motley assortment of weapons. A monk confessed later that at one time or another he had a sword and buckler, a javelin, a breastplate, sleeves of mail, and a gorget. One man took from a tomb Sir Lionel Dymocke's armour and standard. A banner was devised by pinning a painting of the Trinity to a towel fastened to a pole, but later a more suitable banner was made of linen painted with a plough, a chalice, and host, the Five Wounds of Christ, and a horn : the plough to encourage husbandmen ; the chalice in memory of the church jewels they were to lose ; the Five Wounds as they were fighting in Christ's cause ; and a horn for Horncastle.[2]

Many of the gentry joined the Commons, willingly, or by coercion, but in vain did they explain about the subsidy, deny the removal of Church goods, and urge the people to remain at home to attend to their farming operations. All they could do was to persuade them that the Articles should be revised, as " they were

[1] Compare this protest with the conclusion of the Articles of the Western rebels in Chap. XIV.

[2] See Trotter's confession, L. & P. XII. i. 70. Froude has " the taking of Horncastle," which was never besieged, and Gasquet has " for taking of horned cattle." Trotter's evidence reads : " tokeing Hornecastell," which seems more likely to mean " token of Horncastle."

wondrous unreasonable and foolish," and that they should wait until these were submitted to the King.

By this time the rebels had reached Lincoln, and, although they already distrusted the gentlemen, they, " the poor beadmen the commonalty of the shire of Lincoln," signed the revised Articles on October 9th, and these were forwarded through Lord Shrewsbury to the King.

While matters were thus being settled by their leaders in the Chapter-house, news came from Beverley that the inhabitants had risen and desired to know for what they were fighting, and men from Halifax reported that their district was up. Thus encouraged, the " commons must needs go forward, but the gentlemen stayed them at the risk of their lives, saying it would be high treason not to await the King's answer."

A hundred thousand rebels, it was estimated, were assembled near Lincoln. To them a letter from the King was read, but their suspicions were excited by the omission of a paragraph,[1] and they endeavoured to entrap the gentlemen assembled in the Chapter-house ; but these made their escape by another door. The next day the thwarted Commons, threatening revenge, were overawed by finding the gentlemen with their faithful servants in harness, and consented to wait for the King's answer, which was brought that night by Lancaster Herald, and read next day in the Castle garth to the assembled multitude. On that occasion " Mr. Lancaster," the herald, used himself so wisely that, after much persuasion, the Commons agreed to go home, and many of the gentlemen joined the Royal forces.[2]

So ended the Lincolnshire rising, but one hundred

[1] Perhaps this was the sentence thus condensed in the Calendar, " This assembly is so heinous that unless you can persuade them for the safety as well of your lives as theirs to disperse, and send 100 of the ringleaders with halters about their necks to our lieutenant . . ." etc.

[2] Although so successful the poor man was afterwards beheaded for his action on this occasion.

rebels are said to have been taken to London, tried, and condemned by jurors who were undoubtedly coerced by the Crown. All but thirty were pardoned; among those executed being the Abbot of Barlings and a monk of Kirkstead. But these were not the only victims; martial law was proclaimed, and Henry himself gave instructions as to the number of captains of Louth, Horncastle, and Caistor who were to be detained, adding that if Norfolk had proof of a new movement he was to "run upon them (the rebels) and with all extremity . . . destroy, burn and kill man, woman and child (to the) terrible example of others, and especially the town of Louth." He refused to listen to Norfolk's suggestion that he should not further exasperate the people.

So many events in the Western Rebellion of a decade later resembled those described above, that we are tempted to fill certain provoking gaps in the more recent history with details similar to those of the earlier rising. It is not necessary here to touch upon Henry's efforts to collect his forces, his pompous and scornful reply, and his ill-kept promises of pardon, for this insurrection melted as if by magic, and his measures for repression were not completed until after the people had returned to their homes.

This first up-flaring was followed by a greater blaze— as happened in the Western Rising. Henry had scarcely heard of the quiet dispersal of the rebels before a flying post brought news of a rising in Yorkshire, which was destined to assume larger proportions. The acknowledged leader of this was Robert Aske, who had been swept into the previous rising, and had sworn to maintain the cause of God, the King, and the Commons. At first vacillating and undecided, he soon found himself called upon to take active part with the rebels. Proclamations were issued either by him or in his name, and people of the better sort, men of position and title, joined the Commons. They, recognising the determination of the

Commonalty to protest actively against the present *régime*, used their influence to make the movement a reasonable demonstration.   The Articles already devised were re-arranged, modified and extended, and they proposed to perform a peaceful journey to London— the real Pilgrimage of Grace—there to present their petition to the King himself. Aske's frequent, and usually successful, attempts to prevent bloodshed and robberies, and his strenuous endeavour to restrain the people in the later risings, point to his honest conviction that their ends might be peaceably attained. He was determined to have no sordid motives attributed to this Pilgrimage ; it was rumoured that the insurrection was really against the imposition of unjust taxes, so he issued a proclamation denying this and asserting that they had assembled because evil-disposed persons in the King's Council sought to destroy the Church and to rob the whole body of the realm.

" Whether this be true we put it to your consciences, and if you fight against us and win, you put both us and you and your heirs and ours in bondage forever.   Therefore if you will not come with us we will fight against you and all that stop us."

Moreover, the oath administered to the rebels was—

" Ye shall not enter to this our Pilgrimage of Grace for the Commonwealth but only for the maintenance of God's faith and church militant, preservation of the King's person and issue, and purifying the nobility of villeins blood and evil counsellors : to the restitution of Christ's Church and suppression of heretic opinions by the holy contents of this book."

In his own account of the rising, written at the King's command, and in his examinations, he lays great stress upon the fact that these objects, and these alone, were what they sought, again and again reiterating these particular evils and pointing out how universally the insurgents agreed in demanding their redress.

Placing himself at the head of the Yorkshire rebels, and soon joined, willingly or unwillingly, by a number of influential persons, he found himself in command of a large force of men from Yorkshire, Richmond, and the Bishopric (Durham). Lord Darcy, believed to be half-hearted in his opposition, yielded up Pontefract Castle, where the Archbishop of York had taken refuge. With crosses, which had been blessed, borne aloft, and banners unfurled, the Pilgrimage of Grace marched southward, two banners having the pre-eminence—one St. Cuthbert's, the other with the Five Wounds of Christ. York and Hull fell before them.

By the 24th October, a force of thirty-four or thirty-five thousand men was assembled near Doncaster, which Fisher describes as " a gathering fully representative of the military elements of northern society." [1]

Opposed to them, in the Royal force hurriedly sent northward under the Dukes of Norfolk and Suffolk, were the Marquis of Exeter and the Earls of Rutland, Huntingdon, and Shrewsbury, who were gradually assembling all the men they could muster on the southern banks of the Don. They numbered scarcely more than eight thousand on the 26th October, and many, Norfolk admitted, believed in the righteousness of the cause of the insurgents. As he dared not make an attack with such an army, under Henry's instructions, he temporised. As Aske wished to avoid bloodshed, he accepted the suggestion of a conference which Norfolk made to gain time that he might bring up further levies. At this meeting at Doncaster Bridge, the Pilgrim's Five Articles were discussed, and the Duke agreed to accompany two deputies of the rebels to present these to the King in person ; meanwhile a truce was proclaimed.

With difficulty Aske restrained his followers during the next fortnight while the deputies conferred with the King, who detained them unreasonably long and

[1] " Political Hist. Eng.," vol. v. (Fisher), p. 409.

employed underhand means to detach men from the
opposing force in the interval. Finally the envoys
returned " with general instructions of comfort," followed
by the Duke bearing the King's reply, which the Royal
hand had repeatedly drafted, as the Duke insisted that
no ringleader should be excluded by name from its
privileges.

A conference with the King's Commissioners was
arranged to be held at Doncaster, but the rebel leaders
hesitated to attend because of a threatening letter from
Cromwell, the very man who was considered the cause
of the rising, and who was, for various reasons, so
cordially hated in the North that Aske said that the
people would like to eat him.

As the Commissioners advanced the bells were rung
backward, and Norfolk, in alarm, sent desperate letters
to the King, " as though the world should be in a manner
turned upside down unless we," wrote Henry, angrily,
" would in certain points condescend to the petition of
the rebels." But he advised Norfolk, if his force was
insufficient, to temporise further, making any promises,
the King reminding him that " in the end you said you
would esteem no promise you should make to the rebels,
nor think your honour touched in the breach and viola-
tion of the same."

Meanwhile, at their conference at York, the insurgents
urged that the King's actions were so suspicious that the
country north of the Trent should be made sure, and that
they should refuse to meet the Commissioners at all.
But peaceful counsels prevailed, and they agreed to the
Doncaster meeting, and also to call upon the Archbishop
of York to summon an assemblage of divines to discuss
the religious grievances. When the King heard this, he
was very angry, as he had been told that the Northern
gentlemen had unwillingly joined the rebels, yet now
they proposed to treat with him on equal terms. So he
ordered Norfolk to use all means to discredit Aske with

the nobles, while Suffolk was to practise for the surrender of Hull, and Derby was to prepare for immediate advance.

On the 2ud December, imitating Parliament, the Commons and noblemen met in Pontefract Castle, while the bishops and clergy assembled in the Abbey as if in Convocation, and the written demands were discussed and agreed to in a formal manner in each place.

Backed by this authority, and by a force of some 40,000 armed men, Aske went to Doncaster, where, on the 5th December, he met Norfolk. On entering the presence of the King's deputy, he and his companions dropped on their knees and begged a free pardon before discussing the Articles. " Norfolk, who found his opponents too loyal to be divided by treachery, and too strong to be overcome by arms, promised a Parliament, and a free pardon under the King's seal." [1]

Returning to Pontefract, Aske proclaimed the pardon, at which the people murmured, saying they had done naught to require a pardon. But at last he prevailed, and, with the other leaders, returned to Norfolk. In his presence they tore off their crosses and the badges of the Five Wounds, tokens of their Pilgrimage, declaring that they would wear none but the King's badge henceforth.

So the curtain was rung down on the dramatic scene that ended the second act of the Northern Rebellion.

" The king, in whom good faith was not an article of honour," writes Fisher, " viewed the capitulation of Doncaster as a blot on his escutcheon," so he proceeded to wipe it out in his own way.

We presently find Aske, after receiving a gracious letter from the King, with a safe-conduct, journeying to London, warned by his friends to have relays of horses ready for a northward flight as they anticipated treachery. But he went courageously, trusting the promises of the fickle king, at whose request he wrote a detailed account of the causes of the insurrection, the part he had taken

[1] Fisher, *op. cit.* p. 413.

therein, and the remedies he deemed best suited to the existing evils.   Henry received him with that charm of manner which threw a spell over so many who came in contact with him.   He detained Aske until the 5th January, the very last day to which his safe-conduct extended, indeed so long that, in the light of subsequent events, suspicion arises that the King hoped some one would make Aske a prisoner, as might legally have been done when the guarantee lapsed.   It was such a new experience for Henry to find himself in so weak a position that subjects might dictate terms to him, that he was thoroughly angry, and strove thenceforth to get the ringleaders within his grasp by fair means or foul.

But this time Aske returned safely, more or less elated by the reception he had received.   But he found the insurgents less favourably impressed, and not so convinced of the King's good faith.   Therefore, almost immediately on his arrival, he wrote to his Majesty of the dissatisfaction existing.   Their fears are thus summed up :—(1) They think they shall not have the parliament in a convenient time ; (2) the King has sent for the most worshipful men (apparently to obtain possession of their persons) ; (3) they are in doubt of the pardon by reason of a book lately in circulation answering the first Five Articles ; (4) they fear the fortifying of holds, especially as the Duke of Norfolk was to remain at Hull ; (5) the Tenth is demanded ; and (6) Cromwell is in as great favour as ever, which is the gravest trouble of all.

Aske did his best to pacify the people, and was largely successful, with the result that many thought he had been bribed by the King,[1] while the very fact that he exerted his influence, maintaining that the King's word was inviolable, was afterwards brought forward as proof of his treason.

But the district disturbed was very extensive, and though Aske covered amazing distances, he could not be

---

[1] The King gave him a gold chain.

everywhere, and the distrust of the people was increasing, so it is not surprising that they were easily roused by Sir Francis Bygod and John Hallom, whose abortive rising Aske and his companions tried to suppress. It served no good purpose, but provided the King with a plausible excuse for charging the Commons with failure to keep the agreement made at Doncaster.

From this time forward there is nothing but a wholly discreditable story of Henry's perfidy, of his grasping greed and bloody executions, with the mockery of legal forms; truly the brutal revenge of a thwarted tyrant, while on the other hand is the personal heroism and noble self-sacrifice of his victims.

A straightforward story was told and faithfully maintained by Aske through his rigorous and painful imprisonment in the Tower. Sir Robert Constable's account, equally clear, sustained Aske's statements, while the aged Lord Darcy's tale could not be shaken either by pain or terror. Try as they would the inquisitors could find no evidence nor admission of guilt since the pardon had been received—only ample proofs of their efforts to uphold the King, so these instruments of Henry's vengeance could only draw up a series of articles against the leaders, with their comments or misinterpretations attached.

Because Darcy, to pacify the people, wrote that Norfolk would, as agreed at Doncaster, shortly declare a free parliament at York, where they could show their griefs, the inquisitors note : " Whereby it appears that Lord Darcy continues in his traitorous heart, for he rejoices in the parliament, trusting to have his unlawful desires reformed, which is well known to be high treason." Because he wrote that he would be true to God and the King, and would petition for all good common's wealth, they comment : " Shows he continues in his traitor's heart."

Because Aske wrote that the King had granted free election of burgesses, etc., calling attention to the fact that he had not only done his duty to the King but to the Commons, they add : " Shows he continues in his traitor's heart and rejoices in his treasons." Because he wrote, " Bygott intendeth to destroy the effect of our petitions and commonwealth," and because he promised to try to obtain pardons for some who had joined Bygod against their wills, they point out that this proves him a traitor, as he should have apprehended or denounced them.

Because Constable was too ill to act against Bygod, and had urged him to await the result of the promised parliament they say, " He appeareth to consent to Bygod's action."

And so on through a long series of articles : the very fact that they strove on the King's behalf to hold the people in check was proof of their influence and their guilt : when they told the people that instead of rising with Bygod they should have waited until the spring, when the promised parliament might redress their grievances, it was twisted to mean that they merely urged postponement till a more favourable season of the year.

Although letters acknowledging their services had been written to them, such things were now ignored ; no recognition of their efforts to prevent bloodshed was made, though scarce a man had been killed by the Commons : nothing now but wearisome examinations and personal hardships. Only the blood of the victims would satisfy the King and Cromwell ; the former even broke his solemn promise to Aske that he would save his life.[1]

Cromwell was never likely to forget that scene when Lord Darcy, " careless of life and with the prophetic insight of dying men," as Froude writes, turned, when pressed by questions, and cried—

" Cromwell it is thou that art the very original and causer of all this rebellion and mischief, and art likewise the causer

---

[1] Aske mentioned this promise as he was on his way to execution.

of the apprehension of us that be noblemen and dost daily earnestly travail to bring us to our end and to strike off our heads, and I trust that or thou die, though thou wouldest procure all noblemen's heads within this realm to be striken off, yet shall there one head remain that shall strike off thy head."

Bravely they met their fates, quietly petitioning for mercy, but with no abject cry like Cromwell's, when his fall came, and asking for the last rites of the Church on whose behalf they suffered. So they passed from their earthly tribunal, with its mockery of justice, to meet another judgment.

Meanwhile Henry was busy writing to Norfolk " to try and to execute " the northern rebels. When jurors refused to convict against their conscience on slender evidence, their names—sometimes even their persons— were to be sent up to London to be dealt with, and more compliant jurors were to be substituted. Norfolk, smarting under a rebuke for previous leniency, executed recklessly, seventy-four victims being suspended from the walls of Carlisle alone, while a list of those executed by his lieutenants bears witness to a terrible vengeance.[1]

Moreover, with diabolical cruelty, Norfolk caused the jurors at the trials of the rebels to be chosen from their nearest kin and warmest friends in order to test the fidelity of these to the King.[2]

In consequence of the many executions the country suffered from the putrefying of the corpses, and when

---

[1] Froude ignores all this aftermath of slaughter and remarks that only twenty out of 50,000 Lincolnshire rebels suffered, though under martial law each village added one at least to the quota. He praises "the gentleness with which the late insurgents had been handled."

[2] "With few exceptions they are very near of kin to those indicted. They have shown themselves true subjects and have deserved the King's thanks" (Norfolk to the King, L. & P. XII. i. 1172). In his glorification of Henry VIII. Froude gives the relationship of the jurors as a reason why Levering escaped and the consequent necessity of packing the juries. He overlooked or ignored Norfolk's letter boasting of this refinement of cruelty.

these were in some cases cut down and given Christian burial inquisition was made, only to find that it was the work of faithful wives or children, to whom clemency was to be extended.[1]

Nor were the dangers incurred under the law all that these sorrowing relatives suffered : in several instances the contact with the corpses caused the death of those who handled them.

But the King was not only greedy of blood, but of money. If any monk could be convicted of treason by any stretch of the law, all the possessions of his Abbey were confiscated, and many a " religious was hanged "— a sacrilege not then so familiar as it soon became. Before men were convicted by the coerced juries he disposed of their estates, and, a little later, he passed through the North with his then Queen, " like a destroying angel," fining his subjects on any excuse, and obtaining vast sums of money in propitiation. Yorkshire had good reason to remember the terrible vengeance wreaked on all those connected with the Pilgrimage of Grace.[2]

The resemblance between this and the Western Rebellion will be apparent as our story is told. The first tumultuous rising without a leader in Lincolnshire is like the early Cornish disturbance at Helston : the former was provoked by the action of the Bishop's official, the latter by the farmer of the Archdeaconry of Cornwall. The leader of the Yorkshire rising, Aske, held a similar social position to that of Arundell. The Articles which the Northern rebels wished to present peaceably to the

---

[1] To Cromwell's credit has been quoted a note saying that mercy should be shown to the women and children—perhaps it was this instance.

[2] Within a decade Fish wrote " A Supplication of the Poore Commons," intended to embitter feeling against monks, wherein the facts are quite unreliable : after referring to the Northerners' demands for their holidays, abbeys and pilgrimages and how they fell into an uproar, he adds : " Yea had not God wrought on your part in apeesing that sturdye thronge this realme had, even then, been like to have decayed. . . . But nowe (the Lord be thanked therefore) that your Highness hath finished that your godly purpose, without bloodshed of your poore commons " (p. 62).

King had their counterpart in those of the Western men, some subjects being identical, while both protested their loyalty to the King and their desire to change members of his Council. In both risings they bore the Insignia of the Five Wounds.

Even in smaller details the later rising was modelled on the earlier : their aims were religious, ecclesiastical changes started their movement, and they both hoped for help from those who were discontented with the agrarian situation.

Henry's action finds a certain parallel in Somerset's mild treatment of the first movement and the sterner measures adopted to punish the later rebels. Strangely enough one of Henry's instruments, John Russell, survived to execute judgment against the Western rebels. Darcy, Aske, and Constable were the prototypes of Arundell, Wynslade, Bury, and Holmes.

The terror inspired by Henry's awful vengeance probably deterred the Northern men from joining their Western brethren. We can but wonder what would have happened if Arundell had been able to obtain support from men of name and substance at a period when the reins of government had fallen from the hands of a successful tyrant into the nerveless grasp of Seymour.

CHAPTER II

THE MARQUIS OF EXETER'S CONSPIRACY

"Of all the victims of the jealous tyrant the Marquess of Exeter is one of the most noble and guiltless."—GIBBON.

AMONG those who sympathised with the aims of the Pilgrimage of Grace there was one whose career is of particular interest to us. The Marquis of Exeter had been sent northward with the Duke of Norfolk to suppress the insurrection, but he suddenly turned westward instead—some suggest that he deserted, but more probably he was recalled by those in authority who distrusted his loyalty in existing circumstances, and was sent to raise levies for the King in the west, in order to detach him from the Northern Army.[1]

The Marquis was compelled to sit as High-Steward at the trial of Lord Darcy, thus carrying out the brutal principle of forcing sympathisers to condemn their friends under the existing laws. High words, as we have seen, passed at the Council board when that aged Lord

---

[1] Froude points out that Norfolk sympathised with the rebels and was therefore chosen to lead an army against them. He adds, in a note, "The Marquis of Exeter who was joined in commission with the Duke of Norfolk, never passed Newark. He seems to have been recalled, and sent down to Devonshire to raise musters in his own country." We can trace no authority for this statement. Lord Herbert of Cherbury distinctly states, after referring to the rebels at Doncaster, "neer which, the Duke of Norfolk, Earl of Shrewsbury, and Marquess of Exeter were encamped with an army" (p. 414). The Spanish Chronicler, who cannot be trusted but who gives rumours, says that the Marquis with five other gentlemen were given as hostages by the King to Aske (p. 36).

turned upon Cromwell. It was stated that Cromwell, in order to induce the council to condemn Darcy, promised to do his best to save Darcy from loss of life or goods ; but, like other promises, having served its purpose, it was lightly broken. Such action would have helped to embitter the ill-feeling existing between the upstart and the descendant of kings.

The father of the Marquis, Sir William Courtenay, had married Katherine, daughter of Edward IV. This connection with the House of York led Henry VII. to imprison Sir William for fear he might conspire against the occupant of the throne ; as an excuse a charge of having corresponded with Edmund de la Pole was pre-ferred against him. His father, the Earl of Devon, died soon after Henry VIII.'s accession and the son was pardoned, but he died before the formalities connected with his succession to the earldom could be completed.

Sir William's son, Henry Courtenay, afterwards Marquis of Exeter, about five years the junior of the young King, soon became a great favourite with his royal cousin, so much so that the antiquary Pole wrote :—

" He was soe intimate unto King Henry 8, yt hauinge noe issue hee intended to haue made hym his successor unto the crowne, but afterwards hee fell into high displeasure of the Kinge." [1]

Speed, after reference to the favour shown him by the King, says that when Henry went into France, the Marquis was ordained heir apparent, though at his return, upon grave deliberation, he saw it better policy to pluck him down, than was used in setting him up lest in acting his part upon that infective stage, he put the land to as much trouble as the arreared Duke Richard of York had done.[2]

. At the date of our story, Exeter was considered the next heir to the throne. With the exception of James V.

---

[1] Coll., p. 11.   [2] Chron. (1632 ed.), p. 1028.

of Scotland, Henry VIII.'s sisters had only female
descendants living, and as yet no Queen-regnant had
taught the nation that a female sovereign was desirable.
Henry himself urged the lack of a male heir as a reason
for his frequent marriages. James V. was considered
an " alien," and therefore barred from inheriting the
Crown.[1] The view that generally obtained at this
period was " Edward III.'s theory of a Salic law by
which women, while incapable of succeeding themselves,
could transmit their title to their male descendants." [2]

Exeter's disfavour with the King was largely due to
his nearness to the throne, but was increased by his close
friendship with the Poles, who were also of Yorkist
blood, and Henry dreaded a combination of these two
families against himself.

In 1531, after years of honour, during which dignities
and favours had been showered upon him, Exeter fell
under such grave suspicion that he was placed under
arrest and was in danger of losing his life. The public
heard but vague stories of his supposed offences, and
freely attributed his disgrace to the King's jealousy of
his position and power.

Chapuys, writing to Charles V. on the 17th July,
1531, says—

" The young Marquis has been forbidden to go to Court
for some time, because he has been charged with assembling
the people of Cornwall and the neighbourhood. The Queen
thinks this is an invention of the lady, because the Marquis
is her [Katherine's] humble servant." [3]

[1] Michiel, writing in 1557 on the claimants to the throne in the event
of the death of Elizabeth, refers to " a municipal law of this kingdom,
which prohibits a person born out of England from inheriting anything
within the realm." (See " Mumby's Girlhood of Q. Eliz.," p. 231, where it
is noted that Sir H. Ellis attributes this *vulgar opinion* to the law of private
inheritance being applied to the succession.) Nichols (Lit. Rem. Edw. VI.
p. 562) says that the King was made to refer to the daughters of Lady
Frances and Lady Eleanor as " of the whole blood and natural born within
this realm."

[2] " Political Hist. Eng.," VI. (Pollard), p. 84.

[3] L. P., V. 340. " The lady " was Anne Boleyn.

On the 10th September, he reports that a servant [1] of the Marquis had been in prison in the Tower for having suborned various boon-companions to take part with his master, who should be king some day.

It was about this time that it was generally recognised that the King intended to marry Anne Boleyn at any cost—a marriage which was intensely unpopular with the nation at large, and which must have been particularly distasteful to the West-countrymen, as the prospects of the Marquis's succession were likely to be ruined thereby. He was immensely popular in the West, not only because of his ancestral position, but for his personal charm. In a document preserved at Rome there is this quaint description of him—

" The Marquis of Exeter, 36 [years of age], lusty and strong of power, specially beloved, diseased often with the gout and next unto the Crown of any one within England " ; [2]

while Holinshed states that he was beloved by most people " for his sundry virtues."

Of his personal appearance a few years later there is this brief but graphic description. After referring to his ability to speak both French and Latin, Gulphinus Abevan says he " had a long beard and a great cut upon the one cheek, as with a sword, and a like cut upon his nose." [3]

With his charm of manner and with the unpopularity of the King's actions daily increasing, it is not strange that the ardent admirers of the Marquis, especially his servants who foresaw advancement with their master, boasted that he should " wear the garland " some day, and in the ale-house with loosened tongue, bragged of his and their intended doings in the future.

Reports of such boasts reached Cromwell through

[1] This, of course, refers to Kendall.
[2] Brady's Epis. Suc. III. p. 493.
[3] L. & P. XIII. ii. 267 (²).

his spies, and, in consequence, every effort was made to incriminate the Marquis and his followers. To this end two West-countrymen, personal servants of the King, were sent to Cornwall as spies. These were " Roger Becket [1] gentleman huissher of his graces chamber and John Worthe, sewer of the same." [2]

When they reached those parts they were to behave—

" not as being thither sent for the compassing of any such matters to them committed, but as to visit their friends and pass the time with the same in that country using themselves after such secret fashion as they be not espied to intend any purpose other than as before expressed."

That is, they were to espy upon the actions of William Kendall,[3] and to deliver a letter to John Thomas, Serjeant-at-the-Arms, who had already been instructed to watch the same man. If they were able to entangle Kendall or any others, such were to be sent up under close guard to the King, wherever he might be. Attention was called to Kendall's large household for a man in his

[1] Roger Beckett was a younger son of John Beckett of Cartuther in Menheniot. The eldest son, Gilbert, married Elizabeth, widow of Edward Kendall, elder brother of William Kendall, but she died in 1513. A daughter married Thomas Coryton and a son married Peter Coryton's daughter. It is probable that Gilbert Beckett suffered in connection with this conspiracy ; his lands appear among the Crown possessions as " late of Gilbert Beckett, attainted" in 35 H. VIII. His Inq. p. m. is dated 24 H. VIII., that is, 1532–3, about this period. In the evidence of " the old accusation against the Marquis " is the testimony of Gilbert Beckett, Peter Coryton as well as Roger Beckett and John Worthe.

[2] Cotton Appx. 1, 89. This original document is much injured by fire, but an early transcript is among the Harl. MSS. (No. 296). This was printed in Archæologia, XXII. 20, but contains many errors and misleading notes.

[3] William Kendall, of "Westmarght, Duloe and Treworgy," was second son of John Kendall of Pelynt, and was a gentleman of substance. He married Margaret, daughter of Oliver Wyse of Sydenham and widow of Thomas Pyne of Ham in Morwenstowe. He was a quarrelsome and boastful character to judge from his numerous law-suits and from contemporary letters. Edgecombe wrote in 1538 that the two Kendalls, recently made justices, had scarcely enough substance according to the statute, and were the greatest " bayhers " in the country.

position, and to his action in retaining men ostensibly on behalf of his master the Marquis.

The result of their researches the two spies embodied in a " book," [1] the first deposition being that of Gilbert Beckett, brother, and probably host, of the Gentleman Usher. From this it appears that shortly before a quarrel had arisen between Lord Mountjoy, Exeter's father-in-law, and Sir Anthony Willoughby, which not only led to intensely bitter feeling between their servants, but to the death of Thomas Rede, a partisan of Willoughby. At the inquest, held in the West country, the jurors were challenged, but Phillips, the Marquis's servant, interfered and forced them to bring in a verdict that Rede " died of God's visitation," and was not murdered.

Willoughby's cause was espoused by the King and the Duke of Suffolk, which enraged the followers of Mountjoy and the Marquis. They declared they cared not for King nor Duke ; their master, the Marquis, would " wear the garland " some day ; " the King would have a breakfast before Michaelmas day that he had never more such," with similar angry remarks.

All these were carefully noted, and that Kendall was retaining men for the Marquis and that Quyntrell, his recruiting officer, had asserted that if the King married the Lady Anne there would be need of such good men. Another declared that the Marquis was heir-apparent, head of all this country and the " best man's master that ever was," while George Boys of Chard, referring to the Marquis's heirship, said that to support his claim " all men being able to bear a batt [2] would go with them." What the gentleman would do he could not tell.

The result was that an adverse report concerning Kendall, Quyntrell, and another named Harrys [3] was

[1] Probably the identical book is that preserved in the Record Office.

[2] Batt—cudgel, staff (Halliwell's Dict.).

[3] The Marquis had two servants named Harris, and a daughter of John Beckett married John Harrys of Laneast.

made to Sir Thomas Arundell, Sir William Courtenay, and Sir Thomas Denys, to whom letters had been sent on the matter by the King, and Denys was appointed to take the accused to London, where they were lodged in the Tower. Strenuous efforts were made to implicate the Marquis, but, although banished from Court and placed under surveillance, he escaped for the moment. The Lord Privy Seal even failed to prove any serious charge against Kendall and " his boon-companions," who were soon released. Indeed, so slender was the evidence of treasonable practice against Exeter that Montague at the time said that it was a pity the Marquis was so handled, and maintained even that he had a " just suit depending in the law for that matter." [1]

But suspicion still rested both on Kendall and on the Marquis, while the West Country was seething with discontent, keeping on the alert all who were responsible for the peace of the district. In July, 1532, Sir Gawen Carew and Sir Philip Champernowne sent up a " foolish friar, who spake and wrote slanderous words against the King," [2] and many other such disloyal persons were found in the West.

But matters seemed to have simmered down for a time. Exeter returned to his duties at Court, and, though never in favour with Cromwell, managed to keep out of reach of his arm.

Although the Marquis is said to have favoured the King's divorce at first, he repented of it when the marriage with Anne Boleyn was imminent. It was known that he took Queen Katherine's part, so he was hated by her rival. [3] His wife, the Marchioness, wrote frequently to Katherine, and was godmother to the Princess Mary, on whose accession she was made Mistress of the Robes.

---

[1] L. & P. XII. ii. 804.

[2] *Ibid.* V. 1199. Was this Alexander Barclay ?

[3] Owing to his kinship with the Princess he was permitted to kiss her hand, the only person at Court so privileged (L. P. XIV. ii. 744).

Meanwhile his intimacy with the Poles increased. Their mother, Margaret, Countess of Salisbury and widow of Sir Richard Pole, was the daughter of the Duke of Clarence, brother of Edward IV., so they, too, were nearly allied to the Crown. A coalition between the two families was dreaded by the suspicious Henry when he saw signs of his own waning popularity.

Lord Montague and Exeter were on the best of terms during the period between Kendall's imprisonment and the Pilgrimage. The former disliked the life at Court, and longed to join his brother the Cardinal across the sea or else to be in the West with his friend the Marquis, who seemed all-powerful there. Both peers spoke beneath their breath of the evil advisers who surrounded the King, deploring the influence obtained by upstart ministers and the decay of the old nobility.

" Knaves rule about the King," said the Marquis, " but I trust to give them a buffet one day."

" The world will come to stripes one day," prophesied Montague.

Rash words, these, in face of the new treason laws. When Montague had been accused of repeating secrets of the Council Chamber confided to him by Exeter the Marquis had gone even further in rashness, vehemently declaring that he would be bound body and soul for his friend who would in no wise betray him.

Intimacy with the Marquis was counted dangerous ; the King had personally warned several people of the risk, among them Sir Edward Neville, Montague's brother-in-law. Lord Stafford cautioned Sir Geoffrey Pole, while Montague had warned Exeter himself, for Sir Geoffrey had asked the reason of the strangeness between them and received the reply, " My lord Marquis willed it so because there is noted a certain suspicion between us."

When Neville told Exeter of the King's caution to him, and added, " I may no longer keep you company," the Marquis calmly accepted the situation, replying, " I pray our Lord be with you."[1]

Exeter himself had been advised to have nothing to do with Richard Cromwell, so with all these warnings he could not have been wholly unprepared for ensuing events.

All men's lives hung on a thread at this period, but the kinsmen of the Royal tyrant were in special danger. The King long before declared to the Ambassador Castillon that he meant to exterminate " this house of Montague, which is the White Rose."[2]

Cromwell sought eagerly to entangle the Marquis, every action being interpreted unfavourably. He was sent West to raise soldiers for the King against the Northern rebels, and because of his personal influence and position thousands flocked quickly to his standard ; this was construed that he was all-powerful there, and intended to employ these men against his sovereign ; because he told the collectors of the subsidy to postpone collecting[3] it was attributed to his courting popularity for his own ends instead of evidence of a desire to avoid increasing discontent with the King's proceedings at this critical juncture.

After the suppression of the Northern Insurrection a spirit of discontent lingered in the West. Sir Piers Edgcombe wrote that unless the grievance of those who had lost their horses in the King's service in the north was redressed, it would be no easy matter to obtain their services on a future occasion, while Godolphin wrote anxiously of the people's desire for permission to keep their holy days.[4] This latter question developed

[1] L. & P. XIII. ii. 804.
[2] *Ibid.*, 753.
[3] This was also done in Gloucester and Worcester, the collectors for those countries wrote that, considering the late unnatural and " foleus " insurrection they had forborne the taxation for a time (5 Feb. 1537. L. & P. XII. i. 344).
[4] See L. & P. XII. ii. 152 and 126.

into a serious affair which probably had a close connection with Exeter's fate.

Although rumours of a rising in Cornwall reached the City of Exeter early in April, 1537, it was not until the end of the month that Godolphin wrote to Cromwell on the subject. Heading his letter " Jesus," and signifying his duty and due reverence in humble wise, he reported that a friend, a painter by his occupation, had told him that there came to him a man named Carpysacke,[1] of St. Keverne—

" which is a very great parish : they were the first that stirred the Commons to rise when they came to Blackheath : the blacksmith [2] dwelled there,"

Carpysacke desired him to make for the parish a banner with—

" the picture of Christ with his wounds abroad and a banner in his hand : our Lady in the one side holding her breast in her hands, Saint John a Baptist in the other side : the King's grace and the Queen and all the Commonalty kneeling with scripture above their heads making their petition to the picture of Christ that it would please the King's grace that they might have their holy day."

The only witnesses were the painter and his wife : the former asked the fellow why he would have such a banner, and was told that Carpysacke with John Treglosacke had been to sell fish at " hammell " [3] beside Southampton, and two men of that part asked them why they rose not when the Northern men did for the Commonwealth of the Realme and " now we have promised to help them to this," and they swore upon a book. " We are in this mind and have bought us two hundred jerkins of this sort," and some are to be of

---

[1] Carpysack and Treglosack are names of farms in St. Keverne. Thomas and Maurice Treglosack and Reynold, John and Uryn Carnepezak occur as residents in that parish in Henry VIII.'s time. Aug. Misc. Bk. 77 and 78.

[2] Michael Joseph.

[3] Hamble.

" chamlett." The banner was to be carried with them on Pardon Monday and then it would be known who would follow it. Godolphin tried secretly to gain further information, telling the painter that if they came again he was to follow their mind and let him know and tell them to send the " best of their sect " to come to speak with the painter, for there is no " hedy " man dwelling in that parish.

" By the precious Body of God, if they stir . . . I will rid as many as will bide about their banner by the help of my friends and the King's Grace's servants in that part or else I and a great many will die for it. In that I beseech you to put no doubt, for the country is in marvellous good quiet."

But for one thing he desired Cromwell to move the King's Grace—that the people might " hold the day of the head saint of their church solemnly as they were wont to do," then all the country would pray for the Lord Privy Seal's preservation. He apologised because " saving his allegiance " he must notify Cromwell " or else ye should never be troubled withal till some were sent to God or to the devil." Desiring instruction and with prayers for Cromwell's preservation he closed the lengthy letter " Iwritten at my poor house of Gotholghyn, the xxij° day of April." [1]

Cromwell wrote post haste ordering the arrest of Carpysacke and Treglosacke, and instructing Godolphin to inquire particularly the names of those of Southampton who had approached them. Doubtless he felt that now he would succeed in connecting the Marquis with the conspiracy which he was foisting upon the Poles.[2] Warblington, the Countess of Salisbury's house, was

---

[1] L. & P. XII. i. 1001.

[2] He may have found another link of the chain in the information forwarded from Brussels, 26 May, 1536, that Throgmorton was to cross to England with letters from the Cardinal baked in a loaf, and was to land in Cornwall (L. & P. XII. i. 1293).

within a mile of Havant, not far from Southampton, beside which Hamble lay.

But even when Godolphin succeeded in capturing Carpysacke he found it no easy matter to carry out Cromwell's instructions. He was, he writes, in attendance at every gaol-delivery and assizes, but could not bring the judges to deal with the "traitor Carpysacke." Sir John Chamond, at the gaol-delivery, declined to meddle with high treason, having no authority so to do, while the justice of assize (Mr. Willoughby) was no more ready to accept such responsibility, and, by the way, as an instance of Lydford law, it may be mentioned here that Godolphin desired Cromwell to speak to the said justice—

"that his Judgment be to be hanged at Helston Town his end and there to remain in chains where all his parish-men and many more of that quarter shall daily see him, for the country there about thinketh him to be there but at my command. This judgment your lordship commanded me to see it should be done in example of other." [1]

Such were the orders, although at that date no evidence had been heard against Carpysacke. Throughout the correspondence it is evident that Sir William dreaded a rising, as each letter urged Cromwell to obtain permission for the people to hold "the day of the head saint of their church solemnly," or have their holy day, as this would be a great stay to the country.

Nor was he the only one anxious at this moment: on the 21st July, Fitzwilliam, the Admiral, reported that the master of the "Mawdelyn of Trewrew," through the counsel of three priests, refused to allow his ship to be searched by the customer "feigning a pope-holy pilgrimage to a pardon in Brittany." [2]

---

[1] See L. & P. XII. i. 1126, and Cotton Appx. 1, 75.

[2] L. & P. XII. ii. 301. For "pope-holy," see Furnivall's Ballads from MS. I. 226.

In August Godolphin again wrote that the assizes at Launceston, at which Carpysacke should have been "judged and put to execution," would not be held because of the plague, so he suggested that a special commission should be appointed.[1] The fate of the poor man is not known, but it is pretty certain that he was executed, probably at Helston town-end.

All this, happening as it did in a country where the Marquis was credited with holding almost royal sway, reflected much upon his loyalty, raising renewed suspicion against him. About the same date a rumour was afloat that he and Cromwell had had a personal encounter. The story ran that the Marquis had drawn his dagger on the Lord Privy Seal, who was protected by the " harness on his back," probably a shirt of mail worn beneath his doublet, as he feared assassination, and in consequence, the Marquis was sent to the Tower.[2]

Repeating this story, a boasting follower had said that if this were done by Cromwell's order, the Marquis would be fetched out again, " though the best of the realm had said nay." This encounter was reported to have taken place a fortnight before Christmas, 1536.[3]

But the Marquis was to be more nearly touched than he had been by the St. Keverne incident.

[1] L. & P. XII. ii. 595.

[2] The Spanish Chronicler, who is not to be trusted as to facts, gives an account of Cromwell's fall which indicates that the enmity between the Lord Privy Seal and Exeter was recognised by the gossips. When Somerset and Norfolk complained to the King of Cromwell's large household the Marquis called attention to the fact that forty members of the King's guard and five of the Privy Chamber were Cromwell's " servants," and said no minister ought to have such opportunity to do the King harm.

[3] See L. & P. XII. ii. 51. Perhaps this affair was connected with the trouble of the Lady Mary whom the King was trying to bend to his will. Chapuys writes, 1 July, 1536 : " The King on hearing the report of the Commissioners and the prudent answer of the Princess, grew desperate with anger . . . Cromwell was not free from suspicion. . . . At the same time the Marquis and the Treasurer, as suspicious persons, were excluded from the Council " (Ibid. XI. 7). The Marchioness of Exeter declared that nothing grieved her husband more than being put out of the Privy Chamber (Ibid. XIII. ii. 831 (v)).

It must have been late in 1537 or early in 1538 that Sir Edward Neville warned [1] the Marquis that his bear-ward, William Parr, was in danger of being accused of treason under the new law against seditious words.

While attending the Marquis in London [2] Parr was arrested, and, with another servant, John Payne, was sent by Cromwell, under the Sheriff's convoy, to Gloucestershire for trial. There was again danger of failing to obtain a conviction, for all the " honest persons " appointed by Bishop Roland Lee and the justices for the inquest in the immediately preceding cases absented themselves ; in consequence they were summoned to show cause at the next assizes and also before the Star-Chamber.[3] However, the Bishop found some amenable jurors, and on the 26th February, 1537, " those twain, the bear-ward and his fellow," were condemned for treason, their heads and quarters to be sent to eight of the best towns of the shire.

The Marquis was evidently under suspicion in connection with this case, for in a fragment of a deposition Cromwell asserts that when Exeter was asked who informed him of the bear-ward's arrest, he " was the most appalled man that ever he saw," and " would liever die than disclose his friend," while a servant, confessing he heard the news in St. Paul's, refused to say who told him.[4]

But Cromwell's net was closing around the unfortunate representatives of the House of York. Lord Montague and his mother were known to be opposed to the " New Learning," and in sympathy with the Cardinal. The Marchioness of Exeter had been already

[1] It is not evident why Neville's warning was construed as a criminal offence.

[2] The Marchioness confessed that she told Lord Montague that the King had sent to her husband in his house in London for a certain bear-ward (*Ibid.* XIII. ii. 765).

[3] *Ibid.* XIII. i. 371.

[4] *Ibid.* XIII. ii. 961 (2).

implicated with More and Fisher over the Nun of Kent,[1] while the Marquis was suspected of holding to the old faith, a suspicion apparently confirmed later by the evidence of Mrs. Couper, who had been told by Eleys, yeoman of the horse to the Marquis, that the heretics who read the new books would be " sacked " and thrown into the Thames, and—

" if my Lord know any of his servants either to have any of these books in English, or to read any of the same they shall never do him any longer service." [2]

That he might obtain evidence against the Poles, Cromwell employed one Gervase Tyndall, *alias* Clifton, who had already visited Warblington, the Countess of Salisbury's house, where he incurred much hatred. He had suggested examining her chaplains, and it was perhaps in this connection that Wriothesley in September paid for his double journey to and from Lewes with expenses there for several days, as Cromwell was also at that place on the 27th August.[3] At all events, on the 29th August, Sir Geoffrey Pole was arrested, and on the same day, in the West, a Breton priest, examined by Sir Thomas Denys and Serjeant Rowe, was implicating, by his confession, the Marquis of Exeter. This priest, Abevan, declared that Cardinal Pole had come to England about a year before, had had an interview with the Marquis, and was still in this country.

Though his statement was inaccurate, there is no doubt of the friendship of Exeter and the Cardinal. Years after the Cardinal, writing to the Marquis's son

[1] She had sent for the Holy Maid as her children had all died in childbirth and she was expecting another. She desired prayers for this and for her husband's safe return from the wars. (See Cheney in Trans. Roy. Hist. Soc. XVIII. p. 117.)

[2] L. & P. XIII. ii. 820. It is worth noting that Richard Crispyn, then chaplain to the Marquis, and afterwards one of the divines whose liberty was desired by the Western Rebels, was also mentioned in connection with the Nun of Kent (*Ibid.* VII. 1468).

[3] See *Ibid.* XII. ii. Intro. p. xlix.

just released from the Tower by Mary, described graphically his farewell interview with Exeter on his last departure from England for Avignon in 1531, that is, just about the time of Kendall's first arrest. The Marquis, who was ill, sent for the Cardinal. His first words were—

"Lord Cousin Pole, your departure from the realm at this present time shows in what a miserable state we find ourselves. It is the universal shame of all us nobles, who allow you to absent yourself, when we ought most to avail ourselves of your presence : but, being unable to find any other remedy for this, we pray God to find it himself." [1]

Now that they had Sir Geoffrey's evidence, Cromwell and the King decided that the time to strike had come, so wholesale arrests of suspected persons were commanded.

Sir Geoffrey's statements brought many to the block, but when the situation is studied it is impossible not to feel for him pity and deep sympathy. At the worst he was of unstable character, not wholly trusted by Montague or Exeter, nor did he trust himself.[2]

Dreading the rack, he endeavoured to take his own life, " being in a frenzy, like a mad man." He did not—could not, perhaps it should be—disclose anything that would have implicated his friends in a charge of treason except in the reign of Henry VIII., who had invented the "Act of Words." He was but the tool selected by Cromwell to give a legal aspect to the execution of the so-called conspirators, which was already a foregone conclusion.

Sift the evidence, such as it is, put together every careless utterance and boasting action of the followers of Exeter and Montague, with their own comments on the condition of the affairs of the kingdom, and add every

[1] Venetian State Papers, V. 806.

[2] Froude states, without reference, that he had been in command of a company under Norfolk at Doncaster, and was proved to have avowed his intention of deserting in action (III. p. 332).

grain of evidence extracted from Geoffrey by rack and terror, and you have an indictment that would not be accepted by any Court of Justice, except under Henry's new laws, or by judges except those in fear of royal wrath. No, the crime of Exeter and Montague was one that no evidence dragged from Sir Geoffrey could either increase or palliate. They were possible heirs to the throne, and so long as they lived they formed a nucleus around which the discontent against a cruel tyrant might crystallise. To remove them under the guise of a trial in legal form was Henry's endeavour. It is terrible to think that Sir Geoffrey was spared to see his brother Montague, his friend the Marquis and others executed while he lingered in prison, tortured at first by the anticipation of a like fate, for he was not pardoned at once, and then doubly tortured by a conscience that accused him of precipitating, at the least, the doom of his family, to live on a stricken and a broken man : rather far the brief suffering and the sharp end of the so-called conspirators ! [1]

But we anticipate—though it is futile to go into the details of the farce which passed by the name of a trial. Look at the mass of examinations and confessions—unfortunately the Marquis' reply to searching questions is

[1] Morisyne gives this account of Sir Geoffrey's attempt at suicide : " Desperation had wrought her feate, nowe see howe opportunitie made all thynges redye for hym, his keper was absent, a knyfe at hande vppon the table, he rysethe out of his bed, and taketh the knyfe, and with full intente to dye, gaue hym selfe a stabbe with the knyfe vppon the breste. The deuyll had played his parte, nowe se howe god, as he oft dothe, tourned all the deuels hole worke, to his glory, and Geffreyes saluation. The knyfe was blunte, and so dyd perse : but the wounde as god wolde, was not mortall, and yet as moche as bloud came after the wounde Geffrey began at the last to fere god, to fere hel, to remember into what case the deuyll had brought hym, and then beganne to deteste the slaughter of hymselfe, to wishe he has opened al to gether rather than to haue loste his bodye and soule after that sorte " (Invective, sig. E iiij.) Somerset writing in 1548, to an ambassador in France, warns him to be on the lookout for Sir Geoffrey Pole who had recently fled the country (see draft letter, Calig. B. VII. f. 339).

ack and
. not be
Henry's
>f royal
was one
d either
to the
nucleus
. tyrant
ise of a
terrible
brother
xecuted
: antici-
t once,
.ccused
amily,
far the
:d con-

to the
a trial.
is—un-
:ions is

suicide :
made all
:pon the
i intente
e. The
tourned
.. The
lde, was
Geffrey
:ase the
ghter of
ue loste
omerset
he look-
ie draft

not preserved among them—they are no more than the repetition of two or three insignificant remarks, harmless they would be esteemed to-day; study Cromwell's marginal notes and see the vindictive manner in which he stalked his victims, and one feels a sickening sense of the absolute helplessness of the most innocent person who might be caught in his toils till one is indignant and ashamed that such as he should have ruled England for a day.

As regards the trial itself, legal forms were complied with, jurors were empanelled in each county to which the " conspirators " belonged ; before them were placed certain remarks, practically the same phrases were reported as used in different places to different persons, but that mattered not. The course taken to force the jurors to bring in a verdict of guilty may be surmised from a letter from one of the Surrey panel, who states that he was " commanded by my lord Privy Seal to acquaint the King with the secret verdict." [1]

The charges against the Marquis were these : that he held conferences with Lord Montague : that on the 16th July, 1537, in the parish of St. Lawrence Poultney, London —where his town house was—he uttered these words : " I like well the proceedings of Cardinal Pole." And on the 20th August : " I trust to have a fair day upon those knaves which rule about the King. And I trust to see a merry world one day." Of saying to Sir Geoffrey, on the 24th July, at West Horseley : " I like well the proceedings of Cardinal Pole. But I like not the proceedings of this realm, and I trust to see a change of this world." And, on the 25th August : " I trust to have a fair day upon those knaves which rule about the King, and I trust to see a merry world one day." And, on the 1st September : " Knaves rule about the King," and, clenching his fist, " I trust to give them a buffet one day." [2] Such were the only " crimes " laid to his charge.

[1] L. P. XIII. ii. 1089.   [2] See Baga de Secretis, Pouch XI. mm. 25 & 18.

Briefly stated, we have this account of the trial—

" The Marquis being brought to the bar in his own proper person, . . . and the indictments being read over to him, he said that he is in none of these guilty and therefore for good or evil puts himself upon his peers. Whereupon the said Thomas, Duke of Norfolk, Charles, Duke of Suffolk, etc., Earls and Barons aforesaid [among these were his brother-in-law Mountjoy and his enemy Cromwell] of the said Henry, Marquis of Exeter peers, instantly upon their fidelity and allegiance being charged, etc. . . . from the lowest to the highest, say that the said Henry, Marquis of Exeter, etc., is guilty. And on this instantly the King's serjeants-at-law according to the law and custom pray judgment. Whereupon it is ordered that Henry, Marquis of Exeter, etc., be delivered to the said constable and taken to the Tower and thence through the midst of the city of London even to the gallows of Tyburn and there to be . . ."

And here follow the detailed instructions for a traitor's death.[1]

But this bald statement lacks the picturesque, but probably inaccurate details given by Morisyne. From him we glean that while Croft and Colyns, the minor conspirators, stood stiff against the accusation of treason with casting up of eyes and hands, as if they had never heard these before—

" the Marquis, of all the rest stack hardest, and made as though he had been very clear in many points, yet in some he staggered, and was very sorry so to do, now challenging the King's pardon, now taking benefit of the act, and when all would not serve, he began to charge Geoffrey Pole with frenzy, with folly, and madness." [2]

Geoffrey indignantly replied that he fell into a frenzy when he consented to join the conspiracy, and also when he sought to kill himself, and then proceeded to revile his friends and relatives, Morisyne adding: " Geoffrey

---

[1] Baga de Secretis, Pouch XI. m. 10.   [2] Invective. sig. e v.[2]

hath never been taken for any pleasant or sage talker, his wit was wont to serve his tongue but so so."

It is difficult to believe that even in that age Sir Geoffrey would have been allowed to have spoken as he is here reported. Morisyne continues :—

" The Marquis was stiff at the bar, and stood fast in denial of most things laid to his charge, yet in some he foiled and staggered, is such sort, that all men might see his countenance to avouch that, that his tongue could not without much faltering deny. But at the scaffold, when he saw men's oaths, with a multitude of witnesses taken, and his sturdy denial not to save his life, he began either to weigh dishonour less than he did at the bar, or else to think that dishonour standeth in doing traitorously, rather than in confessing it, when it is known to be so, death at hand, taught him and his fellows to provide for the safety of their souls, and to leave the regard of honour there on the scaffold with their bodies. They did acknowledge their offences towards the King, and desired all men that were there present to pray God to forgive them."

He adds that matters of religion were the cause of their treason.

Such formal acknowledgment of offending the King often made on such occasions, even if done at this time, cannot be taken as an admission of treasonable practices. If an illiterate document still preserved is a genuine statement taken down at Neville's dictation, perhaps by a warder, he at all events warmly protested his innocence.[1] Morisyne's story does not lend itself to credence, and he maligned the victims for a purpose.

Although Exeter and Montague were condemned to be hanged as traitors they were spared that particularly horrible death ; perhaps Henry was ashamed to send to Tyburn his near kin and familiar friends such as they, or he may have feared a hostile demonstration from the people if they were drawn through the city. On the 9th December, 1538, they, with Sir Edward Neville,

[1] L. & P. XIII. ii. 987.

were executed upon Tower Hill, and Exeter and Montague, it is said,[1] lie in one grave within St. Peter's ad Vincula. Others who were implicated were hung at Tyburn.[2]

So was done to death the noble Marquis, " to the great grief of the subjects of this realm, who for his sundry virtues did bear him great favour and goodwill." [3]

A further indignity followed six days after the execution, when he was " disgraded " at Windsor from the Order of the Garter, of which he had been until so recently President.[4] " Traditur " and " decolatus " were written against his name.

There was a tradition in Tiverton, Devon, that an old man of the town warned the Marquis shortly before his arrest that on a certain day, unless he saved his life by flight, he would be commanded to London by the King, and would have his head cut off. Exeter " slighted " this warning, and, on the day named, sent for the old man, whom he called a false prophet, and threatened to punish.

" Sir," said he, " there is a party of horse come to seize you, and they are within a mile of the town."

Shortly after the soldiers arrived, surrounded the Castle, and carried the Marquis prisoner to London, where he lost his head.[5]

In the following March William Kendall and Richard Quyntrell were tried, condemned, and executed in

---

[1] Ashmole MS. 861. Anthony Anthony's notes. He also says that Neville was buried in the churchyard.

[2] Wriothesley (Chron. p. 92) describes their execution, and adds : " After the shrives had brought the sayd persons to Newgate, the Kinges shrive, which was Mr. Wilkinson, mercer, returned backe againe to Tower Hill, and there see execution done on the Lord Marques of Exceter, the Lord Montague, and Sir Edward Neville, which three persons were there beheaded, and theyr bodyes were buryed in the chappell within the Tower of London."

[3] Holinshed Chron. p. 807.

[4] Harl. MS. 6074.

[5] Cleaveland, " Courtenay Family," p. 251.

Cornwall, their judge describing them as being " as errant traitours as any within the Realm of Englond who *levyd* and favoured as much in the advancement and setting forth of that traitour Henry, late Marquis of Exceter that his ungracious and traitorous purpose might take effect," [1] and adding an account of the stern punishment meted out to other accused persons at the same time.

But news of the Marquis' execution could not have spread quickly to the West, as, on the 24th December, nearly a fortnight after the event, Sir Thomas Arundell [2] reported some ale-house gossip that had just taken place at Sherborne. When certain persons present said that the Marquis was in the Tower, and was likely to suffer death, Thomas Holman, a tailor, exclaimed that Devonshire and Cornish men would not permit that.[3]

But when the fact became generally known it caused not only consternation but resentment.[4] Henry would not have taken such pains to " explain " the executions had he felt that the public, especially the foreigners, would recognise the justice of his proceedings. Indeed, the injustice was so evident that Chapuys wrote on the 9th January, that proofs of treason were reported to have been found in letters to the Cardinal in the Marchioness of Exeter's handwriting, adding: " Since the testimony of young Pole is not sufficient, these men, *à l'usage de Carintie*, want to form the process after the

---

[1] Willoughby to Cromwell. Titus B. I. 61.

[2] He may have reported this because of the recent admonition he had received from the King (Stowe MSS. 142, f. 14). For correct date see Blake, p. 8.

[3] L. & P. XIII. ii. 1134.

[4] " If anyone living in happier times be disposed to wonder at all this tyranny and injustice, and how it could have been safely perpetrated on prominent men in a high spirited nation like the English, he must remember the merits of the case were not at all clearly or fully set before the public. The mode of trial always bore hard upon the accused, and if the people at large suspected, as they did, that all was not perfectly equitable, matters of state were not theirs to pry into " (L. & P. XIII. ii., Gairdner's Introduction, p. xlvii).

execution," [1] while Castillon forwards to his master on the 16th January, " a little book in English by the King about the death of the Marquis of Exeter and Lord Montague," adding : " *J'entends que c'est leur procèss fait après leur mort.*" [2]

The little book attributed to the King is very probably the rare tract already quoted : " An Invective against the great and detestable vice, treason, wherin the secrete practises and traitorous workinges of theym that suffrid of late are disclosed. Made by Richard Morisyne. Printed by Berthelet, London, 1539." A less bitter invective against living men would have stirred the righteous indignation of any reader, but such vile calumnies against the dead put the writer beyond the pale. Yet this is no doubt the volume described by the King himself as " a pretty book printed in this our realm." [3]

The pens of Cromwell and Wriothesley were busily engaged in writing highly coloured statements maligning their victims. The King himself sent instructions to his ambassador Wyatt, dated the 13th February, 1539, as to informing the Emperor of events, laying particular stress upon his own goodness and generosity towards the Cardinal, Montague, and Exeter, whom he had raised from nothing,[4] and asserting that—

" By the Cardinal's counsel his brother Montague and Exeter conspired to destroy the King and Prince and the ladies Mary and Elizabeth and usurp the whole rule, which the said Exeter had meditated these ten years, all which have been disclosed by Sir Geoffrey Pole, Montague's own brother, and openly proved to their faces." [5]

[1] L. & P. XIV. i. 37.
[2] Add. MSS. 33, 514, f. 11.
[3] L. & P. XIV. i. 280.
[4] This untruth was surely inserted by Cromwell. As both Exeter and Montague were of royal kin they could not be spoken of as upstarts, *raised from nothing*.
[5] L. & P. H. VIII. XIV. i. 280.

This was a deliberate perversion of the truth, no such statement can be traced in the examinations, nor is it put in the indictment. Nor has a most careful search disclosed the letters said to have been found after the trial, and upon which so much reliance was placed to prove the justice of these executions. If they existed, surely they would have been copied and spread broadcast.

It is quite probable that this story failed to deceive those who read it, and certainly failed to palliate the crime. Scepperus writes that the French were horrified by Henry's abominable cruelty,[1] and Bonner repeats a conversation between " Cardinal Below and Mons. de Bise, Captain of Boulogne," which he overheard. One repeated the rumour that the Marquis would lose his head, to which the other replied : " What with hanging, burning, and heading, they make there a good riddance."[2] Evidently they were satisfied that if Henry continued to exterminate the English they would be spared the trouble and would the sooner come to their own.

Nor was Henry content with letter-writing : he felt he must convince his own people. It was necessary to comply with the law and to force Parliament to pass a Bill of Attainder, which included both the dead and living, those in custody and those in exile, none of whom were permitted to speak in their own defence—an act of injustice upon which even Burnet waxes eloquent. These acts, he writes, were—

" of a strange and unheard of nature. . . . It is a blemish never to be washed off, and which cannot be enough condemned, and was a breach of the most sacred and unalterable rules of justice, which is capable of no excuse."[3]

The Marchioness - of Exeter and the Countess of Salisbury had to be included, but no form of trial was allowed them. The former, it is true, had admitted

---

[1] *Ibid.* XIII. ii. 1053.   [2] *Ibid.* 948.   [3] Ref. I. 579.

some vague knowledge of the fact that her husband had had communications of some sort with Montague and Neville, but against the Countess they had to trump up a charge. Although they bullied and ill-treated the aged lady—for she was over seventy years old—she denied vehemently all knowledge of and complicity in the so-called plot, but she confessed that she had written to reprove the Cardinal for his unnatural conduct towards his sovereign : this they held was maintaining treasonable correspondence with him, while some one swore that they had seen her kiss her son. It was no doubt true that in her heart she disapproved of the New Learning, but was that active treason ?

Parliament was not satisfied of her guilt, and though the Bill was pushed forward with unseemly haste, according to Burnet, they still hesitated to condemn the aged lady of the blood royal, whose crime was not proved to the world. At the last moment, when the Bill should have been read a third time, on the 12th May, 1539, Cromwell produced a piece of embroidery, found among her clothes, overlooked at first as harmless or perhaps placed there by her accusers. It was a tunic of white silk, embroidered with the royal arms of England, namely, three lions, surrounded by a wreath of pansies and marigolds, assumed to be a symbol of a marriage between the Cardinal and the Lady Mary. On the back of it was the Insignia, the emblem of the Five Wounds, borne by the insurgents in the Northern Rebellion.[1] Upon such evidence the Bill of Attainder was passed, and Henry took possession of the property of the so-called conspirators, and eventually, upon the rumour of another rising in the North, beheaded the Countess on Tower Hill.[2]

---

[1] See Journal of the House of Lords, 1, 107.

[2] Hilles, writing to Bullinger, 18th Sept., 1541, says that the King went North " to reduce a rebellious and very superstitious people. About twenty persons (of whom about twelve had formerly been monks) had

If Burnet, the prejudiced historian of the Reformation, after so many years had passed, wrote so strongly against the Bill of Attainder, what were the feelings of the people ? Because there was no insurrection in face of the late wholesale slaughter in the North and with this recent reminder of the horrors in store for those who crossed Henry's will, Froude assumes that they accepted the justice of these executions, but as a carefully prepared *ex parte* statement was put forth as to the "fowle worke," the traitors would have made, and gross misrepresentations of facts were circulated, the public could have only vague ideas as to the truth. Evidence of this appears in Lord Herbert's reference to the crime. He confesses his ignorance of their offences, though he found Wriothesley's statement, written before the trial, that their accusations were great and duly proved, and elsewhere he read that they had sent money to the Cardinal.[1]

Sandford, writing later, makes this comment—

" Nor whether the Marquis had been faulty in abetting the treason wherewith Cardinal Pole was charged, or whether the King packt him in that company for instigating several

endeavoured, five months since to raise a new disturbance in those parts : they were beheaded, hung and drawn, after our custom, the June following, at London and York, which are our two principal cities in the Kingdom. The King, before his setting out, beheaded also the mother of our countryman the cardinal, with two others of our oldest nobility. I do not hear that any of the royal race are left, except the nephew of the cardinal, and another boy, the son of the marquis of Exeter. They are both children and in prison, and condemned, I know not why, except that it is said that their fathers had sent letters to Rome to the pope, and to their kinsman, the cardinal " (p. 219). It is curious that history is silent as to the fate of Henry Pole, Montague's son. Chapuys, June 10th, 1541, says that young Pole, who had been allowed to go about within the Tower sometimes, was now strictly guarded and it was supposed he would soon follow his father and grandmother. Marillac says much the same, but adds that, unlike Courtenay, he had no preceptor but was " poorly and strictly kept and not desired to know anything." His " diets " in the Tower begin 6th March, 1539, and continue till 13th Sept., 1542 (L. & P. XIV. and XVII.)

[1] " Life of Henry VIII.," p. 439 (written about 1649).

foreign princes in the pope's behalf to invade the realm, and raise the Cardinal to the Crown : certain it is, that having the Marquis and his partakers upon the advantage, the better to secure his own estate he caused his head with those of the Lord Montague, and Sir Edward Neville to be cut off upon Tower Hill." [1]

But what thought the people in the West, where the gallant Marquis was so well beloved ? They saw in his murderers the oppressors of their faith, and long felt the rankling wound, desiring intensely to avenge his death. When the brutal execution of the aged Countess, delayed in the hope of forcing the Cardinal's hand, completed practically the extinction of the House of York, a rich field had been prepared for the seed of sedition. The members of the Pilgrimage of Grace, Lord Montague, their own Marquis, his servants Kendall and Quyntrell, and now the Countess ! What wonder that they were prepared to welcome any effort made by Cardinal Pole or others, who sought to stir them to rise against their tyrants !

The King had accomplished his purpose, exterminating the White Rose, and Cromwell's vengeance was sated. With fulsome words the much praised Latimer congratulated the latter—

" Blessed be the God of England that worketh all, whose instrument you be ! I heard you say after you had seen that furious invective of Cardinal Pole that you would make him eat his own heart, which you have now (I trow) brought to pass, for he must needs now eat his own heart, and be as heartless as he is graceless." [2]

There were others eating their hearts out in sorrow and grief, but they bided their time, which came not until Cromwell had ended his life on the spot where his victim the Marquis fell, and after the King had finished his tyrannical rule.

[1] Geneol. Hist. p. 420.   [2] Cleop. E. IV. 264.

CHAPTER III

"It is notorious now in the kingdom of England that boys, young men, and men living in the courts of the worldly, are placed in churches and in great offices and prelacies. . . . I knew a foolish youth, eighteen years of age, who was promoted to twelve prebends and a great arch-deaconry of one hundred pounds' value, and to a great rectory, and a secular man received the rents of all the said benefices and spent upon the said youth just as much as he, the secular man, pleased, and never gave an account."—GASCOIGNE.[1]

NEARLY a decade elapsed after the execution of the Marquis of Exeter before the first Cornish rising took place, but in that interval a number of events occurred which had a great influence upon, and a very evident connection with, the insurrection of 1548–9.

To understand what happened, details must be given of the history of two men, William Body and Thomas Wynter, whose actions had an important bearing on the Cornish rising. The latter, Wynter, is generally believed to have been the son of Cardinal Wolsey, by "one Larck's daughter," and was so regarded by many of his contemporaries.[2] The fact that he was obliged to obtain a dispensation points to some such stigma upon

---

[1] This was written in the fifteenth century, but it to a great extent applicable to the following instance.

[2] L. & P. IV. 5581 : 6075 : 2482 and 4824. Among the charges against Wolsey was "Item of his son Wynter and his fellows, the five open pedigrees and acts, and of the great treasure and charges, yea, and promotions and ordinary yearly rents by him, under colors thereof yearly assembled and gathered, and converted to his own use thereby . . ." (*Ibid.* III. 5749).

his birth. His tutor, Volusemus, describes him as son of the Cardinal's brother, while Wolsey himself refers to him as " my poor scholar." The year of Wynter's birth is unknown ; he held a corrody at Evesham which he resigned in April, 1511, and as he was studying at Louvain before November, 1519, he must have been born early in the century.[1] Through the Cardinal's influence he received many preferments ; even for that day he was a remarkable pluralist. Between 1522 and 1528 he is known to have received twenty ecclesiastical positions, the greater part of which he resigned in 1529, on the Cardinal's fall.[2] During all this time Wynter was pursuing his studies at Louvain, Padua, Ferrara, Poissy and Paris. Once only, in 1519, is there reference to his presence in England prior to his recall on Wolsey's disgrace.[3] On his appointment to the Deanery of Wells, in 1526,

Roy's satire, " The Lamentation of the Mass," contains this verse, answering a query whether Wolsey had children :

> " Ye ! and that full proudly they go :
> Namely one whom I do knowe
> Which hath of the churches goodis clerely
> More than two thousand pownde yerely
> And yett is not content, I trowe.
> His name is master Wynter."

See " Furnivall's Ballads," I. 73.

[1] L. & P. I. 1592, and III. 525. He was granted another corrody in Evesham in May, 1532 (*Ibid.* V. 1065).

[2] These, placed as nearly as possible in order were : Milton Prebend, Lincoln ; Palishall, Overhall and Norwell Prebends in Southwell ; Friday-thorpe—resigned for Strenshall—both in York ; Archdeaconry of the West Riding, York ; Chancellorship of Sarum ; Archdeaconries of Norfolk and Richmond ; Deanery of Wells ; St. Peter's Prebend, Beverley ; Lytton Prebend, Wells ; Bedwin Prebend, Sarum ; Provostry of Beverley ; Prebend of St. Stephen's, Westminster ; Rectories of Rugby, St. Matthias, Ipswich and Wynwyck ; Archdeaconry of Suffolk ; and Wardenships of Sherborne Hospital and of St. Leonard's Hospital, York. Wolsey asked for the Deanery of Lincoln for him. See Le Neve's Fasti and L. & P.

[3] Berkinshaw's letter to Wolsey, 29th Nov. 1519, from Louvain, refers to Wynter, adding that " his friend Thomas had returned safe laden with silken raiment and gold worthy of Wolsey's dignity " (*Ibid.* III. 525).

he received a grant of arms,[1] which closely resembled Wolsey's, and in the same year a dispensation was sought for him.[2]

It is doubtful whether he had even then taken deacon's orders, and he writes as late as 1534 that he had not yet been admitted priest, though Wolsey suggested as early as 1528 that Wynter should be made Bishop of Durham, an office the Cardinal then contemplated resigning.[3]

Throughout these seven years Wynter was non-resident, pursuing his studies abroad, devoted to letters and laboriously acquiring languages, he writes. His letters Brewer describes as models of ease, elegance, and pure Latinity. But he lacked his reputed father's energy, ambition, and ability, as well as his delight in the stormy winds and waves of statesmanship, being of a mild and gentle disposition, unable or unwilling to cope with the hardships of life, still less with the harder times and men of his generation. His taste for literary ease prevented him from making any effort to retain his preferments, which were greedily snatched from him on the Cardinal's fall.[4]

Like many scholars, he paid no attention to business matters, so ever lacked money—a characteristic which brings him into our story. In Paris he lived magnificently, associating with the highest in the land, recognised as the Cardinal's kinsman. His frequent requests

---

[1] L. & P. IV. 2054.

[2] *Ibid.* IV. 2482. Clerk there states that in the dispensation no mention is made "de defectu," either in the minute of the old brief or in the new. He supposes that the brief must have been sped *ad partem super defectu natalium*, " as indeed I am well (aware) that I obtained a signature (but know not) that there was ever any bull sped thereon," and desires that search should be made for it.

[3] See L. & P. VII. 280 and IV. 2424.

[4] See Brewer's Intro., *Ibid.* IV. dcxxvi. Clerk (*ibid.* 4294), in 1528, praises his studious habits and describes his mental and bodily growth, saying he has grown three fingers taller and much broader since Wolsey saw him and promises to develop into a very good and comely man's stature.

E

for money disturbed Wolsey, who fell into the habit of asking any friend passing through Paris to report on Wynter's establishment, so we find many picturesque descriptions of his way of living in letters of the great men of the day.[1]

Wolsey not only took a personal interest in him, but entertained a deep affection for him. In one of his last pitiful letters to Bishop Gardyner, then Chancellor, he begs his influence on behalf of his " poor dean of Wells," and afterwards thanks him because by " his greate humanitie, lovyng and gentle recule," the King has been persuaded to accept Wynter as his " poore orator and scoler." [2] Cromwell, succeeding to Wolsey's office, allowed him to keep a few preferments and obtained for him a few others of no great value.

Wynter returned to England on the Cardinal's death, but did not remain here long. On the 15th January, 1532-3, he obtained a licence to remain abroad and to travel with a retinue of three servants, four horses or geldings, ambling or trotting, and baggage as usual. He retired to Padua, where he lived wretchedly, lacking both clothes and money, and subjected to the insolence of Bonner, whom the Cardinal, just before he died, had commended to him " *quasi fratrem fratri.*" He threatened to have Wynter deprived of his preferments, and wrote home complaining of Wynter's treatment of him.

Wynter remained on the Continent until the middle of 1534, when pressing business called him to England. In

---

[1] Bishop Gardyner writes that Wynter is honourably served and has a great household. Lupset reports that he is spending money at a great rate. Wynter himself confesses that he is sometimes compelled to spend " a little more for the sake of his office." Clerk says his expenses are great but due only to " a little evil husbandry " in housekeeping. Russell describes him as treated with distinction because of his connection with Wolsey and suggests that he should have " a worshipful estate to encourage him." His extravagance and lack of means was one of the charges brought against Wolsey.

[2] *Ibid.* 6261 and 6329.

October, 1537, three years later, he obtained the Archdeaconry of Cornwall—a matter which brings him into our story.

Early in his career he must have met William Body, a member of Cromwell's household, and through his pecuniary embarrassments must have soon known him well.

When Body entered Cromwell's service and the post he at first held are uncertain. He is styled " clerk," but appears to have acted as a steward of some sort, to judge from his accounts among Cromwell's papers. In a mutilated memorandum reference is made to " the Juel howse," whereof " William Bodye had the custody," and there is mention of " your letter of attorney to Williamson Cavendish and Body to receive all sums of money due to the King's highness in your name," and of " the bills of money and plate received by Thomas Andrew of Body," as well as " certain jewels of the late Earl of . . . delivered by George Medley to Body and afterwards to Thomas Amerie." [1]

A few years later Body was accused of misappropriating certain articles entrusted to him, as appears from another document in the same handwriting as the above, endorsed " Plate embesylled by Bodye." It is there stated that Body had " begyled Mr. Whalley by his owne seyenge at the weight of Doctor Whythers plate An ale pott & Goblett, A spone & a Paire of pouche rings," as well as a standing cup with a cover gilt and " a vestyment and his Amys." He also obtained " of Doctor Powells plate A challis wth a patent gilt & a pax of parcell gilt wth a Mother off pearle garnyshed," and of Master Plummer's a gilt spoon. From Lord Dacre's possessions he retained " A greatt salt wth a couer gilt & A fforke & spone," and his arms " in goulde sett wth

---

[1] See L. & P. VIII. 301 and IX. 234. Cromwell was appointed Master of the Jewel House in 1532 and the date 15th May occurs in this last document.

Asure. A garter of golde . . . sayved at the meltynge,"
and he "sayved A Coronet of pearls whiche his wyffe
hath taken her parte." Furthermore, it is insinuated
that Body's statement was untrue " that your Master-
shipe had the saphire, the Turkes the Emrade to your
use," that belonged to John Wyther.[1]

Body protested his innocence, and begged Cromwell
to let the matter " lie dead " till his return, when he
would explain all matters relating to the coining of the
plate, of which £50 worth remained unbroken in his
hands. He added—

"I doo not dought by the grace of God you shall fynde
A good and substanciall Reconynge of the same *A prymo ad
ultimum quadrantem* And I praye God do to me as I have and
doo dailie mean to you. . . . I am noon of those that love
to crave but yet I praie god I be not forgoten ffor sethen I
was twentie & seven yeres of Age I never led so pensifull a
somer I pray God the Wynter be more mery to me. I can
Write no more but I commende me to god and to your Master-
shipps tuycion." [2]

Cromwell instructed Cavendish and Lenthall to over-
haul Body's accounts, but the result must have been
satisfactory as Body was retained in a post of trust.

---

[1] L. & P. IX. 235 (? 1535). Dr. John Wyther was Prebend of Mapesbury,
St. Paul's and vicar of St. Giles Cripplegate, in which living he was succeeded
by the famous Robert Crowley. Le Neve gives the date of his death as
1534—there is an inventory of "Mr. Withers' goods within the city of
London, A° 1531," evidently that of a cleric, perhaps taken when he was
first accused. Edward Powell, S.T.P., was deprived of his prebend in
Lincoln for denying the King's supremacy in 1534, and was executed in
1540 (Le Neve, II. 218). Lord Dacre of the North was tried for treason
when Warden of the Marches towards Scotland, 23rd May, 1534, and
declared not guilty on 27th June. In the inventory of his moveables,
taken 16th May, 1534, appear "two gold standing cups, one wrought with
the rose the other plain with Douglas arms, two great standing cups, double
gilt with the lion holding the arms of Scotland on the top of both covers."
(See L. & P. V. 456, VIII. and IX.)

[2] *Ibid.* IX. 124. There is probably a play upon the word "Wynter"
here.

Body had already complained of his difficult position, and had asked that he might serve for his own living without any " co-parcener " or else to obtain the favour of liberty to get his living abroad in the world " with myne handy occupacion," as he was wont to do, and signed himself " your humble servant & slaue." [1]

Perhaps it was in compliance with this request that soon afterwards, in 1536, he was despatched to Ireland on the King's affairs, apparently as a spy. His letter of credence from Cromwell was very ample—

" His highness minding to knowe certainly how ye have provided in that matter [the Geraldine Rebellion] hath at this time destinated and sent unto you this bearer, my servant, William Body, with whom like as his grace's pleasure is ye shall communicate all that you have done therein with the inclinations of all parties to the same. So ye shall give unto him full and undoubted credence in such thinges as he shall declare touching that matter who hath been sufficiently instructed and informed for the declaration of his mind touching that purpose proceeding with him so spedily therein as he may return with diligence." [2]

This was addressed to Lord Leonard Grey, Lord Deputy of Ireland. Body's instructions, said to be in Wriothesley's hand-writing, state that as the King has expended £40,000 in suppressing this rebellion, he desires some " direction " taken for a yearly payment to him and his successors to help to suppress such risings, and requests the Irish Parliament to see to this, while the Lord Deputy and Council are required to furnish Body with the " knowledge of their proceedings in this behalf, and what they have devised for the furtherance of the same." He is to note their reply in writing, and fully " explicate " the same on his return.

At the beginning of July, 1536, Body crossed to Ireland with George Browne, the new and disreputable

---

[1] L. & P. VIII. 152.   [2] *Ibid.* X. 1051

Archbishop of Dublin, whose favour he obtained. Arriving in Dublin on the 15th, he found the authorities starting for battle, or, as he puts it—

" The great hosting doth march forth with all expedition possible to vanquish ' Obryn,' the King's rebellious and mortal enemy and the Geraldines of ' Monster,' " [1]

and he decided to accompany them, to keep the Council in mind of affairs and to see what was doing.

His behaviour on this expedition is graphically described by the Lord Deputy in a letter of the 24th November, 1536 ; his acceptance of the benefice of Swords from the Archbishop, his boast that he was the King's Commissioner, though under the influence of drink he blurted out the truth that he was not, his association with the riff-raff of the camp, his drunken bouts and his abominable language, make a picture of an unscrupulous, low, bragging brute.[2]

Body, for his part, gave a distorted account of the succeeding battle, blaming Grey for not taking sapping tools, which would have been a useless burden, and provision carts, and complained that—

"I amongst others, lay in my harness without any bed, almost famished with hunger, wet and cold from Friday inclusive unto Tuesday exclusive." [3]

An experience which the Lord Deputy reminded him had been the lot of such persons as the Dukes of Norfolk and Suffolk, as well as " my Lorde my brother,[4] whom I had seen lodged wors."

Well might Lord Leonard be alarmed when Body

---

[1] L. & P. XI. 102.

[2] Lord Leonard concludes with : " If he wold not have foreborne me for my auctorite, ne blode, he mought have remembred the tokens I gave hym, which were worth £20, beside the entertaynment I shewed hym."

[3] L. & P. XI. 259.

[4] The Marquis of Dorset.

departed in a great fume, knowing well that threats of vengeance by a great man's servant in these perilous times were often promptly carried into effect—in this case they were fatal to the Lord Deputy, who, a few months later, laid his head on the block on Tower Green.

Nothing has come to light to prove Lord Leonard Grey's estimate of Body inaccurate, while much evidence exists to support his opinion.

After Body's experiences in Ireland, only a few insignificant references to him and his accounts occur in Cromwell's "remembrances," which merely serve to prove that he continued in that statesman's service until his fall. To him was left a legacy in Cromwell's will, which, though dated 1529, had this and other clauses added at a later period.

Following his master's example, who on Wolsey's disgrace rode to London to "make or mar," and became the King's servant, so Body, on Cromwell's fall, transferred his services to a royal master, but in exactly what capacity we can only surmise. He had already served an unscrupulous master in a fashion that suggests a kindred disposition, and no doubt the King, who had a keen eye in the choice of instruments, found in Body a tool ready to his hand for work still to be accomplished. Under Cromwell, "the Mawl of the Abbeys," Body gained considerable acquaintance with the methods employed in suppressing monasteries, and it was while engaged on a kindred task that he met his fate a few years later.

The history of these two individuals having been brought down to 1541, it is necessary to go back to pick up some connecting links before dealing with events in which they were closely associated.

Wynter, on his return to the Continent after Wolsey's fall, wrote several pathetic letters to Cromwell describing his state of poverty and begging assistance, in response to which he received a few benefices of little value. He even found difficulty in obtaining the small income due to him. Apparently, while in this distress, Cromwell lent him money on an assignment of his income as Provost of Beverley,[1] and as these funds passed through Body's hands a deal on his own behalf may have been suggested.

The mutilated Jewel House account quoted contains reference to Wynter's release of " Parson Boleyn," for all actions for Wynwyck and a bond of £2,000 made to Wynter. Later, in dire straits, he offered to sell all the plate left in Cromwell's hands.[2] He wrote urgently to his agent for funds, and returned to England to attend to his affairs. Heeding not the advice " Court not that which will not come, but trust to what you have," he begged preferments from Cromwell and from Wolsey's successor at York. On this occasion he was in England for a longer period than usual—forty-four months absent from his studies, he writes, on the 17th February, 1537, which fixes July, 1534, as the date he started, and there is no evidence that he returned to the Continent before the events about to be described.

[1] L. & P. V. 338 and VI. 841.
[2] *Ibid.* IX. 234. William Boleyn, kinsman of the Queen, succeeded Wynter at Wynwyck and in the Prebend of Strenshall, York.

CHAPTER IV

" When the Bishop of Exeter and his Chancellor were by one Body brought
in a premunire, I reasoned with the Lord Audely, then chancellor, so
far as he bade me hold my peace for fear of entering a premunire
myself."—GARDYNER TO THE PROTECTOR.

LATE in 1537, about Michaelmas, probably, the Archdeaconry of Cornwall was bestowed upon Thomas
Wynter, and there is reason to believe he accepted it
eagerly, not with the intention of assuming the duties
of his office, but as a marketable commodity ; possibly
he had already agreed to transfer it to Body in consideration of the payment of certain debts and a margin
of cash ; if not, the promptitude of the striking of the
bargain is not easily explained.

Wynter was collated to the Archdeaconry on the
8th October, 1537, and was installed by proxy on the 10th.

A month later—the 9th November, according to
Body—he executed a pair of indentures, whereby he,
Thomas Wynter, clerk, Archdeacon of Cornwall—

" granted, demised, betaken and to farm letten " to William
Body " his said Archdeaconry in Cornwall and his prebend
in the Collegial Church in Glasney, otherwise called Penryn in
Cornwall annexed to the same Archdeaconry, and all manner
manors, lordships, lands and tenements, mansions, rents and
services, woods, underwoods, timber, trees, profits, procurations, oblations, emoluments and commodities to the same

Archdeaconry and prebend belonging : together with the advowson and patronage of a priory called ' seynte Jones yn Helstone '
belonging to the same Archdeaconry . . . together also with
all manner ' proxes Synages,' probates of testaments, adminis-
trations, dilapidations, inductions, corrections, commutations,
citations, suspensions, excommunications, monitions, compulsory decrees, sentences and all and singular profits of the seal
belonging to the same Archdeaconry, visitations and the making,
instituting and putting in and putting out of all manner
officials, registers, seals and all manner other officers and
offices, etc., etc., for three years and so from ' three years unto
three years then next following during the term of xxxv.
years.' " [1]

In return, Body was to allow him £30 yearly out of
the revenues, and forthwith paid Wynter £150 " in
manner and form following, that is to say, one hundred
pounds in ready money," and with the remaining £50
promised to discharge a bond of one Grygge, a mercer
of London, for whom Wynter and " ffulke appowell at
Lancaster one of your graces [2] herraldes at Armes,"
stood bound. In addition, with strange generosity,
Body gave Wynter £10 8s. 10d. in cash, and paid his
creditors, John Collett, mercer, Thomas Abraham, the
elder, and Vincent Mundy, the sum of £32 12s. 2d.
Moreover he gave Wynter—

" by the waye of lone thies parcells folowing that is to saye
iiij yardes dimid.[3] of fyne wollen Clothe of the colour of ffrenche
blacke price vj^{li} A nyght-gowne furred wth olde Martorne
and new faced with foynes [4] price vj^{li} And a bible in latten
price xv^{s}."

Afterwards Body stated that he had laid out £90—
i.e. the annual rent for three years reserved to Wynter,
and had also paid the Tenths and Subsidy, amounting

---

[1] See Star Chamber Proceeding, V. 60. [2] The King's grace.
[3] Four and a half. [4] Pole-cat's fur.

to £9 11s. 2d. Altogether it looks as if Body had made an expensive bargain.

The indentures, it was said, were signed in Body's house in London, but there is a conflict of evidence as to what happened on that occasion. Body's witnesses claimed that Wynter then and there signed the lease and also an obligation to perform the same in the presence only of one Stobard, a young surveyor. On the other hand, Fulk Aphowell said Body brought Wynter a bill of attorney, which the latter looked at and said he could not " skill of the sums," so it must be redrawn. Another testified that Wynter had agreed to a certain lease, but that Body had devised a pair of indentures " clean contrary," disagreeing from the agreement, and that Wynter, " not thinking but that the said complainant had faithfully and truly caused the said Indentures to be made," had signed them only to find later that they were not such as had been represented.

But a doubt as to the validity of the sale must have been in Wynter's mind, for, before signing the agreement, he had desired Body to " axe thadvyse of such persons as knew the spirituall lawe " dealing with the subject. Body promptly assured him that he had already consulted Drs. Hewis, Olyver and Darell,[1] who declared that it would stand—a decision which they afterwards denied having given. " Very well," then said Wynter, " you must keep me harmless against the Bishop of Exeter and his successors for and concerning the said Archdeaconry." To which, it was asserted, Body agreed.

Well might Wynter doubt whether it were lawful to sell the spiritual and temporal rights of the archdeaconry for a term of thirty-five years. Considering that he was at least thirty years old, and already had seen many changes in ecclesiastical affairs, he might well question

---

[1] Dr. Hewis and Dr. Olyver were " counsellors in the lawe for the king's parte," when Cranmer, at Dunstable, pronounced the decree of divorce of Queen Katherine. (See Ellis, Orig. Let. 1st Ser. II. 33.)

whether he would have possession of the archdeaconry
for so long a time, apart from the legal aspect of the
transference of his rights, especially to a layman.

However, indentures of some sort were signed at
some date, and one of them was deposited with Stobard,
and Body proceeded to exercise the office of an archdeacon, so far as to collect the rents and profits, which,
we presume, was done through John Broke, clerk, of
Wells, who had acted as Wynter's agent. Possibly it
was due to some confusion in the minds of the authorities
as to whose deputy Broke was that matters were allowed
to remain unquestioned until the expiration of the first
term of three years.[1]

No trace of any action in that interval has been discovered, but immediately on its expiration Bishop
Veysey took cognisance of the matter. He issued first
a "writ citatory,"[2] dated the 20th December, 1540,
directed to John Harrys, late of Penryn, clerk, bachelor
of law, the Bishop's commissary general, to John
Bostock, late of Exeter, gent., and to all clerks and
scholars throughout his diocese, commanding them to
bring the citation to the notice of Thomas Wynter, who
was thereby summoned to appear before the said Bishop
at Penryn, on the 17th February next following (1540–1),
there to answer for indulging in prohibited games and in
other things contrary to the office of an archdeacon and
the honesty of a clerk. Having summoned Wynter to
answer a charge of evil living, the Bishop's deputies,
Thomas Brerewood, Archdeacon of Barnstaple, and John
Croft, late of Penryn and of Exeter, gent., the Bishop's
principal registrar, proceeded to charge him, among the
things contrary to the office of an archdeacon, with
having let to farm the ecclesiastical and spiritual juris-

---

[1] Some deponents went so far as to say that Wynter held the Archdeaconry and collected the "issues, revenues and profits . . . by the space
of four years or thereabouts."

[2] Coram Rege Roll, 35 H. VIII., No. 1130, m. 124.

diction belonging to the archdeaconry to William Body, who was purely a layman, to the subvention of justice and the injury of priestly honesty, and that Body exercised the said office and took the fruits thereof, not only to the extolling of the Roman pontiff, but contrary to the form and statutes of the kingdom. Moreover, Wynter was accused of having sold some large trees growing upon his sanctuary and glebe, which were necessary for the repair and rebuilding of his hospice.

Apparently John Broke, who appeared as Wynter's deputy at Penryn, was not prepared for this charge, so simply asked for a copy of the articles. Thereupon Brerewood proceeded to deprive Body of the farm of the Archdeaconry, to his great loss, as he afterwards complained.

Meanwhile, what had Body been doing? Probably at a date just before the issue of the writ he got wind of the intended proceedings, and one day, the date of which is unknown, a conference was held at a tavern in the Vintry next the Cranes.[1]

Body had sent Peter Ford to tell John Stobard of Lombard Street to bring his copy of the indentures to that inn, where all three met. The document was spread out, and they were quietly reading it over when Ford stopped and pointed out some words interlined in a different writing, which altered the meaning of the document.

Body's temper was never very amiable, and now, roused to anger, he snatched the indenture with violence from Ford, swearing a great oath and demanding what right he had to meddle with his handwriting, and was " sore grieved " with Ford, who, we gather, was a partisan both of Wynter and of the Bishop. In pompous wrath Body left the room.[2]

---

[1] The Three Cranes (mechanical ones for hoisting burdens) was a famous landing-place at the riverside at the foot of College Hill.

[2] Star Chamber Proc. H. VIII. X. 248.

After the conference thus abruptly terminated, Ford visited Stobard in his shop, for he was a scrivener, where, in John Cotton's presence, he reasoned with Stobard on the interlineations, which the latter declared were not his, and he knew not by whom they were written.

Evidently Body took alarm at the suspicion cast on the document, and, feeling his position insecure, he decided to take steps to strengthen it. For this purpose he went to Devonshire, where, about Christmas time, he appeared in the great hall of the Bishop's Palace at Crediton. Here he paid the King's Tenth and Subsidy for the archdeaconry to George Stapleton, the Bishop's servant, and received a receipt in the presence of Richard Martin, John Stephins, and others.

He also took the further precaution of obtaining a letter from the King, written from Hampton Court, on the 6th February, 1541, addressed to the Bishop of Exeter, and the Dean and Chapter there, saying that the King's servant, T. Wynter, archdeacon of Cornwall, had leased to the King's servant, William Body, his archdeaconry for three years to three years for thirty-two years; that Body had spent much money in obtaining the lease, and would lose it should Wynter die. The King asked them to confirm Wynter's grant under the episcopal and chapter seals.[1]

But Wynter, finding his sale condemned in the Episcopal Court, and failing to prove that the indentures were subtly devised and not faithfully and truly executed according to the agreements with Body, now authorised others to hold his archdeaconry and act for him in future. Perhaps by advice of the Bishop he appointed as his deputies John Harrys, *alias* Rowden, clerk, and George Stapleton. The former was prebendary of St. Thomas

---

[1] MSS. in possession of Lord Hatherton of Teddesley, Stafford, quoted in L. & P. XVI. pt. i. 522. This belated application for the sanction of the Bishop and Chapter gives colour to the charge that Body had but recently acquired the archdeaconry and had ante-dated his lease.

of Glasney, superior of the Hospital of St. John next Helston, one of the benefices appertaining to the archdeaconry, and, as we have seen, the Bishop's commissary in Cornwall named in the writ citatory, while George Stapleton was the Bishop's servant who received Body's payments at Crediton. He afterwards deposed that, at the Bishop's request, Wynter, by his own hands, gave Stapleton his " deed and patent " in the house of one Grey, in Fleet Street, at the end of March, 1541. Harrys declared that his commission from Wynter was handed to him by one " Richard Hunne vian a scoler in peryn in the house of Rafe Coche." [1]

These two deputies set out promptly for Launceston, the place fixed for the archidiaconal visitation. Nor were they the only persons to arrive from a distance in that border town.

On the 21st April, 1541, Launceston, with its grim castle frowning down upon the recently finished and ornate church of St. Mary Magdalen, upon the priory nestling in the hollow between the hills, and upon a motley cluster of ecclesiastical and other buildings, must have presented a lively scene.

Body would have arrived in the town the previous night at least, with a train suited to his dignity—either coming from Exeter across the wilds of Dartmoor or from Bodmin, with which place he was in some way connected. Stapleton and Harrys, persons of importance, would have brought their attendants to swell the number of strangers assembled in the place. But on this spring morning the clergy of the surrounding district, who had not already arrived the night before, might have been seen making their way through deep-cut lanes already beautiful with the lace-like drapery of the blackthorn or in some sheltered glade bordered with the pink-tinged apple-orchards. The rich clerics and the

---

[1] Ralph Couch, prebend of Glasney, had the " scole " there.

infirm would be mounted on asses or ambling nags, while others, with sandalled feet, splashed through the muddy roads; many a tonsured crown indicated a recent residence in a suppressed monastery, whence they had issued to become parish-priests.

Where the roads met beside the little river Kensey in the valley they would have joined the townspeople flocking down the steep Launceston Street, and would have climbed the rough ascent to St. Stephen's, to which church John Broke had summoned the clergy to pay their " proxes and synages."

Into the building thronged the multitude, among whom may have been the Mayor and his brethren of the ancient borough of Dunheved, clad in their " scarlets," and followed by a goodly rabblement ready for any excitement that chanced to be afoot. The boasting of Body's attendants, as they cleaned his accoutrements at the inn or groomed his horses at the stable door, would have roused their curiosity.

The hum and buzz of conversation would not have ceased as they entered the sacred building—the reverence for holy places had decreased since the Suppression, when God's houses had been desecrated in blasphemous manner.[1]

Presently Body entered and took up his position in a prominent place. The spring sunshine, streaming through the gorgeous stained glass, would have shone on his rich apparel, his velvet cloak and plumed hat, and gleamed on his heavy gold chain, and glanced from the ornamented sheath of the dagger at his belt. Beside him stood his official, John Broke, and his registrar, John Stephins; perhaps behind his chair was Richard Martin, servingman of Exeter, who received 8d. a day

---

[1] A little later a proclamation was issued forbidding the " shooting of hand-guns at doves and the common bringing of horses and mules into and through the said churches, making the same . . . like a stable or common inn."

to ride about with Body on his visitations, as well as a host of servants and adherents.

Here they had all assembled for the purpose of paying or seeing paid their " synages and proxies, according to the Auncyante Customes there used and hathe been accustomed." [1]

Glancing at the faces of the crowd, had Body any inkling of the trend of events ?   Had his servants, when gossiping in the town, heard any rumour and brought it to his ears ?

Be that as it may, he carried himself with a brave front, and was proceeding to call out names from his book of procurations when the church door was violently flung open, and a crowd burst forcibly and riotously into the building ; then a high voice rang out—

"I forbid you to pay the procurations and synodals demanded by this man Body. I command you, both clergy and people here assembled, to refuse obedience to any process or commandment made by him, by his officials or any other officers ! "

Thus speaking, John Harrys, the venerable priest, pushed his way through the crowd with the help of the stout yeoman, Matthew Collyns, followed closely by John Wyse, a worthy gentleman of Launceston,[2] and accompanied by sturdy companions.   The people recognised the Bishop's commissary, one armed with authority, so made way for him to advance quickly.

Reaching the spot where Body stood, Harrys roughly snatched the book from the hands of the farmer of the archdeaconry.

Startled by the sudden interruption with the " owte cry," and by the violence offered to him, Body instinctively sought his dagger, half drawing it from its sheath.   Finding his guest Harrys in personal danger,

---

[1] Star Chamber Proc. V. 60. "Synages and proxies " = synodals and procurations.

[2] Probably one of the Wyses of Sydenham.

F

John Wyse pushed forward to the rescue, and laid violent hands on Body, and, on his resistance, knocked him down, it was asserted. In the twinkling of an eye, Body found himself and his companions thrust and pushed and hustled outside the church, with the door shut fast behind them.

Seeing the temper of the crowd, Body could but call upon his supporters and turn, shouting and threatening, to the multitude.

" You will rue this day," would have been the burden of his cry, well interspersed with oaths. " You have to reckon with a servant of the King, one who was of the household of my lord Cromwell, the hammer of the monks. My patron will see to it that you suffer for what you have done ! "

' With imprecations and curses, Body, the hot-tempered, would have taken horse quickly for London, stopping perhaps in Exeter, to lay a train which was to deal destruction to some of those in authority.

Against the rioters, the " fautors and maintainers " of Harrys, he brought an action in the Star Chamber. Here he poured out his grievances in a mass of verbiage : how he had legally obtained the temporal and spiritual jurisdiction of the archdeaconry by indenture, how he had been interrupted in the execution of his duties, how violent hands had been laid upon him in St. Stephen's Church, and how he was deprived of the profits due to him, which were now paid to Harrys and Stapleton.

Then began swearing and counter-swearing, so diametrically opposed that it is evident that some did ' not handle the truth carefully : depositions and counter-depositions, answers and replications, each totally denying the other, which form a huge mass of documents, whence this story is gleaned, though unfortunately the result of the case is not forthcoming.

But Body had not by any means played his last card.

He forthwith brought an action against the Bishop of Exeter and his deputies who had acted at the Court in Penryn. These, Body maintained, had come within the Statute of Præmunire. His contention was not unnoticed in Parliament, where an animated discussion took place between Bishop Gardyner and Lord Chancellor Audeley. The former held that as the bishops were now authorised by the King and not the Pope, none of them could fall into a præmunire, and he withstood the Chancellor's arguments so vehemently that Audeley, to quote Gardyner's words, " bade me hold my peace for fear of entering a præmunire myself." [1]

However, as the authorities upheld Body's contention, the matter was brought into court, and " Thomas Brerewood, late of Exeter, clerk and professor of ecclesiastical law, and John Croft, late of Penryn and of Exeter, gent., principal registrar of John, Bishop of Exeter throughout his whole diocese," were arrested and imprisoned in the Marshalsea, whence, early in February, 1543-4, they were brought into the Court of King's Bench, there to answer for their breach of the Statute of Præmunire, in contempt of the Crown and to the damage of William Body of £3,000. [2]

After reciting the course of events at Penryn and pointing out the offence committed, the record states that the accused defended the injury, but said that they could not deny the action, nor that they were guilty of all the premises. The Court considered the matter

---

[1] Harl. MS. 417, i. 86. The Statute of Præmunire, passed in the reign of Richard II., asserted that " The crown of England hath been so free at all times, that it hath been in no earthly subjection, but immediately subjected to God in all things touching its regality, and no other, and ought not to be submitted to the Pope." By the same statute it was enacted that " They who shall procure or prosecute any popish bulls and excommunications, in certain cases, shall incur the forfeiture of their estates, or be banished, or be put out of the King's protection. . . . By a statute of Henry III. the Pope's canon law had no place in England, except so far as the king and parliament permitted " (Hook's " Archbishops," VI. 389).

[2] Coram Rege Roll. 35 H. VIII. Hil. 1130 m, 24,

until after Easter, during which period the prisoners remained in custody, and then delivered adverse sentence upon them. Body was to recover his damages and twenty shillings costs, Brerewood and Croft were put outside the King's protection and forfeited their goods and chattels to the King, and were again committed to the Marshalsea.

Croft remained in prison until the following June, when, under letters patent, dated the 27th May, 1544, after the payment of a fine of £100 he was released, and furthermore, on the same date, " William Body at London, viz. in the parish of the Blessed Mary of Bow, in the Ward of Chepe, by deed of release, etc.," freed the said John Croft from all further actions, debts, trespasses, etc., whereupon the said John was released from prison.

But, as for Brerewood, his release was of another sort. Whether serious illness made them open the prison doors or whether he died within the Marshalsea, is not evident, but in the early summer of 1545, i.e. five weeks after Easter, his executors appeared in Court, armed with similar letters and with Body's release, and were quit of further actions.

Brerewood's will is dated the 22nd May, 1544, five days before the date of the letters patent and of Body's release.[1] It was proved the 2nd March following. He refers to money accounted for by his servant, John Parre, " since my coming out of Devon " ; he leaves to each of his servants a black coat and twenty shillings " to bring each of them home " ; he arranges for a " solemn obit in the Cathedral Church after the order

---

[1] P. C. C. 23 Pynnyng. Brerewood was fellow of All Souls, Oxford, 1511; B.C.L. 1511–12 ; D.C.L. 1527 ; Canon of St. Paul's, 1518 ; of Exeter, 1523 ; Rector of Colyton, 1524 ; Archd. Barum, 1528 ; Rector of Ilfracombe, 1530 ; Prebendary of St. Endellion, 1533, of Crediton, 1536 ; Rector of St. Ewe, 1536, of Bradninch, 1538 ; Chaplain to the King, Chancellor to the Bishop of Exeter and " consiliar " of Launceston Priory. Oliver says Archd. Totton, 1533. See also Chapter XI.

of a single canon "; and adds this reference to h
trials—

"I will that all such sums of money as the Bishop of Exet
shall depart and give towards my charges and costs of my la
trouble shall go towards the performance of my will."

No doubt through this action Body had a fair measu
of revenge, ruining one opponent and causing the dea
of another, or at least shortening his life by anxieties a
the rigours of imprisonment.

So ends the episode of bringing the Bishop of Exete
officials within the all-embracing grasp of the Statute
Præmunire.

isoners
entence
es and
re put
t goods

June,
, 1544,
ed, and
ody at
f Bow,

passes,
prison.
er sort.
prison
is not
weeks
armed
d were

Body's
g. He
, John
aves to

for a
e order

, Oxford,
1518; of
Rector of
n, 1536;
rg, Chan-

CHAPTER V

DISTURBANCES IN CORNWALL IN 1548

" As with the first spread of Christianity, so with the spread of the Reformation, the towns went first and the country reluctantly lagged behind."
—FROUDE.

THE ecclesiastical changes at this period were more quickly felt by the townsmen, who readily adapted themselves to the new order, but the slow-moving countrymen, conservative by nature, resented the suppression of the monasteries and the desecration of all that they had held sacred. The greater the distance from London the more intense their opposition to the changes—in Cornwall, as well as Yorkshire, they forcibly resisted the imposition of the new orders.

As early as 1536 Cornwall showed signs of resentment. Writing from Penryn—a place prominent in our story—on the 5th September in that year, Dr. Tregonwell, the King's Commissioner, referred to rumours of the disturbed state of the county because it was reported that he was to remove crosses, chalices, and other idols from the churches, but, on the contrary, he found every one ready to obey the King's injunctions, the country being as quiet and as true to the King as any other. The people were even marvellously pleased that his Highness promised to allow them to keep their " *festum loci*," and he hoped no more would be heard of irreverent handling of the Sacrament of the Altar.[1]

---

[1] L. & P. XI. 405. His last remark seems strange, as there is little reason to believe that the Cornish people displayed such irreverence.

Scarcely six months later Godolphin wrote the letter, quoted in Chapter II., about the proposed stirring at St. Keverne, which ended with the request that Cromwell would move the King to permit the people to "hold the day of the head saint of their church solemnly as they were wont to do"—a petition repeated in another letter a fortnight later; evidently, in spite of the King's promise, the custom was forbidden.

An order issued in 1538 added to the resentment of the people. In April, 1539, Sir Piers Edgcombe, having promised to inform the King of any "grudge or miscontentation" among his subjects, wrote that he had heard from a right true, honest servant of much secret and several communication among the people who feared and mistrusted that the command that each incumbent should register the names of all those wedded, buried, or christened, would lead to additional charges.[1]

his fear was shared by the members of the Pilgrimage of Grace.[2]

Much fresh fuel was added to these flames by the events already described; yet into this county, after a lapse of two years, during which no trace of his movements has been found, William Body came, either as a Commissioner connected with the Chantry inquiry, or, more probably, in his capacity of archdeacon, to see that the injunctions of this year, 1547, were carried into effect according to the Bishop's instructions, and this, too, after his obnoxious conduct at Launceston and his action against the Bishop's officials. To aggravate matters, he made Penryn his headquarters, though his

---

[1] L. & P. XIV. i. 816.

[2] Hilles, writing to Bullinger from Strasburg, the 18th June, 1548, reports that there are in England "papists who, by their false rumours, endeavour to excite the people against the king and nobles of this realm. Their lies are to the effect that the king is intending to oppress the people by a new and unheard of kind of tax; namely, that when any person marries, he must pay half a crown to the king; and so in like manner for baptising an infant, or burying the dead" (Zur. Let. I. 263).

selection of this place was not surprising, for as archdeacon he was *ex officio* prebendary of St. Thomas of
Glasney at Penryn, and had there a " mansion pertaining, with gardens and grounds limited within itself and a
small wood adjoining." But among his fellow-pre-
bendaries was John Harrys, the active commissary at
Launceston, who had held his prebend a dozen years,
and had been appointed some thirty-five years before
prior of "St. Jones yn Helston," pertaining to the
archdeaconry.[1] John Moreman, of whom more will be
heard, had recently resigned his prebend in the same
College on his appointment to a canonry in Exeter, but
he still held the neighbouring living of Menheniot. It
was to Penryn that Wynter had been summoned in
1541. So doubtless there was much ill-feeling against
Body in this district.

Here, contrary to his instructions, Body commanded
the clergy to assemble to hear the Injunctions of
Edward VI., which carried further Henry VIII.'s
tentative steps towards ceremonial changes. These
removed the two remaining lights and the Easter
sepulchre, and abolished the washings, crossings, shift-
ings and blessings accompanying the Mass ; crosses,
lights, and bells at the communion of the sick and the
burial of the dead, as well as other ceremonials, superstitions, pilgrimages, etc. In fact, a clean sweep was
to be made of all that was styled " popery," a course by
no means liked by the rural population. Moreover, all
this was accompanied by another dip of the royal hand
into ecclesiastical revenues. What seems to have
touched the Cornishmen very nearly was the query
relating to the alienation of Church lands, jewels, and
goods. No doubt this suggested similar inventories that
preceded the annexation of monastic property, and
they may have recalled stories of that time when

---

[1] Aug. Of. Misc. Bk. 132.

commissioners were reported as riding along the highways decked in the spoils of desecrated chapels, with copes for doublets, tunics for saddlecloths, and silver reliquaries hammered into sheaths for their daggers,[1] and they did not wish to have their church treasures, mostly bought with their own contributions, thus contemptuously treated. Doubtless Body's enemies used this discontent to further their own ends.

The day appointed by Body is uncertain. The order for the Royal visitation was dated, Strype says, the 1st September, 1547 ; some injunctions issued by bishops under it are dated the 3rd of that month, but in remote Cornwall the visitation itself was probably much later. On the 17th October, the Council wrote Bishop Veysey that if he had not already attended to this matter he was to take steps " undelayedly " to inquire into the sale and alienation of Church goods. But the letter of the Privy Council, whence the following account is gleaned, is dated the 17th December,[2] and reads as if written immediately after receiving the report of Sir William Godolphin and his colleagues : so the day fixed was probably towards the end of November or early in December.

Having assembled a multitude of incumbents and churchwardens of all the parishes of the district on one day, in order to avoid " his own pain," [3] Body—

" further handled himself after such a manner as thereby the people were persuaded that the ensearch to be taken tended only to effect as if thereupon a confiscation should have ensued to the King's Majesty's behalf, much contrary to the Council's intent, who meant but only to see the same preserved entirely to the churches, without embezzling or private sales, as by

---

[1] See Froude, III. 98.

[2] P. C. Letter Book, Harl. MS. 352, f. 65. See also Dasent's Acts of P. C. II. 535, where it is inaccurately transcribed.

[3] *I.e.* to save himself trouble.

the copy of that their letter subscribed with the same Body's
hand returned herewith unto them might evidently appear."

If precedents counted, the people might well fear
confiscation, especially as much was being, and had been,
absorbed ; while royal promises clearly asserted had
been broken, so they might well question one which was
only implied.

The hostile demonstration made by the assembly at
Penryn was so " tumulteous " that the local authorities
were much perturbed, and, either on their own initiative
or on Body's appeal, Godolphin, Militon, and St. Aubyn
wrote an account of events and sent it post haste to the
Council. In the latter's reply, quoted above, they
instructed the Justices to commit Body to ward for a
week and then bind him by recognisances under a good
sum to appear before the Council by a certain day to
answer complaints that he did " misuse himself." They
were also to show the copy of the Council's letter,
endorsed by Body, to the substantial persons of every
parish, declaring how greatly they had mistaken it—
" the very purpose whereof ran to the preservation of
the church jewels, and prohibition of private sales
thereof, rather than otherwise." Finally, they were to
inquire out two or three of the chief stirrers up of this
business and commit them also to ward—a piece of
even-handed justice rather unusual at this period. The
Council were to be informed of the course of events, but
unfortunately no record has been found of what happened between this and the following April, when Body
was not only at large, but returned, under a letter from
the Council dated in February, on an iconoclastic
mission.

This letter, directed in the first instance to the Archbishop, after pointing out that " the lively images of
Christ should not contend for the dead images, which be
things not necessary," signified to him to give orders

immediately that all images remaining in any church or chapel must be removed, and he was so to notify all bishops, who were to use such foresight that this should be quietly done, "with as good satisfaction of the people as may be." Evidently they anticipated that the destruction of images would not be calmly accepted. Bishop Veysey received such instructions and Body, as a special commissioner sent from London, it is said, went to Cornwall on this mission. His movements there can only be surmised, but probably he visited several churches in the hundred of Kerrier, perhaps including Penryn, before he reached Helston, on the 5th April.

By that time feeling throughout the district seems to have been thoroughly roused, and a demonstration of some sort determined upon. Helston may have been selected as a parish particularly opposed to Body by the influence of John Harrys, who held the Priory of St. John the Baptist, about a quarter of a mile from the parish church.[1]

Previous to the day appointed, much gossip, excited conferences, and seditious speeches prepared the people, so they were not surprised when, one fair, spring morning, the Common bell rang backwards in several parishes in the district. They would have flocked to the village green and thronged into their church for mass. On emerging a procession would have been formed, the parish cross, if still left to them, at its head. A new crusade was being preached, they must prevent this iconoclast from executing his mission, and their parish priest led them forth on this pious errand.

As far afield as Gwennap on the north, and Grade on the south, small companies advanced, but Constantine

---

[1] This cell was close to the ancient toll-house on the old Penzance road beside the river, which is the boundary between Helston and Sithney, and within the latter parish. The middle arch of St. John's bridge is believed to be part of the old bridge. A stone coffin-cover with a cross carved on it inserted in a garden wall marks the site of the old priory.

and St. Keverne supplied large contingents ; while stray persons from Redruth, Illogan, and St. Peran-in-le-Sand were swept into the throng, or perhaps joined it after its arrival in Helston.

It is not surprising that Constantine was a centre of disaffection when we learn that two of the chief land-owners there were John Harrys and William Wynslade. For some reason feeling ran high at St. Keverne. Godolphin's account of a conspiracy there we have already had, and he mentions it as the home of Michael Joseph, the blacksmith, connected with the earlier rising.[1] The parish was at this period one of the largest and most thickly populated in the county, a seaport containing a hardy race of fishermen. The terrible Manacles, which jut out beneath it, have been the scene of many a wreck, and there may have been here a body of " wreckers " ready to join in any mischievous excitement.

With them was their priest, Martin Geffrey, who played a prominent part in the end, though it is not known whether he was an instigator of the movement, or was carried away by it, or was simply held responsible for the conduct of his flock.[2]

From St. Keverne, then, some ten miles from Helston, advanced an excited crowd of fisherfolk and farmers. From Constantine, which lies almost equi-distant between Helston and Penryn, and which probably shared in the recent excitement at the latter place, came a detachment,

---

[1] See Chapter II., p. 29.

[2] Sir Robert Rawe had been instituted to the vicarage of St. Keverne, the 14th May, 1547. Although Richard Rawe, husbandman, was one of the rebels tried, there is no record of Robert Rawe, clerk, charged in this connec-tion, yet the next institution recorded at Exeter is 24th Jan., 1549–50, Thomas Poley, S.T.P., the benefice being then vacant *by the attainder of the last vicar.* In 1544 Martin Geffrey was a stipendiary priest paid by the parishioners of St. Just in Roseland. Possibly he succeeded Rawe, but his institution is unrecorded ; the reference to the last vicar's attainder supports this theory rather than that of his having been a curate-in-charge. The church of St. Keverne is a very large structure with several very curious architectural features.

chiefly agriculturists, prominent among whom were the brothers Kylter,[1] the ostensible leaders of the movement, to one of whom was accorded the title of " yeoman."

Just outside of Helston all would have joined forces, and perhaps William Kylter harangued the crowd, now numbering close on a thousand men ; a strange assembly of sailors and husbandmen, armed with a motley assortment of weapons, swords, staves, sticks, hauberks, bows and arrows, breastplates, and other articles. He would have urged them to rise against the unjust, even unlawful action, of those who controlled affairs during the King's minority. They had but to lead the way, and the whole nation would unite to sweep the Protector and Council from power and restore their old religion. Then would they regain their church-plate and jewels, and prevent further sacrilege like that they had already witnessed in some churches ; above all, they would re-establish the abbeys, with their charities ; again would the chantry priests' voices resound through the sacred buildings in prayers for their dead ancestors, whereby, too, their own pains in purgatory would be relieved.

" Look," he may have exclaimed, " at the Pilgrimage of Grace ! How nearly they succeeded ! Why, the King himself was forced to treat with the Commons, and only gained his evil ends by treachery ! "

Perhaps he had been employed against the Northern men, and could have furnished details of the struggle. His appeal would have engaged the sympathy of many. Could they not recall those days, scarce a dozen years ago, when rumours of the rising filtered down to these remote parts ? Some may have spoken of it with bated breath as they rode along the highway,[2] expressing

---

[1] William Kelter or Kylter appears on the Subsidy Rolls as of Constantine between 1543–46 assessed upon xxˢ of goods. He was also a witness to a transfer of land made by John Wynslade of Pelynt to his wife in 1544.

[2] L. & P. XII. i. 298.

approval of the movement. They remembered that some of the " most tallest men " had been requisitioned for the King's service,[1] that they, lacking horses, had taken those of the stay-at-homes ; nor had they forgotten that many of their sons and more of their horses had failed to return from the expedition, while the men who did come back brought tales of the King's treachery and cruelty—that one woman, at least, had been barbarously hanged and quartered as a traitor !

Truly had Sir Piers Edgcombe warned Cromwell that if the owners of the horses failed to obtain redress the King would be ill-served another time. So it was easy for Kylter to rouse the crowd with unlawful and seditious words.

" Forward to the town, to the church, and have out this vile traitor and image breaker ! " would have rung out the cry.

Body, meanwhile, was already in Helston, and probably at this moment engaged in his iconoclastic task, assisted by his own men, for, judging from the temper of the people, he would not have been well served by local carpenters and masons.

The approach of the threatening crowd may have been heralded by a breathless messenger, who startled the Commissioner's escort as they lounged at the churchyard gate or rubbed down their horses that browsed among the graves. The rattle of their accoutrements and their shouts would have warned those within the church that some danger was afoot, making them emerge hastily. Only a blustering bully, to judge from his previous record, and aware that he had not enough men to withstand the enraged populace, Body sought refuge in a house, near at hand. None too soon, for the excited crowd, gathering in numbers as it advanced,

---

[1] L. & P. XII. i. 152.

surged into the churchyard, only to find themselves for the moment disappointed of their prey. Hot on his scent the boldest pushed forward to his place of refuge, which was quickly surrounded by the mob.

Foremost of all was William Kylter, followed closely by Father Geffrey. Dragged from his hiding-place, apparently undefended by his attendants,[1] Body was brought forth in the sight of the crowd. What happened then ? Did they demand their church jewels ? Did they take away his book of accounts ? Did they force him to climb the cross and cast his ledgers with the English Bibles and Service books into a fire ? Did they threaten to hang him, tear him limb from limb, behead him as he had beheaded their images ? Did he in piteous wise beg for merey, for mercy from an enraged multitude, who had long detested his autocratic manner and evil doings ? The picture cannot be certainly filled in, but it is possible that a scene similar to that at Louth was repeated here.

At some moment Body was struck down, stabbed with a knife and despatched by William Kylter and Pascho Trevian. The mob may have been awed to silence when the consequences of killing such an official dawned upon them, and some bold man may have denounced them as murderers, or one in authority may have commanded them to disperse. Again the records fail us.

We next find them returned to the old cemetery, perhaps listening to Father Geffrey's reassurances as to the righteousness of their cause in the eyes of God. In the midst of his discourse a Justice of the Peace, with armed retainers, may have appeared to demand the murderers. Boldly defying him, John Pyers, a sailor from St. Keverne, stood forth and cried—

"If any of you dare to arrest a member of our

---

[1] No one else is said to have been injured in this fray.

company for the death of William Body, we are ready to rescue him." [1]

Few men would have been bold enough to go counter to the wishes of such an ugly-tempered crowd, so he doubtless retired discreetly to await reinforcements.

From the cemetery, pushing and jostling, the throng moved to the market-place. The four roads converging here were now blocked by an eager, excited crowd, anxious to know what was doing, ready to join their friends.

It would have been from the steps of the market-cross that John Ressiegh, yeoman, of Helston, harangued the multitude, pointing out their religious grievances and the injustice inflicted by the present Council of the King. Details are lacking, but his speech must have dealt chiefly, if not wholly, with the evil doings of the Royal visitors, the suppression of religious houses, the confiscation of ecclesiastical lands and goods, the alteration threatened in the Church services and the destruction of images and shrines. Finally he summed up with—

"Let us have again all such laws and ordinances touching the Christian religion as were appointed by our late sovereign lord, King Henry the Eighth, of blessed memory (God rest his soul), and none other, until the King's Majesty that now is accomplish the age of four-and-twenty years, and whosoever dare defend this Body and follow such new fashions as he did, we will punish him likewise ! " [2]

---

[1] This seems to be the meaning of the words in the indictment : "That if any man wolde revenge the death of the said William Body, that they were there ready to rescue the same."

[2] There are two versions of this speech, or proclamation ; the one in the Launceston indictment reads : "That they wold have all suche lawes and ordynances touchyng cristian religion as was appoynted by our late Soueraigne lord Kyng Henry theight until the kynge maiestie that now is accomplish thage of xxiiij yeres." The other from the indictment of Martin Geffrey and his comrades reads : "that thei wolde haue all suche lawes as was made by the late Kynge Henry theight and none other, vntyll the Kings maiestie that now is accomplish thage of xxiiij[to] yeres, and that whoso wolde defende Body or follow such new faschyons as he dyd thei wolde

Resseigh's peroration must have been received with cries of assent, and made a fitting conclusion to the day's proceedings. The good people of Helston then retired, probably, to their homes to discuss events, to extend hospitality to their country neighbours or to toss in restless slumbers.

All the next day the town continued in a ferment, and tumultuously received the Justices who hastened to assemble at the scene of the murder, to learn the truth of the rumours that had reached them, to set in motion the machinery of the law, and, if possible, to allay the excitement of the people. But in this last respect their efforts were vain, their attempts to arrest the murderers and ringleaders were stoutly resisted.

The next day, the 7th April, the crowd in Helston increased to three thousand persons, who disturbed the usually sober town. They did unlawfully and feloniously, armed in manner of war and then and there did openly conspire war, against the Lord the King and his true subjects; that is, against the Justices of the Peace and other officers, who sought to enforce the law. In the excitement this mixed and unruly assembly committed divers thefts, spoliations, and other evil deeds. Finally, in reply to the appeals and threats of the Justices, who were arranging to bring the guilty parties before the sessions, and had already made prisoners of some of them, they proclaimed and voiced these felonious words—

" That on Tuesday next at the general sessions to be holden at Helston, we will be there with a greater number to see if any man will be avenged therein ! "

punyshe him lykewise." These, with the other proclamation are in English in the midst of the Latin indictments. This point, that matters of religion should remain unchanged during the king's minority, was the one for which Bishops Gardyner and Bonner went to prison and which was maintained by the popish party, and, indeed, by Cranmer. It was demanded in the Articles of the rebels of the following year. Its presence in this speech indicates that Resseigh was prompted by some one familiar with this argument.

G

The Justices, recognising the temper of the people, went in fear of their lives, and dared not hold the proposed sessions. In consequence of the turbulent state of affairs, they changed the venue, and committed those apprehended to the Sheriff's keeping to be produced before a Special Commission of Oyer and Terminer at Launceston.

Meanwhile, letters describing these startling events had been written by Sir William Godolphin and his colleagues to the King and Privy Council, and were sent by William Welche, who arrived in London on the 8th April. He received £4 as a reward for bringing them, and was " dispatched from hence to them again " with the Council's reply.[1]

On his mad gallop to London Welche roused the country. From the Plymouth Municipal documents we learn that the authorities, alive to the danger, prepared to aid the King. Twenty-eight shillings and eightpence were paid to Henry Blase " for hym & his companye the viij[th] of Aprel, when they Rode w[t] Sir Richard Eggecomb into Cornwall agaynst the Rebells there," while a " dowsen of bowestryngs " were provided at the cost of eightpence.[2]

As Sir Richard dashed westward to the rescue, many rallied to his standard—a clatter of hoofs, a gathering at the village cross, a hasty collection of " harness," a donning of armour and weapons, amid the excitement of wives and children and low-breathed curses from those who sympathised with the rebels, a mounting of shaggy ponies or plough-horses, while a frugal meal was snatched by the weary riders from Plymouth way as they rested on the green, and then all together they disappeared with more clatter, more clouds of dust or more splashings of mud, to enact similar scenes at the next halting-place.

Soberly afterwards the churchwardens recorded how

---

[1] Aug. Of. Misc. Bk. 257, f. lxix, and P. C. Reg. 1548, f. 302.
[2] Hist. MSS. Com. Rept. IX. 277.

they sold their church goods—at Morval, to provide men
" to ride westward for to help to resist the last commotion " ; at St. Veep, for " conduct [1] men and for meat
and drink and for their wages and horses when the parish
went west to resist the commotion " ; and at Lanteglos
with Polruan " to pay xxvi^{ti} men their wages and for
their horses which men were sent forth by the whole
parish for to help to resist the last commotion in the
west part " ; at St. Winnow, to repay William Lowry,
" their captain when they went westwards in the King's
majesty's affairs against the rebellers of the west in five
pounds x^s which the said William Lowry at the request
of the whole parish disbursed " ; at " St. Nyghtens
by St. Winnow," " for meat, drink, and horses for the
carrying of men of the said parish when they went west
to resist the last commotion " ; at Boconnock, " borrowed
of one John Deyngell and John Coyche four pounds for
the charge of xviij^{ti} men and as many horses for their
meat, drink, and wages when they rode westwards for to
help resist the last commotion." [2]

The whole country must have been in a blaze : at
Launceston 13s. 4d. was paid to Henry Marker " at the
Commotion time by the commandment of the Eight
man " ; [3] while further north still we can trace the
excitement in the entries in the Stratton Churchwardens'
accounts : " for the business that was in the west part,"
x^s, for " bread and cheese for them, and xxxj^s iiij^d
given to Mr. Thomas Arundell to pay them that went
west at the business." [4]

---

[1] Conduct = hired.

[2] Church Goods. $\frac{1}{32}$. Cornwall. 3 Ed. VI. The spelling has been
modernised but it is very quaint. The repetition of the same phraseology
and spelling suggests that a scrivener went from parish to parish in a given
district to write up churchwardens' accounts.

[3] Accounts of the Guild of All Hallows, St. Thomas, Launceston.

[4] Add. MSS. 32, 244. f. 19. In the High Cross wardens' accounts of
the same place is entered " for the church harnys when ye besynys was be
west vj^d " (Add. MSS. 32, 243).

The hurrying feet sped westward or southward to uphold the Justices at Helston so rudely threatened in the exercise of their duty. The change of venue being arranged, these armed men would have provided an escort for the officers and their prisoners to prevent a rescue on their journey to Launceston.

The coming and going of official messengers, the collecting of witnesses, the sifting of evidence, and other business would have filled the ensuing month, an anxious interval for the whole county.

At last, about the 19th May, a weary horseman rode up the steep street towards Launceston Castle, his jaded horse spent with the rapid journey from his last stage, for he had ridden post from London, yet, in spite of his fatigue he cheerfully greeted the people, who augured well therefrom. It was rumoured that he not only bore the official writs for the trial, but also a general pardon. Like wild-fire the news spread, and the Castle Green was soon thronged in order to hear the dignified official, in his gorgeous robes, read out the proclamation dated at Westminster, the 17th May.

Pardon! Yes! but there are exceptions. The names are announced amid breathless silence, and yet when the proclamation is fastened up, it is eagerly scanned by those who can decipher the writing, to make sure of the name of a friend who might unluckily have been mentioned. Twenty-eight, there are in all, and many a heart must have ached with dread. Yet there is hope even for these, as the Grand Jury has not found a true bill against them. But that is not long delayed.

On the 21st May the Special Commission of Oyer and Terminer assemble, seven men of name and weight in the county, headed by Sir Richard Grenville,[1] while the names of the Grand Jury are almost as familiar, and

---

[1] The other Commissioners were Sir William Godolphin, Sir Hugh Trevanion, John Harris, sergeant-at-law, William Carnesew, Thomas St. Aubyn and William Bere.

included Humphrey Arundell and Robert Smyth.[1] Before them was laid the indictment of twenty-two prisoners, six having been selected by some preliminary process to be tried in London. The very parchment from which the clerk read is, presumably, the one still preserved with many an interlineation and erasure.

Against the following a true bill was found, and their trial fixed for the 28th May : William Kylter of Constantine ; John Kylter of the same ; John Kelyan of Loggan ; William Amys of Grade ; Oliver Ryse of St. Peran-in-le-Sand ; Richard Rawe, Pasco Trevian, Martin Resse or Resseigh, Henry Tyrlever, John Trybo the elder, and Thomas Tyrlan vian, all of St. Keverne. Two of these, John Kylter and Kelyan, were yeomen, Trevian, Tyrlever and Tyrlan vian were mariners, and the rest husbandmen. The following names were erased : John Williams of Parva Ruan, miller ; Richard Trewela of Redruth, yeoman ; John Chykose, Alan Rawe, Laurence Breton or Franke, Michael Vian Bretton, all of Gwennap, and all husbandmen but Franke, a groom ; John Tregena, husbandman ; James Tregena, James Robert, Michael John, Maurice Tryball, all mariners of St. Keverne, and Hugh Mason, otherwise Wavers, otherwise Parker. Against these, with the exception of Robert, no further action was taken.[2]

[1] The other Grand Jurymen were John Trelawney, whose son-in-law Wynslade was active in the rebellion of the following year, Richard Chamond John Trewenack, Degory Grenville, Richard Buller, John Dymok, John Amadas, John Bechamp, Sampson Manhitton, Walter Coode, John Langdon John Glynn of St. Columb, John Cosworthy, Thomas Tregowick, Thomas Spore, John Lowry of Polruan, and William Chiverton. Some of these may have been sympathisers with the rebels and therefore selected for the purpose of trying their fidelity.

[2] Most of these are place names derived from farms in these parishes. The last is so effectually erased that it is difficult to decipher, but both here and in the Privy Seal list it seems to be Mason, not Mascue as given in the copy of the Proclamation in Titus, B. II. Several errors have crept into the printed lists, notably Froude's miscount, due to lack of punctuation which led him to divide one name into two. *Vian* means " the little." Franke and Breton were obviously aliens.

After days of anxious waiting the day of the trial dawned. Launceston is again astir ; the country people from the remote districts agog with excitement as to the fate of their comrades, gathered with the rest at the Castle, where armed Cornishmen, augmented by smarter, but not more sturdy, trained soldiers, guarded the approach.

Leland, but a few years before, wrote of the large and ancient Castle standing upon " the knappe of the hill by south a little from the parish church," much of which then remained ; the " moles " on which the keep stood, was of a terrible height, " the arx of it, having several wards, is the strongest but not the biggest that ever I saw in any ancient work in England." Within was a chapel and a hall for " syses and sessions," which Norden, in 1584, describes as very spacious and in the base court and still used for the assizes of the whole shire. To this hall the ten men to be tried passed through the crowd, under the Sheriff's escort, emerging from that dark, dankish dungeon, infested with foul toads and other filthy vermin, where with bare stone-floors for beds and hard stones for pillows they had been confined.[1] Blinking at the transition from their gloomy cells to the bright May sunshine they passed wearily through the throng of friends and strangers.

All that pomp and state could do to impress the spectators would have been done. Aloft, upon the highest bench, sit the Judges sent down in commission in the middle. Next, on each side, are the Justices of the peace according to their degree. On a lower bench in front, are other Justices, gentlemen and their clerks. Before them and below is a table for the Custos Rotulorum, the Escheator, the Under Sheriff, and the writing clerks. At the end of the table is a bar made with a space for the " inquests," and the twelve men to enter

---

[1] See Robbins' "Launceston," pp. 102 and 109.

when they are called ; behind that another bar, where stand the prisoners, brought thither by the gaoler, chained to each other. " Then the Crier crieth and commandeth silence. One of the Judges briefly telleth the cause of their coming and giveth a good lesson to the people." Then the prisoners are called by name and bidden to answer.[1]

The Custos Rotulorum produces their indictments, and the presiding Judge commands William Kylter and Pascho Trevian to be first arraigned. After all forms have been duly complied with, these two say they cannot deny that they are guilty of high treason, felonies, and murders, but the others plead not guilty, and put themselves upon God and the country for good or for bad.

" Ye have pleaded not guilty," says the Clerk of the Court, " being asked how ye will be tried ye have answered by God and the country." Turning to Ryse, Kelyan and Robert, and indicating the jurors, he adds, " Lo, here be these honest men in the place of the country and if ye have anything to say to any of them look upon them well for ye stand upon your life or death."

Twelve men are duly sworn, and at each name the Crier ticks off, " one, two, three," etc. Formal questions are put and answered, and evidence is produced, but no record of this remains, for, writes Sir Thomas Smith—

" this is to be understood, although it will seem strange to all Nations, that do use the Civil Law of the Roman Emperors, that for life and death there is nothing put in writing but the Indictment only."

Finally, the Jury return their verdict : Ryse and Kelyan are not guilty ; Robert is guilty of murder only, but has no goods and chattels.

The same form is gone through for John Kylter,

---

[1] See Smith's " Common Wealth," p. 186 *et seq.*

Amys, Richard Rawe, Tyrlever, Trybo senior and Tyrlan vian, with a different jury, and all are convicted of high treason.

The worst is now known, and the tension in the Assize Hall is, for the moment, slackened.

The Commissioners, who are close at hand, give judgment: Those guilty of high treason, the seven named above, with William Kylter and Pascho Trevian, are condemned to be drawn through Launceston to the gallows, to be there hanged, and while still living to be thrown to the ground, their entrails removed and burnt before their eyes, and their heads amputated and their bodies quartered; these to be carried where the Lord the King may wish them to be assigned. But James Robert, guilty of murder, having no goods, chattels, or lands, is to be hanged only. Downcast and sad, the men returned to their cells to await execution, which seems to have been delayed. Indeed, at the outset a hitch occurred; when the scribe came to the words in the verdict "drawn . . . up to the gallows of—— " he stopped abruptly, leaving a blank space. Evidently a doubt arose, perhaps a question of difference of procedure between ordinary cases and those of high treason, or else as to the jurisdiction within which the criminal lay. The recently dissolved Priory of St. Stephen's had possessed "right of gallows," but this had fallen to the Crown. The gallows on the Castle Green pertained to the Duke of Cornwall, a title now merged in the Crown. High treason was a crime against the Crown: at which of the gallows were the prisoners to be executed? [1]

While these nice technicalities were being discussed, efforts were made to obtain pardons, or at least a mitigation of the brutal and brutalising sentence, and perhaps it was while matters were in abeyance that the curious event, recorded by Carew, happened—

[1] The Priory gallows were erected on the site now occupied by the schoolhouse beyond St. Stephen's Church, Mr. T. C. Reed informs me.

" For activity one Kilter, committed to Launceston Gaol for the Cornish commotion, lying there in the Castle green upon his back, threw a stone of some pounds' weight over the Tower's top which leadeth to the park."

Although some thought the number appointed to be executed in Cornwall was over great,[1] the Council would not admit it. They were determined to strike terror into the rebels' minds, and to crush the rising with a firm hand, so they wrote on the 3rd June, commanding the Commissioners in Cornwall to proceed with as convenient speed as may be to execute the traitors there, as they tendered the King's pleasure, and, in order that errors might not occur, they enclosed a list of those who were to suffer ; but this is lost, and we know not whether others than the above were included. But all hope for the condemned was not relinquished.

In the Privy Council Register, under the 16th June, is entered the payment of—

" John Harris, sergeant at Law, Henry Chiverton, and John Roscarrock, for their charges riding to Cornwall, tarrying there and returning from thence in the King's Majesty's affairs." [2]

These may have brought up a petition for pardon of those against whom no true bill had been found, for it is recorded on the Patent Rolls that a pardon was issued the 3rd September for all treasons committed before the 1st July by John Williams, Richard Trevela, Laurence Britton, Alan Rawe and Michael John ; and on the 6th October William Amys was pardoned, but nothing is found to show that the rest did not suffer a traitor's death.

But these were not the only victims in the West country. Beside those killed in encounters between the people and the authorities, others were executed. The

[1] P. C. Let-Bk. f. 79.   [2] Dasent's ed. p. 204.

Plymouth Municipal Records give details of the execution of the " Traytor of Cornwall " ; this nameless one was drawn to the Hoe, and there hanged and quartered in the presence of the Under-Sheriff of Cornwall. A vivid picture of the scene can be reconstructed : the wretched victim is brought to the town, wine is provided for his escort and dinner for the Under-Sheriff; a horse is supplied to draw him to the place of execution, gallows are erected on the Hoe and a dozen of faggots and a quarter of reed are provided for burning the entrails and boiling the head and quarters. The head and one quarter are set up on the Guildhall by two poles secured by cramps of iron, and finally a shilling is paid for the gruesome task of " carying a quarter of the traitor to Tavistock." [1] The disposition of the other quarters is not recorded, doubtless they were set up in some neighbouring town in order to bring home to the inhabitants the punishment of all would-be traitors. Nor is this likely to have been an isolated instance of a victim executed locally, though it is the only one discovered. Helston and Penryn would not have been without like ghastly reminders of the end of traitors, either quarters brought from Launceston or of local executions. John Militon, Sheriff of Cornwall, received £40 on the 12th December following for " his charge in taking and execution of certain rebellious in the County of Cornwall." [2] This may refer to the Launceston executions, but quite possibly it included others elsewhere in the county.

But there were yet other rebels, those selected and sent up to London : Sir Martin Geffrey, late of St. Keverne, clerk, John Peers, mariner, who made the

---

[1] See Worth's Plym. Mun. Rec. p. 115.

[2] Aug. Of. Misc. Bk. 257. f. 81. The date of the Launceston executions may safely be placed between 3rd Sept., the date of the recorded pardon, and a day early in December, as time must be allowed for sending up the charges and for having them audited.

proclamations, Edmund Irish, smith, and John William Tribo, junior, all of the same place; and William Thomas, otherwise Nenys, mariner of Mullion. They journeyed to London under the convoy of William Militon and William Veale, arriving on or before the 15th May, on which day £38 0s. 9d. was ordered to be paid their escort "toward their charges for bringing hither vj rebelles prisoners, out of Cornwall." [1]

Five of these rebels are identified above; the sixth is uncertain; the only one in the proclamation unaccounted for is Richard Hodge, whose name there occurs between two who were sent to London. He may have died from the rigours of imprisonment or from some injury received previously in the fray at Helston.

Two days after the above entry was made, the 17th May, the proclamation of pardon already mentioned received the King's signature. Probably Militon brought word that the authorities were satisfied that they had all the ring-leaders in custody, and it was deemed wise to deal leniently with the other Cornishmen. But a month elapsed before these five rebels were brought to their trial.

On the 11th June, 1548, Sir John Gage, Constable of the Tower, conveyed them in custody to Westminster Hall, where they were arraigned before the Justices and a Middlesex jury. They pleaded not guilty, but the verdict was adverse. The Court sentenced them to be taken back to the Tower, and thence drawn to the place of execution to be hanged and quartered. This was not done for nearly a month. Wriothesley records, under the 7th July—

" A priest was drawen from the Tower of London into

---

[1] P. C. Reg. (Dasent I. p. 198). In the above quoted Aug. Of. Misc. Bk. the corresponding entry is " William Meliton, Paide him the xvij of Maye for the charge as well in apprehendinge and bringeinge out of Cornwall hither to London six rebelles and prisoners as by a warrante dated the xvth of Maye appeareth the some of xxxviij^h ix^d." .

Smithfield and there hanged, headed, and quartered, and his members and bowels burnt, which was one of the causes of a commotion in Cornwall, where one Bodie, a gentleman and one of the King's commissioners, was slain, and other of the said traitors were put to death in divers other parts of this realm. His head was set on London Bridge and his quarters on four gates of this city." [1]

Geffrey seems to have suffered alone, and either strong petitions for mercy reached the Council or they were satisfied with the vengeance taken, for three of his companions, Irish, Tribo, and Thomas, received special pardons on the 10th August, and the fourth, Pyers, obtained his on the 13th September. So in the end all, except the following, out of the twenty-eight excluded from the proclamation of pardon, escaped execution :— William Kylter, Pascho Trevian, John Kylter, Richard Rawe, Martin Resse, James Robert, Henry Tyrlever, John Trybo the elder, and Thomas Tyrlan vian. Possibly even some of these were pardoned, but the record has escaped notice.

So William Body's death was avenged by the execution, if we are not mistaken, of ten known rebels and a number of others unrecorded.

The writers who have described Body's death give an account which differs in many particulars from the above, which is based on authoritative documents, chiefly the original indictment.

Odet de Selve, the French Ambassador, in a letter to his master of the 15th April, 1548, refers to the scarcity of soldiers and the doubts entertained by the Council, not only of the French King and the Scots, but of their own subjects, who, a few days before had risen in the

[1] Hamilton's ed. II. p. 4. The Grey Friars' Chronicle has " the vij day of July after there was a priest that came owte of Cornewalle drawne from the towre of London unto Smythefelde and there was honged and heddyd and qwarterd for slaying of one Boddy that was kynges commyssyoner in that country for chauntries " (p. 36).

county of Cornwall and had killed and made into a thousand pieces some commissioners, who had gone there to remove images, because they had cut down and broken the Crucifix of a church, which the people had insisted should be left.[1] This was probably the version current in London.

Holinshed refers to the " devilish attempted outrage," when—

" Certain seditious persons in Cornwall fell upon one of the commissioners named master Bodie, sent thither with others for the reformation of matters in religion . . . for the which murther a priest being apprehended arraigned and condemned, was drawn into Smithfield and there hanged and quartered the seventh day of July . . . other of his complices and associates were executed and put to death in divers parts of the realm." [2]

Norden, writing about 1584, under Helston, has—

" In this town one Kilter, and his most wicked adherentes, murthered an innocent gentleman, one Mr. Bodye, as he was exequitinge a Commission in the town for reformation of matter of Religion : and the year following it grew to a general rebellion." [3]

And under St. Keverne—

" In this parish, near the south sea shore, was the first occasion given of the Cornish Comotion by one Kylter and other wicked persons, who through their multitude and mighty favourites aspired high, and went far, yet came they short of their purpose, and fell as rebels." [4]

Carew writes a little later—

" The last Cornish rebellion was first occasioned by one Kylter, and other his associates of a western parish called St. Keverne, who imbrued their wicked hands in the guiltless

[1] Corres. Polit. p. 328.　　　　　[2] P. 917.
[3] See Spec. Brit. p. 46.　　　　　[4] Ibid. p. 47.

blood of one M. Body, as he sat in commission at Helston for matters of reformation of religion." [1]

Speed, about 1611, after stating that the idols in all churches were overthrown, continues—

"Whereof great stirs presently happened and in Cornwall the first. For the King's Commission being put in practice, and these gay golden Images cast down, broken and burnt, their Priests accounted the Act sacrilegious, and one of them as Baals for zeal sought to make his sacrifice with blood, but sparing his own sheathed his knife in the heart of Master Body a Commissioner, employed about the same business : which fact was so favoured among the rural Commons of Cornwall, and Devonshire (who ever gave voice for the papal continuance) that in rebellious manner they combined against the King."[2]

Of slightly later date is Sir John Hayward's account, upon which modern writers have usually based their version. After several references to the destruction of images and the distaste of the people for these innovations as well as remarks on the " unseasonable and un-seasoned fashions " employed which indicated hostility against images, he says—

"But in the meantime such tempests of sedition tumbled in England, more by default of Governours, than by the people's impatience to live in subjection, that not only the honour, but the safety of the state was thereby endangered. For as the Commissioners before mentioned passed to divers places for the establishing of their new injunctions, many unsavory scorns were cast upon them, and the further they went from London, as the people were more uncivil, so did they rise with insolency and contempt. At the last, as one Master Body a commissioner was pulling down images in Cornwall, he was suddenly stabbed into the body by a Priest with a knife. Hereupon the people more regarding Commotioners than Commissioners, flocked together in divers parts of the Shire, as clouds cluster against a storm : and albeit justice was afterwards done upon the offenders, the principall being hanged

---

[1] Cornwall, p. 237.   [2] Chronicle, p. 805.

and quartered in Smithfield, and divers other of his chiefe complices executed in divers parts of the Realm. Albeit so ample a pardon was proclaimed for all others within that Shire touching any action or speech tending to treason, yet could not the boldness be beaten down either with that severity, or with this lenity be abated." [1]

So the story, containing a grain of truth, grows. But Strype's version is simple : referring to the open rebellion in Cornwall, he adds—

" In this confusion, William Body, Gentleman, one on the King's side, was slain. But at length they were quelled, and begged the King's mercy and obtained it, yet the chief ringleaders were excepted and reserved for execution." [2]

C. S. Gilbert, of the modern writers, embroiders the story a little, and describes Body as " performing his duty in Bodmin church," instead of at Helston. [3] Davies Gilbert says that Mr. Body, going to do his duty in Helston church, " a priest, in company with Kiltor of Kevorne and others, at unawares stabbed him in the body with a knife of which wound he instantly fell dead in that place." [4]

Froude states—

" The preachers provoked a rising in Cornwall in the summer of 1548, and a royal commissioner named William Body, was murdered in a church. But a priest who had been concerned in it, was hanged and quartered in Smithfield, twenty-eight other persons were put to death in different parts of the country and the riot was suppressed."

In a note he adds that he infers that twenty-nine suffered in all because the pardon excluded that number. [5]

---

[1] P. 53.

[2] Eccles. Mem. II. i. 143.

[3] P. 16.

[4] P. 191.

[5] V. 97. Only twenty-eight are named in the proclamation including the priest. " Preachers " is more commonly applied to those of the " New Learning."

Even Dr. Gairdner falls into some errors, calling Body a royal agent stabbed by a priest, attributing the disaffection to the rumours of new taxation, and giving over thirty persons excepted by name.[1]

Putting together these stories we have : Body, an innocent man (save the mark !), murdered in Helston church in the act of destroying images, stabbed suddenly, at unawares, in the back by a priest and Kilter. For this twenty-nine or over thirty were, apparently, executed.

But the evidence now produced shows that Body, who had already provoked a riot, was followed to Helston, where he was found taking refuge in a house.   Kilter and Trevian seem to have been the actual murderers, while not more than ten, if as many, of those excepted from the pardon, suffered death.

---

[1] " Hist. Eng. Church in Sixteenth Cent.," 256.   Robbins (" Launceston Past and Present," p. 93) says Body was stabbed to instantaneous death by William Kylter while demolishing images at Helston.   Kylter and twenty-nine comrades suffered death.   He styles Kylter a priest.   " Plymouth . . . in War and Peace " has : In defence of the Mass an uprising occurred, but it was easily suppressed, and only " one bodye was slayne in the fight ! "

CHAPTER VI

THE RINGLEADERS

" Periods of revolution bring out and develope extraordinary characters :
they produce saints and heroes, and they produce also fanatics and
fools, and villains : but they are unfavourable to the action of average
conscientious men and the application of the plain principles of right
and wrong to everyday life."—FROUDE.

THE year 1549 opened darkly, threatening to be a period
of revolution. In the early months risings occurred in
many counties : Hayward mentions Sussex, Hampshire,
Kent, Gloucester, Warwick, Essex, Hertford, Leicester,
Worcester, and Rutland, and adds—" partly by authority of gentlemen, and partly by entreaty of honest
persons they were reduced to some good appeasement." [1]
Strype asserts that the first insurrection was at North-
hall and Cheshunt, in Hertfordshire, and he includes
Somerset, Wilts, Surrey, and Yorkshire among the disturbed counties. [2] The spirit of discontent was indeed
abroad, the people flocking together " as clouds cluster
against a storm."

The question of the hour must have been, what would
happen if these sporadic movements were united under
a leader of master mind, who could bring together into
a compact force those who objected to the agrarian and
the religious situation ? Such a combination was dreaded

[1] " Edward the Sixth," p. 58.

[2] He gives Oxford and Berkshire, but these were more closely connected
with the later risings.

H

by Somerset's party, and it would have ended the control which they had established with so much scheming and trouble. On the other hand, the opponents of his autocratic rule sought eagerly for such a leader. Was he to be found ? Would he succeed in combining the different elements, and, above all, would he command the allegiance of all classes of society ?

It has been pointed out that the theory was held that a remonstrance presented by representatives of both estates of the realm could force the abdication of a monarch constitutionally. How much more easily could they displace the " Governours " of a king in his minority.

From this point of view the leaders of the Western Rebellion must be considered, and, after studying all available information, it must be admitted that they did not fulfil these conditions, not being sufficiently representative of the higher estate, and to this, in some measure, their failure must be attributed.

The acknowledged leaders were Arundell, Wynslade, Bury, and Pomeroy. The only title among them was that of Sir Thomas Pomeroy, Wynslade was an " Esquire of the White Spur," and Arundell was a member of one of the most powerful West Country families.

HUMPHREY ARUNDELL, born about 1513, was son of Roger Arundell [1] of Helland, Cornwall, a scion of the Lanherne family, by his wife Joan, daughter and heir of Humphrey Calwoodley, of Calwoodleigh, Devon. On the death of his parents, in 1536 and 1537, he inherited large estates in both counties.[2] Of his early years little is known, but he was probably brought up in the use of arms. Hayward describes him as " a man well esteemed

---

[1] Roger was a younger son of Thomas Arundell of Lanherne, by his wife Katherine, daughter of Sir John Dinham. He died 12th June, 1536. Humphrey Calwoodley, Roger's father-in-law, resided at Helland, near Bodmin, and was implicated in the Perkin Warbeck conspiracy of 1497, being attainted but not executed. He died in 1507 and his daughter was restored in blood : she died 28th Sept., 1537.

[2] Leland mentions him as " a man of mene lands," *i.e.* of *many* lands.

for his military services," and in a list of men supplied for the army against France, is entered "Humphrey Arundell, himself and X on fote."

It is frequently asserted that Arundell was Governor or Captain of the Mount, *i.e.* St. Michael's Mount.[1] Some writers declare that after the Dissolution the Mount was granted to him,[2] and one adds that after his execution " Edward VI. sold or gave the government and revenues to Job Militon." [3] But John Militon was Captain and Farmer of the Mount as early as 1522 under Syon Abbey, and a grant of its revenues to his son William in 1534 by the Abbess was confirmed by Henry VIII. and re-granted by Elizabeth to his descendants.[4] As Arundell is so persistently considered ruler of the Mount, it can only be suggested that he was the military

[1] None of the contemporary chroniclers mention this, nor does Hoker in his account of the Siege of Exeter, though in his edition of Holinshed he styles him "Humfry Arundell esquier, gouernor of the Mount." Foxe (ed. 1563) calls him "governor of the Mount," and so do Carew and Speed. Godwin (1630) has " Captain " and Heylin (1660) has " Commander."

[2] Lysons's " Cornwall " has, " In 1533 it was given with all its revenues (valued at 110^l 12^s per annum) to Humphrey Arundell of Lanherne." Hals values it at 200^l and gives the same date (Add. MSS. 29, 762 f. 116^d).

[3] Davies Gilbert, II. p. 191. He gives 33 Henry VIII., 1542.

[4] On 4th Feb., 1534, John Militon and his son William obtained a grant from the Abbess for thirty years of the farm of St. Michael's Mount, among the conditions being the maintenance of an Arch-priest and two other priests. The Minister's Accounts of Cornwall have continuous references to the Militons, father and son, sometimes one sometimes the other, as " farmer " of the Mount, but John is called Captain of the Mount until his death in 1549. About 1551 William Militon failed to pay the charge for the priests : as far back as 1542-3 the salary of the minor priests had been transferred to support a gunner, and the Arch-priest prior to 1552 obtained a post as teacher of grammar at Penryn. For a long time the charge for the sustentation of the priests is entered as in arrears in the accounts until the original lease terminated and the authorities investigated the matter. Thereupon Militon claimed that he was not bound to pay this as under Edward VI. all chantries had been suppressed. The Lords finally decided this claim in his favour, and a new lease for forty years was granted by Elizabeth, with special provisions for the maintenance of five soldiers and of all the instruments of war there as well as its defence against all enemies, rebels, and traitors. On the expiration of this lease the Earl of Salisbury obtained it.

officer in command of the five or more soldiers employed, under the terms of his lease, by Militon to defend the " fortlet," or perhaps in charge of some soldiers sent by the King to augment the garrison when a French attack was feared.[1]

Humphrey Arundell married Elizabeth, daughter of Sir John Fulford, by whom he had two sons, Humphrey and Richard, and a daughter.[2] Soon after his execution his widow married Thomas Cary of Cary,[3] and died on the 24th November, 1565.

JOHN WYNSLADE was of the family of Wynslade of Wynslade,[4] in Buckland Brewer, who " for their great revenues," writes Risdon, " were dignified with the title of ' Esquires of the White Spurs.' " [5] He held large estates in both counties, his chief residence being Tregarrick, in Pelynt, where he kept great hospitality. He was the son of William Wynslade [6] by Joan, daughter and heir of John Eston of Eston. John married first Jane, daughter of Sir John Trelawney, of Menheniot, by Jane, daughter of Sir Robert Holland. This latter Jane was the widow of John Kendall, of Pelynt, and mother of

---

[1] Carew (1602) distinctly states that as soon as he left that stronghold it was garrisoned against him.

[2] Chancery Proc. Eliz. Ser. II. 6.80. He had also an illegitimate son, Giles, born about 1534, for whom he made provision in 1544 by leasing land from John Wynslade. After Arundell's execution, and perhaps earlier, Giles formed one of the family, living with the widow, "who had the governance of him by reason of his tenderness of age " (Court of Requests, 78.83 and 86.21).

[3] She had eight children by Cary.

[4] Sometimes spelt Wydeslade.

[5] "Devon," p. 246. "The King himself, together with a title, giveth arms or createth esquires by putting about their necks a silver collar of S S, and (in former times) upon their heels a pair of white spurs, silvered : whereupon at this day in the west parts of the kingdom, they are called white spurs, for distinction from knights, who are wont to wear gilt spurs ; and to the first begotten sons only of these doth the title belong " (" Weever's Fun. Mon. " p. 357). Lysons (" Cornwall," p. cxxix) says the Coplestones of Lamerton also held this title.

[6] William Wynslade was son of Richard Wynslade by Marina, daughter of John Byrt of Bochym, who was a great heiress.

William Kendall, who was executed in connection with the Exeter Conspiracy—that is to say, John Wynslade's wife Jane was half-sister to William Kendall. By her he had one son, William. After her decease, about 1544, he married Agnes, whose surname is unknown. Apparently they had no children. Soon after his execution she married John Trevanion of Carhayes.[1]

WILLIAM WYNSLADE, son of John, had already grown to man's estate at the time of the Rebellion, and resided at Mithian, in St. Agnes, which belonged to his father. Although he took an active part in the Rising, he was released with other prisoners. He was afterwards known as " of Vgmore in Co. Glamorgan." For some reason he fled the kingdom in 1579.[2] He married,[3] apparently before the Commotions, and had two sons and a daughter.[4]

---

[1] See Exchq. Com. 531 and Exchq. Dep. 26–27 Eliz. Mich. 26 and 27–28 Eliz. Mich. 18. John Wynslade had two brothers, Robert and Luke, and three sisters ; Philippa married Nicholas Barret, perhaps related to Roger Baret, priest, one of the rebels ; Joan married Humphrey Bonville of Ivybridge, who was released on recognizances in 1550; and Anne married Richard Cole of Woolfardisworthy. Wynslade's kinship was remarkable ; William Kendall, the conspirator, his half-brother-in-law, married the widow of Wynslade's first cousin, Thomas Pyne of Ham. Edmund Kendall's widow married Gilbert Beckett, brother and host of Roger Beckett. (See Chap. II.)

[2] Perhaps in connection with the Jesuit plots of that date.

[3] He may have been the William Wynslade who married Jane, daughter of Nicholas Babington of Ottery St. Mary.

[4] Tristram and Daniel. Of the former Carew writes : " He led a walking life with his harp to gentlemen's houses, where through and by his other qualities, he was entitled Sir Tristram ; neither wanted he (as some say) a ' bele Isoud,' the more aptly to resemble his pattern " (p. 309). His name really was Tristram ; he was captured by the Spaniards, but before that he had laid claim to certain Courtenay estates, saying his grandmother, Jane Trelawney, was grand-daughter of Edward, Earl of Devon, and on the death of Edward, son of Henry, Marquis of Exeter, these estates should have reverted to her heirs, a claim he was not able to substantiate (Chancery Proc. Eliz. Ser. II. 230. 64). Daniel Wynslade followed up the claim but devised a different pedigree : he said his grandfather, John Wynslade, married Jane, daughter of . . . Kendall (she was daughter of Jane Holland, widow of John Kendall, by John Trelawney). This Kendall had married Anne, daughter of Sir Hugh Courtenay by his second wife—a lady ignored by

John Bury is thus described in a contemporary tract :—

"The chief captain of all, saving one, was the Marquis of Exeter's man, and setteth forth the matter of the Cardinal so much, as indeed he maketh no other matter. His name is Berry, one of them which subscribed the Articles." [1]

A thorough search through the detailed lists of the Marquis's servants does not disclose this name. According to his own account at the time of the first disturbance in Exeter, in June, 1549, he was servant, *i.e.* wore the livery of, Sir Thomas Denys, and he resided at Silverton. He had estates at Hartland, Ugborough, Tavistock, Plympton, Widecombe-in-the-Moor, and elsewhere. [2]

He was the son of Lewis Bury or Berry [3] by his wife Margaret, who afterwards married Thomas Darke. The latter had the guardianship of John for four years, and then gave it to John Ashe of Sowton, who married Bury to his daughter. [4]

Robert Smyth, of Tregonack, in St. Germans, who bravely led a charge at Fenny Bridges, was son of Thomas Smyth, of the same. He married first, before 1522, Elizabeth, daughter of John Skenock, of Trewint,

genealogists (Harl. MS. 660, p. 162). Daniel also sought to recover some estates given by John Wynslade in dower to his second wife. (See Exchq. documents, quoted above.) Joan, daughter of John Wynslade, was " contracted and affied " to John Jolle, of Warbstowe, Cornwall, who " doth entend by the sufferans of god to marie according to the Lawes of Holie Church," but owing to difficulties over the marriage settlement the marriage did not take place and a lawsuit ensued (Chancery Proc. Eliz. Ser. II. 102, 76).

[1] " A Copie of a Letter." See Appendix K. Oddly enough his Christian name is omitted from all the copies of the Articles preserved.

[2] Lysons says he leased the manor of Canonteign from Lord Russell (" Devon," 103).

[3] He was probably of the Berrynarbor family and his wife's name may have been Cove ; through her John inherited the estates of John Kyrton.

[4] " Court of Requests," 8. 292.

in Blisland, where he usually resided.[1] His second wife was Katherine, daughter of Lawrence Courtenay, of Ethy. He survived the Rebellion, dying the 28th April, 1569, leaving two sons, Robert and John, by his first wife.

THOMAS HOLMES came also from Blisland, and was a servant to Sir John Arundell. He was of the yeoman class, and probably, as representing them, was selected for execution, having been a particularly active rebel.

— COFFIN, gentleman, was also one of Sir John Arundell's servants, but his Christian name is un-obtainable.[2]

SIR THOMAS POMEROY, son and heir of Sir Edward Pomeroy, of Berry Pomeroy, was born about 1503. He sold his ancestral estates, the Castle, Park, and Manor of Berry Pomeroy, to the Protector Somerset, with whose descendants they still continue.[3] Pole says that Sir Thomas " consumed his estate, & decayed his house." [4] Perhaps his hatred of the purchaser of his property or his recklessness, for he had nothing to lose, made him espouse the rebels' cause. While he was fighting against the Government, papers granting him monastic lands in Cornwall, were passing through the Augmentation Office.[6] Prince describes him as a " commander in the

---

[1] Blisland or Bliston is near Helland, Arundell's home. Blisland, Helland, and St. Columb, which to-day seem so remote, were formerly on the main line of traffic. Maclean states that until 1769 the western road from Launceston lay through Bodmin, passing close to Blisland and Helland, and then by St. Lawrence and St. Wenn Churchtown to St. Columb.

[2] Richard Coffin of Porthledge, who died in 1555, had four brothers and a sister ; the latter married John Kestell of Kestell, perhaps related to Kestell (or Castell) who betrayed Arundell.

[3] Lysons (" Devon," p. 43) says he made over his property to Somerset to save his life after this rebellion, but he questions this in a note, pointing out that at the time of Sir Thomas's attainder the Protector was in the Tower and was shortly afterwards beheaded. Pomeroy was never attained. Vivian (" Visit. Devon," 607) states that Sir Thomas sold it to Seymour, 1st Dec. 1547.

[4] Collections, p. 281.

[5] This included, among others, the Chapel of St. John by Helston, held by John Harrys, the active enemy of Body.

wars under Henry the VIII. in France." He married
Jone, daughter of Sir Piers Edgcumbe.[1]

WILLIAM FORTESCUE bears a well-known Devon
name, but it has not been possible to identify him with
any William living at that period.

JOHN WISE may have been the John Wyse of Sydenham, born about 1527, closely related to the wife of
William Kendall.

JOHN BOCHYM, of Bochym, and his brother, probably
ROBERT BOCHYM, priest, JOHN and JAMES RESOGAN, or
Rosogan, of St. Columb, JOHN PAYNE, Portreeve, of
St. Ives, —— DREW, perhaps of the Kenn, afterwards
Killerton, family, WILLIAM MAYOW, of Clevyan, in
St. Columb, are found among the rebels. From all this
it is evident that the best of the county families of Devon
and Cornwall contributed to the ranks of the insurgents.

As representatives of the Commons, we have the
Mayors of Torrington and Bodmin, the tailors, labourers,
etc., of Sampford Courtenay, certain merchants of
Exeter, and other such.

The Church was represented by many priests beside
those mentioned above : John Wolcock, William Alsa,
James Mourton, John Barrow, Richard Benet, John
Thompson, and others.[2] But, above all, were the Canons
of Exeter, already in prison, whose release was demanded.

RICHARD CRISPYN appears in the Oxford Registers
as "of Devon." He probably belonged to the ancient
family that dwelt at Woolston, in West Alvington.[3]

---

[1] "Worthies," p. 649. Perhaps his connection with the Edgecumbes
favoured his escape from attainder. He is described in a deposition of
1553 as "a symple gente": apparently on the strength of this Maclean
attributes his escape to his "weak intellect" ("Life of Sir P. Carew," p.
156, *n.*).

[2] For such information as has been found concerning the above, see
Appendix L.

[3] A Robert Crispyn held land at Ide of the Dean and Chapter, which
passed to his son John in 1526. In Richard Crispyn's will mention is made
of his brother John, and a John Crispyn was " fermour or proctour to one

He was fellow of Oriel College from 1514 to 1527, when he was appointed Rector of Woodleigh.[1] On the 28th March, 1530, he was instituted to Harberton, which he held with the chapel of Halwell and Woodleigh, in 1536.[2] He was also Chaplain to the Marquis of Exeter,[3] and was made Canon of Exeter the 15th June, 1541.[4]

He was of the party opposed to Dean Heynes,[5] and to this fact, in some measure, may be attributed his subsequent imprisonment. He incurred the violent enmity of one Philip Nycolles, who made notes of a sermon preached by Dr. Crispyn, on the 13th March, 1546-7, at Marldon at the "month's mind of Master Otes Gilbert."[6] Nycolles published a book confuting it in the following April. This may have been one of the sermons for which Crispyn was imprisoned, so quotations from the reply are here given.

" Among other things, I remember you envied Luther very sore, only because he would have the Scriptures to be the touch stone, or trial of all other doctrines. And calling Luther, as it were, into disputations with all his disciples, you put forth three questions which be these.

" First, if there rose any heresies or dissensions before the Gospel was written (as there did indeed, between Simon Magus and Simon Peter, and over the circumcision) ask Luther and his disciples, who now shall discuss the matter, and who should

Mr. Richard Crispyn, the vicar of Harberton," and a Thomas Crispyn held that office under another vicar later. (See Records of Consistory Court, Exeter.)

[1] His name occurs among the " well-learned " doctors " not abiding in Oxford but in Devon " (L. & P. V. 6). Foster's " Alumn : Oxon : " gives also : B.A. 20th Feb. 1513-4 ; M.A. 14th July, 1519, junior proctor 1522, B.D. 1527, D.D. 1531-2.

[2] See Taxatio made by Bp. Veysey.

[3] John Dering told him of the Nun of Kent's prophecies concerning the King, but Crispyn apparently escaped implication in the so-called conspiracy (L. & P. VI. 1468).

[4] He was one of the keepers of the Chest of the Fabric of the Cathedral in 1547.

[5] See Chapter XI.

[6] Otes Gilbert, father of Sir Humphrey, died 18th Feb. 1546-7.

be the touch stone to try the matter. The Gospel, can not, for it was not then written.

" The second question is. If one should deny Matthew's Gospel or say Matthew wrote it not : how can it be proved by Scripture ? It can not you say, for Scripture speaketh not of it.

" The third question did deceive the ignorant people, which have little or no knowledge. If there be dissension or strife about the understanding of the Scripture, and both allege Scripture, as the Arians did, who brought two places of Scripture for the defence of their error, in such case you ask who shall be judges : or by whom shall this be determined ? Or rather to use your very words : where is Luther's touch stone ? The Scripture can not be touch stone you say, for both bring forth Scripture. Wherefore there must needs be another touch stone. Where is Luther now, quoth you. What answer can be made to these questions ? For Luther's touch stone will not serve. Your answer was therefore, that Luther must give place and say with you, that it is the Holy Ghost that would be touch stone.

" Thus you triumphed upon Luther and his disciples meaning by Luther's disciples such (I suppose) as hold his opinion, as though you had overcome them that could answer nothing.

" This is easy to do, when the man hath the talk himself. But for so much as you wished Luther there at your sermon or some of his disciples, to answer to your questions, I think verily you will be content to hear a poor man answer." [1]

---

[1] See Nycolles' " Copie of a letter sente to one Maister Chrispyne, chanon of Exeter, for that he denied scripture to be the touch stone or trial of al other doctrines whereunto is added an appologie and a bulwarke in defence of the same letter." (Lambeth Palace Library 31. 8. 17.) The border of the title page is almost exactly the same as the " Copie of a Letter " given in Appendix K. Among the Cecil Papers at Hatfield is a letter from this same Nycolles to Sir William Cecil urging him, in strong language, to warn the Queen (Elizabeth) against idolatry, the papists and covetousness at Court and advising more preaching to be ordered by her. It is dated 1560. He had already printed a volume on the " History of the XII men that were sent to spye out the Land of Canaan." He applies the story of the oppression of Israel under Pharaoh to England under the Pope and rails against the preachers of the day. Originally published in 1548 it was re-published later, reference to " a gratious Judith " (Elizabeth) being substituted for " a yonge Josias " (Edward).

Nycolles published this reply with a dedication to "the right worshipfull and his syngular good Maister syr Peter Carewe," with a "bulwark" or supplement added the 7th November, 1547.

It is probable that Sir Peter, thus appealed to, laid the matter before the authorities, with the result that Crispyn had to answer a charge of heresy,[1] and remained confined in the Tower until his death, which took place between the 9th September and the 10th December, 1551.[2]

JOHN MOREMAN, S.T.P., "clarum et venerabile nomen," was born at South Hole, in Hartland, about 1490, and was educated at Oxford. He was fellow of Exeter College, 1510–1522. Prince says that he obtained this position—

"with no small difficulty, being opposed therein, with great violence and a powerful influence by one Mr. Atkins, of the same college, who having obtained letters from Bishop Holdham of Exeter on his behalf, assured himself of the place. But Mr. Moreman, for his more eminent learning and accomplishments, as is most likely, found that favour in the house that he carried the fellowship."[3]

Atkins's failure so grieved the Bishop that he bestowed large revenues, intended for this college, upon Corpus Christi.

In 1522, Moreman was instituted to Instow, his first living in this diocese; in 1528 he held Holy Trinity, Exeter; and in 1529 he was instituted to Menheniot, in Cornwall.[4] Here this very industrious man, as Prince

[1] Crispyn gives the same reason as Moreman's for his imprisonment—the accusement of the Dean of Paul's for his preaching in the West.

[2] That is, between the writing and proving of his will (P. C. C. F. 36 Bucke). Moreman was one of the executors, but owing to his continued imprisonment John Stephyn (probably the Canon) was appointed to act for him.

[3] Worthies, p. 600.

[4] He was also Principal of Hart Hall, 1522–7, Canon of Glasney, 1532, Canon of Exeter, 1539, Vicar of Colebrook, 1546.

says, undertook the honourable fatigue of instructing youth in school-learning.   The Chronicler Hoker was one of his pupils, and gives this account of him :—

" He was of a very honest and good nature, loving to all men, and hurtful unto none : and that he was the first in those days, that taught his parishioners and people to say the Lord's prayer, the Belief, and the Commandments in the English tongue, and did teach and catechise them therein." [1]

It is, therefore, the more remarkable to find him associated with the rebels who objected to the use of English in the Church service.   He had evidently endeared himself to the people, and this, with opposition to Dean Heynes' action, led them to demand his release.   He was one of those sent to examine Thomas Benet, the anti-papist, and, with his colleagues, endeavoured to avert his fate.[2]

Prince suggests that he was imprisoned in the Tower either for refusing the oath of supremacy or for over-zealousness for certain points in the Romish religion. But his own statement, made in prison, was that he—

" was committed to the Tower for preaching in the West country by the accusement of the Dean of Paul's and other commissioners there and he was examined by the Lord Archbishop of Canterbury as he saith and his sermons whereupon he is accused is in the Fleet with his stuff there." [3]

He was apparently imprisoned, with Dr. Crispyn, early in 1547.[4]

Dr. Moreman was highly esteemed at Oxford, and had been one of the small company of Divines who had opposed the Divorce.[5]   He was one of the prisoners personally released by Mary on her accession, and seemed

---

[1] Add. MSS. 5827, fol. 45ᵈ.
[2] See Chap. XI.
[3] S. P. Dom. Ed. VI. IX. 48.
[4] See Harl. MSS. 249, f. 40.
[5] See " Grysilde the Seconde," p. 76, among Katherine's chief friends Moreman is mentioned.

destined to high preferment ; Prince suggests that he was in such grace with the Queen that, had he lived longer, he would have " ascended the top of preferment in the Church." In the Convocation of 1553, he was appointed to dispute with the Protestant Divines, especially with Mr. Cheney, Archdeacon of Hereford, who argued against " the darling doctrine of those times, transubstantiation." His selection—

" must be acknowledged a great honour, and argues a very high opinion the convocation had of the man, that he among so many eminent and learned men, should be pitched upon for so great an undertaking." [1]

After his release Moreman resided at Exeter, and was " appointed to be the Dean of the said Church, but before he was possessed thereof he died about the beginning of Elizabeth." [2] He does not appear even to have been elected Dean. He died between the 20th May and the 14th August, 1554.

These two " grave priests " are found at the opening of the Rebellion imprisoned in the Tower for upholding the ancient forms of religion, and as its representatives, their release was demanded by the West Countrymen. [3]

[1] Worthies, p. 601. Foxe (VI. p. 397) gives this disputation at length and shows much animus against Moreman. Ridley (Works. Par. Soc. p. 362) wrote to Cranmer, " It is said also, that Justice Hales has recanted, perverted by Dr. Moreman."

[2] Harl. MSS. 5827. Hoker had written " presented " but corrected it to ". possessed." It is incorrectly asserted that he was appointed bishop on Veysey's death.

[3] There is a curious entry relating to these two Divines in the Chapter Act Book at Exeter (3553. fol. 60), dated 1554, relating to the payment of their dues as Canons during their confinement in London. The Privy Council had written to the Dean and Chapter on this subject as they desired their " dividentes " paid so that there would be money to pay for their diets in the Tower. (See P. C. Reg. 29th May, 1552, and 25th March, 1553.)

CHAPTER VII

" It is certain that the majority of persons, most of all those who are quite
unused to analyse the causes which lead to a result, ascribe to one or
two events, occurring concurrently with an effect which makes them
anxious or distresses them, the whole effect of which they complain."
—THOROLD ROGERS.

WITHOUT going into the details of the economic and
ecclesiastical changes of the period it is necessary to
consider certain points which bear upon our subject, and
particularly the state of affairs as it appeared to the eyes
of the populace.

That it was a time of crisis as well as a period of
suffering for the masses is undoubted. Burnet draws [1]
a vivid picture of the distress and attributes the condition of things to various causes : the destruction of the
monasteries, the enhanced rents caused by the transfer
of their estates, the injustice of the enclosure of their
common-lands and the enforcement of wages fixed at the
landlords' pleasure, and he concludes : " By this means
the Commons of England saw they were like to be
reduced to great misery."

An earlier writer [2] draws an even more gloomy picture
of the terrible condition of the Commons, whose children
could be brought up only to " garnish gallow trees."

This serious state of affairs is attributed to two
primary causes : the enclosure of common-lands and

[1] " Reformation," II. 234.
[2] " An Information and a Petition," 1548.

the changes of ownership with other alterations arising from the suppression of the monasteries ; while there were subsidiary causes, such as the debasement of the currency, Court extravagance, etc.

The question of enclosures was by no means a new one. In 1489, efforts were made to deal with it by legislation, and in 1514 an " inquisition of enclosures " was undertaken. But the effects of these attempts were by no means satisfactory, so it continued a burning question down to the period of which we are treating. But it was less acute in the West than elsewhere. Already much of the land in Devon,[1] including wastes, had been enclosed, and was to a considerable extent in the hands of husbandmen, who raised thereon sheep of which, it is said, there were more than in any other county,[2] as may be inferred from its great woollen trade.

Before this time Henry VIII. had disparked all the Marquis of Exeter's parks in this district, expecting great benefit to the commonwealth by tilling and pasture, but this caused great discontent among the gentry, who were thus debarred from their recreations and pastimes,[3] and, presumably, corresponding satisfaction among the people.

In Cornwall, also, the land was already largely given to pasture, which the tinners, not able to use themselves,

[1] Hoker writes : "For the husbandman, be he poor or rich, be his bargain (farm) great or small, he hath always some sheep, be they more or less and it is supposed and by some affirmed that the number of sheep in this country is as great or greater than in any shire in the land " (Harl. MS. 5827, f. 10).

[2] One of the complaints of the earlier Articles concerned the tax on sheep.

[3] Hoker (Harl. MS. 5827). He says this was done at the instance of Sir Richard Pollard, and that in consequence of the discontent of the gentry the King so chid and fell out with him " that he took it in such grief as he never enjoyed himself but died." He also refers to the benefit derived by the husbandmen from the divided fields which allowed change for cattle while the hedges provided firewood. In the " Commonweal of this Realm of England " (ed. Lamond, p. 49) Devon is mentioned among the counties in which the commons were most enclosed and which were, therefore, the most wealthy. Hoker also states that the most part of the county was enclosed.

let out to "foreigners" of neighbouring counties.[1] The fact that at this period, when throwing open of enclosures was a frequent cause of actions in the Courts, the Star Chamber and the Court of Requests had before them so few cases from the West relating to enclosures, indicates that agrarian discontent could not have been an important factor in the Western Rebellion.[2]

But the Dissolution of the Monasteries had more influence on the situation here. The monastic land was granted chiefly to courtiers who had no connection with the district, while often the outlying members of the estates passed to persons of lesser rank. Frequently the properties continued to be managed by the same bailiffs or stewards who had served the monasteries, but with the difference that they displayed a greater desire to increase the revenues of their new masters, doubtless aware that their tenure of office depended largely upon a more favourable balance-sheet. Where the smaller estates were managed by the new owners personally, it would appear that greater friction existed than of old between landlord and tenant.[3]

---

[1] Carew's "Survey" (ed. Dunstanville, p. 61). Mr. W. J. Blake, in his "Rebellion of Cornwall and Devon," has gone very fully into this subject, and I am indebted to him for several suggestions. He quotes from Carew, and concludes that it is proved " that the land was mainly given to pasture so that if any enclosures took place at this time they would obviously be beneficial as increasing instead of decreasing employment." Both he and Prof. Gay strongly controvert the theory that the Western Rebellion was due to the enclosure question.

[2] Prof. Gay, who carefully examined the records of both courts, found in the Star Chamber four enclosure cases in Cornwall and three in Devon ; and in the Court of Requests none for Cornwall and one for Devon (Trans. Roy. Hist. Soc. XVIII. p. 208, n.). Mr. Blake states that in Edward VI.'s reign there are none in either court for Cornwall but two in each for Devon, and one of these cases was tried in both courts. He also refers to the litigious character of the Cornishmen and to the size of the two counties, adding that of the 716 cases of Edward's reign 65 refer to Cornwall and 64 to Devon ; while in Henry VIII.'s reign a rough calculation shows that 13 per cent. of the total cases came from these two counties.

[3] This statement is based upon a careful examination of Chancery Proceedings relating to Devonshire.

For a while old monastic leases were usually respected and allowed to run out their time, but many were called in by the new lords of the manors on the ground of the illegality of some of the recent monastic leases, while others were surrendered by timid tenants who feared that some flaw might be found if their leases were submitted to the common-law courts, so they sought safety in leases from the new lord, granted at enhanced rents and accompanied by oppressive admission fines.[1]

Much land, especially in Devonshire, where the proportion which had been retained by the monks for their own cultivation was large, was thrown upon the market. This supply of new holdings tended to depreciate the lettable value of the old and a fall in rents would naturally be expected, but instead such evidence as we have goes to prove that the rents either remained as of old in spite of deterioration and glut of the market, or were enhanced,[2] especially, one student of the subject points out,[3] higher rents were demanded from the poorer tenants, while the richer, better able to resist such demands, were more fortunate. Such differentiation was an added grievance to the populace, while all the tenants, seeing such momentous changes around them, must have felt their own position insecure, so that they would be likely to do their best to obtain immediate returns instead of pursuing an economic system of husbandry—in such cases further deterioration would have taken place in the interval between the Dissolution and 1549.

Moreover, the new owners or their deputies persisted in reviving ancient claims in order to deprive tenants of their privileges. Some of these claims had already been successfully contested by tenants in the law courts,

[1] See " Leadam's Court of Requests," p. lxviii.

[2] *Op. cit.* He refers to an increase of rents on one estate amounting to 122·48 per cent.

[3] Hibbert, " Dissolution of the Monasteries," p. 99,

particularly in regard to rights of common pasture. The more prosperous tenants now carried their complaints to the Court of Requests, or elsewhere, causing more friction between landlord and tenant—resulting frequently in forcible destruction of fencing on the one hand, and forcible ejection of beasts, with injury to the same, on the other.

Writing of such riots, Ascham says—

" Who are the real authors ? Those who have everywhere in England got the farms of the monasteries, and are striving to increase their property by immoderate rents. Hence the exaggerated price of things. These men plunder the whole realm. Hence so many families dispersed, so many houses ruined. Hence the honour and strength of England, the noble yeomanry, are broken and destroyed." [1]

This discontent with the state of affairs, which found expression throughout the country, it was thought could be removed by legislation on the matter in dispute. To this end, in spite of protests from his colleagues, Somerset had appointed commissioners, armed with extraordinary powers, to investigate the question of enclosures. But this inquiry succeeded in doing little more than add fuel to the flame—the landlords complained of interference with their rights of adjudication in manor courts, while the failure to enact satisfactory laws to deal with the difficulty roused further discontent among the disappointed peasantry—indeed, its chief result was to cause a more embittered feeling between the classes and the masses. It is, therefore, not surprising to find that the whole country was in a ferment, and that the people took violent steps to assert their claims. Disturbances, extensive enough to be styled insurrections, pervaded England.

Here, then, was a grievance associated in the minds of the people with the dissolution of the monasteries, and

[1] Epistles,

also with the changes in religious observances. These lands had been held by monks, who, in the light of recent experiences, were looked upon as easy-going landlords.

The taxes, which they had been told would be lightened by the application of monastic funds, were as heavy as, or heavier than, ever. The courtiers who had, they considered, profited most by the transfer of ecclesiastical property, were now engaged—for to them the ruling Council seemed to consist of the most successful spoilers—in making innovations in religion, which, to the peasants' vision, appeared to lead to further advantage to the gentry at their expense ; the chantries, more or less benefiting their class, founded by their richer neighbours, or else belonging to the guilds to which they and their ancestors had contributed, were now to go the way of the monastic spoils. Looked at from their point of view the secularisation of ecclesiastical property and the changes in religious formulas were inextricably interwoven.

It should be borne in mind that, although there had been momentous alterations made by Henry in the government of the Church, these appeared to be little more than matter of academical discussion to the populace. They knew that the supremacy of the Pope had been set aside, but as regards the payments formerly sent to Rome and now transferred to the new Supreme Head, they were, if anything, heavier than before— breach of the rules of the Church was superseded by breach of Henry's laws, which was more swiftly and severely punished. So far as they personally were concerned, the changes seemed to be for the worse.

The alterations gradually introduced into the Church services by Henry were not radical nor extensive, and many of them were ignored in the remoter districts. The substitution of English for Latin in the less important parts of the servce was not, it would seem, universally enforced, and already they had been familiarised with the use of English in their Prymers as regards the portion of the service with which they were more directly concerned, so that it was no startling innovation to hear these read in English by the priest. The ritual in the parish churches had not yet been shorn of its gorgeous accessories ; true, the monastic churches with their wealth of display had been largely denuded or destroyed, but not all of these had been open to the use of the public.

They were a devout race, the English. An Italian who visited this country early in the sixteenth century, wrote :—

" Although they all attend Mass every day, and say many Pater Nosters in public (the women carrying long rosaries in their hands, and any who can read taking the office of Our Lady with them, and with some companion reciting it in the church verse by verse, in a low voice after the manner of churchmen) they always hear Mass on Sundays in their parish church, and give liberal alms, because they may not give less than a piece of money, of which fourteen are equivalent to a golden ducat ; nor do they omit any form incumbent upon good Christians."[1]

So it was that in the parish churches the Mass continued to be celebrated after the ancient " use," often with full musical setting and impressive ritual without any great alteration. The images abused by superstitious uses had been removed ; English litanies may have been read, but the service itself had undergone no fundamental alteration evident to them. But now the people were forced to realise that amid the many changes their own parish churches were to suffer—not only to be stripped of their precious ornaments, but robbed of part of their supporting funds, while the services were to be deprived of much of their impressive character. The dull, daily routine and the drab surroundings of the home-life of the poorer classes, which

[1] " Relation of the Island of England," p. 23.

heretofore had been brightened by the beauty and warmth of the ancient ritual, were no longer to have this relief—something beside spiritual comfort was to be lost.

Robbed of their secular rights by courtier landlords, and now to be deprived, as they believed, of their spiritual solace by the command of the Protector and the Council—all of whom were associated in their minds with the appropriation of Church lands and the loss of their privileges as tenants—they were roused to revolt against the governing body, drawing a clear distinction between the King and his guardians, self-appointed as they considered.

Another point demands notice. It was a period of great distress amongst the poor, who, by the extinction of the monastic establishments, had sustained serious loss in the way of charity. The amount distributed by the monks is much disputed, but there can be little doubt that after their eviction the alms were considerably diminished—daily doles to poor tenants and neighbours had been freely given, while distributions of gifts and money at " month's minds " and obits had done something to alleviate distress.[1]   At an early date after the Dissolution it was recognised that the hospitality enjoined upon the holders of abbey lands and the distribution of charity by the successors of the monks very inadequately supplied the place of monastic generosity.

Apart from the charity distributed, the Dissolution had other effects on the people—a considerable body of workmen was displaced. In some cases those who had been employed continued to serve the new owners—the

---

[1] Few records of these charities are preserved, but Hoker gives "The order for relieving the poor people in the monastery of St. Nicholas, late dissolved," from which it appears that in the " Poor Man's Parlour " seven poor men were daily fed before the monks had their dinner and after that meal all the poor tenants as well as those who dwelt in St. Nicholas' Fee, received generous doles of food and drink.   On Good Friday a penny was given to every applicant.   See " Oliver's Mon.," 116.

bailiffs, stewards, etc., who had obtained generous rewards out of the spoil,[1] frequently received higher salaries, while most of the agricultural labourers and a certain number of servants were still employed, but the poorer dependants and personal attendants were the greater sufferers. Such persons as cooks, bakers, barbers, gate-porters, custodians of chapels, those who kept clean the monastic buildings, laundresses, personal servants of the superiors and the old servants kept on out of charity were not by any means absorbed in the new establishments,[2] so a great many were added to the already large number of unemployed.

The most recent estimate of " religious " in England at the time of the Dissolution places their number at 7000, excluding the friars, while there were about five times as many lay persons connected with the monasteries—in round numbers 42,000 persons directly affected by the change.[3] Of these the nuns were rendered absolutely homeless and practically destitute, having little or no means of adding to their meagre pensions. The number of monks who received Church preferment at first could not have been great, but a considerable number obtained church livings as they fell vacant. Still, there must have been a large addition of monks to the ranks of the poor, and this at a time when strict laws, recently passed, were in force punishing both the receiving and giving of alms.[4]

The pensions, of which so much has been made as supplying means of support, were, except in the cases of

---

[1] Hibbert points out that such officials were, very wisely, generously treated to avoid discontent among a class in a position to make itself heard.

[2] The number of servants allowed to the nobility even was restricted by statute.

[3] Savine's " English Monasteries," p. 265. The number of friars is not given, nor does this estimate seem to include the "conversi," those preparing to become monks. Obviously the collegiate churches with their staffs, dissolved in 1545, are not counted.

[4] See Act 27 Henry VIII. c. 25, s. 28.

heads of houses, by no means generous, nor were they paid with regularity.[1] In Devonshire, the average pension granted to a monk was £5 10s. a year—elsewhere it has been estimated at about £6. The wages of an agricultural labourer of that period has been worked out from statistics by Thorold Rogers [2] at 2s. a week, or 4d. a day, with 302 working days to a year, making £5 8s. their average annual wage, while the cost of their board and lodging as allowed is reckoned at 1s. a week—a sum which would have been a very small allowance for the monks, who, as a community, had been able to live in comparative luxury. The occupations by which the monks could eke out their pensions were not many, and the market was already overstocked with applicants for situations.

It is therefore evident that the ranks of the unemployed and distressed must have received an appreciable addition from the classes affected by the Dissolution.

Chapuys, writing on the 8th July, 1536, says—

"It is a lamentable thing to see a legion of monks and nuns who have been chased from their monasteries wandering miserably hither and thither seeking means to live, and several honest men have told me that what with monks, nuns, and persons dependant on the monasteries, there are over 20,000 who know not how to live." [3]

[1] In some lists of Staffordshire houses Hibbert notes the name of a single monk who received a " reward," a small sum by way of gift such as was distributed to the lower servants, but no pension. It is suggested that in such cases the particular monk was recalcitrant. There seems to have been no fixed rule for the distribution of pensions. It must have depended largely upon the good pleasure of the suppressors ; some monks seem to have found favour while others did not.

[2] "Six Centuries of Work and Wages." See pp. 327, 354, and 388. "In 1542 board and lodging are put at 1s. a week ; but in ten years from this time it rises to an average of 3s. a week " (p. 354). Without placing too much reliance upon these estimates they may be taken as some indication of the purchasing power of the pensions as compared with the earnings and cost of living of the common labourer. While the price of labour and of living increased in a decade there was no corresponding rise in the pensions.

[3] L. & P. XI. 42.

In the face of the statistics quoted above, this does not seem a great exaggeration of the truth.[1]

The situation, then, at this period was very serious. The peasantry were thoroughly discontented with their lot, and not without cause. They were jealous of the upstart landlords, who had no claim upon their gratitude, as their predecessors had had—a mass of men had been advanced from obscurity to dazzling positions of apparently boundless wealth, while the peasants' lot had at the same time deteriorated. When the discontent had reached a serious pitch, a fresh grievance was added in the appropriation of the possessions of the chantries in which they had a far more personal interest than in the monastic possessions.

It is easy in these circumstances to imagine that the clerics who were now added to the dispossessed class, found the ground ripe for their agitation, and were able to convince the peasants in the West that theirs was a religious crusade, and that by defending the rights of the Church they were doing God service.

And care was taken that no claim for personal benefit,

[1] It is difficult to arrive at the proportion of " religious " to the whole population. It would seem that Thorold Rogers, basing his estimate on the poll-tax of 1377, places the population at that time at $1\frac{1}{2}$ millions and at the end of Elizabeth's reign it is put as $2\frac{1}{2}$ millions. From this it might be approximately correct to fix the population at the end of Henry's reign at 2 millions. The figures given above as the number of religious, 42,000, do not include the friars, the staffs of Collegiate Churches, the stipendiary priests and those connected with the " Hospitals," some of whom were dispossessed. In Devon there were two large collegiate churches with an official staff of, at least, 40 and 44 respectively, while in four smaller ones there were 27—a total of 111, without counting servants in their employ and dependents. A certain number of these canons or prebendaries were also members of the Cathedral body or held livings, but the break up of these establishments must have affected a considerable number of people. In 1542, according to a return made by Bishop Veysey, there were 414 stipendiary priests in Devon alone. The number of friars and those who belonged to other foundations is not obtainable. On the whole it does not seem unreasonable to place the total number throughout the country affected by these changes at 50,000 in a population of 2,000,000. This must be considered only a suggestion based on the figures given above.

such as the throwing open of enclosures, should be advanced—they only asked that half of the Abbey lands should be restored to their ancient use, *i.e.* the funds should be devoted to religious uses and for the relief of poverty. Rightly or wrongly, the populace looked upon these as the purposes for which the lands had been given and which had been fulfilled by the former holders of the estates, and in rising against the domination of the Council of Edward VI. they believed they were opposing the very men who had obtained the largest share of the spoils of the Church, and who were now bent on depriving them of their Chantry-lands— the very men, too, who were forcing upon them a new service-book, which they could not understand, and which they distrusted because it might shelter beneath it some unknown advantage to the upper classes at their expense.[1]

---

[1] Godwin in his "Annales of England" (p. 230), gives a paragraph in italics as if it were a quotation, summing up the complaints of the Commons. "The free borne Commonalty was oppressed by a small number of Gentry, who glut themselves with pleasure, whiles the poore Commons wasted with daily labour do like pack horses live in extreme slavery. But howsoever, the calamities incident to this present life may with a constant patience be endured, the soule is to be redeemed even with a thousand deaths. Holy Rites established by antiquity are abolished, new ones are autorized, and a new forme of Religion obtruded. To other evills death gives an end ; but if they suffer their soules to be contaminated and polluted by this kinde of impiety, what thing is there that can equall them in miseries, to whom the end of these present ones is but the beginning of some more horrid, namely of the paines infernall, which no death can ever terminate. Why then should they not go to the Court, and appoint the King yet in his minority new Counsailours, removing those who now ruling as they list, confound things sacred and prophane, regarding nothing els but the enriching of themselves with the publique Treasure, that they may riot amid the publique calamities." Resuming ordinary type he adds : "This was the common complaint and resolution, especially of the Devonshire Rebells, who having among them made choice of their Chieftaines, did indevour to vnite themselves with the rest of their fellow Rebels."

CHAPTER VIII

"You need fear nothing if quiet may be maintained at home. If the
beginning may be resisted the intended folly may easily be interrupted."
—GARDYNER.

ALL England was, indeed, in a state of ferment : a train
had been laid which required but a spark to set it off.
The exciting cause at Bodmin is unknown, but the first
movement is said to have taken place on the 6th June,
1549. Nearly a year had elapsed since the execution of
Sir Martin Geffrey and the other rebels. In Cornwall the
stern measures adopted failed to extinguish the flame,
their very cruelty probably served to keep the mutinous
feeling smouldering so that it was ready to burst into a
serious conflagration at a moment's notice. The memory
of the sufferings of the previous year and of the terrible
executions made many anxious for vengeance—two, at
least, of the jurors, Arundell and Smyth, sympathised
with the rebels, and perhaps to them may be attributed
the more or less successful efforts to mitigate the sentences.

Bodmin was a noted centre of disaffection : it was
the headquarters of the insurrection against the taxes
which was headed by Thomas Flamank and Michael
Joseph—hence they started for London to be defeated
at Blackheath in June, 1497.[1] A few months later

---

[1] Joseph was a native of St. Keverne, not of Bodmin as usually stated.
See p. 29.

Perkin Warbeck assembled his followers here and had himself proclaimed Richard IV.

The temper and state of feeling there is well shown by an incident given by Carew—

" I should perhaps have forgotten the free school here . . . were I not put in mind thereof through a fore-hanseling of this rebellion [of 1549], by an action of the scholars, which I shall report from some of their own mouths. About a year before this stir was raised, the scholars, who accustomably divided themselves, for better exploiting their pastimes, grew therethrough into two factions : the one whereof they called the old religion, the other the new. This once begun was prosecuted amongst them in all exercises, and now and then handled with some eagerness and roughness, each party knowing and still keeping the same companions and captain. At last one of the boys converted the spill of an old candlestick to a gun, charged it with powder and a stone, and (through mischance or ingraciousness) therewith killed a calf : whereupon the owner complained, the master whipped, and the division ended." [1]

This was but a reflection of the opinions held by their elders throughout the county. Gilbert describes the Cornish people flocking together in a tumultuous and rebellious manner at the instigation of the priests in divers parts, committing many barbarities and outrages : though the justices sent many to gaol they had not power to suppress the insurrection, which under Arundell soon broke out into actual rebellion against the Prince.[2]

Arundell's home, Helland, was but a few miles from Bodmin, and here he seems to have been, on temporary leave of absence from the Mount, because of his wife's delicate state of health. It is generally assumed that he was at the Mount and volunteered to lead the insurgents or even instigated their rising, but his own account was that, hearing of the belligerent condition of

---

[1] " Cornwall," p. 293. [2] Davies Gilbert, " Cornwall," p. 191.

the Commons, who threaten to force the gentlemen to join their rebellion, he and two companions hid in the woods for two days, but his wife, whose confinement was hourly expected, sent for him. While he was with her a Bodmin man called and begged him to join the rebels, and, on his refusal, a company of them came and carried him away by force. The next day he wrote to Sir Hugh Trevanion, recently Sheriff of the County, asking what he ought to do, and was advised to " tarry with the rebels and to be in their favour to the intent to admitti-gate their outragious doings." Even after he had signed their Supplication, he, feigning sickness, returned home, but the rebels did fetch him again and enforce him to go with them.[1]

Whether willingly or unwillingly at first, he, in the end, accepted the position of leader of the insurgents. The motley company assembled by this time at Bodmin under Arundell, perhaps assisted by Smyth and Holmes, made their way through the narrow lanes and by the high road to the old British fortification known as Castle Kynock, lying half a mile to the south-west. Arundell was appointed their general, while as captains, majors, and colonels, they had John and James Rosogan, William Wynslade, John Payne, Robert and John Bochym, and several priests, vicars, and curates,[2] who endeavoured to establish some sort of military discipline. While engaged in training their irregular forces, arranging ways and means, and discussing plans, news came from the Mount that " divers gentlemen with their wives and families had possessed themselves thereof." [3]   To reduce his old garrison Arundell promptly despatched a party of horse and foot, picked men, who had served under him, and had known the " fortlet." The besieged endeavoured to resist the attack, which was skilfully

[1] See his examination, S. P. Dom. Ed. VI. IX. 48.
[2] See Davies Gilbert's " Cornwall," II. pp. 87 and 191.
[3] *Ibid.* p. 192.

arranged; waiting till the low tide laid bare the connecting strip of sand, the rebels crossed to the Mount, and, by assault won the plain at the hill's foot. They gained the even ground on top by carrying great trusses of hay before them to—

"blench the defendants' sight and deaden their shot : after which they could make but slender resistance : for no sooner should one within peep out his head over those enflanking walls, but he became an open mark to a whole shower of arrows."

The women's dismay and lack of victuals forced a surrender—

"to those rakehells' mercy, who, nothing guilty of that effeminate virtue, spoiled their goods, imprisoned their bodies, and were rather by God's gracious providence, than any want of will, purpose, or attempt, restrained from murdering the principal persons." [1]

Flushed with victory, the little company returned to Castle Kynoch, where some six thousand men [2] had already assembled, some peacefully recruited among the discontented, others intimidated by force of arms— many unwilling gentlemen and reluctant knights and esquires being imprisoned in Bodmin.[3] The news of the success at the Mount, the firstfruits of their valiant comrades, was regarded as of good omen, and brought many to their standard. Their camp, indeed, grew so formidable that John Militon, the Sheriff of Cornwall, " with all the power of his bailliwick durst not encounter it " as long as Arundell was in command, so the leaders had freedom to consult together on their common

---

[1] Carew, p. 380. Gilbert (II. p. 193) says they surrendered for lack of food and ammunition, and the fears and cries of women and children, on condition of free liberty to depart with life " though not without being plundered."

[2] D. Gilbert, II. 193.

[3] See Indictment of the Rebels.

interests and to draw up a manifesto of the justice of their cause and the grounds for taking up arms. It is often said that this mixed multitude of men of diverse professions could not agree upon this manifesto—some wanted no justices because they were so ignorant that they could not construe Latin without their clerk's help, who with the attornies imposed upon them for their own ends, while the judges were themselves corrupt and partial; lawyers should be abolished, as they cheated the people and made extravagant charges; others objected to court-leets and court-barons, because of the expense of prosecutions therein.

"But generally it was agreed amongst them, that no inclosure should be left standing but that all lands should be held in common : yet what expedient should be found out and placed in the room of those several orders and degrees of men and officers, none could prescribe." [1]

Yet the Articles " hammered out " contain no reference to justices, lawyers, or enclosures. Religious questions alone were dealt with, and no dissent is elsewhere recorded. Probably, while Arundell busied himself with military affairs, the priests carried out an active propaganda, inflaming the people further against the religious innovations ; to them may be attributed the preparation of the Articles which were at this time sent to the King, and were in substance as follows :—

1. That curates should administer baptism at all times of need, as well week-days as holy-days.

2. That the Bishop should confirm their children when they resorted to him.

3. That Mass should be celebrated without any man communicating with the priest.

4. That they should have reservation of the Host in the churches.

---

[1] Gilbert gives this expansion of Foxe's statement—it is strange how his prejudiced view is thus further distorted.

5. That they should have holy bread and holy water.

6. That service should be sung and said in the choir, and not set forth like a Christmas play.

7. That priests should not marry.

8. That the VI. Articles set forth by Henry should continue till the King came of age.

They prayed God save the King, as they were his, both body and soul.[1]

To these Articles the King " so far condescended " as to send a written answer and promised pardon to all who would lay down their arms, but these overtures " were not only rejected by the rebels, but made them more bold and desperate." [2]

While the insurgents awaited the King's reply, the restraints of camp-life became irksome, and some of them got quite out of hand, threatening the lives of the imprisoned gentlemen : according to the Indictment they tumultuously paraded the streets of Bodmin, crying—

" Kill the gentlemen and we will have the Six Articles up again and ceremonies as they were in King Henry the Eighth's time."

It was evidently high time that inactivity should cease, and, besides, there was difficulty in feeding so large a company.

" The General therefore resolved, as the fox who seldom chucks at home, to prey upon other men's goods and estates further off, for the army's better sustenance,"

as Gilbert has it.[3]

A Council of War decided to advance to London

---

[1] For a full account of these Articles, see Chap. XIV.

[2] D. Gilbert, II. p. 194.

[3] The Cornishmen of Flamank's rising are said to have paid scrupulously for the provisions consumed on their march. The Indictment of 1549 charges the rebels with " feloniously and traitorously despoiling the lieges of the King of their goods and chattels by force of arms," but this may refer to a later period of the strife.

to enforce by their presence their just demands, and to
obtain some security for their fulfilment, rather than to
accept the condescending reply of the King, whom they
considered but a tool in the hands of the Protector and
Council, so a few days later they started bravely—

"with unanimous and traitorous assent and consent, with
banners unfurled, swords, shields, clubs, cannon, halberts,
lances, and other arms, offensive and defensive, armed and in
warlike manner." [1]

Above them floated the banner of the Five Wounds of
Christ : before them was carried—

"(as the Jews did the ark of God, in the times of old), the
pyx, or consecrated host borne under a canopy, with crosses,
banners, candlesticks, holy bread and water, to defend them
from devils and the adverse power." [2]

As they passed, chanting or cheering, was there by
the roadside any tottering old man who could recall that
May day, scarcely fifty years ago, when he, in the first
flush of his youth, marched gaily forth from Bodmin with
that other band of insurgents ?   And did he remember
with foreboding the terrible field of Blackheath, and how
he, with the broken remnant of the force, returned to
their Cornish homes ?

Strong in the righteousness of their cause, relying
partly on the Protector's unpopularity and on the
assistance of those who had other grievances, they
started, full of faith and courage, that summer's day on
their eastward march across the almost trackless waste
of Bodmin Moor, and then by Polson Bridge into Devon.

But a considerable body of men was detached and
sent to Plymouth, no doubt to rouse the country in that
direction. It may have been under the command of
Robert Smyth, as his ancestral home was at St. Germans,
and he was well suited, therefore, to appeal to the

[1] See Indictment.   [2] Heylin. Eccles. Rest. p. 76.

neighbouring gentry. This company would have followed the old Roman road, through Liskeard, then passing Menheniot—whose rector was imprisoned in the Tower—and so to the banks of the Tamar. Here their advance may have been checked, not only by the difficulties of transport, but by a hastily-collected band of local gentry under Sir Richard Grenville, who disputed their way—a man who had been at the head of the Commission that tried the rebels of the preceding year. If so, their efforts were ineffectual, and they were forced to take refuge in Trematon Castle, Grenville's stronghold, which the rebels proceeded to besiege, encamping in three places against it. But lacking great ordnance—

" they could have wrought the besieged small scaith had [Sir Richard's] friends, or enemies, kept faith and promise: but some of those within, slipping by night over the walls, with their bodies after their hearts, and those without mingling humble entreatings with rude menaces, he was hereby won to issue forth at a postern gate for parley: the while a part of those rakehells, not knowing what honesty, and far less how much the word of a soldier imported, stepped between him and home, laid hold of his aged, unwieldy body, and threatened to leave it lifeless if the enclosed did not leave their resistance. So prosecuting their first treason against their Prince with suitable actions towards his subjects, they seized on the castle; and exercised the uttermost of their barbarous cruelty (death excepted) on the surprised prisoners. The seely gentlewomen, without regard of sex or shame, were stripped from their apparel to their very smocks, and some of their fingers broken, to pluck away their rings: and Sir Richard himself made an exchange from Trematon Castle to that of Launceston, with the jail to boot." [1]

[1] Carew, p. 265. Baring Gould (" Book of the West. Cornwall," p. 161) describes the remains of Trematon and ascribes its destruction to these rebels; but this is unlikely as they lacked artillery to reduce so strong a building; moreover, Leland (*circa* 1538) describes its then ruinous condition (III. f. 20), Norden (*circa* 1564) and Carew (1602) describe its state of decay without attributing it to the rebels.

K

Their victory, however won, must have put heart into the rebels and inspired the natives with fear; Carew describes the strongly fortified island of St. Nicholas in Cawsand Bay, and adds that—

"when the Cornish rebels . . . turmoiled the quiet of those quarters, it yielded a safe protection to divers dutiful subjects who there shrouded themselves," [1]

while others must have sought refuge elsewhere.

The insurgents pushed on towards Plymouth, where the town offered ineffectual resistance, but the castle withstood them for a time, to judge from an entry in the municipal records made in Mary's reign; it runs—

"The city of Exeter and the Castle of Plymouth were valiantly defended and kept from the rebels, until the coming of the Lord Russell. . . . Then was our steeple burnt with all the town's evidences in the same by the rebels." [2]

The town itself may have yielded through treachery, as hinted by the Privy Council later.

A small force may have been left to continue the siege, while the rest, with the recruits who joined, marched towards Launceston by way of Tavistock, where would still have hung that grisly relic, the quarter of the traitor who suffered on the Hoe a year before. When they reached the main road from Launceston, it must have been swarming with insurgents, in a straggling column, pushing across the wilds of Dartmoor to Crediton, where, by the 20th June, a considerable force had been collected.

But affairs in Devon in the meantime require notice. News of the Cornish doings would have already reached them; messengers sent to Court would have warned the

---

[1] Carew, p. 239.

[2] Worth's Plym. Mun. Rec. p. 16. Leland says that Thomas Yogge "paid of late years for the making of Plymouth Church. The town paid for the stuff" (III. f. 22). This may account for the muniments being stored in the strong, new steeple.

country, and there were other means of spreading
information. Sir Thomas Smith complains that the
watchmen, formerly useful, are now mischievous, being
men who do nothing but spend the night inventing
mischief, which they pass from one to another faster
than any post. If they think themselves strong enough
they will stop travellers—

" Let one of those Runabouts come, or campmen, to tell
the news, straight they call up their neighbours, and make
exclamations out of all truth and reason." [1]

Already plans had been laid for risings in other
counties, Devon among them, and early in June they
were on tip-toe of expectation. The first stir in this
county occurred on the 9th June, three days after the
Bodmin rising, according to the indictment, and it
should be noted that religion was again the dominant
factor.

Whitsunday had been selected, very appropriately,
for the universal adoption of Divine Service in the vulgar
tongue in place of Mass in Latin. This change was
actively opposed in the little village of Sampford
Courtenay on the borders of Dartmoor. Exactly why
the movement began here is uncertain, but the incumbent
may have been a prominent agitator. Nearly three
years previous, William Harper had been instituted on ·
the presentation of the most serene lady Katherine
(Parr), Queen of England. He had been her Clerk of
the Closet, and perhaps, in view of a possible breaking-up
of her establishment, this provision was made for him.
His subsequent history suggests that he favoured the old
form of religion.[2] Probably after the death of his
mistress he retired to Devon to spend his declining years,
for he must have been nearly seventy, in this parish.
The Princess Mary must have known him, and to him,

[1] S. P. Dom. Edw. VI. Vol. VIII. No. 433.
[2] For further information about Harper, see Appendix E.

without doubt, the Council referred when they complained of her chaplain at Sampford Courtenay as one
of the " chief stirrers, procurors, and doers in these
commotions." [1] She vehemently denied that any chaplain of hers was in the county.[2]

On the eve of that memorable Whitsunday the
agitators must have been busy warning those on the
outlying farms that the expected signal had come, and
describing the prowess of their Cornish brethren. Consequently, on Sunday, the crooked street leading up to
the parish church would have been unusually crowded—
some curious to hear the new service, others intent on
preventing its performance. Groups of excited men
discussed the latest news from Cornwall, and some one,
probably, harangued the eager listeners on the evils of
the day—how the wealth of the abbeys had been
swallowed up by the insatiable courtiers who coveted
the treasures of their churches and of their guilds.
Already their own chantry at Sticklepath had been
granted to Sir Anthony Aucher. Moreover, they urged,
this new-fangled service did away with old customs, and
was but part of a scheme to deprive them of their faith.
It was no longer a matter of Church government, the
supremacy of the King or Pope, but of their fasts and
feasts, their images, holy water, palms, and all the outward symbols of their religion which were to be swept
away, and they were no more to worship God, their
Divine Father. To conservative Devonians all this
seemed incredible, although backed by tales of the Commissioners' sacrilege. So, with stern visages, clenched
fists, and low mutterings, many would have entered the
church.

What were the feelings of Father Harper, as, clad
no longer in his gorgeous vestments, he entered the
chancel and glanced at the set faces of his congregation ?

---

[1] S. P. Dom. Edw. VI. VIII. 30.   [2] Add. MSS. 27, 402, f. 40.

Cognisant he no doubt was of the bitter feeling and perhaps of threats to prevent the new service being performed, did he hesitate ? Did he see present some justice of the peace, come to see that he complied with the law ? Did he even exhort the congregation to listen reverently to the new service and not disturb the peace of the holy day ? Or did he, while gauging the danger, trust that the moment for action had not really come, and that his flock might not take active part ? Or did he believe that a demonstration of force would make the government, who were in a critical position, hold their hands ? We can only surmise his thoughts, all we can say is that he performed the new service, and that no demonstration on that day is recorded.

The service ended, like a swarm of bees, the people issued from the church, angrily complaining of the loss of their gorgeous ceremonial. They listened more eagerly to the agitators, and departed after agreeing to meet the next day and take active measures.

When Monday came a larger and more hostile crowd assembled, many attracted also by the usual Whitsun Ale festivities. They gathered near the church, and when the priest was about to enter the building two ringleaders, Thomas Underhill, a tailor, and William Segar, a labourer, demanded what he meant to do, and what service he meant to say.

" In obedience to the law set forth I must say the new service," answered Father Harper.

" That you will not ! " exclaimed the leader. " We will have all such laws and ordinances touching Christian religion as were appointed by King Henry (God rest his soul !), until the King's majesty that now is reaches the age of twenty-four years, for so his father appointed it."

The roar of approval greeting this speech would have shaken the resolution even of a man desiring to uphold the new order, so Father Harper gave way, and—

" whether it were with his will or against his will he replied
to their minds and yielded to their wills and forwith ravessheth [1]
himself in his old popish attire and sayeth mass and all such
services as in times past accustomed." [2]

Having listened reverently to the " old ancient "
service, the triumphant and excited crowd streamed out
of the porch, either betaking themselves to their sports
or listening to inflammatory speeches and fresh tales of the
Cornish doings. News of their own actions spread like
wild-fire. The local justices, informed of these exciting
events, hurried to the village to keep the King's peace.

From North Tawton came Alexander Wood, of
Ashridge, and his son-in-law, Mark Slader, of Bath :
Sir Hugh Pollard, from King's Nympton, and Anthony
Harvey, of Columb John, joined them—

" being advertised how disorderly and contrary to the laws
things had been done in the church at Sampford and how that
the common people were clustered and assembled together
to continue and maintain their lewd and disordered behaviour ; "

so they wisely provided themselves with a suitable
escort. They were minded—

" to have conference with the chief players in this interlude
as well for the redress of the disorder already committed as
also to persuade and pacify the rest of the people."

Hearing of the approach of the Justices, the ringleaders consulted together, and being " so addicted and
wholly bent to their follies that they fully resolved themselves wilfully to maintain what naughtily they had
begun." So, putting on a bold front, when the authorities

---

[1] Reveshed = clothed. See Halliwell's Dict.

[2] Hoker, p. 57. In the footnotes " Hoker " refers to the Guildhall
MS. as printed by the Devon and Cornwall Record Society : " Bod.
Hoker " to the Bodleian Library MS. and " Brice ed." to the extract from
Holinshed published by Brice in 1765. See Appendix D for a description
of Hoker's MSS.

arrived near the churchyard, they declined to parley with them unless the Justices left their escort and went " asid into a certain several close not far off."

The gentlemen took counsel together. Some were loath to go to extremes, though they had a sufficient force, it is said, to have repressed the few persons then assembled ; it is even hinted that these sympathised with the aims of the rioters. Perhaps for this reason, or else " because they thought in such a cause to use the best and quietest ways for the pacifying of them," they decided to accept these terms, and entered the close unattended, and—

" there having had conference a pretty while together did in the end depart without anything done at all whereof as there rebounded [1] some weakness in the said Justices which were so white-livered as they would not or durst not to repress the rages of the people, so thereof ensued such a scab as passed their cure and such a fire as they were not able to quench : for the commoners having now their wills were set upon a pin that the game was theirs and they had won the garland before they had run the race." [2]

Flushed with this victory, the mob was in no mood to listen to remonstrances, yet there was one bold enough to speak plainly to them. William Hellyons, a neighbour respected for his amiable character, a " Franklin, a gentleman," urged them to stay their rebellion and return to their due obedience ; but he was taken prisoner at the Town's end and carried to the Church-house, the rebels' headquarters—

" where he so earnestly reproved them for their rebellion and so sharply threatened them of an evil success, that they fell in a rage with him : and not only with evil words reviled him, but also as he was going out of the Church-house and going down the stairs, one of them named Lithibridge, with a bill

---

[1] ? Redounded.

[2] The last part of this sentence in the Guildhall Hoker is unintelligible, so the reading of the Holinshed edition is here given.

struck him in the neck, and immediately notwithstanding his pitiful requests and lamentations, a number of the rest fell upon him and slew him and cut him in small pieces." [1]

This was the first blood shed in Devonshire, and it may well have given pause to the people when they recognised the seriousness of their action, but they felt it was less wise to draw back than to go forward to join the Cornish rebels.

In the awed silence that had fallen on the people, Father Harper must have stepped forward and 'ordered the burial of the mangled remains, though he felt obliged to see that the body was laid north and south, to indicate that Hellyons was an outcast from the Church, a heretic.

Thus, " nothing forecasting what might ensue, nor yet accounting what folly it is to triumph before the victory," the Sampford men summoned their neighbours to join them.

The news of their doing was—

" as a cloud carried with a violent wind and as a thunder clap sounding through the whole country : and the common people so well allowed and like thereof that they clapped their hands for joy : and agreed in one mind to have the same in every of their several parishes."

Making their way to the main road, the little company of Sampford Courtenay men joined the advanced contingent of the Cornish men marching to Crediton, to which place malcontents flocked from all parts of the county. Near to this town was Yewton Arundell, which belonged to their general, so, among his friends and adherents, he made this his headquarters. He had,

---

[1] Jenkins (Hist. Exeter, p. 112) styles him " a Fleming by birth, who had for some years resided near Sampford." But Hoker does not refer to his nationality. He may have belonged to the ancient family who spelled their name Hellions, Helions, or Hilion. See Lysons, clxvi and 544. Lethbridge is a common Devon name.

Photo by Chapman & Son, Dawlish.]

SAMPFORD COURTENAY CHURCH HOUSE.

probably, already arrived, and was endeavouring to train the raw levies of Devon while he waited for the rest of his Cornish following to come up.[1]

[1] Chancellor Edmonds remarks : " It is a pathetic thing to read the Collect for Whitsunday with its prayer for a right judgment in all things, and to think that the first result of ordering it to be said in the mother tongue was a series of battles, sieges, and executions which make up the terrible history that began to unroll its woes outside the Barns of Crediton " (Mem. Old. Dev. p. 87).

CHAPTER IX

THE BURNING OF THE BARNS

"The world will never mend till we fight for it."—LORD HUSSEY.

WHEN the first news of the western insurrection reached London is not known. The Privy Council Register contains entries relating to the Scilly fortifications, but these had been long in progress, and to the payment of forty marks on the 15th June to " Myles Coverdale sent into Cornwall." He had been sent as an itinerant preacher, with Tong, to reconcile the people there to the changes, but with small success. Four days later there is a heavy payment—£433—for 140 black corslets and 70 white and black demilances. This may have been in the regular course for soldiers already sent to Scotland, or the armourers may have required a payment on account before supplying arms for the West, for the Government credit was then notoriously bad.

At this moment the Council had their hands full with French and Scotch affairs, as well as with the economic and agrarian crisis, not to mention their own internal dissensions, when messengers brought news of outbreaks in Hertfordshire, and of smouldering discontent else-where ; rumours of risings came from Somerset, Glou-cester, Worcester, Wiltshire, Hampshire, Sussex, Essex, Kent, Yorkshire, Rutland,[1] and Norfolk. It must have

[1] The Rutlandshire rising has received little notice but was evidently of some importance. The Earl of Huntingdon writes, 12th Sept., 1549, of a rising there for which already divers had suffered and that next week many in Leicester were to be arraigned (Lodge's " Illustrations," III. p. 163).

SIR PETER CAREW.

From an Engraving by J. J. Chant after the Portrait at Hampton Court.

been the last straw when a man, exhausted with hard riding, brought certain information of an outbreak in Cornwall under a person of such local importance as Arundell, and close on his heels came the bearer of letters from the Devon justices about the Sampford Courtenay movement, which at first they thought could be suppressed by the power they had, but now feared would result in a combination with the Cornish rebels.

Hasty letters had been sent by Somerset on the 11th June, the very day after the Sampford movement, warning the authorities in various counties to be ready to cope with any rising, whether it were for " seeking redress of enclosures," or, as in some places, " through the instigation of seditious priests and other evil people set forth to seek restitution of the old bloody laws." [1]

Oxfordshire and Berkshire were at this moment added to the list, and in despair some member of the Council urged active repressive measures. Westcountrymen, familiar with affairs at Court, with a knowledge of local feeling and respected in the district, should be sent to quell the Western rising. One of the Carews [2] would be well fitted for this task, but both would be better, it was suggested. Sir Gawen, who was at hand, was ordered to prepare to start at once, while hasty messages were sent to Sir Peter, who was resting from active service and enjoying a prolonged honeymoon on his bride's Lincolnshire estates. These men were after the hearts of the more determined members of the Council, who were well satisfied with their appointment. But, faithful to his

---

[1] S. P. Dom. Edw. VI. VII. 31.

[2] Hoker writes of Sir Peter : "Sharp was his understanding, pithy were his arguments, and deep was his judgment . . . such was his experience in martial affairs, that he could pitch a camp, martial a field, set array, and order the battle, with such wisdom, dexterity, and policy, as should be to the best advantage and safeguard of the army, and the most annoyance to the enemy " ; beside skill in government and knowledge of a soldier's duty he knew all that appertained to wars both by land and sea (" Life," p. 115).

own ideas as to the best course to be pursued, Somerset gave them instructions. Leniency—leniency, he reiterated. True, the people are in open rebellion, and affairs are serious, but try to persuade them by gentle means and use no force until compelled. Such were the orders embodied in a minute to the " Sheriffs, Justices of Peace, and rest of the gentlemen in Devonshire touching them that would not read the book of services," which distinctly recognises the true cause of the insurrection, and, as it played an important part in subsequent proceedings, must be given at length.

" Trusty and well-beloved, we greet you well.

" And where we are advertised that certain of our subjects hath of late in that our county of Devon repined and rebelled against the most godly proceedings (in the last sessions) of parliament at Westminster in the last sessions thereof, concerning the book set forth by our authority in full parliament of the rite and ceremonies to be used in our church of England and Ireland and all our dominions, of which we do much marvel that any of our subjects should be so ignorant, disobedient, and disloyal unto us to gainsay the act of all our whole realm and the common agreement of both our spirituality and temporality there gathered together, and although the same doth deserve most extreme punishment as against rebels and traitors ; yet of our abundant mercy (with the advice of our most entirely beloved) are desirous to shew to all our loving subjects by the advice of our most entirely beloved uncle the L(ord) P(rotector) governor of our person and protector of all our realms, dominions and subjects, and the rest of our Privy Council, we are content to accept this hitherto done to have been done rather of ignorance than of malice, and at the motion of some light and naughty persons than of any evil will that our loving subjects doth bear to us or to our proceedings.

" And therefore at the suit of divers gentlemen who hath made humble suit for them by the advice aforesaid have pardoned, and by these presents do pardon, all the said contempts and offences heretofore past. So that the said offenders shall never hereafter be troubled nor vexed for any such offence hereafter past and done, upon condition that hereafter they do behave themselves towards us as the duty is of loving and obedient subjects. In obeying the godly laws and statutes (made in our parliament) by our authority promulgated and set forth. The which thing we will ye shall promulgate and declare accordingly, willing, and straightly charging you and every of you if any manner person after this our writing, pardon, and commandment shall eftsones attempt to repugne or resist our godly proceedings in the laws by us and our Parliament made by gathering or assembling in companies or otherwise to apprehend the same. And to see our laws and statutes duly and severely executed against all such offenders as appertaineth.

"In witness whereof we have signed this present with our hand.

"By us under our signet at our manor of Richmond the XXth June, 1549, and in the third year of our reign." [1]

Armed with this letter the Carews hastened westward, empowered to use—

"by the advise of the justices all the best means and ways that they might for the appeasing of this rebellion, quieting of the people and pacifying of the country : and to cause every man quietly to return to his home and to refer the causes of their grief and complaints, if they had any, to the King and Council." [2]

But the point which must have appealed to these soldiers would have been the last paragraph—"and to see our laws and statutes duly and severely executed against all such offenders as appertaineth;" or, as Hoker glosses it : "and if they then refuse so to do

---

[1] This is copied from the draft in Somerset's writing preserved at the Record Office (S. P. Dom. Edw. VI. VII. 37). The portions within brackets are erased. This is evidently the King's letter, under his hand and privy signet, upon which Sir Peter Carew relied when before the Privy Council. (See Hoker, p. 81.) It will be observed that, although being a draft it is unsigned, it was intended by the form of its ending to have the King's signature alone.

[2] See Hoker, p. 50.

they to use such other good means and ways as might be for the suppressing of them."

Thus "the emissaries of peace went forth with the wings of war."

"The foresaid two knights having received their commission under the king his hand, came in post to the country and making their repair to this City [Exeter] do forthwith send for the Sheriffs and the Justices of the peace of the county,"

before whom this letter was laid and the situation discussed. News had come in that—

ı' a great company of the commons were assembled at Crediton, which is a town distant about seven miles from Exeter, and that among them were the Sampford men."

So, together with the chief men of the county, they "took counsel and advice what was best to be done, and what ways meetest to be taken," and finally all agreed that the Carews, with a suitable escort, should ride to Crediton—

"there to have conference and speeches with the said commons and to use all the good ways and means they might to pacify and appease them, they then supposing and being persuaded that by good speeches and gentle conferences they should have been able to have compassed and persuaded the said commons."

In accordance with this decision, on or about the 21st June, a little company under Sir Peter's command, set out from Exeter.

Meanwhile the rebels had not been idle, being—

"by some secret intelligence advertised of the coming of the gentlemen towards them and they fully resolved not to yield one iote [iota] from their determinations but to maintain their cause taken in hand, and to this end do arm and make themselves strong with such armour and furniture as they had." [1]

[1] See Hoker, p. 60.

Not only so, but they put Crediton in a state of defence. They—

"entrenched and rampired the high way at the Town's end leading towards Exeter and had hanged up great plough chains uppon them and fortified the same with men and munition." [1]

On either side of the road from Exeter and adjoining, the entrenchments were two barns ; the walls of these they pierced with "loops and holes" for their shot, and "complenished" them with men well appointed with bows and arrows and other weapons in order to prevent entrance to the town. [2]

Carew's advance-guard, as they neared Crediton, were surprised to find their progress barred by this mighty "rampire," and turned back to warn their comrades of the obstruction. Dismounting, they held a hasty conference, and decided to advance on foot, anticipating no resistance if they came in that fashion, but when they reached the rampire—

"they found the contrary : for they not only were denied to come near the rampire but utterly were refused to be talked withal : no offers of persuasions nor motions of conference at all to be allowed for the sun being in Cancer and the midsummer Moon at full their minds were embrued in such follies and their heads carried with such vanities that as the man of Athens they would hear no man speak but themselves, and thought nothing well said but what came out of their own mouths."

Sir Peter, as Froude says, "accustomed to cross swords with the French chivalry, was not to be daunted by village churls," and the other gentlemen—

"upon such checks taking the matter in evil part to be so irreverently and discourteously intreated : with one consent do agree to make way over the rampire."

---

[1] See Bod. Hoker, f. 2ᵈ. [2] See Maclean's "Carew," p. 48.

But this proved no easy task; the defenders of the barricade were ably seconded by picked soldiers, who shot from the shelter of the barns, so that the Carews were " fain to retire and give place with the loss of some and the hurt of many."

The insurgents triumphed for the moment, and their shouts of victory must have galled the little company. But presently a tiny puff of smoke, followed by a larger volume and by a sharp crackling of flames in the thatch and straw, startled those in the barns, where non-combatants would have now arrived to watch the dis-comfiture of the enemy. Under cover of the recent excitement, a serving-man, named Foxe, belonging to Sir Hugh Pollard's household, had set fire to the barns [1] " unawares of the gentlemen," [2] determined to smoke the rebels out, like vermin, from their holes.

Startled and alarmed for their own safety, the occu-pants took to flight, the panic spreading to the defenders of the rampires, so that when Carew's force presently advanced, they found these deserted. Cautiously they entered the town, only to find there a few poor, old people, " the residue trusting better to their heels than to their arms fled to a further place."

With no enemy to encounter, and no general with whom to treat, the besiegers were non-plussed. Nothing could be done. Their company was not large enough to hold the straggling town, surrounded as it must be by the rebels. After their barren victory, they could but return, covered with glory, to Exeter, where they could boast of no gain and no success in suppressing the rising. They could only point out that it was a serious matter, requiring more men than were at their disposal.

So letters were despatched, giving an account of the affair, and urging the Protector to hasten the prepara-tions which he had in hand.

---

[1] See Hoker, p. 61.   [2] Maclean's "Carew," p. 48.

But the rebels were in no wise daunted. They had bravely defended their rampire, and had driven back the enemy. It was only because of a fire, maliciously set, that they were forced to beat a hasty retreat. Moreover, this cruel and unsportsmanlike conduct was used to rouse the people, the "Burning of the Barns" became a watch-word.

"The noise of this fire and burning was in post haste and as it were in a moment carried and blasted throughout the whole country and the common people upon false reports and, of a gnat making an Elephant, noised and spread it abroad that the gentlemen were altogether bent to overrun, spoil and destroy them : and in this rage as it were a swarm of wasps they cluster themselves in great troops and multitudes, some in one place and some in another fortifying and entrenching themselves as though the enemy were ready to invade and assail them."

Among the places fortified was the little village of Clyst St. Mary, two or three miles from Exeter.[1]

By this time the whole district was in a state of turmoil, and the people were ready enough to display indignation at any thwarting of their will, and especially in the circumstances would they attach great importance to any insult or even slur upon matters pertaining to religion, so it can be readily understood what excitement was caused by an event recorded at length by Hoker, who perhaps laid stress upon the story because the hero was the father of the famous Sir Walter Raleigh, the latter being well known to the historian.

"It happened that Walter Raleigh, Esquire, dwelling not far from thence as he was upon a holiday [2] then riding from his house to Exeter, overtook an old woman going to the parish church of St. Mary Clyst who had a pair of beads in her hands : and asked her what she did with those beads : And entering into further speeches with her concerning religion which was

[1] For reference to an interpolation in the text, see Chap. XVII.
[2] Brice ed., p. 41, has " a Side Holiday." Perhaps Corpus Christi day.

reformed by order of law to be put in execution did persuade with her that she should as a good Christian woman and an obedient subject yield thereunto, saying further that there was a punishment by the law appointed against her and all such as would not obey and follow the same and which would be put in execution upon them : This woman nothing liking nor well digesting the matter went forth to the parish church where all the parishioners were then at the service and being impatient and in an agony with the speeches before past between her and the gentleman beginneth to upbray in the open church very hard and unseemly speeches concerning religion, saying that she was threatened by the gentleman, that except she would leave her beads and give over holy bread and holy water the gentlemen would burn them out of their houses and spoil them, with many other speeches very false and untrue and whereof no talk at all had passed between the gentleman and her : notwithstanding she had not so soon spoken but that she was believed : and in all haste, like a sort of wasps, [they] fling out of the church and gat them to the town which is not far from thence and there began to entrench and fortify the town, sending abroad into the country round about the news aforesaid and of their doings in hand : flocking and procuring as many as they could to come and join with them : And they fearing or mistrusting lest the gentlemen which were then at Exeter would come upon them, they first fortified the bridge which lieth at the end of the town towards the city and laid great tree overthwart the same as also planted certain great pieces of ordnance upon the same, which they had procured and fetched from Topsham, a town not far from thence : but before they came into the town they overtook the gentleman, Mr. Rawley, aforesaid and were in such a choler and so fell in rages with him, that if he had not shifted himself into the chapel there and had been rescued by certain mariners of Exmouth, which came with him, he had been in great danger of his life and like to have been murdered." [1]

[1] See Hoker, p. 62. Upon this incident a modern historian has based the statement that the sailors as a class were opposed to the cause of the rebels. It is hardly sufficient evidence to enable one to judge the sentiments of the seamen because Raleigh was rescued by a few mariners, who may have been men in his employ.

Raleigh took care that an account of his hair-breadth escape should reach the Carews, and the fears of the people at Clyst St. Mary were speedily fulfilled.

Sir Peter, on his return to Exeter, called the Justices and gentlemen to a further conference, laying before them an account of his own action at Crediton and Raleigh's adventure, and pointed out that Clyst St. Mary—almost at their gates—was put in a state of defence, adding rumours of the ugly temper of the people. After some discussion, it was agreed that the rebels' stronghold should be approached, adopting the same tactics as before. The two Carews, Sir Thomas Denys, Sir Hugh Pollard, and others, were to ride to Clyst St. Mary and use " all the best means they might for the pacifying and quieting " of the peasants.[1]

It was too late when this decision was reached, to do anything that night, but early next morning, being Sunday, a little cavalcade issued from the South Gate and trotted down the Topsham road. As they approached the bridge near Clyst St. Mary, they were surprised to find another rampire barring their way. Not having learnt from experience, Sir Peter alighted from his horse, and, mistrusting nothing, was going on foot towards the bridge. But already the burning of the barns had been attributed to him, and he was a known supporter of the innovations, so it was not strange that, owing to this " rancor and malice against him, a gunner, John Hammon," " an alien and a smith " of the neighbouring village of Woodbury, deemed it a worthy act to rid the world of this troublesome heretic. Some one pointed out Sir Peter, and " he having charged his piece of ordnance there lying, levelled the same to have shot and discharged it at him," but Hugh Osborne, servant to " sergeant Prydeox," stayed his hand.

[1] Denys and Pollard had not gone to Crediton but had then remained in Exeter (Bod. Hoker, f. 3ᵈ). The Burning of the Barns seems to have been on Friday, the 21st ; Raleigh's adventure and the conference on Saturday.

As they could not enter Clyst St. Mary, the gentlemen sent a messenger—

" to advertise them that they were come to talk friendly with them, as also to satisfy them if they had any cause of grief or were by any body misused."

What wonder that a company in arms against the rulers who were imposing distasteful changes were " staggered a while " by such a message and " motion."

Their munitions of war, their fortified bridge, their threatened discharge of a great piece were met by a mild inquiry as to whether they had any cause of grief or were misused ! Well might they mistrust these gentlemen and " cast many doubts," imagining that such gentle words hid some treachery—that once within their fortifications the mask would be thrown off and a massacre follow. The leaders discussed the matter with some heat. Sir Peter they would not have, but a deputation without an escort might be entertained. Sir Thomas Denys, their neighbour at Bicton, known to all, and believed not to be heartily with the new party, Sir Hugh Pollard, and Thomas Yarde, unattended, might pass into the town if they gave their " faith and promise that no hurt should be done or offered to be done unto them," [1] " by the residue of the gentlemen which were at large upon the heath." [2] Upon such conditions only would they be content to talk.

Agreeing to this arrangement, being now about ten o'clock in the morning, these three gentlemen entered Clyst St. Mary, and there tarried most of the day, " in much talk and to no purpose, as in the end it fell out."

As for the other knights and gentlemen, left kicking their heels by the side of the stream, they, too, as the hours wearily passed, mistrusted on their part; indeed, as—

---

[1] Hoker, p. 64.   [2] Bod. Hoker, f. 3ᵈ.

" the day did draw towards night [they] began to mislike of the matter, some speaking one thing and some another : yea and some of them in plain speech said they would ride over the water and issue into the town : But the friends and servingmen of the two knights, respecting the promise made before their entry into the town but especially their masters' safety, which by the breach of promise might be put in peril did utterly mislike and were grieved with those speeches and whereof began a little quarrelling among themselves but forthwith pacified and quieted : And yet some one or two of the company rode to the water's side and with their staves searched the depths thereof, for at that bridge the water at every tide (by reason that the seas are so near)swelleth up and reboundeth."

Prominent among those who probed the mud was Sir Peter Carew's servant, Richard Carwithen.[1] These noisy threats and the attempt to find a ford roused the wrath of the keepers of the bridge, and they, mistrusting their opponents, gave the alarm and made much ado, and even " some of them began and grew into such rages that the gentlemen within the Town began to distrust their safety." [2]

At long last, well after sunset apparently, the three gentlemen, with downcast faces, issued from the town, and, crossing the bridge, joined their comrades unscathed. Carew eagerly demanded how they had sped, but received only a surly, " Well enough." Perhaps these emissaries had boasted before leaving Exeter of greater powers of persuasion and fuller knowledge of the Devon peasant than Sir Peter had shown at Crediton, and were now reluctant to admit their failure. Turning their horses' heads towards Exeter, they rode forward, silent and depressed.

---

[1] Perhaps son of Richard Carwithen of Pawnston, St. Giles in the Heath.

[2] Froude says an alderman of Exeter was permitted to enter Clyst St. Mary. None of these gentlemen can be so described, and two of them were knights. He represents both of the Carews as present, probing the mud with their *lances* to find footing for their horses and says that Sir Peter would have dashed through at all hazards had not the people mutinied at his back. This does not tally with Hoker's description which is given above.

Arrived within the city they drew rein at the Mermaid Inn,[1] where many justices, gentlemen, and civic officers had gathered to sup together.   Before the servants they talked of indifferent matters, for they could trust no one ; but when they were alone, Sir Peter again demanded what had passed at the interview, insisting on full details.   The reply was unsatisfactory, but it showed that the rebels of Clyst St. Mary were in league with the others, having their catch-words by heart.   The ambassadors reported that—

" the commons had promised and were contented to keep themselves in good and quiet order and to proceed no further in their attempts so that the King and the Council would not alter the religion but suffer it to remain and tarry in the same state as King Henry the Eighth left it and until the King himself came to his full age."

A silence fell on the company—they had expected other things, and liked not this answer.   For a time they were in " a great dump or study but in the end misliked and discommended both the matter and the manner of their dealings."   High words ensued—Sir Peter, backed by Sir Piers Courtenay, Sheriff of Devon—

" openly, sharply and in plain terms inveighed against them for their slender, or rather sinister, dealings in so weighty a cause : wherein they all ought to have used all means to have suppressed their outrages than to have maintained their follies : and therefore as there was a blame in them, so was there a plain rebellion in the other."

Sir Thomas Denys and Sir Hugh Pollard were not slow in replying, saying they had done their best, excusing themselves, and they would have purged their sincerity herein.   There was multiplying of words, crimination and recrimination, charges and counter-charges, retort direct and retort oblique, even danger of

---

[1] Cotton and Woollacombe, p. 51.

blows. Sir Peter's failure at Crediton was cast up at him, and other words were bandied to and fro with increasing heat, till " they brake asunder without further dealings and every man shifted for himself, some one way and some another way."

But the high voices in the improvised council-chamber of the inn were overheard, dissensions among the gentlemen lent courage to the friends of the Commons ; swift messengers notified their leaders, who quickly matured their plans. It was so late now that few who lived outside the city returned home that night, but when the day dawned and the Mayor urged that the city was not provisioned for a siege so that they must retire with their followers to their country-seats, they found themselves entrapped.

The Commons had blocked the highways, casting great trenches and laying huge trees " overthwart " the roads, while some were set to watch in order to bar the way when the gentlemen rode forth. Many gentlemen were captured " because they would be taken and so left loose at liberty ; but many who escaped were driven to hide themselves in woods and in secret places in great fear and peril." [1]   Others, among them Walter Raleigh, for whom a special watch was set, were imprisoned and " kept in duras during the whole time of the commotion and abode great hardnes and were in peril of life and limb." [2]

Only six or seven, according to Hoker, remained in the city, among them Sir Roger Blewet, knt., John Beauchamp, Bartholomew Fortescue, John Courtenay and John Peter, Customer. [3]

But very early Monday morning, by some unblocked way, Sir Peter Carew, who had slept at the Mermaid, [4] galloped post haste eastward to report the state of affairs to the Council.

[1] Bod. Hoker, f. 4ᵈ.   [2] Hoker, p. 65.
[3] Brice, Hoker, p. 46.   [4] Cotton and Woollacombe p. 51.

The Mayor, John Blackaller, and his Brethren, fore-seeing trouble to the city, took many precautions. Already, on the 15th June, affairs had been considered so serious that the "twenty-four" had agreed to dispense with the usual Midsummer Watch, which for many generations had assembled in Exeter on St. John's Eve. It was a ceremonious gathering when the mayor and other city officers, accompanied by the members of the great trade guilds, each clad in armour and livery, bearing cressets, torches, banners and emblems, went in procession through the streets and then marched round the city walls to inspect them and see that the defences were secure, after which they all sat down to a generous feast.

At a critical moment like this such an assembly would be dangerous—feeling ran high and armed men, on some slight variance, might find themselves involved in a serious encounter, so it was wisely arranged that the usual display and rejoicing should not take place this year, but instead ten honest householders from each quarter should be selected in place of the Watch to make the round of the city walls. But even this was considered insufficient, so on 22nd June it was enacted

"that for divers reasons considerations had and made for the discharge of the Watch against Midsummer now next coming it is thought good . . . that for the better safeguard and good order in the same city . . . that the corporation of tailors, weavers and tuckers, shoemakers, and bakers and brewers shall every of the same [four] corporations severally by themselves bring for the Watch . . . X men in harness, householders or honest and discreet inhabitants. And in every quarter one constable or more as shall be thought good by the mayor." [1]

Having thus made all the preparations which they could devise for the welfare of the city they could but patiently await events.

[1] Exeter City Muniments, Chamber Act Book, No. 2, f. 103.

CHAPTER X

THE COUNCIL'S ACTION

" He that with himself earnestly imagineth how much blood must needs
be shed, what a number must needs be slain, how many good towns
shall be robbed and spoiled, how many farmers and honest householders shall be utterly undone, how many gentlemen for lack of their
rents shall be fain to lay their lands to mortgage or utterly to sell
them away, how many honest women shall be defiled, how many
virgins ravished : He that setteth the bloody field before his eyes,
here legs, there heads, these deadly wounded, those utterly dead, is it
possible that any man can so cast off humanity, so hate men, that he had
liever have so many dead, as needs must die in such cruel division,
than to have them alive and his friends ? "—CHEKE's " Lamentation."

MEANWHILE the authorities in London were not idle.
Messengers from the West brought news of the growing
seriousness of affairs, and after the conference at Exeter,
the Carews reported the local opinion, suggesting that
the Sheriff of Devon and his bailiwick were not strong
enough to cope with the rising, which required a more
formidable force than could be raised in the county.
Preparations for such a contingency had already been
begun, but the question of who should take command
was most anxiously debated.

Many people expected that Somerset, whose military
renown had been increased by his recent campaign in
Scotland, would have put himself at the head of the army
for the West. A few weeks later Sir William Paget,
then an ambassador abroad, hearing how ill things sped,
wrote to the Protector, warning him that the weak course
adopted was unwise.

" Call together," he advised, " the strongest men in the country and be guided by their authority. Put yourself at the head of the 4,000 almayn horsemen now idle at Calais, send for your trusty servants, for Lord Ferris and Sir William Herbert to bring horsemen from Wales and such as they dare trust, and for the Earl of Shrewsbury and his followers. With such a force under your command advance into Buckingham-shire, appoint three or four justices of England to resort to the next town where you rest, join to them local justices and select twenty or thirty of the rankest knaves to come before them. If they come peaceably to justice, let six be hanged of the ripest of them without redemption, the rest to remain in prison. Let the horsemen take enough in the towns to make the rebels smart for their villany. Take into the king's hands the privileges of offending towns, send some of the chief doers away from their wives to be soldiers at Boulogne or in the North. In such manner make your progress through the country. By this means you shall be dread, which hitherto you are not but of a few that be honest men. By this means you should deliver the king an obedient realm." [1]

Some belligerent members of the Council would have given similar advice, urging the sharp and swift suppres-sion of the rising, but such a course did not commend itself to Somerset, whose—

" good fortune now began to fail him when the mischief did appear with the face of danger, and could not otherwise be redressed but by force of arms ; instead of putting himself at the head of an army the Lord Russell is sent down with some slender forces to give stop to their proceedings."

Lord Russell was one of those who had risen into prominence in the late king's reign through his courtier-like abilities. He had held offices of trust about the Court, where he was in high favour, and had been em-ployed on diplomatic missions. He had developed into a stern soldier, merciless to his opponents and possessing a vein of brutality noticeable in a period none too

[1] Titus, F. III.

JOHN, LORD RUSSELL.

From an Engraving by H. Robinson after the original in the collection of the Duke of Bedford.

gentle, yet he had certain endearing qualities which had won him by this time the title of *Father Russell*.

Already he was known in this district, for when, in 1539, it was decided to establish a " Council in the West Parts," similar to that in the North and elsewhere, he was chosen President, endowed with ample—almost regal—powers, and for some time continued to exercise his office, hearing causes and reporting to the King.[1]

He was one of the executors of Henry's will, and now held the office of Lord Privy Seal under Edward. He had already begun to accumulate estates in the West, and at his death was a very large landowner.

" A person of stout spirit, proper for such a service and a man of great interests in that county as well as the state was sent down to Exeter, with a convenient power of men of war both on foot and on horseback." [2]

[1] Titus, B. I. 161 (quoted L. & P. XIV. i. 743). He had power to assemble and direct the Council and had in it a negative voice. He was to be treated in all respects, except kneeling, like the King himself. The Council had among its members the bishop and dean of Exeter, Edgcumbe, Denys, Sir J. Arundell, the elder, Sir T. Arundell, Godolphin, Sir Hugh Pollard and Sir Hugh Paulet ; its jurisdiction extended over Devon, Cornwall, Somerset and Dorset ; it could punish contempt of its orders and seditious words, by pillory, cutting off of ears, wearing of paper or otherwise at discretion. They attended at gaol deliveries, enforced laws relating to retainers and the acts against the Bishop of Rome. It is not quite certain when the Council ceased to exist but there are letters from Russell, chiefly dated from Exeter, throughout the rest of the year, which seem to refer to matters of the Council, *e.g.* L. & P. XIV. i. 743 and ii. 371.

[2] Blomefield's " Norfolk," III. p. 230. Lloyd, in his " Worthies," writes : " Sir John had a moving beauty that waited on his whole body, as that standing one doth upon the face and complexion : such a grace and comeliness waited on his noble mein, as exacted a liking, if not a love, from all that beheld him . . . our knight's comportment and carriage was neither dull nor vapouring, neither gross nor affected, but of a becoming temper, at equal distance with the clown and the pedant, what's contemptible, and what's invidious. But both these were set off with his person, of a middle stature, neither tall to a formidableness, nor short to a contempt : straight & proportioned, vigorous and active, with that pure blood and spirits that flowed and flowered within his swelling veins & disposed him to these natural and innocent, those manly & noble, exercises of dancing &c. Dancing I say, which he was not exquisite in, for that is vanity : nor

It was on the 20th June that warrants were issued for £300 all together for the Lord Privy Seal " as parcel of his diets," and a further warrant on the 23rd was granted " for conduct coats and transportation of soldiers levied in London for service," probably part of his escort.

His instructions, embodied in a " memorial," are dated the following day, and were supplemented by a Privy Seal authorising him to call upon all subjects to serve the King in the counties of Devon and Cornwall, with Dorset and Somerset added as an afterthought— this being dated the 25th.[1]

So it would have been about that date that pre- parations for his departure were concluded, and he started with a force deemed sufficient by the Council, but by him considered inadequate, as he knew the temper of the West-countrymen, and was too old a soldier to believe that so small a force would be likely to succeed. The Council were, however, restricted by the low state of the treasury and afterwards constantly complained of the cost incurred in maintaining his army.

His orders were to summon the local justices of the peace and other the good men of each shire on his arrival in the county, to hear their account of the condition of their districts, and to be guided by their advice.   Where he found the people " out of frame " he was to discover the cause thereof and travail by gentle persuasion to bring the people with gentleness to become obedient subjects.   If he failed in that, he was to assemble men to repress by force such as obstinately troubled the country and bring them to the " knowledging " of their

ignorant of, for that is meaness, but a graceful exercise, (wherein he were carelessly easie, as if it were rather natural motion, than curious & artificial practising) which endeared his severe virtues to that place where the worth that riseth must be complaisant and pleasing as well as service- able & useful " (p. 320).

[1] See S. P. Dom. Ed. VI. VII. 40.   This is given by Pocock but very inaccurately.   Also Privy Seals, June 3, Edw. VI.

bounden duty in this behalf. In case of invasion by foreign enemies, he was to use his dexterity and courage to repulse them, and, for the better order of defence, he was to give commands, if it had not been already done, for the setting up and watching of the beacons in accustomed places along the coast. And to further the quietness of the country he was to give special charge to masters and fathers to have " an earnest continual regard to the good governance of their children and servants," and particularly to command all clothiers, dyers, weavers, fullers, and all other artificers, to be kept occupied in order to avoid occasion of unlawful assemblies. Above all, he was to see that his Majesty's orders touching religion were well obeyed and executed. " If any light seditions or vain bruits and rumours shall spread " he was to make every endeavour to find the " beginners and first setters forth," whom he was to commit to ward and further punish according to their deservings. He would be kept " undelayedly advertised from us of all occurrants of importance," and he, on his part, was " once every month at the least to advertise hither the state of the country ; any other matter of importance to be signified oftener."

It is evident that they had not yet grasped the seriousness of the rising, and believed that it could be put down by gentle means. The day before the date of the above document they had, presumably for the purpose of strengthening Russell's hand, issued a licence to Mr. Gregory to preach in the disturbed district ; and followed it on the 24th by one to Dr. Reynolds : they were to be army chaplains to his lordship with special instructions to " openly declare with sincerity the Word of God in such public place and auditory as the same Lord Privy Seal " should solicit them.[1] But at the last

<hr/>

[1] Petyt MSS. No. 538, fol. 431. This MS. is in the Inner Temple Library, and permission was most courteously given for the comparison of it with Pocock's transcripts which are printed in his " Troubles Connected

moment they seem to have substituted for them Miles Coverdale, who had been preaching in the West.

The Council appear to have entertained no doubt as to the cause of the Western rising, for, as we have seen, their " memorial " to the authorities in Devonshire was " touching them that would not read the book of services."

It is possible that Russell left London on the 24th, leaving his commission to be brought on and his army to advance at a moderate pace [1] while he pushed on to Salisbury. Thence he wrote to the Council, his letter being sent, perhaps, by the messenger Stowell, who also took to London with him information as to " the whole state and proceedings of the busy people in Devonshire," [2] most probably the report of the local justices.

From Salisbury he made his way to Hinton St. George, the seat of the Paulet family, near Chard, where he established himself for a time. Scarcely could he have settled down for a moment's rest after his journey when he heard a clatter of hoofs and a breathless parley. A hastily opened door disclosed the dishevelled figure of Sir Peter Carew, travelworn and weary, who had turned aside from the London road to report the course of events to his lordship. Russell listened eagerly as Carew detailed his experiences in the West : the conference with the local justices, the advance to Crediton, the Burning of the Barns, the unsatisfactory parley at Clyst St. Mary, the hasty departure by partly-barricaded ways, and his dash to Hinton St. George when he heard that Russell was there. Having finished his tale and

with the Prayer Book " (Camden Soc. 1885). The inaccuracies in his transcripts are so great that it has been thought best to quote the originals, adding the page in Pocock : this is on p. 7.

[1] Hoker says Carew met Russell at Hinton St. George. As Sir Peter left Exeter on the 24th and was due to arrive at London on the 26th, it seems probable that Russell started in advance of the main army as suggested above.

[2] Pet. MSS. 432. Pk. p. 15.

given his opinion on the formidable character of the rising, they discussed ways and means for suppressing it. After a brief rest while Russell wrote praying the Council for more men and money, Carew again took horse and travelled eastward. Following Sir Peter's advice Russell rapidly made preparations for going westward to Honiton, where he knew the Carew mansion at Mohun's Ottery would afford him good quarters.

Hastening to Court, Sir Peter found himself the centre of interest. He at once reported the state of affairs in the West to the King, who " not liking the disloyalty of his people promised to seek out a speedy remedy and so commanded him to the Council for the same." [1]

Bluntly and straightforwardly, undaunted as would be one accustomed to the ways of the Court, in the presence of the Council he repeated his story. He drew a gloomy picture of the disturbed state of the country, told of the conference in Exeter, of his advance, on local advice, to Crediton, his lack of opportunity to reason with the rebels, the burning of the barns—and here the serious result of such action caused exclamations from all sides. The Protector turned fiercely on him, saying that his instructions had been exceeded, peaceful and conciliatory measures were to have been used towards the deluded Commons, and here was Sir Peter burning their houses down about their ears and driving the poor wretches to extremes—by such ill-advised doings Sir Peter was himself the very cause of the serious aspect which the commotion had now assumed.

" Aye, true, I used strong measures, your Grace ; but only because I had no chance of being conciliatory. They attacked me, and I had to defend myself and my men. Beside, I have done naught for which the King's warrant is lacking."

---

[1] Hoker, p. 81.

" How now ?   What say you ?   You have the King's warrant for your rash actions ? " exclaimed a member of the Council.

" Yea, here it is, bearing the King's own hand and signet," Sir Peter replied, producing the folded document, and running his finger down towards the bottom of the page, " hear this—

" ' If any manner person after this our writing, pardon, and commandment shall eftsoons attempt to repugne or resist our godly proceedings in the laws by us and our parliament made by *gathering or assembling* in companies or otherwise, to apprehend the same, and to see our laws and statutes duly and severely executed against all such offenders as appertaineth.' [1]

What say you now ?   Was I not justified in trying to apprehend them and use due severity upon them ? " he added triumphantly.   Then, glancing up from the paper, surprised at the silence, he saw that all looked towards Somerset, who appeared abashed and crestfallen.

" Let me see that paper," commanded Lord Chancellor Rich.   " This is no authority," added the unscrupulous lawyer, when he had examined it, " this is no sufficient warrant.   For such actions as yours ye require the King's commission under the Broad Seal, and this is naught but a letter.   You ought by the law to be hanged for your doings."

" What !   ' Given with our hand and under our signet,' " quoted Carew, pointing to the words at the bottom.

" But you should have the authority of the whole Council."

" That I have," he answered.   " See, it reads ' By the advice of our most entirely beloved uncle, the Lord Protector, and the rest of our Privy Council.'   If my lord the King and the Duke's Grace say they have that

---

[1] S. P. Dom. Ed. VI. VII. 38.

authority, it is enough for me—unless you tell me that my Lord Protector has no power in this matter."

Silence fell on the company, and meaning glances were exchanged as he finished speaking. It would not do to let it be known that there were dissensions within the Council, so they postponed the discussion of the matter until, having concluded his account of the Clyst St. Mary conference and of his escape, Sir Peter withdrew.

Hard words were said by Warwick's party concerning Somerset's arbitrary proceedings, but in the end it was decided that Carew's excess of zeal must be overlooked, first, in order to avoid trouble which he might cause, and secondly, because he was a man of so much local knowledge and influence that he would be of great assistance to the Lord Privy Seal. For this purpose they agreed to send him back to the place which was evidently becoming the seat of war. But once bitten, twice shy— not only did Sir Peter demand, but he received letters from the King in Council stating that he had not acted *ultra vires*. Armed with this and with letters to Lord Russell promising that men and money, a sufficient help, should be sent down with speed, Carew promptly started.

He found the Lord Privy Seal ensconced at Mohun's Ottery, and presented the letters, probably adding a vivid description of the scene at the Council meeting. Here the two soldiers awaited the promised " supply and furniture," and would have discussed the Council's letter of the 29th June, containing such minute and futile directions for Russell's action, ignoring the rapid development of affairs in the West while they were dallying and disputing over the cheapest means of suppressing the rising. Well might the young King be—

" much grieved and in double perplexity because at this instant like tumults and rebellions were in like order began in sundry other places of the realm, and partly also because he was enforced to give over the appointed attempt for the conquest

M

of Scotland and to employ the strangers and soldiers retained for that service to the quenching of the fire at home, nevertheless minding to follow the first and to appease the last he sent courteous letters, gracious proclamations and many merciful offers unto all the Commons if they had had the grace to have accepted of the same." [1]

But the Council's letter throws some interesting light upon events in Devon as well as gives some curious advice to Lord Russell. We trace the hand of the Protector, proud of his recent successes in Scotland, in both the military and other schemes set out, which he tries to make palatable to the veteran with a prefatory compliment—" not doubting but at your coming into those parts [by] your wisdom and good policy shall we finish those stirs," and adding that they advised according to their understanding of affairs, " remitting nevertheless the alteration thereof as good occasion shall seem to your wisdom." [2]

He was to appease the multitude assembled at Sampford Courtenay—who, by the way, had long since moved on to Crediton—and to this end, leaving Exeter " in good safety for all purposes of your return "—it was so effectually surrounded by the rebels that Russell could not approach it—he was to advance with his " power of horsemen and some convenient number of ' hagbutes footmen ' " and half a dozen or so of double-basses.[3] In this war-like array, before attempting any enterprise against them, he was to make a final conciliatory attempt. He was to—

" let them understand their disobedience and the causes of their, griefs to be only devised of very falsehood by such as mind traitorously to the King's Majesty and their utter destruction, and therefore it is thought that the great number of them be but seduced and deceived with false rumours, so that if they

---

[1] Hoker, Bod. MS. f. 4ᵈ.   [2] Pet. MSS., f. 432.   Pk. p. 15.
[3] Heavy guns.

will depart to their houses like good subjects and remit the
redress of their griefs to the King's Majesty, who hath only
power that to do and none more ready, then they shall be taken
as the King's subjects, having erred by ignorance. And if
otherwise they will maintain themselves in any assemblies they
shall be sure to be used as high traitors and rebels to the King's
Majesty and the Crown, and that shall they feel forthwith
without any extremity to be spared."

But Lord Russell's exhortation, presumably delivered
as he sat on horseback, armed *cap-à-pie*, in the main
road at the entrance to Sampford Courtenay, was not to
end here. He was to enter into the particulars of their
grievances—those special " bruits and rumours."

Among these, for instance, was a report that " after
the payment for sheep they should pay for their geese
and pigs and such like," which he was to say was utterly
false, invented by some seditious traitor. As for the
" article of Baptism," they were to be referred to his
Majesty's book, " even the last sentence of the first side
of the leaf entreating of baptism," [1] and he was to advise
them to read the whole book that they might see how
much deceived they were.

Russell was also to cause to be—

" bruited abroad sundry wise, that these men thus assembled
be wonderfully abused and that by the provocation only of
certain popish priests, which colour all their doings with other
seditious rumours and means nothing else but to subdue the
people to the pope."

Should this oration fail to pacify the people he would
then be at liberty to proceed as he might think best, but
they advise—

" your horsemen may lie aloof, making now and then offers
to the town, and sending certain harquebutters of horseback
to the place of advantage, to the intent the rebellors may be

---

[1] This refers to the permission to have the children baptised at any
time if it were proved necessary.

drawn to the utter parts of the town, where they have chained up their passages,"

and to back these up by his basses, which were to annoy the people as soon as the horsemen returned, thus he would—

" slay such numbers of them as we think plainly the press thereof will cause them suddenly to give over and shrink, and if not but that they shall break or issue out upon you, then we doubt not but that your horsemen, being instructed before of your L[ordship's] good policy, shall utterly distress them and overthrow them."

But, above all, he was to endeavour to capture a certain ringleader, who was reported to have taken refuge in the church steeple, with some half-dozen com- panions, where he was " keeping his fond office." This man was to be punished before all others for example's sake, and he and his companions were to be dealt with by rack or terror to force a confession of the names of those who were the beginners of the disturbance.[1]

The Lord Privy Seal was to keep to this peaceful policy for two or three days, meanwhile sending a couple of trusty, likely persons—

" with good wise instructions to become partakers of the said multitude, and to profess much earnestness therein, to the intent to get some credit and authority among them,"

to relate his Lordship's power and to point out the terror of committing treason : so—

" upon the fear of their own lives the same men so suborned may wax faint and fall to fear by degrees, that it may be without suspect and not only to begin to flee themselves but also to move others so to do."

---

[1] Sampford Courtenay church possesses two curious architectural features : a staircase up the tower in the thickness of the wall, the inner surface being of carefully dressed and curved blocks of granite, instead of having an external turret for the staircase ; and a staircase turret at the west end of the south aisle, which gives access to the roof of the latter.

Lord Russell was also instructed to cut off their supply of victuals in order to reduce them by famine.

Meanwhile, for the further ordering of affairs, the Council proposed sending him two commissions and a proclamation. One commission "for oyer and determiner of all riots," etc., the other "for the inquiry of decays and unlawful enclosures." The proclamation was for assessing and taxing the excessive prices of victuals.

As if all this were not sufficient to occupy the Lord Privy Seal, he was particularly instructed to search out Mr. Blaxton, one of the Cathedral body, an ecclesiastical Commissary, who had been "dispersing amongst them false and seditious advertisements of the alteration of religion" and to make him, by letters, preaching or otherwise "stir and provoke" the people within his jurisdiction to be obedient, telling them that nothing was meant towards them but—

"true and good establishing of their faith and the profit of the Commonwealth. And so finally to order, that people may be revoked to more quiet or the said commissary to be brought out of his credit, whereas if he should remain without amend- ment much harm might follow."

Indeed, this lengthy letter would have afforded ample food for thought and comment to Lord Russell and Sir Peter, and we can imagine their feelings of mingled amusement and annoyance as they studied it.

After this there is a provoking gap in the Council's correspondence with Russell until the 10th July, when they acknowledge several letters of his dated the 8th instant. But from other sources we obtain glimpses of their action in the interval. On the 2nd July they issued a proclamation to regulate the price of victuals, on the 8th another dealing with "tale tellers and runa- gates," people of no occupation, who went from place to place spreading seditious tales and stirring up the people, and a third about the same date, on the subject of enclosures. As a matter of fact, there were eight proclamations issued in July and five in August. Considering the disturbed state of the West, Russell must have been surprised to receive one denouncing those who failed to yield obedience on the 11th July, and another pardoning those returning to their allegiance, on the 12th.

The Protector's pen was also busy assuring Paget, the ambassador, that the stirs in Essex, Kent, Hampshire, and Devonshire had been renewed but were nearly suppressed, so he must contradict the slanderous reports spread by the French ; by writing and publishing a reply in the King's name to the rebels' demands, and by composing letters to the Princess Mary calling upon her to conform to the orders of the Council as propounded to her by Doctor Hopton. But, turning for the moment from the actions of the Council and of Lord Russell, let us describe the state of affairs in and around Exeter.

CHAPTER XI

" Tush, this gear will not tarry ; it is but my lord Protector's and my lord
of Canterbury's doing."—LATIMER.

THE dislike of religious innovations, so prevalent in
Cornwall, was scarcely less intense in Exeter, then, as
long afterwards, the Metropolis of the West. As a
commercial centre it had more communication with the
outer world, but even such a widening influence did not
lead to a ready acceptance of the " New Learning."

The Cathedral, naturally the headquarters of the old
faith, was considered a hotbed of disaffection, and this
influence made itself felt in the City. Evidence of the
state of opinion there is found in a letter from an imprisoned friar, excusing himself to his Master Provincial.
He had been appointed to take the place of Dr. Charnock
as preacher in the Cathedral on the Third Sunday in
Advent, 1533, as well as on Quinquagesima Sunday.
Of the Cathedral body he writes :—

" I perceived that they were not inclined to the fashion of
the world that goeth now, and specially the master of the
—— Close, for I heard certain of them preach before me. I
was but little acquainted, so I thought I must approve their
sayings, unless I would be *asinus inter simias* I should have
been taken as a wondering stock among them." [1]

---

[1] The details he gives of his sermon are interesting. His reference to
those who acted as " cushion-bearers " to their masters and those who dwelt

The aversion to the " fashion of the world that goeth now " must have caught the attention of the authorities, who soon after sent the King's favourite preacher, Latimer, to convert the Exonians. Hoker says that he delivered his first sermon here in June, 1534, in the churchyard of the Friars beyond Southgate, the Grey Friars or Franciscans—

" to the great annoyance of all the friars, with the exception of their guardian, John Cardmaker, alias Taylor, who from an admirer became a preacher of the same doctrine and for the testimony thereof was burnt at Smithfield, May 30, 1555." [1]

But the authorities took other steps than preaching to overcome the prejudices of the Cathedral body. To make clear the situation it is necessary to describe its members.

John Veysey, *alias* Harman, had been consecrated Bishop of Exeter in 1519 ; already, soon after leaving Oxford, he had been attached to the household of Elizabeth of York, queen of Henry VII., and rapidly developed into an accomplished courtier, so that through the son's reign with its ecclesiastical troubles, he steered a safe course. His intimacy with Cardinal Wolsey, with whom he was at Magdalen College, Oxford, secured his rapid advancement,[2] and when the Cardinal's hat was

in King's houses gave offence and probably led to his imprisonment. His second sermon contained reference to the mystical body of Christ and to the danger caused by the changes in church government. Dr. Charnock mentioned was one of Queen Katherine's friends associated with Moreman, and was a Dominican.

[1] Oliver's " Monasticon," p. 332.

[2] He is sometimes called Voysey. Among his preferments were the incumbencies of Chalfont St. Giles ; St. Mary's, Chester; Clyfton Reynes ; Ashton ; Norton Bryan ; St. Michael's, Coventry ; Wolverhampton ; Sutton Coldfield, and Myvod. Canonries or Prebends in Exeter, Salisbury, and St. Stephen's, Westminster. Archdeaconries of Chester and Barnstaple. Chancellor of Lichfield. Deaneries of Exeter, Chapel Royal, and Windsor, with certain chapleries. He was Registrar of the Order of the Garter, President of the Council of the Marches of Wales, and a Commissioner on the Inquisition on Enclosures.

received at Westminster, with great ceremony, Veysey read the Papal bull bestowing it. He also formed one of the brilliant company of the Field of the Cloth of Gold.

His position at Court does not seem to have been affected by Wolsey's fall; his abilities caused Henry VIII. to appoint him tutor to the Princess Mary, and, although he must have been known to incline to the cause of Queen Katherine, he was able to retain his position through the King's matrimonial and ecclesiastical changes,[1] no doubt his duties in the Marches of Wales and in the household of the Princess helped to keep him out of danger; however, he was present at the consecration of the first Protestant Archbishop, Cranmer.

His duties at Court kept him away from his diocese after the early years of his episcopate, in which he had shown zeal and energy there, but he made occasional visitations, notably in 1538, when he enjoined upon the clergy that they should—

" every Sunday declare in English, or in *Cornish where English is not used,* all or part of the Epistle or gospel of that day, or else the Pater Noster, Ave Maria, Creed, and Ten Commandments, as interpreted in the book called ' The Institution of a Christian Man,' declaring especially the second and fourth commandments, for want of the knowledge whereof it is thought many of the unlearned people of the diocese have been blinded, following their own superstitious fancies, and omitting to do the works of mercy and other acts commanded in Holy Scripture."

He added that incumbents should reside, chantry priests should teach, with other wise instructions.[2]

In the following year he received an admonition because, owing to their lack of spiritual instruction, labourers and artificers left their work from noon till

---

[1] A priest at Sutton Coldfield used seditious words against Anne Boleyn, but the Bishop was able to prove that he was not implicated in the charge (L. & P. VI. 733).

[2] L. & P. XIII. 1106.

evensong on Saturdays after the custom of the Jews; fishermen would not fish on the abrogated Saints' days, smiths would not shoe horses on St. Lewis's day, etc., for the suppression of which superstitions the Bishop was to take prompt steps.[1]

He has been accused of alienating more episcopal estates than did other bishops of the period, but the letters from Henry and from Edward's Council suggest that he was wise to yield gracefully to their imperative demands—those bishops who resisted or remonstrated lost almost as much—Winchester, Norwich, and Durham, for instance—while such favourites as Cranmer and Ridley were forced to relinquish a great deal. Scarcely a bishopric escaped a large loss of revenue, and Exeter, in proportion to its possessions, does not appear to have lost more.

A curious injunction to the people of Veysey's "dyowse" commands them to have a

"better regard unto their livings and specially to refrain their greedy appetite from that insaciable serpent of covetousness wherewith most men are so infected that it seemeth each one would devour another without charity."

It is signed, among others, by Somerset and Bedford, whose own greedy appetites had caused them to swallow many plums of the See.

The Bishop, indeed, attempted to check this spoliation by arranging with the Chapter that all deeds relating to the transfer of ecclesiastical property—of the See or of the Chapter—should be countersigned by both the Bishop and the Chapter—this seems only to have served to record the passing of the property and the names of the new owners.

Another grievance many writers have against Veysey is his compliance with the Council's demand for the

---

[1] Wilkin's "Concilia," III. 846.

resignation of his bishopric. On the 14th August, 1551, he was " peremptorily enjoined to surrender his see," [1] and, in existing circumstances, no other course remained open to him, and he may well have desired rest from active service in his advancing years.[2] Added to this, it is said, Coverdale, his bitter opponent and a strenuous advocate of the new order, had been his co-adjutor during the previous year, which could not have conduced to peace. When the order, which placed him " in fear as well of soul as of body," [3] reached him, Veysey may have counted himself lucky to have been allowed to retire to his native town of Sutton Coldfield, there to expend his annuity in benevolent enterprises.[4]

But scarcely two years' retirement were permitted him. Mary, on her accession to the throne, having satisfied herself that he was still capable of performing the duties of his office, immediately restored him to his see.[5] In spite of advancing years, he revisited the distant West, and spent two months attending to diocesan affairs. Returning to Sutton Coldfield, he was soon after seized with a fatal illness, dying at the end of October, 1554.[6]

[1] Patent Roll. 5 Edw. VI. pt. i. m. 34. Therein he is *required* to render up and resign, though the next patent, granting the see to Coverdale, refers to Veysey's " free resignation."

[2] The date of his birth is uncertain. If aged 103 at his death, as his monument says, it would have been 1451, but his admission to Oxford in 1482 makes 1465, given by some authorities, more probable. In 1539 Russell describes him as " sore diseased with the gout," and suggested that he might well absent himself from Parliament. Russell posed as his friend, but availed himself of royal letters to force the bishop to alienate large estates to him.

[3] Pat. R. 1 Mary, pt. ii. m. 10.

[4] He gave very generously to Sutton Coldfield, adding to the church and establishing charitable institutions. He was son of William Harman, alias Veysey, by Joan, daughter of Henry Squire. He had a brother Hugh ; a sister, Amicia, wife of John Leveson, and another, Amelia, wife of William Gibbons.

[5] 3rd Sept., 1553.

[6] He was buried in the parish church, where a sumptuous monument, erected long after, records that he was 103 years old.

In 1537, when the authorities made their important move, the Chapter contained many devotees of the Old Faith. Reginald Pole had been appointed Dean in 1527, but, on his attainder with Montague and Exeter, though not deprived by ecclesiastical sentence, the King counted the deanery void. The Precentor, John Ryse, god-father of the Chronicler Hoker, had died at an advanced age in 1531,[1] apparently his office had not been filled. William Leveson,[2] a nephew of the Bishop, was appointed Chancellor in this very year. Thomas Sowthorn had been made Treasurer in 1531. Thomas Bedyll, having died in September, 1537, was succeeded by Thomas Wynter as Archdeacon of Cornwall,[3] with the strange results already described.[3] George Carew, made Arch-deacon of Totnes in 1534, was a man of distinction, brother of Sir Gawen and uncle of Sir Peter Carew ; his marriage with Anne, daughter of Sir Nicholas Hervey, of the Privy Bedchamber of Henry VIII., probably accounted for his rapid advancement to posts of honour.[4]

Thomas Brerewood, appointed Archdeacon of Barn-staple in 1528, has also had his doings described.[5] Robert Weston was Sub-dean until his death in 1539, when Nicholas Weston succeeded. Among the other sixteen Prebendaries were William Horsey, William Parkhouse,

[1] Hoker records that Ryse had been chaplain to Edward IV., that he was a great housekeeper, of good hospitality, liberal to scholars and good to the poor. Also that he built the priest-vicars' college and appointed Hoker's father his executor. Shortly before his death at about the age of 90, he founded the Mass of the Holy Ghost in the Chapel of St. Mary or the Charnel-house. There may have been a Precentor appointed, as Heynes in 1537–8 was granted the *next* presentation.

[2] The name is frequently spelt phonetically, Luson. He succeeded another nephew of Veysey's, John Gybbons.

[3] See Chap. IV.

[4] The D. N. B. has a brief notice of him but only as the grandfather of his grandson, the Earl of Totnes. Through lesser benefices he advanced to the deaneries of Bristol ; Christ Church, Oxford ; Windsor and Exeter ; as well as to the Mastership of the Savoy. His recorded livings in Devon are five.

[5] See Chap. IV.

John Holwell, John Stephyn, and William Fawell, titular Bishop of Hippo.

Already the Chapter had attracted the vigilant eye of Cromwell; he had received, between 1529 and 1531, a set of "Articles against the Canons residenciary of Exeter,"[1] which complained of their refusal to allow John Holwell, chaplain to the King, to take up residence on the excuse of having no residence available. However, they yielded to the Royal command, after protest. Other such cases occurred—Richard Manchester brought an action to recover the first-fruits of his prebend, and William "Hippo" claimed a residence, and was backed by a letter from the authorities.[2] Such contumacy called for close scrutiny, and the disaffection over the "King's Proceedings" was apparent. The vacancy of the Deanery at this juncture, through Pole's attainder, offered an occasion to set matters right. Cromwell had promised the Lord Chancellor that the office should be given to his nominee, Thomas Brerewood—at least £100 would accrue to Cromwell in that event.[3] But the King's choice fell upon a fit instrument—upon Simon Heynes, recently master of Queens' College, Cambridge, and Vice-Chancellor of that University, whom Henry, in 1535, had appointed to preach there "against the supremacy of the Pope and to reconcile the minds of the students to its abolition."[4]

The King's letter to the Chapter, dated the 6th April, 1537, recommended as their future ruler—

"our trusty and well-beloved Chaplain, Master Simon Heynes, who is our Ambassador and agent in the parts beyond the sea for certain our affairs and necessary business there,"

and required them not to prevent him from securing his

[1] L. & P. V. 1785.
[2] See Star Chamber Proceedings, XVII. 412, and L. & P. IX. 191.
[3] L. & P. XII. i. 764 and 835.
[4] Oliver's "Bishops," p. 477, *n.*

distributions, quotidian dividends and other emoluments.[1] This was brought by Richard Chamber, with a
letter from Heynes, to Treasurer Sowthorn, who sent him
on to the Bishop. The latter commented that the letters
were drawn " slenderly "—had he been of council they
would have been more effectual and of more pith ; but,
as this was the King's letter, he would obey it as far as
he could. He would institute him to the prebend at
once, but there must be a form of election, especially as
the King wished him put in by the most assured way ;
so it was best to give the three weeks' notice needed and
follow the old law " whatever chance should befall the
King." [2] The matter was discussed by the Bishop, the
Treasurer, the Archdeacon, and the Chancellor, who used
Latin as Chamberlain did not understand that language,
but when the Chancellor said, " *No, no, cave ad enter,*" [3] he
guessed that he meant that if any chance should befall
the King he would be the first to put Heynes out because
of the non-compliance with ancient forms.

On the 4th June Heynes was put in possession of
the canonry and prebend " void by the resignation of
Reginald Pole," and the citation for the election as
Dean was affixed to the Chapter-house door, and on
the 16th July they complied with the royal command.[4]

When Heynes arrived and " protested " to begin
residence, he refused to pay caution money as demanded
by the statutes and " laudable, usual and approved
custom of the Church of Exeter," for he had come for the
avowed purpose of doing away with these, and began as
he meant to continue. The Canons would not consent

---

[1] Dean and Chapter Archives. Letter 75.
[2] L. & P. XII. ii. 182. A similar claim was made in the reign of
Elizabeth. See Wilkin's " Concilia."
[3] Perhaps *Caveat emptor.*
[4] Chamber filled in the interval by examining the decanal possessions—
the Dean's house was in bad repair, its garden a wilderness, and the more
distant holdings and farms were wholly condemned.

to his admission, and postponed the matter to be considered by a fuller Chapter. The latter allowed him, in obedience to the royal commands, to begin residence, while the Dean agreed to make payment provided the custom was not abolished by the King, which he, naturally, expected would be done to support his authority. On his part he demanded to see the Injunctions recently left by the King's Visitor, but no one knew where these were unless Brerewood had a copy—one exasperated Canon remarking that "they imported nothing," but that they should do as of old. The Dean wrote asking Cromwell to send such injunctions, signed with his own hand, as he wished kept and promised to see them executed within the Close. He added—

"I like the people of this town very well and I may not mislike no kind of men until I know their condition thoroughly, but as far as I have seen, the priests of this country are a strange kind, very few of them well persuaded or anything learned." [1]

The Dean proceeded to take matters with a high hand, claiming unusual privileges and emoluments as well as pre-eminence and jurisdiction over the Cathedral body. He refused to recognise "old, ancient customs," and would not provide wax for candles to burn before the High Altar, which preceding deans had maintained. He obtained Cromwell's support in his quarrels—for the Chapter would not tamely submit to his innovations, though their fear of his Royal master usually carried the day, especially as the Dean would make them solemn promises, which were lightly broken if occasion served. He himself was greedy and grasping to the last degree, yet rebuked the Canons for covetousness and for taking

---

[1] Hoker states that Heynes had many adversaries "as his brethren the Canons of this Church as namely Willm luson chancellor. . . . Thomas Southern, Treasurer, Adam Traverst, Archdeacon of Exeter, John Holwell and Thomas Wyse, Mr. Cryspion and Gregory Basset" (Common Place Bk. 1550).

good coins from the Chapter chest, leaving nothing to pay his emoluments.[1]   At one time they so far rebelled as to charge him with grave offences ; that during the year preceding the 24th July, 1550, he had destroyed or caused to be destroyed many beautiful statues of saints, laudably erected by the faithful, which had not been abused by superstitious pilgrimages : he had torn up and removed over £40 worth of monumental iron and brass ; he had obliterated and cut the choir books to the extent of twenty marks damage ; by indiscreet removal of the monumental iron and brass he had mutilated columns, walls, and pavements, injuring most of them, and he had taken away and extinguished the light which had burned continually for three hundred years before the High Altar and the Body of Christ, which previous deans had been obliged by the ancient foundation to maintain.   All this was done with grave scandal.[2]   The Dean vehemently denied these accusations, and the matter was referred to arbitrators, but the result is not recorded.

A little later a more serious charge was brought against him, with the result that he was summoned before the Privy Council to answer " certain things objected against him touching his own evil opinions and the maintaining also of sundry persons in the like." [3] According to Strype, his accusers were Sowthorn and Brerewood, who declared that the Dean had preached against holy bread and holy water, and that in one of his sermons he said—

---

[1] Heynes submitted to the King certain " Articles for the Reformation of the Cathedral Church of Exeter." Harl MS. 604, f. 59. See Olivers' " Bishops," p. 477.

[2] See Reynolds' "Anc. Dioc. Exeter," p. 172. Hoker records that Heynes, as Commissioner for the removal of images, " had defaced and pulled down an Image called St. Saviour which was builded in the outside of the north wall of the chancel of the parish church of St. More in the sand, for which he was marvellous hated and maligned at " (Com. Pl. Bk.).

[3] P. C. Reg. (Dasent) I. p. 79.

" that ' marriage and hanging were destiny : ' whence they would have gathered treason against him because of the King's marriage, as though he had an eye to that." [1]

His defence did not satisfy the Council, so he was committed to the Fleet on the 16th March, 1542–3, and a letter was written to the Bishop of Exeter and the Chapter commanding them to certify what they knew concerning his evil opinions.[2] Their book of " articles " on the subject was submitted to men learned in ecclesiastical law, and on the 3rd May certain bishops were appointed to examine the informations and report with all diligence. On the 4th July, after nearly four months' imprisonment for his " lewd and seditious preaching and sowing otherwise of many erronious opinions," he appeared before the Council. " After a good lesson and exhortation, with a declaration of the King's mercy and goodness towards him," he was dismissed, and set at liberty under heavy recognisances.[3] Soon after he returned to Exeter to quarrel with the Canons afresh.

About this period the distribution of capitular estates was accelerated ; courtiers, backed by the King, demanded plums, while canons were not above profiting, and the Dean, above others, tried to feather his own nest.

Opposed as they were to the Dean and to all the religious innovations which he represented, it is remarkable that when the crisis came and the city was besieged by those who wished to retain the ancient forms, the Canons, or rather such as remained within the walls, upheld the civic authorities, even sending their servants to keep watch and ward. Yet their devotion to " popish superstitions " was in no wise abated, for on Mary's accession they openly rejoiced at her " reformation of

[1] Vol. II. ii. p. 53.
[2] See P. C. Reg. (Dasent) II. pp. 98, 117, 118, and 150. Sir Philip Hoby was imprisoned with him.
[3] See note 4 on previous page.

abuses." Under Elizabeth many of them retired to the more congenial atmosphere of Hereford, becoming veritable thorns in the flesh of the authorities.[1]

And the citizens of Exeter, what opinions did they hold ? Many particulars of the Canons' opinions on the innovations have been preserved, but, not unnaturally, the civic records contain less ample accounts of the opinions of the citizens on the subject. In fact, the latter were still inclined to leave theological discussion to the clergy and were conservative enough to follow the religion of their forefathers, so they seldom came in conflict with the law in this connection. Those who ventured to express new opinions often met with terrible fates.

Such an one was Thomas Dusgate,[2] who, having been influenced by the " New Learning " at Cambridge, had sought Luther's opinion on celibacy. On his return from this visit he felt obliged to leave the University, and retired to Torrington, where he married, and kept a school under the name of Bennet. Later, he removed to Exeter, and frequented the Cathedral services, where " Dr. Moreman, Crispin, Caseley, with such others bare

---

[1] It is strange how many of them survived. A picturesque glimpse of them is found in the affidavits connected with the Carews' plot in Elizabeth's favour—a supper at Canon Holwell's, was attended by Sir Thomas Denys, Dr. Moreman, Treasurer Sowthorn, Canons Gregory and Smart (see Maclean's "Carew," App. E.). At Hereford Leveson, Blaxton, Mugge, and Friar Gregory had been received with a torchlight procession and were reported to have mass in their houses ; to keep " scoles " of popery and to maintain enemies of religion. Blaxton and Mugge are styled " stubborn persons " against whom processes could not be executed as they were supported by members of the Cathedral there. Leveson disobeyed an order to make open profession of the new faith and refused to read a homily. Altogether, they were contumacious to the last. (See Bateson's " Letters of Bishops " and S.P. Dom. Eliz. Add. VI. 522.)

[2] See Foxe, V. p. 18. Hoker, who contributed this account of Bennet, was only seven years old at the time of the martyrdom, so he quotes from the papers of a minister resident in Exeter at the time. The style suggests Philip Nycolles. (See Chap. VI. p. 105.) Foxe mentions no other martyr in the diocese prior to the Marian persecutions, and only one in her reign.

swing," while the preachers were Drs. Baskerville and David, and "Doctor I-know-not-who," as well as Gregory Basset, a Grey Friar, who in picturesque language is described as having held Lutheran opinions, but had recanted.[1] Dusgate so resented these sermons that he fixed a bill on the Cathedral door denouncing the Pope as Anti-Christ.

The unknown offender was cursed with bell, book, and candle, and Dusgate's conduct at that service roused suspicion. Soon after, his boy was caught affixing another bill to the "Little Stile," and Dusgate was brought before the magistrates. On his confession he was handed over to the ecclesiastical authorities, confined in the Bishop's prison, and then brought into the Consistory Court, before the Bishop, Chancellor Brerewood, and "other of his lewd clergy and friars." Here he set forth his opinions so well that most of the Court had pity and compassion upon him, and made every effort to convert him. The most busy of all was Gregory Basset, who even spent both day and night with Dusgate in prison, and, with others, for eight days held disputations with him. In view of Dusgate's language against those in authority, it is not surprising that, continuing obdurate, he was condemned as a heretic.

They procured a writ "*de comburendo*" from London on the 15th January, 1531, whereupon he was delivered to Sir Thomas Denys, then Sheriff of the county. Izacke states that the stake was ordered to be set up on Southernhay, "which the Chamber would not suffer," [2] so he was burned at Livery Dole, outside the city limits.[3] If there was a dispute it was probably a question of jurisdiction.

Some spectators at the execution are reported to have

---

[1] See note 2 on previous page.

[2] "Exeter," ed. 1677, p. 116.

[3] Oliver ("Bishops," p. 122) denies that Denys erected almshouses on this spot in expiation, as they were not begun until more than thirty years after Denys' death. Jenkins ("Exeter," p. 437) says they were founded in 1591.

displayed unwonted brutality. Hoker, himself, indicates that the citizens had little sympathy with his
opinions ; the hate of the people at that time, by means
of ignorance, was hot against him, scarcely a suspicion
rested upon any.

" Few or none, unless a shearman or two, whose houses, I
well remember, were searched for bills . . . knew anything of
God's matters, or how God doth bless their curses in such case." [1]

The only sympathiser named is William Strode, of
Newnham, by Plymouth, already imprisoned for heresy,
who wrote letters of comfort to Dusgate.

Latimer's sermon, in 1534, as we have noted, produced apparently only one convert, Cardmaker. When,
in the following year, the suppression of the smaller
houses began in Exeter with St. Nicholas Priory, it was
actively opposed. The Commissioners sent two Breton
carvers [2] to destroy the rood-loft in the church, reports
of which reaching certain women, they broke down the
locked door and drove the men from their sacrilegious
work ; one man took refuge in the tower, but was so
hotly pursued that he leapt from the window and broke
his ribs. John Blackaller, then an alderman, hearing
of the fray, and thinking by fair word or foul to pacify
the women, was speedily on the scene, but he received a
blow that sent him packing. The Mayor and his officers,
with better luck, apprehended the women and lodged
them in ward ; so strenuous, however, was their opposition
that they were reputed to be men in disguise. The
Commissioners thanked his Worship for his diligence, but
begged him to release the women. [3]

[1] See Foxe, V. p. 20.
[2] Local workmen were seldom employed.
[3] The women were Jone Reeve, Elizabeth Glanfield, Agnes Colleton,
Alys Miller, and Jone Rede. In 1536 Blackaller, as mayor, signed an
account of the disturbance sent to the Marquis of Exeter. The women
had been found guiltless of traitorous intent, their purpose being to " let
two Breton carvers, who boasted that they would pull down the crucifix

The inference to be drawn from these stories—that the citizens were averse to the innovations—is supported by Hoker's statements elsewhere. He also records the fate of a citizen, who was accused of speaking against those in authority. John Bonyfant—a gentleman, an attorney, and an owner of considerable property in the city and vicinity—in 1539 dined with John Northbrook, his tenant, who coveted the house he occupied; Adam Wilcocks, proctor of the spiritual court, being also a guest. The conversation turned on certain prophecies then current: that a "molde warpe" should come cursed of God's mouth and vengeance should befall him,[1] and a Welsh prophecy that a dun cow should ride the . . .[2] and then great changes should happen. Various interpretations were suggested, but they agreed that these must both refer to the King, who should come to destruction. After burning the written prophecies, they went with Bonyfant to his home. While walking on together, Northbrook suggested that they had all talked high treason, and that Bonyfant, being a lawyer, and a crafty man, would probably disclose all secretly to the Mayor, and accuse them to the jeopardy of their lives, so it was best to "play sure," and accuse him first to the Mayor. Rousing his Worship, for it was late, they made the accusation, Northbrook advising that the gates should be watched till morning. Very early Northbrook

---

of the said church with all the saints there, calling them idols." Seditious bills against the mayor for imprisoning the women had been posted. Oliver gives the story at length ("Mon." p. 116). The mayor was William Hurst.

[1] This was from the "Boke of profecyed," by Mistress Amadas. See her confession, Cleop. E. IV., f. 84. Furnivall ("Ballads, etc.," I. 476), quoting this story, refers to Shakespeare's *Henry IV.*, pt. i. act iii., and to Holinshed's account of the division of England between Glendower and his allies. Chapuys writes: "This people . . . is peculiarly credulous, and is easily moved to insurrection by prophecies, and in the present disposition is glad to hear any to the King's disadvantage (Spanish S. P. 1531-3, No. 1154).

[2] Indistinct in MS.

called on Bonyfant, and, "pretending good," advised him to escape to a neighbour's house, to which he soon brought the searchers, who found Bonyfant in hiding, and fetched him to the Guildhall. At the villain's suggestion proceedings for high treason were begun by asking the accused if Northbrook was his friend, and, when he declared he knew him to be an honest man, Northbrook entered and said, "I cannot say the same of thee—thou art a very traitor, and I accuse thee of treason." Later, Wilcocks supported the charge, and, in spite of denials and countercharges, Bonyfant was committed for trial, condemned, and hanged and quartered on Southernhay, on the 10th August. Hoker adds that Wilcocks "fell amased and was dystracted of wyttes, his tounge rotted yn his hedd and dyed most myserable," while Northbrook obtained his house, but lived in great infamy all his days, and his issue had bad success.

Although before 1549 there was undoubtedly an anti-papal party of considerable dimensions, including such noted citizens as Bodley, Prestwood, Periam, and Hoker himself, a large proportion favoured the old religion—such as Blackaller, Hurst, Peter, and Smith. Hoker writes of the two sorts—

"the one and the greater number were of the old stamp and of the Romish religion. The other being of the lesser number were of a contrary mind and disposition for they wholly replyed [1] themselves to the reformed religion. . . . The first were so addicted to their own fantasies and their bottles were so far seasoned with the old wine, that they cannot abide nor hear of any other religion than that they were first noselled in : wherefore to keep and observe that was their only endeavour, and in respect whereof they regarded nor king nor kaiser, passed not for kin nor friendship, regarded nor country nor common-wealth, but were wholly of the opinion of the rebels and would have no reformation of religion. . . . The magistrates and chieftains of the city, albeit they [were] not fully resolved and

---

[1] The Bod. Hoker has " who relyinge to the Kinges proceedings.'

satisfied in religion yet they not respecting that but chiefly
their dutifulness to the king and commonwealth, nothing liked
the rebellion . . . but . . . do all things to defend the city
and themselves against their rebellious attempts . . . and to
keep the citizens in peace and quietness : whereupon the
favourers of the old Romish religion, being inwardly grieved
that they could not have their will nor . . . have the gates . . .
opened that these good and religious men, as they termed them,
might come in they used private conferences,"

either over the walls or by letters sent by privy messengers, or by open speeches in times of truce, or by written
messages attached to arrows or other wicked devices
tending to betray the city and set up their religion,[1] but
in the end it pleased the Eternal God so to rule the hearts
of the magistrates that though devoted to the Romish
religion they respected their duty to their prince and
their commonwealth, and openly professed that they
would never yield as long as they lived and were able to
keep the city.

" The Mayor himself, William Hurst, John Buller, John Bryt-
nall, William Periam and others of the ancients of the city were
by sundry means, ways, devices and reasons persuaded to conjoin themselves in this rebellion with the commoners : they all
with one mind and one voice gave a flat answer, that in the city
they had been brought up, there they had gotten their livings,
there they had sworn their fidelity and allegiance to their king
and prince, there they had hitherto served him and they would
so continue so long as they could to the uttermost of their
powers : and which their promise and advowries (the Lord be
praised) they performed." [2]

There can be little doubt from the above quotations
that Hoker believed that the " New Learning " had
found few adherents in Exeter.

---

[1] Hoker, p. 71.　　　　[2] Ibid. p. 74.

CHAPTER XII

"Thus hath this ancient little city been from time to time in many and
    sundry storms and troubles, but in the most extremity of them they
    never forgot the due allegiance to their sovereign prince, nor their
    faith and duty to their commonwealth."—HOKER.

BUT while Lord Russell lingered at Honiton, Arundell
and his combined forces had not been idle.   It is evident
that a council of war had been held at which it was
decided that, before taking active warlike steps, an
humble petition should be forwarded to the king asking
redress of their grievances.   Already, as we have seen,
the Cornishmen had made seven demands which had
the approval of the united body, but to these they now
added another article on the new service in English.
Leaving this subject for another chapter we will follow
the course of events in Devon.

Remembering the experiences of the Northern rebels,
when Henry had been frightened by warlike demonstra-
tions into listening to their demands only to betray
them when the show of force was withdrawn, the Western
men deemed it wise to back their requests with evidence
of their strength.

Already they had blocked the roads and captured
willing and unwilling gentlemen.   They appear to have
scattered themselves over the country, sheltering with
friends, inciting others to join them, and arming themselves, like a strong man, to keep the peace.

Flamank's companions in 1497 are said to have—

"marched without any slaughter, violence or spoil to the country, showing that remarkable forbearance from pillage or wanton destruction characteristic of the Celtic race."[1]

There is no reason to suppose that these rebels were less kindly disposed to their neighbours, who, in truth, were inclined to sympathise with them. The charges of rapine and robbery brought by their opponents were probably unfounded, being based on the usual actions of soldiers in an enemy's country, but these were among friends. They may have been true at a later period when there was serious opposition to their doings, but at first they sought by gentle conduct to win favour.

While they awaited the King's reply to their demands, the leaders tried to put matters on a military footing, as a refusal must find them ready for action. They seem to have established a council of war consisting of three Cornish gentlemen, three Devon gentlemen, and three representatives of the people—Arundell, John Wynslade, and Holmes, for Cornwall ; Pomeroy, Bury, and Coffin, for Devon ; and Underhill, Sloeman, and Segar, of the people, all, we believe, of Sampford Courtenay. These nine controlled the army, and decided matters of moment, while eight " Governors " commanded as many camps, of whom four signed the Articles—two of these were priests, Thompson and Barret, and two represented the civic element, Bray and Lee, mayors respectively of Bodmin and Torrington.

Hoker writes—

" The commons being now entered in their follies and having driven the gentlemen to flight do openly show themselves traitors and rebels and therefore assembling themselves do appoint out Captains to direct and order both themselves and their proceedings : and as the common proverb is, like lips

---

[1] E. C. Batten, Somers. Arche. Soc. Proc. XXV. p. 53.

like lettuce, so as is their cause are the Rulers, the one being
not so bold and evil as they wicked or worse : The Captains
then are these : Underhill, a tailor, Mawnder, a shoemaker,
Seager, a labourer and Ashridge, a fish-driver, with sundry
others such like the worst men of all others, though most mete
for this service." [1]

His object was to disparage the rebels, representing
them as of the lowest class, but he somewhat grudgingly
adds—

" But it was not long before that certain gentlemen and yeomen
of countenance both in Devon and Cornwall were contented to
carry the Cross before the procession and to be guiders and
captains of this Rebellion : Some of them are notoriously noted
in Chronicles and were executed for the same : some are yet
living but being sorry and ashamed of their folly I do suppress
their names." [2]

Hayward describes the leaders as priests unworthy to
be named, importunate incensors of rage, men of some
academical learning in discourse, but their minds not
seasoned with any virtuous or religious thought.[3]

Holinshed states that this assembly numbered little
less than ten thousand—

" stout and valiant personages, able indeed (if their cause had
been good and favoured of the Lord and giver of victories),
to have wrought great feats.   But being (as they were) rank
and malicious traitors, the almighty God confounded their
devices, and brought them to their deserved confusion." [4]

---

[1] P. 66.   Bod. MS. reads : " The Comons advertised of the departure
of the gentlemen from out of the Cittie take hearte of grace and nowe
thinking the gaine to bee on their side doe openlie show them selues to bee
Traitors and rebells and assemblinge them selues togeather doe appointe out
Captaines, the chiefest of them att the ffirst were Vnderhyll a Taylor,
Maunder, a shoemaker, Seager A husband laborer and Aysherydge a
fisshe driuer wth sundrie other such like."   A fish-driver was one who fished
with a drift-net.
[2] Bod. MS. f. 5.
[3] See " Edward VI.," p. 55.
[4] Chron. p. 917.

Russell still lingered at Honiton, whether because of secret instructions " to drill on the time," or because he was more of a statesman than a soldier, or else lacked strength to encounter the enemy,[1] but in any case, his inaction was interpreted as due to fear.[2] Fresh rumours of taxes on sheep, cattle and food, and a circumstantial report of the King's death,[3] with other " slanderous bruits were spread abroad by those children of Belial, whereby the cankered minds of the rebels " were hardened and made stiff, and the " rebellious rout " grew to an obstinacy, deaf to all persuasion, and more resolute in their pestilent actions.[4]

Under these influences the people grew restless, and demanded bold action, such as the capture of Exeter,[5] as some one suggested, either by persuasion or force, anticipating little opposition, as many of the citizens, even the Mayor and some of his brethren, were known supporters of the old form of religion. Therefore, as Hoker puts it—

" the principle and chief captains in Devon being fully resolved by their own power and authority to maintain and continue the religion according to the Romish Church and utterly to impugne the reformation thereof established by Act of Parliament, and to support the Idol of Rome whom they never saw in contempt of their true and lawful king whom they knew and ought to obey : these I say send messengers unto the Mayor of this City, whose name was John Blackaller, to move and pray him to join with them, they, thinking that they having access to and from the City and the help of the citizens should not want money, or anything else to serve their turn. The

---

[1] Heylin, p. 75. Drill, probably from " driling," a Devon word for wasting time. See Halliwell's Dict.

[2] Hayward, p. 60.

[3] The King mentions this in his journal and how he went in procession through the city to confute it.

[4] See Holinshed, p. 924.

[5] Hayward (p. 60) says that as they were " unable to support themselves with their own estate or by waste of villages, they aspire to the spoil and subjection of cities."

Mayor forthwith advertiseth unto his brethren this motion : and albeit some and the chiefest of them did like and were well affected to the Romish religion yet respecting their duty to God, their obedience to the King, their fidelity to their country, and safety of themselves, gave their full, resolute and direct answer that they would not join nor deal with them at all." [1]

Blackaller, the leader of this bold company, is described as " a merchant, and only exercised in that trade [and] had small reach in matters of policy or martial affairs." Thrice mayor of Exeter in each year " grew some troubles," but he took such special care in regard to its government that he never attempted anything therein but by the advice and counsel of wise, grave, and expert men, and " God so blessed him, that he prospered and had good success in all his doings." [2]

The Mayor's reply was " nothing liked," so a second messenger required and commanded them—

" to maintain the Catholic religion with them, and do as they did or else they would besiege them and perforce compel them thereto."

To this threat they gave the same answer, adding that—

" they in their doings were wicked and bad men, and they did and would repute them enemies and rebels against God, their King, and country and so renounced them." " The foresaid Captains, stomaching at their answer do agree and conclude to besiege the City and to assail the same, thinking and hoping in short space to purchase that perforce, which (having many friends and favourers of their doings within the City) they thought to have had with a good will and of a free offer at the first." [3] " The Mayor and his brethren upon good advice guarded and watched with sufficient men armed both by day and by night : the Rebels according to their determination

---

[1] Hoker, p. 67.   [2] Brice's Hoker, p. 65.
[3] See Bod. Hoker, f. 5.

relying themselves upon a vain hope, thinking that notwith-standing the answers before made, yet because the most part of the citizens were of their opinion and of the like affections in religion would not resist them : as also that they had many friends within the City, more ready to join with them, than to follow the Mayor, if they might have the choice what to do." [1]

These negotiations must have occupied several days, and before the gates were shut many of the disaffected joined the rebels.

Those were anxious times for the citizens. The Mayor and his brethren must have awaited the result of their bold refusal with some trepidation. It was almost impossible to tell who among the inhabitants would uphold them, there were dissensions in their own body, and they dreaded the members of their own households, for they knew not who would play the traitor—friends of the rebels lingered in the city to act as spies and to lend them aid.

The hearts of the Mayor and his brethren must have beat high when word was brought that the rebel host was advancing in force. Hastily donning their robes and insignia they joined the crowd hurrying to the gate commanding a view of the approaching army. A solemn procession drew near, for Arundell would have recognised the importance of impressing the people, and would have used every item of pomp and ceremony.

In the July sunshine, for it was the second day of that month, the watchers saw the glitter of metal ; here the gold and silver ornaments in the religious part of the procession, there the steel of the armed men. In front was the banner of the Five Wounds, fluttering in the breeze, swaying as it was borne along, then came a company of priests, robed and chanting solemnly ; in their midst, beneath a gorgeous canopy, was the sacred pyx, in a cloud of incense rising from swinging censers,

---

[1] See Hoker, p. 68.

acolytes, and singing boys in cottas and cassocks, bearing huge tapers, marched beside it. A familiar sight this to the onlookers, accustomed from childhood to see such ceremonials when the priests sang the Litany as they marched in procession around their churchyard. Involuntarily the watchers, to whom the new services were unfamiliar, would have been moved by the forbidden display. Could these be wicked men who reverenced thus their old ceremonials ? Was it worse to rebel against the King than against the Holy Catholic Church ? A stirring and a searching of heart would have troubled those not well grounded in the new faith. Behind the religious procession came the man appointed to act as herald for the rebels, surrounded by a fitting escort, preceded by trumpeters. As the clerics neared the gate they stood aside, lining the way, and ceased their chanting. After a brief pause came a flourish of trumpets and the herald stood forth and made proclamation : If after this third demand the inhabitants refused to yield peaceably and to join their fellow-countrymen in protesting against the new orders so illegally imposed during the King's minority, then would their host advance, enter by force, and spoil the city.

"But the walls of Exeter," says Heylin, "fell not down before this false ark as Dagon did before the true." [1]

Then the Mayor flung forth a defiant answer : They would be true to their King, observing the laws promulgated by the Council concerning religion ; they were ready to suffer if need be for their loyalty, the city refused to treat with such as they, let the rebels do their worst.

If at first his voice trembled, surely ere he ended it rang true and clear, and a murmur of assent rose from his brethren and the Justices beside him, who had hastened to support him. Turning with dignity, he

---

[1] "Eccles. Rest.," p. 76.

walked back to the Guildhall, there to hold conference as to the best ways and means of defence, while the populace lingered to see what the insurgents would do.

A great number accompanying the herald jeered at the citizens, threatening to starve them out like rats in a hole. Later they returned, bringing their wives, horses, and panniers, persuading themselves and promising them by such a day and upon such a day to enter into the City, and then to measure velvets and silk by the bow and to lade their horses home with plate, money, and other great riches.[1]

But for the moment the crowd dispersed, the citizens to contemplate sorrowfully the prospects of a siege. Some among them surely could remember Perkin Warbeck's attack in 1497, when they—

"with ordnance battered the walls, fired the gates, undermined it and with mighty ladders scaled them and left nothing undone which might be to compass their attempt," [2]

while the memory still lingered of a previous siege in 1470, so they knew what to expect and for what to prepare.

So passed Tuesday, the 2nd July, when the gates were closed and the city surrounded. The rebel forces spread themselves in a circle—

"from St. David's Down to St. Sidwell's Church, across the wide waste of the Southernhay, even to the Southgate along the open banks and flats by the river from the Watergate past Westgate to Snayle tower." [3]

"The Mayor and his brethren forecasting what would ensue provided all things meet and necessary wherewith to defend themselves and to annoy the enemy. The City therefore is viewed for armour : men are mustered : Soldiers are retained : Captains in every ward appointed : wardens for the day and watchmen for the night assigned : ordnance at the

---

[1] See Hoker, p. 68.   [2] Ibid. 55.
[3] Cotton and Woollacombe, p. 53.

gates and upon the walls placed : mounts in convenient places erected : and all things else done as that present state and necessity required." [1]

When the rebels from the vantage ground of houses in the suburbs shot down the citizens in the streets, not only were these mounts erected to shelter them, but the suburbs were set on fire ; when the gates were burned " rather a benefit than a hurt " [2] followed, for the defenders added fuel to the flames, preventing the near approach of the enemy until they had cast up a strong rampire, shaped like a half-moon, so that when the seditious pushed their way in they were slain " from the corners like dogs." [3] At the foot of St. Edmund's Bridge they erected a *chevaux de frise* to prevent entrance at that point.[4]

Frequently they were called upon to foil the enemy's devices. It was rumoured that the wall by the West-gate was to be undermined, so John Newcombe, of Teignmouth, a tinner, who was much indebted to Alderman William Hurst, offered his services to counter-mine. Not knowing the exact spot threatened, he took a pan filled with water, which he moved from point to point, watching the ripples on the surface until he was satisfied by their greatest motion that he had detected the mine. Here he countermined until he was near enough to make a small opening through which he could see the unsuspecting enemy at work filling the cave with gunpowder, pitch, and other combustibles, and over-heard mention of the time fixed for the explosion, so he took prompt measures to prevent it. Instructions were given to all citizens residing on that slope of the

[1] See Bod. Hoker, f. 5ᵈ.
[2] See Hoker, p. 69.
[3] Hayward, p. 60.
[4] Exeter City Muniments, Receivers Account, 3 & 4 Edw. VI., " le chippis de vulnera " would literally mean a palisado or sharp stake for wounding, here it is obviously a series of such stakes used for a barricade.

hill to provide themselves with a tub or hogshead of water at their fore doors, and all the wells or streams at hand were made to fall that way and dammed up. Having nearly pierced the remaining wall between the mines and having constructed a channel to his own mine, on a given signal all the tubs were emptied into the kennels and the conduits were made to overflow, with the result that the torrent of water rushed down the hill, and so entered and drowned the place which had been mined.[1]

Although they could meet the external enemy's stratagem with stratagem, yet the enemy within was more difficult to cope with, " for the serpent of division and the fire of malice entered into the City many being envenomed with the one but more skalled wth the other." [2] Those who held to the old forms found opportunity to help the besiegers, sometimes by secret messages and sometimes by bold and audacious acts. Under cover of truces and parleys the rebels persuaded and conferred or by friendly conferences devised to " compass their intents."

A certain John Wolcot, member of the " common counsell," once perpetrated a piece of open treachery. In the ordinary course he became captain to ward the gates, and one morning on his rounds he found certain friends at the Westgate, probably by arrangement. After some consultation he suddenly went out by the wicket gate, taking the keys with him. Outside he held conference with some one high in authority, making promises that he was unable to perform. After attempting to fulfil his undertaking he was returning with two companions when, either suspecting treachery or desiring a valuable hostage, the rebels laid hands upon the three men, who, however, with some difficulty escaped, but the facts becoming known, Wolcot was severely censured.

---

[1] It is said that a violent thunderstorm occurred at the same moment, the Powers above lending their aid.   Charldon mentions this in his sermon.

[2] Hoker, p. 71.

On another occasion the rebels bribed the soldiers hired to keep the Castle to admit a company through a postern gate, and an hour was fixed—

"but whether the same by secret advertisement were discovered, or whether the matter were mistrusted, or whether it pleased God to move the hearts of certain men to take the view of the Castle and of the manner of the soldiers' usage there : It is most certain that by the repair and resort of certain men under the colour to walk and see, the treachery was espied and the practices discovered and their whole devices prevented." [1]

Once, when the Mayor had summoned all the commoners to appear at the Guildhall in their armour a tumult arose, the "Papists being then the greater number," and thinking in some way to gain an advantage, one of them, Richard Taylor a clothier, bent his bow and—

"did nock his arrow minding to have stricken the man to whom he leveled the shot, but guaging his hand and missing his mark, he struck his own and best friend, John Peter, the King's customer, a gentleman of good countenance and credit who had died thereof had not the arrow lighted upon one of his rib bones." [2]

When truces existed, strenuous efforts were made to induce " by sundry means, ways, devices and reasons " several of the "auncients of the Citie," including the Mayor, "to conjoin themselves in this rebellion with the commoners," but they flatly refused, declaring that they had been born, brought up, and had sworn allegiance there to their prince, and so intended to remain to serve him as hitherto.

But perils from rivalry among the defenders had also to be considered, many were too rash in their sallies to

[1] See Hoker, p. 73.

[2] *Ibid.* Guaging = engaging, entangling. Hoker adds a marginal note in Holinshed : " This Taylor died after a prisoner of debt," as if that were a judgment upon him.

attack the besiegers or to capture cattle to provision the city and emulated each other, those under suspicion of sympathising with the rebels tried to clear themselves by acts of audacious bravery. This became such a peril that a grave council was held, when a hundred of the chief men banded themselves together by a kind of self-denying ordinance, and also agreed that if the city should be forced to yield they would meet at Bedford House, and issue by the garden postern either to escape, or, if they met with resistance, to stand to their defence and die in the Crolditch. Details were arranged, and a captain appointed. Meanwhile they formed themselves into a special committee to trace out tricks and treachery, supplementing the guard and walking about from sentry to sentry. To their care much credit for the safety of the city was due.

" Howbeit, the Devil, the Author of all division and strife, who cannot abide any unity, concord and agreement in good causes, did here also hurl in a bone among these men whereof had ensued a great detriment to the common state and over-throw to themselves had it not in due time been prevented."

One of Lord Russell's servants, Bernard Duffield, was in charge of Bedford House. Hoker styles him a " man of very good service, practice and experience," but from other sources it appears that he was a froward and overbearing man, who took things with a high hand. One night he led a company forth through the Bedford postern, and had considerable success. They slew several of the enemy, took a few prisoners, spoiled others of their goods and captured some " slynges and basses." [1] But they did not all escape scot-free : some were taken, others hurt. Among them, John Drake, Receiver of the city in the previous year, was shot through both cheeks by an arrow, " which he brought into the City with him." John Symons, a cook, died of his wounds, while John

---

[1] Pieces of ordnance.

Goldsmith, a Flemish servant of Richard Helyard of the Goldsmith's Company, had a remarkable experience. Having encountered a rebel who nearly slew him with a bill, Goldsmith fell down and yielded himself prisoner. The soldier had mercy and spared his life, whereupon Goldsmith treacherously turned his handgun upon his conqueror, discharging it into the very belly of his unsuspecting victim. Having thus slain him, he despoiled him and returned to the city.

Well pleased with their success, they planned other adventures, but John Courtenay, a younger son of Sir William of Powderham, and step-son of Sir Anthony Kingston, who had already served with distinction under Lord Lisle, declared that such sallies ought not to be permitted from any fort or city in the present state of distress and extremity ; they should only be undertaken by very special order of the " general or chief Captain or some urgent necessity." But Duffield resented Courtenay's interference, " being very loath to lose any of his credit : or to desist from that he with others had determined."

A quarrel ensued, and, finding his remonstrances vain, Courtenay appealed to the Mayor, who assembled his brethren and called Duffield before them. The matter was fully debated, and at last it was—

" concluded that it was very hurtful and dangerous to that present state that any such issue out should be granted or permitted : and therefore they prayed the said Duffield to stay his determination and be contented : but he being impatient and thinking his credit to be stained if he should be debarred or denied to do that which he had faithfully promised did utterly refuse to yield to this the Mayor his request, as also by continuing of talks fell out in foul and disordered speeches."

Such proceedings could not be permitted, so the court, " to avoid further inconveniences," commanded him to prison. But the end was not yet. Duffield had a daughter, Frances, a young lady who inherited her parent's impetuous and imperious temper. Hearing that her father was in ward, and " taking in grief that so great an injury (as she termed it) should be done to her father, came more hastily than advisedly unto the Mayor," and demanded his release. It was late in the evening, and when this was denied her—

" she waxed so warm that not only she used very unseemly terms and speeches unto the Mayor but also, contrary to the Modesty and Shamefacedness required in a Woman, especially young and unmarried, ran most violently upon him, and strake him in the face : "

or, as it is elsewhere expressed, " but also disorderly used her hands and suddenly strake the Mayor in the face."

Some over-zealous bystander, fearing " it had been a set Match of some further Inconveniences," rushed wildly forth, shouting that the Mayor was killed. Forthwith the common bell was rung and every one ran to the Guildhall, fastening his armour as he went. In the confusion, Frances Duffield escaped to Bedford House, but the mob, although assured of the Mayor's safety, were on the point of following her to " fetch her out,

"when Blackaller forecasting that Inconveniencies might ensue, and respecting the Necessity of the present State, was not only contented patiently to wrap up those Injuries, but also earnestly requested the Commoners to do the like."

Pacified by his speeches, they escorted him to his house and quietly departed. But presently he was disturbed by a heavy knock at his door, and, on opening it, found there the representatives of the Cathedral, Archdeacon Pollard, Treasurer Sowthorn, Chancellor Leveson, and Canon Holwell, with their servants in warlike array. Having heard of the fray, although somewhat belated, they had hurriedly rushed to the Guildhall, only to find it deserted, so repaired to his house to assure themselves that he had suffered no injury, to offer their services and express their regrets. The Archdeacon even added, " that in proper Person he would herein stand in his Behalf against all Persons whatsoever, that would attempt or offer to do him wrong."

After polite and friendly speeches, he bowed them out with respectful thanks. Daily thereafter the Archdeacon called or sent to make inquiries.[1]

But although attacks were repulsed, internal dissensions suppressed and treachery prevented, there remained a yet more difficult task for the Mayor, one whereof—

" the greatest danger and peril was feared : and this was famine or penury, which of all other turmoils and perils is most dangerous : and no other plague to it to be compared : for no force is feared, no laws observed, no magistrate obeyed nor common society esteemed where famine ruleth." [2]

Already the price of provisions had been greatly enhanced throughout the kingdom, and as the scarcity in the city, ill-provided for a siege, made itself felt, the cost of food would have naturally increased.

" Albeit theare were good store of drye fishe, rice, prunes, raisons, and wine at very reasonable prices," yet bread was not to be had, so that

" in this extremity the Bakers and householders were driven to seek up their old store of puffyns and bran wherewith they in times past were wont to make horse bread and to feed their swine and poultry and this they moulded up in clothes for otherwise it would not hold together and so did bake it up and the people well contented therewith." [3]

---

[1] The above account combines the three versions of the course of events given by Hoker in the Guild Hall MS. (p. 77), Brice ed. (p. 64) and Bod. MS. (f. 8ᵈ.).

[2] See Hoker, p. 79.

[3] From Toulmin Smith's " English Gilds," p. 336, we learn that the bakers of Exeter were obliged to " make butt ij horse-lofys to a peny,

When cattle were captured in the raids made outside the walls, the larger portion was given to the poor, while the prisoners fettered in the King's gaol had a share as long as it lasted, but at length were fed on horseflesh, which they learned to like.

A brewer, named Reve, endeavoured to profit by his neighbours' distress, and tried to persuade other brewers to combine to raise the price of beer.[1] While, on the other hand, the people were encouraged, during the twelve days when the famine was sharpest,

"by an aged citizen who brought forth all his provisions, and said that as he did communicate unto them his store so would he participate in their wants : and that for his part, he would feed on the one arm, and fight with the other, before he would consent to put the city into the seditious hands," [2]

for the people naturally,

"were very soon and easy to be persuaded, or rather of themselves contented to yield unto the enemy to be fed for the time with the stolen fat of his flesh-pot than to abide for a short time a little penury in hope of a deliverance and then to be filled with saturity and plenty." [3]

One cause of anxiety to the Mayor was the care of the poorer citizens ; for them, however, he arranged that there should be a

"general collection set and rated throughout the whole City for their relief : and thereby they were liberally every week

and of clene beanys, vppon payne of xij. d." (Elsewhere the horse-loaf was made of "al maner of corn.") He also remarks, under the "Old Usages of Winchester," p. 366, that "The making of horse-bread was formerly a regular part of the baker's business." Harrison, in his "Description of England," writes that poor labourers were sometimes reduced to eating "horsecorne, I meane, beanes, peason, otes, tares, lintels" (p. 153). Halliwell gives "puff-loaf" as a kind of light bread, but "puffyns" must have some other meaning here.

[1] Cotton and Woollacombe, p. 85. See Exeter Chamber Act Bk. 2, f. 104ᵈ.

[2] Hayward, p. 62.

[3] See Hoker, p. 79.

considered : which thing being some increase to their stock
and store was the better to their content : all such victuals
as were to be had within the City they either had it freely or
for a very small price." [1]

Beside this, the plate of most of the parish churches
was sold, part of the proceeds being given to the poor
and the rest going towards paying the soldiers' wages.[2]

Moreover, the Mayor listened readily to the complaints of the poor and endeavoured to redress their
grievances. Frequently he exhorted them and " persuaded with good words patiently to abide and be contented not mistrusting but that God shortly would send
a deliverance."

But the anticipated assistance tarried until they were
reduced to dire straits and were in grave danger of being
forced to yield the city. Their condition being known to
the rebels a more strenuous effort was made, in collusion
with their adherents within the city, to capture it—a
final attempt, for they must have known of Russell's
success at Woodbury Common and his threatened
advance.

On the very last Sunday of the siege, which was
raised the following Tuesday, about eight o'clock in the
morning the rebels among the citizens in every quarter
of the city, " having their consorts in a readiness to join
and serve with them if need so required," " gadded up
and down the streets," under the leadership of John
Vincent, John Sharke, and others, the bellwethers of the
flock, "walking with their weapons and in their armour as
to fight with their enemies." Suddenly they shouted—
" Come out, you heretics, you Two-penny book men ! [3]
Where be ye ? By God's Wounds ! By God's Blood !
We will not be penned in to serve your turn. We will

---

[1] See Hoker, p. 60.
[2] Invent. Ch. Goods.
[3] Perhaps a reference to the Service-Books, cheap compared with the
ancient missals.

go out and have in our neighbours. They be honest and godly men."

Our chronicler explains—

"their pretence and meaning being then that if any of the contrary side had come out they would have quarrelled with them and so have taken occasion to set upon him and so raised a new tumult. But by the providence and goodness of God it so fell out that some being in their houses and some at their parish churches the Mayor and magistrates were first advertised hereof before the others heard anything of the matter: and they according to their wisdoms pacified the matter,"

making the rioters return to their houses. The chief disturbance occurred in Southgate street and at the Southgate, where "there was a little stir, which being soon stopped, there ensued no hurt thereof other than a broken pate or two," for the warders of the gate were faithful citizens, and had the larger company on their side. So in the end it came to no effect, "because the Lord kept the City." [1]

[1] See Hoker, p. 75.

CHAPTER XIII

THE SIEGE OF EXETER. WITHOUT THE CITY

" And if the besetting of one house to rob it, be justly deemed worthy
death, what shall we think of them that besiege whole cities for desire
of spoil ? But herein hath notably appeared, what cities hath faithfully served and suffered extreme danger."—CHEKE.

WHILE affairs were going thus inside the city what were
the besiegers doing ? We have no verbose chronicler of
their deeds, so must glean what we can from the worthy
chamberlain's tale and supplement it with items gathered
elsewhere.

The captured gentry who refused to join the insurgents were imprisoned in the tower of St. Sidwell's
Church, just outside the Eastgate. Here Walter Ralegh
was confined, his unnecessary reproof of the old woman
of Clyst St. Mary or some other cause led the rebels to
treat him uncivilly, and, it is even asserted, his life was
threatened : perhaps by way of reprisal, as he was one
of the persons of greatest importance among their
prisoners, and the citizens made violent threats regarding
the rebels whom they captured. Another man incarcerated in the same place was Thomas Colyford, of
Collumpton, who, in a deposition a few years later, refers
to other " soferers " released with Mr. Ralegh and
himself.[1]

The rebels, after demanding that the Mayor should
yield the city, encamped around the walls and placed

---

[1] Exeter Mun. Records.

officers in command of the different sections and introduced as much discipline as possible in their army.

They thoroughly invested the city, cutting off all access—

" They plash down trees, brake down bridges, keep watches and wards in every place so that no man could pass to or [from] the city without their sufferance : the markets are stopped, victuals are kept from it and all dealings and intercourse shut and cut off : and having as they bragged, penned and shut up the townsmen in a coop or mew, they plant their ordnance against every gate and in all other such places as best to serve their turn and to hurt them within, they burned the gates, they brake up the pipes and conduits as well for the taking away [of the water] coming to the city, as also to have the lead to serve for their shot and pellets." [1]

But, as we have seen, the besieged counted the burning of the gates a benefit, and they suffered not from the loss of their conduits, as they had springs of sweet water within the city.

The rebels proceeded to undermine the walls, the Cornish contingent, with their skill in such work, rendering particularly useful service, but failed because of Newcombe's countermine.

" They left nothing undone which might be to annoy the citizens, for some times they made alarums as though they with all might and main would have given the scale : and indeed they had provided ladders for the same purpose : sometimes they by policies would seek to come to the gates to burn them : and herein they used this stratagem : They provided a cart laden with old hay and driving the wheels before them would come to the gate without danger and so set fire in the gate : notwithstanding they scaped not scot free for both at the Westgate and at the Southgate their coming being perceived

---

[1] Hoker, p. 69.

the great port pieces [1] were charged with bags of flint stones and hail shot and as they were approaching unto the gate the gate should be secretly opened and the said port pieces discharged and so they were spoiled divers of them." [2]

To prevent such attacks the citizens thenceforth kept the gates open with huge fires burning within and with rampires thrown up for defence.

The rebels likewise

" would keep themselves close in sundry houses in the suburbs near the walls and would so watch the garrets that if any within the city would look out at the garrets " [3] " they with their shot did shrewdly gall and annoy as also killed divers of the city watching and warding within upon the walls, which was the cause that some part of the said suburbs was burned and some part beaten down and spoiled," [4] " and so drave the rebels out of those holes : besides this they had in sundry places their great ordnances so set and placed that in certain streets and places none could go but in peril and danger of their shot, which their devices were choked by making of certain mounts to shadow the streets from the same." [5]

Their batteries were set up on the high ground around the city, probably on the Pinhoe and Pennsylvania sides as well as, we are told, on St. David's Down to the west,

[1] Jenkins, writing of the siege of Exeter in 1497, has the following note : " One of those Port Pieces was remaining [in the author's memory] and laid on the left side of the passage under the East-gate : it was composed of flat iron bars, strongly hooped together with iron (similar to a cask), and was near twelve feet in length, and twelve inches diameter at the mouth (as far as memory can answer :) it did not seem to have ever been fixed on a carriage as it had no trunnions, but strong iron rings on the sides, for the purpose of moving it from place to place : and probably when it was discharged it was placed on a mount, or logs of wood laid, for the purpose of elevating it. . . . There is a cannon of the same sort in the armoury of the Tower of London." (Hist. Exeter, 1841, p. 91.) It is quite likely that this very port-piece was also used in the later siege.

[2] Hoker, p. 70.
[3] Hoker, p. 71.
[4] Hoker, Bod. ed. fol. 6ᵈ.
[5] Hoker, p. 71.

not far from St. David's Church, then outside the city limits.[1]

The heavy piece of ordnance on this side was under the control of a very skilful gunner, who could handle his piece well, " a stranger and alien," who did much damage to the city, and by one well-aimed shot, slew a man named Smith as he stood at a door in North-gate Street. So pleased was he with his successes that he boasted that he could set fire to the whole city by means of fire-balls, so that it would be burnt to the ground in four hours, " do they what they would," which would have been quite possible in view of the fact that it consisted largely of timbered houses at that time. His comrades were so delighted with this idea that they fixed a day and hour for the execution of his design. But at the last moment the proposal came to the ears of the worthy Vicar of St. Thomas à Becket, just outside the city at the foot of Exe Bridge. With all speed he collected as many soldiers as he could and hastened across to St. David's Down, where the crowd had assembled to see the gunner carry out his promise. The Vicar demanded that no such attempt should be made, remonstrating earnestly, saying that " he would in no wise suffer so lewd an act and wicked a thing to be done."

" Do what you can," he cried, " by policy, by force, or by dint of sword, and I will join you and do my uttermost, but to burn the city, which would be hurtful to all and profitable to none, I will not consent thereto, but will withstand you with all my power."

This short, thick-set man, hot with indignation, as he harangued the crowd, made a favourable impression upon the people, with whom he was popular. A fine

---

[1] In the inventories of Church Goods of 1552 that of St. David's is the only one recording that the church was robbed. Although no robber is specified, it is quite possible the rebels were guilty. They did not despoil St. Sidwell's, but left their opponents to do that.

athlete, famous as a wrestler—for he was Cornish by birth—a good shot, clever with the long-bow and cross-bow, able to handle well a hand-gun or " piece,"

" a good woodman and a hardy and such a one as would not give his head for the polling nor his beard for the washing . . . a companion in any exercise of activity and of a courteous and gentle behaviour."

Such as he would receive a respectful hearing, and " so stout he was in this matter that he stopped them of their further enterprising of so wicked a fact." [1]

While Hoker admired this vicar, Welsh, for certain of his good qualities, he denounced him vehemently for his action on another occasion.

One of the difficulties encountered by both the besieged and besiegers was the prevention of spying and treachery. The rebels had adopted the device of attaching letters to arrows, which they shot into the city towards the haunts of their friends, and also communicated with such of these as sallied forth secretly or openly, and even tried to gain entrance by bribing soldiers or by persuading men like Wolcot to help them to enter the gates.

But the spies were not confined to their side, and they found it needful to take precautions to prevent messages from being sent to the outer world. They did not always succeed, as Russell was able to communicate with the Mayor.

But on one occasion, at least, they caught a man red-handed. This was a tinner of Chagford, named Kingwell, servant to Mr. John Charles of Tavistock, a justice of the peace. He was captured conveying letters between his master and " my lord "—probably Russell.

He was taken in the early days of the siege, and every

[1] The above is taken from Hoker's account of him (p. 93). For further information concerning him, see Chapter XIX.

effort was made to persuade him to join the rebels, but he was

"earnest in the reformed religion which was then termed the King's proceedings and an enemy of the popish state : And being a sharp inveigher against the one and an earnest defender of the other it procured unto him great hatred and malice : when the rebellion was begun he sought by all the means he could to escape away but he was so narrowly watched that he could never have any opportunity so to do : They used all the devices they could to recover him to their opinions, sometimes fair words sometimes with threatenings and sometimes with imprisonments : but still he inveighed against them calling them rebels and traitors both against God and the King and 'foreprofeceide' unto them that destruction and confusion would be the end and reward of their doings."

Such a fire-brand and encourager of mutiny could not be allowed to continue in these evil courses, and, all other means failing to reclaim him to "their disposition," he was by Welsh's order taken out of prison and "forthwith brought forth before 'Cayphas and Pylate' and condemned to be hanged."

It would seem that in some way he was within the jurisdiction of this vicar, but just who were "Cayphas and Pylate" Hoker fails to tell us. Still, it would appear that there was a formal trial of some sort, and clear evidence of his conveying of letters was laid before his judges. It was also proved that he obstinately continued to use seditious language likely to cause mutiny in the army ; so there was nothing for it but to condemn him to be executed. So he was brought to "an elm tree in Exe Island without the West-gate of the city before the house of one Nicholas Cove, and there hanged " as a terror to other spies and messengers.[1]

Afterwards the part he took in bringing to judgment this red-handed and contumelious spy was brought up

[1] See Hoker, p. 92.

against the vicar as one of his greatest crimes. Hoker even puts it forward as a palliation of his own terrible fate as well as for the execution of rebels without form of law, although in the above case all such forms had been observed.[1]

Arundell, indeed, had no easy task, with his ill-trained troops, to sit down patiently before a walled city. They had " no great artillery to open a breach, and yet without reason they gave an assault, and used divers means to mount the walls." [2]   A few guns they had, among them the one trained upon Carew at Clyst St. Mary bridge, and it is said [3] some were taken from Plymouth and other forts of the King, probably including those of St. Michael's Mount, St. Mawes, Pendennis, and Trematon Castles ; but these could have been but of small calibre, as the difficulties of transport would have prevented them from bringing larger guns.   " But the more madness they showed in their attempts with the greater loss were they driven back." [4]

The difficulties of capturing so strong a position are mentioned by Heylin : to the resolution of the citizens was added, he says—

" the natural defences of the city (being round in form, situated on a rising hill, and environed with a good old wall), gave not more encouragement than some insolent speeches of the rebels." [5]

---

[1] Nicholas Cove of the parish of St. Edmund on the Bridge, in which Exe Island is situated, made a deposition on 4th Aug., 1552, that when he and Thomas Westcote heard " on the opening on the gates of the city " in 1549 that some plate belonging to St. Edmund's church was being shifted by the rebels from one house to another they took the same and divided it between them.   A part of this a deponent believed belonged to St. Thomas's. (See Exeter Mun. Doc.)   One John Cove, a tanner, who had been at Doncaster with the Marquis of Exeter, the evening after his return in 1537, had an extraordinary escape from drowning which Hoker records in his Common-place Book.
[2] Hayward, p. 60.
[3] Spanish Chronicle, p. 180.
[4] Hayward, p. 60.
[5] Eccles. Restaurata, p. 76.

Blomefield, in defending Norwich from the aspersions cast on it by Sir John Cheke, who extolled Exeter's prowess, says—

" Exeter is a city (if I may credit the accounts we have of it) placed on a hill having a castle, the site of which is eminent, and above both the city and the country adjoining, for they do all lie, as under the lee thereof, the city is strongly ditched and walled round, and is not easily to be gotten by force, and was well provided with cannon, and other weapons of defence." [1]

Finding assault beyond his powers, Arundell was forced to content himself with closely investing it, using all pretexts and devices to seduce the citizens and hoping by dissensions or starvation to obtain the city. It was a dangerous task to attempt, as the inaction of a siege would be more than likely to cause deterioration in his heterogeneous army. His success in keeping the besiegers in more or less good order speaks volumes for his ability as a general and for their devotion to the cause.

Even admitting that Russell was supine, and by his inaction encouraged them—for they thought it was the fear which they inspired that made him hold aloof— still there was always the danger of attack from that side by trained, hardened soldiers, under skilful captains, with the likelihood of the royal army being augmented at any moment. There can be little doubt that the people in the surrounding country sympathised with the insurgents, and were particularly incensed by the use of foreign soldiery to suppress their countrymen— otherwise we cannot account for the fact that 2,000 rebels, as mentioned by Hoker, or even the 10,000 men, as estimated by others—and these usually described as a rabble rout—were permitted to besiege Exeter without fear of the inhabitants of the locality.

[1] Norfolk, Vol. III. p. 229.

The picture of this motley army drawn by the historians, increases our amazement at even this temporary success. Not only were they the scum of the earth, if we are to believe several chroniclers, people " such as poverty or fear of punishment might plunge into any mischief," [1] men who had

" grown to an obstinacy, seeming so far from admitting persuasions to submission, that they became resolute in their pestilent actions, wilfully following the worst, which they knew full well would redound to their detriment, but they were prone to dissensions among themselves, [2] rather without a Lord than at liberty to accomplish their misery they fall to division, of all calamities the worst, and so broken in their desires, that they could not learn either wherefore they came, or what they would have done . . . every man regarding what he followed, but not what might follow thereof . . . and they esteemed bold obstinacy for bravest courage, and impudent prating for soundest wisdom." [3]

Yet with such material Arundell was able to besiege Exeter for six weeks, and to give pause to Lord Russell with his trained and hardened veterans at Honiton.

[1] Hayward, p. 56.   [2] Hoker, p. 67.
                [3] Hayward, p. 56.

CHAPTER XIV

THE ARTICLES OF THE REBELS

> " But now let us weigh well the cause of those that rebel for religion sake,
> which is thought by some a most urgent and weighty cause. Here
> men will say, that if they be constrained by superior powers to forsake
> any part of their faith, by which they are well assured to be saved,
> that then they must rather obey God, than man : and put their lives
> in jeopardy, rather than will leave their religion. This is very well
> said, and every Christian man must so do."—CHRISTOPHERSON.

As they contain the reason for all this tumult, the
" Articles " of the insurgents require careful consideration.

Following the custom adopted in previous risings, the
rebels of the West embodied their grievances in certain
Articles, which were presented to the King. As a
matter of fact, at different dates Articles varying in
number and contents were forwarded ; sometimes
" Articles or Requests," sometimes a " Letter," again a
" Supplication," but all amounting to much the same in
substance. None of them is dated, and it is only by
internal evidence and references to them in other documents that we can approximate their time of issue.
Only two of these have the signatures of the rebels ; the
others must be reconstructed from their replies. The
earliest of all seems to tally with the set of Articles given
by Foxe in his edition of 1570, so these are copied below.
The first English edition of his " Acts," of 1563, gives
the Fifteen Articles word for word. Why he substituted
in his later and fuller account of the rising the Eight

Articles, which there is reason to believe were issued first, is a matter for conjecture ; perhaps they could be more easily ridiculed.

For convenience the different versions may be thus described and numbered—

I. Set of Eight Articles, as given in Foxe's edition of 1570.
II. Set of Nine Articles, as deduced from Somerset's Answer.
III. Set of Fifteen Articles, as signed by the rebels, in the Lambeth Palace tract.
IV. Set of Sixteen Articles, as signed by the rebels in the Corpus Christi tract.

From the Council's letter of the 29th June,[1] it may be inferred that the King had already received a statement of the Commons' grievances, and from his reply, known as the " King's Message," it is evident that this document closely resembled No. I.—most likely it was identical—supplemented by certain " bruits and rumours " as to taxes to be imposed not only upon sheep, but upon pigs and geese, and that the people objected to any alteration of the laws relating to religion *until the King came to his full age.* Foxe's version of 1570 is as follows :—

Articles No. I.

The Articles of the Commons of Deuonshire and Cornwall sent to the kyng. . . .

First for asmuch as man, except he be borne of water and the holy Ghost, can not enter into the kingdome of God, and for asmuch as the gates of heauen be not opened without this blessed Sacrament of Baptisme, therfor we wil y^t our Curates shall minister this Sacrament at all times of nede, aswell in the weeke dayes as on the holy dayes.

Item, we will haue our children confirmed of the Byshop when soeuer we shal w^tin the Dioces resort vnto him.

[1] Pet. MSS. f. 432, Pk. p. 16.

Item, for asmuch as we constantly beleue that after the Prieste hath spoken the wordes of consecration being at Masse, there celebratyng and consecrating the same, there is very really the body and bloud of our Sauiour Jesu Christ God and man, and that no substance of bread and wine remaineth after, but the very selfe same body that was borne of the virgin Marie, and was giuen vppon the Crosse for our redemption : therefore we wil haue Masse celebrated as it hath bene in tymes past, without any man communicatyng with the Priestes, for asmuch as many rudely presuming vnworthely to receiue the same, put no difference betwene the Lordes body and other kinde of meate, some saying that it is profitable to no man except he receiue it, with many other abused termes.

Item, we wil haue in our Churches reseruation.

Item, wee will haue holy bread and holy water in the remembrances of Christes precious body and bloude.

Item, we will that our Priestes shall sing or say with an audible voyce, Gods seruice in the Quier of the Parishe Churches & not Gods seruice to bee set forth like a Christmasse play.

Item, for asmuch as Priestes be men dedicated to God for ministring and celebratyng the blessed Sacramentes and preachyng of Gods word, we will that they shal liue chaste without Mariage, as S. Paule dyd being the elect and chosen vessell of God, saying vnto all honest Priestes, be you folowers of me.

Item, we will that the vj Articles, whiche our soueraigne Lorde Kynge Henry the eight set forth in his latter daies, shall be vsed and so taken as they were at that tyme.

Item, we pray God saue king Edward, for we be hys, both body and soul.[1]

It must have been with Articles such as these before them that the Council wrote to Lord Russell, after denying the rumours about the taxes—

" and for the articles of Baptism, of not baptising their children from Sunday to Sunday, the same is likewise false, as may

---

[1] "Acts and Monuments," ed. 1570, p. 1268.

appear by the King's Majesty's book, even in the last sentence
of the first side of the leaf entreating of baptism, and so likewise, may they credit all them that spread such rumours by
the trial of that one, if they will peruse the book."

Turning to the leaf to which they refer we find their
complaint thus answered—

" the people are to be admonished, that it is most convenient
that Baptism should not be administered but upon Sundays
and other holydays, when the most people may come together.
. . . Nevertheless (if necessity so require) children ought at
all times to be baptised either at the church or else at home." [1]

Nine days after this letter was written, that is, on
the 8th July, the King set his hand to the document
entitled " A Message sent by the King's Maiestie, to
certain of his people, assembled in Devonshire." This
was issued by Grafton, the King's printer.[2]

While referring to their demands concerning Baptism,
Transubstantiation, Confirmation, the Mass and the
Service in English, his replies are not in that order.
The marginal references run : i. Baptisme : ii. Sacrament : iii. Service in English : iiii. Masse : v. Confirmation : The Sixe Articles : The King's Age. The
Message, though somewhat contemptuous in tone, is
couched in quiet language until the final threat. In
substance, it amounts to this : He had heard that they
were assembled in a seditious manner, yet, as they were
misled by evil disposed persons working upon their
ignorance, he would make reply. He reproves them for
their unlawful assemblies and for having summoned
them in his name. The causes put forward are all false,
and the people who suggest them are rank traitors,
heretics, papists, etc. I. For Baptism, they are referred

---

[1] See Prayer Book, ed. 1549, under Baptism.
[2] This is addressed to the rebels in Devon only, and refers to that
county as being in rebellion, making no mention of Cornwall.

to the first side of the first leaf of " our book," set forth with the consent of Parliament. II. For the Sacrament, he makes so much difference between consecrated bread and other bread that he considers the latter of no profit but to maintain the body, but the other is food for the soul. As for Baptism, Confirmation, Mass and the English service, this has long been debated in Parliament and agreed upon by learned men. III. For Matins, the service in English is the exact translation of the Latin. IIII. For the Mass, the learned clergy have brought this to the very use as Christ left it, as the apostles used it, and holy fathers delivered it, indeed somewhat altered from that the Popes of Rome for their lucre brought it. V. For Confirmation, " Think you that a child christened is damned because it dieth before Bishopping ? " They should be confirmed when they have reached years of discretion, and have learned what they have professed in Baptism. For the VI. Articles, " know ye what ease you have with the loss of them ? " They were bloody, but were then needed, but are now removed out of pity. " For the King's age, In the end of this your request (as we be given to understand) ye would have them [the laws concerning religion] stand in force until our full age." Be we of less authority, be we not your king now ? Are we not your rightful, anointed, crowned, sovereign king, your liege lord ? It has been marvelled that we so young in years have reigned so nobly, so royally, so quietly. Why should Devonshire give the first occasion to slander our realm ? We have condescended of love to write rather than to war against you as rebels, but unless you repent we will extend our Princely power and draw the sword against you as infidels and Turks.

A long and detailed reply to this message exists in a tract in French, which the preface states is a translation of the response of the people of Devon. Although its genuineness has recently been called in question its substance is worth considering as representing the opinions of the insurgents.[1]   Under three headings they group their replies.

(a) As to the first article, where we are accused of rebellion because we are united and assembled, and have abused your Majesty's name, and so forth.—To this, while protesting their faithfulness to the King, they declare that in altering matters of religion the King's governors have assumed a position reserved to God or his vicars, and are forcing his Majesty into errors of faith during his minority.   They have assembled for no seditious purpose, but because of the care which each one has for his own soul.   While admitting that reformation within the Church may be needed, they insist that this should be done only on the advice of the bishops.

(b) As to the second article, concerning five points of faith, that is to say, of Baptism, of the Mass, of the Sacrament, of the Service in English and of Confirmation.—They claim that these ceremonies have been accepted by the universal consent of Christianity, and should not be changed except by the evident inspiration of the Holy Spirit.   As for Baptism, there are difficulties in bringing children to be baptised at stated times—such as the predilection of parents for certain days, and, in cases of illness of the infant, the trouble of obtaining witnesses and notaries to prove the necessity.   As to the Sacrament, they claim that Transubstantiation has been accepted for fifteen hundred years, and in so high a matter no change should be lightly made.   The same reasoning applies to the alterations connected with Confirmation, the Mass and the service in English, even when the ordinances made by the King's governors in his name may be accompanied by some appearance of reason.

(c) As to the third and fourth articles : we are accused of ignorance and rebellion—of ignorance

---

[1] For the history of this tract, see Appendix H.

because we demand that the statute of Six Articles
should be revived, which your Majesty says has been
cancelled and annulled as too violent, bloody, and
greatly prejudicial to the liberty and repose of your
subjects ; of rebellion in that we demand that the ancient
laws remain in force and others that have been made
should be suspended until by the grace of God you reach
the age of discretion and knowledge.—If, as is said, the
Six Articles are so cruel against us, our sincerity in
desiring their restoration is evident. Their repeal should
be by Act of Parliament, not by the King's governors,
who make changes in the laws without due consideration,
such action inviting sedition—at least the late King's
laws should continue in force until you are of age.
Regencies of uncles and tutors have heretofore been
injurious to this realm—instances are quoted—and it is
to prevent similar mal-administration that we are
jeopardising our bodies, goods, and souls. Already
England's reputation has suffered by the abuse of power
by those in authority, which is demonstrated by reference
to the breach of Henry VIII.'s agreement with Scotland,
and other affairs. The King is urged to spend the money
employed in going counter to the wishes of his people
in re-establishing the kingdom in prosperity and reputation.

They conclude with a peroration, reminding the King,
among other things, of the cruelty towards certain
subjects used by the ministers of the late king, against
faithful promises, made upon oath, and they declare that
they would rather sacrifice their lives for their sacred
cause than relinquish their faith at the bidding of the
King's governors.

Not long after the receipt of the King's Message
another set of articles, with but slight modifications,
perhaps to please the Cornishmen, who had by this time
joined the rebels in Devon, were sent to the King. They
called forth a diatribe, of which several rough drafts, in

Somerset's handwriting, exist in the Record Office.[1] This begins by stating that the King has already caused to be sent an answer to a greater part of their Supplications, which had been presented on their behalf by a gentleman to the Lord Privy Seal.

From this document we gather that the Articles related to nine different subjects upon which Somerset comments.

Articles No. II.

I. Baptism : " Ye are put in fear that your children should not be christened but upon the holy day."

II. Confirmation : " The order of confirmation ye seem not to mislike but you think your children shall not learn it except they go to school."

III. The Sixe Articles and the Statute that made words treason.

IIII. The blindness and unwillingness of curates to set forth the King's Proceedings.

V. Communion in common, which, they seem to hint, leads to impropriety, and the curates' refusal to baptise and bury, which is contrary to the King's orders.

VI. Objection to the English service, because all Cornishmen do not understand it.

VII. Objection to the New Book, because it was passed without the King's knowledge.

VIII. The remission of the " relief of cloth and store sheep."

IX. Famine : " Ye complain of Dearth of victuals and other things."

There is reason to believe that this " Answer " was completed about the 24th July. For, as it says, the King's Answer had then already been printed, and also it contains a reference to the intention of the French—

" at this present time to land in Cornwall or Devonshire and there as our ' espiall ' showeth to take a gentleman's house which is almost an Isle and more than half environed in the Sea." [2]

[1] S. P. Dom. Edw. VI. Vol. VII. No. 6.

[2] Leland, writing of Pendennis, says: "The King hath builded a

In a letter of the 24th July to Lord Russell the Council enclose one from " Mr. Hobbie," declaring the intention of the Frenchmen to take " some place in Cornwall," so it was probably about the same date that the above answer was written.

On the 25th July the Council signed a brief reply " to the supplicacon of the Commons of Cornwalle," [1] which they seem to have substituted at the last moment for Somerset's wordy tirade.

From the fact that this " Reply," which was enclosed in a letter to the Lord Privy Seal, dated the 27th July, begins with a reference to " Humphrey Arundell's poyson," the very first time his name is mentioned in this correspondence, we are tempted to hazard the conjecture that between the writing of Somerset's Answer and the date of this Reply they had received the demands of the rebels which were set forth in the Fifteen Articles, signed by the four chief Captains and the four Governors of the Camps, for by this date the insurgents were besieging Exeter, and this document was sent up by the Commoners who were in divers camps " by East and West of Excettor." [2]

The tone adopted in these " requests " is that of men in a position to dictate to the Council, and they end with a demand that two of their number, both Cornishmen, should have a safe-conduct under the King's Great Seal to pass and repass " with a Heroalde at Armes."

If our conjecture is correct it follows that Somerset's " Answer " would have been out of date, as it did not

Castell callid Pendinant and longgith to Mr. Keligrewe. It is a Mile in Cumpace by the Cumpace, and is *almost environid with the se*, and where it is not the Ground is so low and the Cut to be made so litle that it were insulated " (Iter. f. 10).

[1] Pet. MSS. f. 443, Pk. p. 37.

[2] The body of this agrees with the Articles as set out in Foxe's edition of 1563, but his has this heading : " The Articles or requestes drawen and sent vp in the names of the Deuonshire and Cornishmen, encamped in armour : to be subscribed and graunted vnto, with thaunsweres afterward followyng vnto the same."

deal with several points raised ; moreover, the insolent tone of these demands would account for the Council's decision to substitute a brief, stern order that any one who should "receive, take, or hear any such letter or writing" as that of Humphrey Arundell, should be treated as a rebel, and punished accordingly.

These Requests as given in the "Copye of a Letter," in the Lambeth Palace Library,[1] read as follows :—

Articles No. III.

The Articles of vs the Commoners of Deuonshyre and Cornwall in diucrs Campes by East and West of Excettor.

Fyrst we wyll haue the general counsall & holy decrees of our forefathers observed, kept and performed, and who so euer shal agayne saye them, we hold them as Heretikes.

Itē we will haue the Lawes of our Souerayne Lord Kyng Henry the viij concernynge the syxe articles, to be in use again, as in hys tyme they were.

Item we will haue the masse in Latten, as was before, & celebrated by the Pryest wythoute any man or woman cōmunycatyng wyth hym.

Item we wyll haue the Sacrament hange ouer the hyeghe aulter, and there to be worshypped as it was wount to be, and they whiche will not therto consent, we wyl haue them dye lyke heretykes against the holy Catholyque fayth.

Item we wyll haue the Sacramēt of ye aulter but at Easter delyuered to the lay people, and then but in one kynde.

Item we wil that our Curattes shal minister the Sacramēt of Baptisme at all tymes aswel in the weke daye as on the holy daye.

Item we wyl haue holy bread and holy water made euery sondaye, Palmes and asshes at the tymes accustomed, Images to be set vp again in euery church, and all other auncient olde Ceremonyes vsed heretofore, by our mother the holy Church.

[1] See Appendix K.

Item we wil not receyue the newe seruyce because it is but lyke a Christmas game, but we wyll haue oure olde seruice of Mattens, masse, Euensong and procession in Latten, as it was before. And so we the Cornyshe men (wherof certen of vs vnderståde no Englysh) vtterly refuse thys newe Englysh.

Item we wyll haue euerye preacher in his sermon, & euery Pryest at hys masse, praye specially by name for the soules in purgatory, as oure forefathers dyd.

Item we wyll haue the Byble and al bokes of scripture in Englysh to be called in agayn, for we be enformed that otherwise the Clergye, shal not of lōg time confound the heretykes.

Item we wyll haue Doctor Moreman and Doctor Crispin which holde our opinions to be sauely sent vnto vs and to them we requyre the Kinges maiesty, to geue some certain liuinges, to preach amonges vs our Catholycke fayth.

Item we thinke it very mete because the lord Cardinal Pole is of the kynges bloode, should not only haue hys pardon, but also sent for to Rome & promoted to be of the kinges coūsayl.

Item we wyll that no Gentylman shall haue anye mo seruantes then one to wayte vpō hym excepte he maye dispende one hundreth marke land and for euery hundreth marke we thynke it reasonable, he should haue a man.

Item we wyll that the halfe parte of the abbey landes and Chauntrye landes, in euerye mans possessyons, how so euer he cam by them, be geuen again to two places, where two of the chief Abbeis was with in euery Countye, where suche half part shalbe taken out, and there to be establyshed a place for devout persons, whych shall pray for the Kyng and the common wealth, and to the same we wyll haue al the almes of the Churche boxe geuen for these seuen yeres.

Itē for the particular grieffes of our Countrye, we wyll haue them so ordered, as Humfreye Arundell, & Henry Braye the Kynges Maior of Bodmā, shall enforme the Kynges Maiestye, yf they maye haue salue-cōduct vnder the Kynges great Seale, to passe and repasse, with an Heroalde of Armes.

By vs

HUMFREY ARUNDELL
BERRY
THOMAS UNDERHYLL
JOHN SLOEMAN
WILLIAM SEGAR

Chiefe Captaynes

JOHN TOMPSON Pryeste
HENRY BRAY Maior of Bodmā
HENRY LEE Maior of Torriton
ROGER BARRET Prieste

The foure Gouernours of the Campes.

It was to the Articles in this form that Cranmer wrote an answer, couched in extreme language.[1]   From internal evidence it is clear that he composed this after the condemnation of the leaders in November, and before their execution in January.

There is reason to believe that long before this Answer was published, indeed, soon after the above fifteen articles were issued, a revised version, with slight additions, appeared over the same signatures. The " Copye of a Letter " in the library of Corpus Christi College, Oxford, has appended to it a set of sixteen articles, which has the following modifications and additions, excluding variations in spelling :—

Articles No. IV.

These are the same as No. III. except

Item viii. has " we wyll haue oure olde seruice of Mattens, Masse, Euensong and procession in Latten *not in English* as it was before."

---

[1] Cranmer's answer is variously estimated ; his admirers praise in extravagant terms both his language and his arguments, while those less prejudiced in his favour consider his exclamations and vituperations poor substitutes for sound argument.

Item x. reads : " we wyll haue the *whole* Byble. . . ."

Item xii. reads : " we thinke it very mete because the lord Cardinal Pole is of the kynges bloode, should not only haue hys *free* pardon, but also sent for to Rome & promoted to be *first or secōd* of the Kinges counsayle."

Item xiii. ends : " we thinke it reasonable, he should haue a man, and *no mo.*"

Item xiiii. ends : " almes of the Churche boxe geuen for these seuen yeres, *and for thys article we desire that we may name half of the Commissioners.*"

Item xvi., which is entirely new, not being in the preceding, reads : " *for the performance of these articles, we will haue iiii. Lordes. viii. Knightes. xii. Esquyers. xx. Yomē, pledges with vs vntill the Kynges Maiestie haue graunted al these by Parliament.*[1]

To this set of Articles Nicholas Udall wrote a lengthy reply addressed to his countrymen of Devon and Cornwall. He quotes each article at length and discusses them separately. The date of this document is also uncertain, but as he begs them to leave their " camping, and with most humble submission to cry to God and to your king for mercy and pardon," and exhorts them to beware the vengeance of God, and—

" remember and reconcile yourselves before it light upon you, when neither your traitorous captaines nor Popish ceremonies shall be able to save or help you,'"

it seems probable that it was written before the relief of Exeter.

It should be noted that the first set of Articles contains no reference whatever to agrarian discontent, enclosures, or upstart gentlemen, and even in the second set, those answered by Somerset, there is but one point

---

[1] It was this set of Articles that the Welsh Chronicler had before him when he made his translation, for he mentions the hostages given in the XVIth Article though he gives the number different in one instance. See Appendix I.

not pertaining to religion, *i.e.* the "relief of cloth and store sheep." The signed fifteen Articles (No. III.) while not mentioning that subject, suggests restrictions on the retinue of gentlemen and the redistribution of Abbey lands, partly for religious purposes, and these points are but slightly extended in No. IV.

In all other respects they confined their demands to matters relating to religion. In this they differed from the leaders of the Pilgrimage of Grace, for the Articles of the latter dealt with the dissolution of the monasteries and consequent poverty, the "statute of uses," tenths, first-fruits and subsidies, and the removal of the King's evil Councillors and certain bishops.[1]

We find an even more curious set of demands signed by the prime-movers of the insurrection in Norfolk, which began before the Western Rebellion was concluded. Here were twenty-nine Articles, dealing with fees, leases, grants, taxes, enclosures, free commons, copyholds, wardships, bondmen, and the removal of offending officers. Only seven of these articles relate to priests, who were objectionable from a secular point of view—*e.g.* priests were not to be allowed to buy land, nor to let such as they have except to temporal men—three only touch them on religious grounds—

> "parsons and vicars that be not able to preche and sett forthe the worde of god to hys parissheners may be clerely putt from hys benefice, and the parissheners there to choose an other, or elles the pateron or lord of the towne."

[1] Froude combines many demands gleaned from various sources, including such things as the demise of the Crown, the legitimation of the Princess Mary, the rental of lands, the statute of handguns, the election of knights of the Shire and matters of common law and fees. He comments, "A careful perusal of these articles will show that they are the work of many hands, and of many spirits. Representatives of each of the heterogeneous elements of the insurrection contributed their grievances; wise or foolish, just and unjust, demands were strung together in the haste of the moment" (Vol. III. p. 158 *n.*).

" No prest shall be a chaplain residential, steward nor no
other officer to eny man of honor or worshippe, but only
to be resydent vppon ther benefices, wherby ther paris-
sheners may be enstructed with the lawes of god."
" Euery propriatorie parson or vicar havyng a benefice of
x^{li} or more by yere shall eyther by them selues or by
some other person teche pore men's chyldren of ther
parisshe the book called the cathakysme and the prymer."[1]

Even in the first two of these there is a worldly touch,
quite at variance with the strictly religious tone adopted
in the West Country, while in the last is a demand
diametrically opposed to those of the Western rebels,
who had no affection for the " cathakysme and prymer."
The long accepted confusion of the aims of the two
rebellions would be utterly inexcusable except on the
ground that the risings synchronised, and that the ringleaders were tried together. Any careful student of the
subject will perceive that the two insurrections were
caused by entirely different grievances, but it was the
policy of the Government of the day to confuse the two
in order that they might be the more readily condemned
by the different parties of their opponents.

It has been suggested that the priests prepared the
Articles of the Devonian and Cornish rebels, a fact the
more readily believed when we reflect that they deal
so exclusively with religious questions, and that their
conciseness and their clear statement of demands
indicate a scholarly source which is not traceable in the
diffuse, verbose, and heterogeneous articles of Kett's
followers.

Several of the subjects dealt with by the Western
rebels call for comment or elucidation, particularly such
points as are not treated fully or correctly in the various
replies given in the Appendix.

It has been so frequently reiterated that the Princess

---

[1] See Russell's " Kett's Rebellion."

Q

Mary and the Bishop of Winchester *invented* for their own purposes the theory that the laws relating to religion should remain unaltered during the King's minority, that a clear refutation of the charge should be made. Collier even twists this theory so as to make it apply to laws of all sorts—

" they were made to believe, that, during the king's minority the state had no authority to make laws but that the constitution was to continue on the old footing." [1]

In the 28th year of Henry VIII. an Act was passed—

" by which all laws made while his son was under twenty-four years of age, might be by his letters patent, after he had attained that age, annulled as if they had never been." [2]

This Act had been repealed by Somerset as soon as he attained power. His opponents, who resented his usurpation of kingly authority, and objected to a Council ruled by him, declared that, while certain prerogatives might be transferred to that body, the headship of the Church was a personal matter, and could not be so delegated to a mixed body of men, and also that changes relating to religion could properly be made only by a person of mature judgment. In these circumstances the whole question of religious alterations must remain in abeyance until the King reached years of discretion. Therefore they insisted that the laws and ritual of the Church should continue as the late King had left them, and as it was clear that Henry had intended that they should remain.

Far from Gardyner and Bonner cunningly inventing this theory [3] to please themselves, they based their objection upon an Act of Parliament, which they maintained ought not to have been repealed to suit the

---

[1] "Eccles. Hist.," V. p. 330.
[2] See Burnet's Ref. II. i. p. 83.
[3] See Latimer's " Sermons," Parker Soc. ed. p. 117, note.

Protector's own purposes, for it was really designed intentionally to restrain the Council.

The Princess Mary, holding the same opinion, reiterated her willingness to obey her father's strict injunctions, and refused to acknowledge the usurped power of the Council in—

" making (as they call it) laws both clean contrary to his proceedings and will,[1] and also against the custom of all Christendom, and (in my conscience) against the law of God and his Church." [2]

For maintaining these principles the Princess suffered persecution, and Gardyner and Bonner were imprisoned.

But, strange to say, the very person most concerned in having these two bishops imprisoned, Cranmer himself, had held a similar opinion not long before. Morrice, the Archbishop's secretary, relates, to his master's credit, that when it was suggested that the innovations in religion which he held had been prevented by Gardyner in the previous reign could now be carried out as that bishop was powerless.

"Not so," quoth the Archbishop. "It were better to attempt such reformation in King Henry the Eighth's days than at this time, the King being in his infancy. For if the King's father had set forth anything for the reformation of abuses, who was he that durst gainsay it? Marry! we are now in doubt how men will take the change, or alteration of abuses, in the church; and therefore, the council hath forborne especially to speak thereof . . ." [3]

So, too, Morrice records that Cranmer withstood Northumberland, as he styles him even then, in the first year of King Edward, concerning the disposition of the

---

[1] It is not certain that the word " will " is here used in the sense of testament.

[2] Lansd. MSS. 1236, f. 25.

[3] Foxe, V. p. 563.

Chantries, which should not be dealt with, he declared, until the King was of lawful age.

But an even more remarkable fact is that the chief person concerned, the very one on whose behalf Somerset and his companions with vehemence were insisting should be considered capable of altering, or permitting to be altered, matters relating to religion, gave most solemn instructions on his death-bed to prevent such action in the future, for in his will Edward VI. wrote—

" In the young years of any of my heirs, my executors are not to enter upon any wars, except on occasion of invasion, *nor to suffer religion to be altered.*"

It is by no means clear why the use of the vulgar tongue in Divine Service was so violently opposed. The use of English in church was not very uncommon, and most Cornishmen were fairly familiar with the language, so that they could have followed the new service readily, as they did the Latin Mass, etc., by means of prepared manuals. Already the Cornish language was dying out ; Norden, in 1584, records that scarcely one, except from some very remote district, failed to be able to converse in English with a stranger. Even their own friend, Cardinal Pole, is believed to have advocated at one time the use of the vulgar tongue in church, while both Cranmer and Ridley,[1] in Mary's reign, stated that the best-learned, both of the old and new learning, gospeller and papist, held that the common prayer should be in the common tongue. The reasons against the change were chiefly that the universality of the Church on earth required a uniform language.[2]

But at first there was a clear distinction drawn between the propriety of using English in the Litany, Gospels, Epistles, and Lessons, and the undesirability of using it in the " solemn mysteries." Even Cranmer at

[1] See Jenkins' "Rem. Cranmer," I. 375, and Ridley's Works, 340
[2] See Tunstall's remark quoted by Gasquet and Bishop, 89.

one time feared that the use of the mother tongue in this part of the service might lead to a decrease of reverence.[1]

The question of the new service resembling a Christmas *play*, as in the earlier Articles, or *game*, as in the later sets, is a puzzle. The only suggestion, and it is nothing more than a suggestion, that can be put forward is that there had been under Cromwell's direction an immense amount of ridicule of sacred things spread abroad by means of parodies of miracle plays. Some of these which have been preserved contain much that is blasphemous, and the method of introducing Biblical characters is disgusting. These plays were in English, and in giving Holy Writ in the vulgar tongue as the new service did, the Western men may have seen some analogy between the two.

The subject of the " Relief of Cloth and of Store Sheep " is dealt with in Chapter XIX.

In the later sets of Articles the one demand not connected with religion is the thirteenth, which in modern English reads—

" We will that no gentleman shall have any more servants than one to wait upon him unless he can afford to spend a hundred marks and for each additional hundred marks we think that it is reasonable he should have another man."

This suggested restriction has been much ridiculed by modern writers as unthinkable and impossible, forgetful that in those days legislation in regard to personal liberty was much more stringent, descending to the minutest details, and much was accepted without demur which would now be resented. The young King in an essay wrote that in the ideal Commonwealth no merchant would have more than £100 worth of land, no farmer more than one or two hundred marks, no artificer above one hundred marks, and no labourer much more

---

[1] See Hook's " Archbishops," VII., 266.

than he could spend. The petition presented as the result of the Commission of Enclosures requested that—

"no person of any degree, in possession of more than a hundred marks a year in land should farm any part of it beyond what his household required."

Burnet refers to several books issued about this date that " proposed a sort of agrarian law that none might have farms above a set value or flocks above a set number of ten thousand sheep." [1] From this it is evident that the restriction proposed by the rebels was quite in keeping with the ideas of the period.

The restoration of Canons Crispyn and Moreman would have been a recognition of the triumph of the opinions of the Old School. They were the representatives of the West country clergy who still held to the ancient forms of religion, they were loved and respected in their diocese, and they were martyrs, imprisoned for preaching the doctrine for which the rebels were contending. So, too, would have been the recall of Cardinal Pole and his elevation to the Council where he would have prevented the rash advance of the reformers, Somerset and Cranmer, and might have even caused a return to the old *régime*. He was quite prepared to listen to the call of the people, and approved their " just demands," as he styles them. He wrote to Somerset when he received the news of the insurrection that—

"should all others fail them, though, for the honour of God and personal advantage, it may be supposed there will be no lack of many who will favour and assist them, I, to speak clearly and frankly to you, as is my wont, will never fail endeavouring (if required and requested by them) by every effort and all the means in my power, that they be not abandoned and unassisted, provided they contain themselves within

[1] Burnet, "Ref.," II. i. p. 234. Merriman (p. 373) refers to an Act proposed in 1534 which forbade any man to keep more than 2,000 sheep and required every farmer to put one-eighth of his land in tillage.

the limits of their just and religious demands, as I see they have done hitherto." [1]

Their cause was his : for years, he admits, he had striven to bring England back to its ancient ways, and now the Western men were engaged in that Crusade.

[1] S. P. Venetian, V. p. 265.

CHAPTER XV

" Of men and harnes which longeth to batayle
  We haue ynoughe : and captaynes excellent,
  With strength ynough, bold corage and counsayle.
  We lacke no thyng that is expedient,
  As wyt, and wysdome, wyse practyse and prudent."
                          BARCLAY's " Ship of Fools."

BEFORE continuing the history of events it is well to consider the composition of the Royal army and their action, or inaction, prior to their final advance to the relief of Exeter.

As has been said, Sir Peter Carew, on his return to Devon, found Lord Russell ensconced in the family mansion at Mohun's Ottery, about four miles from Honiton. Perhaps his lordship occupied the " chamber next ouer the gayt housse," furnished with a bed, its tester of white and red silk embroidered, its curtains of sarcenet to match, the sheets fine and the coverlet of arras ; a " cheare " of crimson satin embroidered, edged with gold lace, and another of red cloth ; while the whole room was hung with arras and its six windows had " clothes of green saye." Sir Peter may have occupied the " King's Chamber," which had hangings of black and yellow saye.[1]

While the Lord Privy Seal waited here for the promised " supply and furniture," he was engaged, with

---

[1] Inventory of Mohun's Ottery, 1554.

Sir Peter's assistance, in making local levies, holding frequent conferences for this purpose with the gentlemen in the vicinity who remained loyal. But he was not very successful in his efforts. His hope of obtaining 2,000 footmen was not fulfilled, while the few he did gather, discouraged by the failure of the promised help from London, were inclined to join the rebels, with whose aims they were much in sympathy. In consequence, he found himself—

"daily. more and more foresaken of such of the common people as who at the first served and offered their service unto him : and havinge but a very small guard about him he lived in more fear then he was feared : for the Rebells daily increased and his company decreased and shrank away and he not altogether assured of them which remained." [1]

He complained to the Council of this difficulty in a letter of the 8th July, suggesting that letters of thanks should be sent to the gentlemen for their services, and that money distributed to their servants would improve matters. In response to this the Council sent the desired letter and authorised the payment of £100, and also sent an order to the mint at Bristol to supply him with £500, at the same time warning him that the rate of pay should not exceed 6d. a day for foot-soldiers and 9d. for light horsemen. [2]

As for his place of residence, he was to choose such as made it most easy to annoy the rebels and keep the adjacent country quiet. He was to intercept the enemy's food supply in order to bring them to great misery, and was also, apparently even in defiance of truth, to spread abroad "rumours of their devilish behaviours, cruelty, abominable 'levings,' Robberies, murders, and such like," to cause "such detestation of them among the common people, and few, we think, will repair towards them."

[1] Hoker, p. 82.   [2] Petyt MS. f. 435, Pk. p. 22.

For their part the Council complained that it would be very hard to send " in a short time such a number of footmen as with plain force might be able to meet with the rebels," adding that to attempt the setting on without a sufficient force would be dangerous. Still, they were preparing to send soldiers, 150 Italian " harque-butters," four hundred foreign horsemen, and a thousand " almayn " footmen. The first-named were under the command of Paolo Baptista Spinola, an Italian, born of a noble house in Genoa,[1] who, at an audience of the Privy Council on the 4th April, had offered his services with a band of Italians proposed for Scotland.[2] On the 1st July he received 300 crowns for 150 Spaniards [3]— probably they were Italians and Spaniards together— no doubt the very " harquebutters " referred to above. They figure in subsequent letters as four-score harque-butters and in histories as " 300 shot."

The four hundred " horsemen strangers " seem to have been a mixed lot of " Albanois," " Almayn," and Italian men under Jacques Jermigny, and Pietro Sanga.[4]

These two detachments started westward prior to the 18th July, but the Almayn footmen were detained " partly for the disorders of these parts hereabouts," write the Council, " and namely for that they be odious to our people abroad in so much as we can hardly move them to receive them without quarel here at hand." [5]

These " disorders " were the risings in Buckingham-shire, Berkshire, and Oxfordshire, which were sup-pressed by Lord Grey de Wilton with such sternness and brutality.

---

[1] Holinshed, p. 919.
[2] Hayward, p. 62.
[3] P. C. Reg. (Dasent ed.), p. 272.
[4] Gasquet mentions Malatesta as in the West.
[5] Pet. MS. f. 438, Pk. p. 29.

From what they wrote it is evident that the Council relied from the first upon the employment of foreign mercenaries, hitherto never employed to suppress an insurrection at home. They were particularly obnoxious to Englishmen, as the Council admitted ; it was said that every year they became more ferocious, bloodthirsty, and dishonest, which, considering the reputation they had already gained early in the reign of Henry VIII., must point to an extreme brutality. Guistiniani, writing in 1516, speaks of the " inhumanity of the Germans, who do not content themselves with plundering, but burn and kill, filling every place with death and slaughter," their ferocity being only exceeded by that of the Switzers, who boasted of " irrigating and inundating the earth with human gore." [1]

The overbearing manners of the mercenaries were always keenly resented by the people.[2] When they were sent to quell the insurrections of 1549 the Commons declared that they were but a " handful of an armful to follow, driving on the design to subject England to the insolence of the foreigner." [3] Hoker describes the " Burgonians " as abhorred of the one side and nothing favoured of the other.[4]

But it was even difficult for the Council to obtain these mercenaries as the credit of England at that moment was at a very low ebb, so that the payment of troops was most irregular. About this time the discontent of the foreign soldiery was so great that they refused to take service except in numbers large enough to compel good treatment. Dymock writes—

" If they should go less in number than three or four thousand men, they affirm they should be brought to the butcher's stall, ' for they heard from those who had returned from

[1] " Four Years at the Court of Henry VII.," I. p. 233.
[2] For a graphic account of their insolence, see Hume's " Life of Romero."
[3] Fuller's " Ch. Hist.," II. 322.
[4] Hoker, p. 96.

England that they were more ordered like wild beasts than Christians both in the scarcity of victuals and payment,' " [1]

and that they lacked both food and fuel.

Moreover, when it came to suppressing a rising on account of religion, the devout sons of the Pope declined to take part, while even the rough " rakehells " who consented felt obliged to seek absolution for fighting to maintain heresy.[2]

But such scruples did not deter some of the Germans, who were ready to uphold the new religion. It is reported that the Duke of Lunenburg said that though the pay was small and the hurt and damage great, yet he was content to help the King, who favoured the Word of God.

These mercenaries were gathered from various quarters, " for the most part from sea-towns," [3] and were usually of a very low class, but at this juncture the Council, in spite of the detestation in which they were held, recalled those who had already started towards Scotland in order to send them to Lord Russell's assistance.

Pollard writes that the employment of mercenaries—

" has been attributed to all manner of sinister motives on the part of the Government, such as distrust of the English soldiery, and a design to impose religious changes on the people at the point of foreign pikes. It was really due to sheer necessity." [4]

But colour is given to these charges by the Council's letters, for they distrusted the mixed force under Russell's command, especially the men from the neighbouring counties, who would " most faintly fight " against the Devonians ; while Hoker says that the Lord

---

[1] S. P. Foreign. Ed. VI. No. 144, 6 May, 1549.

[2] Morysine writes from Augsburg, 14th April, 1551, " Many Spaniards and Italians this Lent went to the Bishop of Rome's Nuncio to be absolved, for that they had served in the wars the King of England " (*ibid.* No. 319). These may have been employed at Boulogne, but others probably did the same.

[3] Soranzo's Report, Ven. S. P. V. 548.

[4] " Protector," p. 212,

Privy Seal was not altogether assured of the loyalty of the meagre force which remained attached to him. Burnet, writing of the German troops, says that—

" the true secret of it on both sides was this : that the bulk of the people of England was still possessed with the old super-stition to such a degree, that it was visible they could not be depended on, in any matter that related to the alterations that were made : whereas the Germans were full of zeal on the other side so that they might well be trusted to : and the Princes of Germany who were then kept under by the Emperor, so that they neither durst not nor could keep their troops at home, but hoped they might at some better time have occasion to use them, were willing to put them in the hands of the present government of England. Howsoever, this had an odious name put on it, and was called a ruling by strangers, so that it very much shook the Duke of Somerset's popularity." [1]

This use of foreign soldiers was one of the complaints against Somerset made by his brother, the Admiral.

But, to return to Lord Russell, who, while waiting for the promised reinforcements, was busy in Devon, striving to increase his army as well as weeding out doubtful adherents and suspected spies, leading anything but a life of peaceful ease. He also summoned supposed delinquents, among them Sir John Arundell, who was believed to sympathise with his kinsman, and was also accused of attending mass and ordering a procession on Corpus Christi day. Afterwards he pleaded that illness had prevented him from obeying his Lordship's summons, and excused himself to the Council.

But Russell was also much occupied in writing letters

---

[1] " Hist. Ref. " III. p. 389. The matter has been bitterly discussed. The Roman Catholic writer, Corbett, goes so far as to charge Bishop Hooper with recommending the use of German troops to bend the neck of the English to the Protestant yoke, but his authority is not given. Soranzo, in his report, states that the English sometimes subsidised German soldiers, and had employed as many as 10,000 at a time, and that they gave Court-penick a pension of 2,000 ducats. There are many references in the Privy Council Register to the payment of mercenaries.

to the Council, and though few of these remain, their substance can be surmised from the Council's replies. He often reiterated his complaint of the difficulty of raising levies and his lack of trust in those he did obtain. Meanwhile he was further discouraged by rumours that the rebels had captured Exeter, and that a rising had taken place near Salisbury, which, if successful, would cut off his direct line of communication.[1]

At this critical juncture Russell summoned the neighbouring gentry to discuss the situation with him and his officers. On the advice of those from Dorset he actually retired from Honiton into Somerset.[2]

Sir Peter Carew evidently did not attend this conference. As yet the Privy Council had not granted Russell's request that the Carews might be added to his council,[3] and Sir Peter may have been absent on some small expedition. But as soon as he heard of his Lordship's movements he took horse and rode post haste after the slow moving forces.

He overtook Russell on Black Down, where he had some " speeches and conference with him," and—

" declared what inconveniences were likely to ensue to the encouraging of the enemy, the undoing of the whole country, and the great dishonour unto himself, if he should leave the country and give the enemy scope and liberty to go forward." [4]

Indeed

" had he departed according to his first determination, there had grown thereby a greater fire than all the waters of

---

[1] An " uproar " is recorded at Harnham Hill, near Salisbury, in 1549, but perhaps this was on account of enclosures in the spring. See Hoare's " Mod. Wilts," VI. p. 261.

[2] He probably intended to make for Taunton, where he would be able to communicate with London by another road which runs well north of Salisbury, joining the main road at Andover. From Taunton he could have fallen back on Dorset.

[3] For the Council's consent on 12th July, see Pet. MSS. 437.

[4] Mclaean's " Carew," p. 52.

five shires about would have been able to quench." But with "such pithy reasons he carried him, that leaving his former determination [Lord Russell] doth return again unto Honiton." Here "daily waiting and look[ing] for the promised help and supply which came not he was in an agony and of a heavy cheer : not only for the want of men and money which he had long in vain looked for but also because he had spent all that he had brought with him and could not tell how otherwise to help and provide to supply his present need." [1]

The Council still gave unsatisfactory replies to his frequent appeals for funds, though, to be sure, a phrase in a letter from the Protector of the 12th July sounds like *carte blanche*, but it is far from clear. After referring to the number of men that might be required, he adds—

"for as the impossibility to have men stayed hitherto, So presently by this your fresh advertisement to mind to take footmen, we have given order to the Treasurer or Comptroller of the mint of Bristol, the King's Receiver, to Croche our Receiver, to pay upon your bill, that ye shall like to demand." [2]

It does not appear that Russell availed himself of this generous order, but he was not slow to accept a significant hint in the same letter. " In like manner what ye can get of merchants to be repaid here take it. It shall be answered with thanks."

Fortunately there were merchants ready to meet his requirements, even on such indifferent security, in three Exeter men, "following and attending upon him," Thomas Prestwood, John Bodley, and John Peryam, all wealthy merchants. [3]

" These men understanding the heaviness and grief of his Lordship make their resort unto him and promise to help and

[1] Hoker, p. 82.
[2] Pet. MS. 436, Pk. p. 25.
[3] Prestwood had been recently mayor of Exeter ; Bodley was the father of the founder of the Bodleian. All three were connected by marriage—Bodley was Prestwood's step-son and had married Peryam's sister-in-law.

relieve his agony and want : and forthwith did procure upon their credit from the merchants of Bristol, Lyme, Taunton and elsewhere such a mass of money as which when he had received his grief was eased : for forthwith he so provided and furnished himself with such necessaries and with a great number of men that he was now in the better safety as also the better able to encounter with the enemy : and it was not long after that he had a further supply from the king even to his content." [1]

Letters, men, and money were not the only things supplied to Lord Russell by the thoughtful Council. They added a series of curious proclamations. One of these, dated 11th July on the printed broadside, is entitled "A Proclamation, for the punishment of the rebelles of Devonshire and Cornwall." Its substance is as follows :—

" Whereas divers evil disposed persons, are at this present rebelliously and traiterously assembled in sundry companies . . . in Devon and Cornwall . . . shewing themselves, not only to contemn and disobey his most royal majesty, his laws, ordinances and most godly proceedings but also to levy war against his highness . . . (the King is nevertheless pleased that all his) said subjects, which . . . do continue in their unlawfull, and disobedient assemblies and within — days, next after this Proclamation, shall not willingly and obediently submit them selves unto the right honorable lord Russell shall be deemed rebels and traitors."

For their punishment and to encourage those who withdrew from these rebels, and as all property of such traitors belongs to his Majesty, the King is pleased to order that the goods, etc., of such as continue in rebellions and treasons shall pertain to such persons—

" as shall first have, take, possede and attain to the said goods and chattels or shall enter such manors, lands, etc., and they

---

[1] Hoker, p. 83. £2,000 were paid on 19th July and £1,000 on 30th July. See P. C. Reg. pp. 302, 306.

shall hold and possess the same by right of such forfeiture as if granted by letters patent." [1]

It is worthy of comment that the Council devised this Proclamation for the express purpose of sowing dissensions among the rebels. Replying to Lord Russell's remark that if the proclamation had been carried into effect there must have ensued great seditions, troubles, strife and contentions, they write—

" Marry, that was indeed the very end of the making of the proclamation, to set such division and strife amongst themselves, as for desire of revenge, or fear of loss, the countrymen should rather have tarried at home and been occupied that way then assemble together against the king as they did." [2]

This proclamation was supplemented by another, dated, if the printed copy is correct, the 12th July—the following day. It is entitled " Concerning the effect of his majesty's pardon granted to certain of his subjects, lately having made unlawfull riots and assemblies." [3] This refers to the proclamation of pardon recently set forth, and declares that as it is " the reputation of his Majesty's mercy, to defend and save harmless all such which submitted themselves to his mercy," so ought he also to punish " his obstinate subjects with justice." He, therefore, commands that such repentant subjects shall not be molested by "actions, suit, violence or compulsion " by those who suffered injury or loss at their hands prior to the issue of that pardon.

A third proclamation, dated the 16th July, four days later, was " for the executing of a law Martial for pain against rebellors and their upstirrers," but this dealt

---

[1] The " Tudor Proclamations " copy of this has a blank before " days," while Grafton's has the figure 3 inserted. The Council's letter of 10th September mentions six days (Pet. MS. 463ᵈ).

[2] Pet. MS. 463ᵈ, Pk. p. 70.

[3] Tudor Proclamations.

R

only with those who destroyed enclosures, having no special reference to Devon and Cornwall.

There are no letters from the Council which might have enclosed these Proclamations.[1] The next one after that of the 12th is dated the 18th July.[2] In this they promise that if Sir William Herbert does not join him Lord Russell will be provided with a skilful man on horseback. ' They also say that

"the Lord Grey, who, by advertisement even now we perceive to have chased the rebels of Bucks, Oxfordshire, and these parts to their houses and taken cc of them and a dozen of the ringleaders delivered unto him whereof part at least shall suffer pains of death to the example of all malefactors." [3]

They inform him that the strangers, horsemen, and " Italian hagbutters footmen " will be with him as soon as they possibly can, being already on the way thither. They authorise Russell to transfer the ordnance from Purbeck to Corfe Castle or to Poole, as he thinks fit, to keep it from the rebels who threaten to capture it.[4]

Meanwhile Mr. Travers and Mr. Dudley had brought instructions to Lord Russell, who sent a letter to the Council by the same messengers on the 18th. In this he pointed out the smallness of his own army and the increase in that of the rebels, as well as the absolute necessity of a " main force," without which he could neither relieve Exeter nor assault, nor even resist, his opponents. From Dorset and Somerset he did not expect to raise more than a thousand footmen nor more than six or seven hundred horse : the difficulty in the latter county being due to the evil inclination of the

---

[1] Russell may have removed these letters for his defence when his actions were called in question by Warwick's party and never replaced them.

[2] For the reasons proving that the letter dated by the transcriber at the beginning the 17th and at the end the 27th should be assigned to the later date, see Appendix F.

[3] Pet. MSS. 438, Pk. p. 29, Grey's ruthless execution of his orders is dealt with elsewhere.

[4] *Ibid.*

people, who openly spoke traitorous words against
the King. Moreover, he sadly lacked ammunition, he
reminded them.[1]

It is impossible to gauge the exact strength of the
opposing forces at this period. The Council make an
estimate in a letter of the 28th July ; they reckon that
if both Cornwall and Devon gathered all their force they
would not have

"above vij^m men tag and rag that should come to fight, and
yet some we are sure they leave behind to keep their houses
and the towns and one thousand of them is in Exeter. So
that things accounted as they should be esteemed the rebels
cannot be thought to be in the whole against you past iiij^m
men (and the more part unarmed) as indeed they have been
esteemed by some that hath viewed them : your band already,
we take it, to be no less than about iiij^m more or less : and yet
better armed with harness and having arquibusses, which they
have none." [2]

This estimate seems not far wide of the mark as

to calculate Russell's force with fair accuracy, although
they quote him as saying that he could count upon only
1000 foot and 600 or 700 horse from the district.[3]

[1] Most of the above is gathered from the Council's reply (Pet. MSS.
439), but a portion of Russell's letter is to be found in S. P. Dom. Edw.
VI., VII. 41, which gives a description of the district. Pocock, who trans-
cribes it very inaccurately (p. 11), assigns it to June, but without giving
any reason. Its heading, which he has placed at the end, identifies it.

[2] Pet. MSS. 446, Pk. p. 44. vij^m = 7000 and iiij^m = 4000.

[3] Working out such data as we have and accepting the Council's
"4000 more or less," it would seem that Russell brought with him a very
small force. The Council sent 150, or eight score Italian "hagbutters"
under Spinola ; 400 foreign horsemen under Jermigny and Sanga, and
1000 "almayn" foot, between 10th and 18th July : i.e. 1550 or more
mercenaries. Russell's local levies are estimated at about 1700 : together
these account for more than 3200 of his entire force, leaving about 800
as his original escort. These would have been for the most part foreign
or native mercenaries and retainers of gentlemen. The latter might
easily have been suspected of sympathising with those of the old faith.
The trained English soldiers in this force must have been comparatively few.

Replying to Lord Russell's letter, the Council expressed their surprise that a man of his experience could write of desperation and impossibilities, and they then proceed to point out in detail facts which must have been obvious to a general of such long service. For instance, he ought to take possession of all the horses in the district, no matter who owned them, as he would thus increase his own strength and " decay " that of the enemy, who might use the horses themselves. Thus furnished, " though they be x^t tymes so many in number," he could, with 500 horse and a reasonable number of footmen properly disposed, cut off their supplies and prevent their skirmishing by using his " hagbutters," who would " bicker " with the rebels on their march, taking a great advantage on them of their victuals and otherwise, as shall be to them " impeschment," and yet at all times when it shall appear by the " renforce " of the enemies convenient to retire, they may draw themselves back and the footmen also with them in surety. And in this wise the enemy encountered by force of horsemen, hagbutters, and politic handling of the matter by interruption of their victual, shall be weary of their life and abate their pride after they have met with men of " conduct." They are surprised that he can gather so few men while the rebels brag that they will have ten thousand " to seat on your back " out of Somerset and Dorset, as they avow their number is so great so be your numbers mentioned so much under foot. As for shot, whereof ye complain to have lack, shift is to be made there by lead, whereof we doubt not there is plenty within the limit of your commission, and for powder the same hath been sent hence unto you.[1]

Roofs, conduits, etc., of monasteries and churches must have still remained in some places close to Honiton,

[1] Pet. MSS. 440, Pk. p. 31. Bicker=skirmish. Conduct=hired, *i.e.* trained in this instance.

and, if he had not already taken possession of all available lead, he would now have accepted their hint.

Wherever he cannot trust the people to possess them he is, according to these instructions, to collect all the "hagbutters," bows, arrows, shot, powder, and other munition and bestow them in some castle, as at Bristol or elsewhere, as he may think best, where they may be out of the hands of the enemy.

He is also to issue proclamations in Somerset and Dorset like the last one sent for Cornwall for forfeiture of lands, etc., adding to it—

"If they shall not come unto you to serve according to their duties and obedience to their sovereign lord and show themselves as prest and ready to fight against those rank rebels and papists of Devon as becometh good subjects, they shall be both deemed and taken for traitors and forfeit their lands, copyholds and goods without redemption to themselves, wives and children, and be without hope of pardon to the perpetual disherison of themselves and all that depend upon them : the matter of copyholds being so general a living to the number of those shires [this] shall be as much a terror as any other thing that can be possibly devised." [1]

As the rebels freely sent spies into Russell's camp, he was to send trusty men into theirs. As for soldiers, they cannot send those under Lord Warwick, as they had anticipated, because they heard only yesterday that the counties of Essex, Suffolk, Norfolk, and Kent are not in such good order and quiet as they could wish, the people having risen on account of the land-question, etc., not as in the West for other reasons. As soon as the Earl has quieted these, as they expect him to do in two days, he would depart towards the Lord Privy Seal. In the meantime, Lord Grey had started with two hundred and fifty horse and eight score hagbutters under Spinola, while William Grey is advancing with two hundred men

---

[1] Pet. MSS. 440, Pk. p. 32. Prest = ready.

from Reading, and Russell is asked to extend favour particularly to the last-named.[1]

All this time Russell had not been wholly idle : he had so governed those parts by his continual labour and wisdom, that hitherto the enemies dared not come forth out of their dens, " for so would you call them if you saw the lanes, the hills, the woods and straight passages betwixt us and them," wrote the pamphleteer.[2]

One forward movement he seems to have made about this time. Finding advance to Exeter by the high-road impracticable, he tried to make a *detour* by way of Ottery St. Mary, at which place he spent a night, " where as it fell out, he was in more fear than peril." [3] But the rebels, getting wind of his proposed advance over West Hill, cut down all the trees between that town and Exeter, laying them across the road.[4] In revenge, and also to prevent the place from being a refuge for his opponents, Lord Russell burnt the town and thought to return to Honiton, but, according to the King's Journal, the rebels kept a bridge behind him, and compelled him, with his small force to set upon them.

If we could place any reliance upon a pamphlet issued about this time Lord Russell continued to hold

---

[1] William Grey, the lewd ballad-maker, was a favourite with both Henry VIII. and Somerset. Among his " merry ballads " is " The hunt is up," and another, written against Cromwell, is " Trolle on away." He also wrote " A New Year's Gift " to the Protector. (See Puttenham, " Arte of Eng. Poesie," 1589, p. 32.) He was sent to the Tower with Somerset in October, 1549. In the list in S. P. Dom. Edw. VI., IX. 48, his name, " William Grey, of Redyng," follows " Wolfe of the Privye Chamber." He was released on heavy recognisances in February, 1549-50. It is not known why this poet was employed to lead soldiers from Reading, for which he received £50 for expenses and 40s. for calling for the payment on 7th August, 1549 (P. C. Reg. p. 558).

[2] See Appendix K.

[3] Hoker, p. 82.

[4] The King's Journal. It may be that some confusion exists between this excursion and the later battle of Fenny Bridges in his account, but there is not enough data to help us to decide whether the rebels held a bridge behind Russell twice or only once.

some outlying post towards Ottery—perhaps at Alfington
—for there is a " Copy of a Letter," signed by " R. L."
and dated from " a village nygh sainct Mary Otery, the
xxvii of Julie." Unfortunately, this is open to the
suspicion that it was composed by order of the Government, and published for the purpose of spreading their
views on the rebellion and of discrediting the rebels.
The language is very vehement, while the detailed discussion of principles in so pointed a manner makes it
unlikely that it was written by an officer on active
service. But it is interesting in any case, as it most
emphatically attributes the origin of the rising wholly
to the dissatisfaction felt by the people with the alterations in matters of religion—he asserts that the rebellion
was inspired by popish priests or the Evil One himself,
and represents the rebels as despicable rascals. To the
letter is added a copy of the Articles of the rebels upon
which the writer makes some comment.[1]

The Lord Privy Seal kept the Council informed of
his movements, sending off their messenger, Mr. Travers,
about the 22nd July with a description of some small
success, perhaps the encounter at the bridge, which
called forth their congratulations on his good beginning
and an expression of thanks for their good and faithful
service to the gentlemen who had aided him, adding
a fervent hope of " as good success to follow to the King's
Highness and all the realm's comfort." [2]

As a further encouragement to Russell, the Council
sent another proclamation, dated, according to Grafton,
the 22nd July, and addressed to the " Bailifes, constables
and Hedboroughs," whose duty it was, it pointed out, to
pacify and stay their neighbours, showing them the
dangers and perilous sequel of such " heady " and disobedient attempts, and also to apprehend the sowers
and spreaders of lewd tales and rumours stirring to riot,

[1] See a transcript of this pamphlet in Appendix K.
[2] Pet. MSS. 424, Pk. p. 35.

but, on the contrary, these officers had been the very
ringleaders and procurers by their example and exhortation, and had even levied forces in the King's name,
abusing their authority. If they continued to allure
others to join their unlawful assemblies for seditious
proceedings or procured harness, weapons, or victuals for
the rebels they were to be deemed traitors, and suffer
accordingly.[1]

The Council were also engaged in trying to increase
the force at Lord Russell's disposal. They held correspondence with Sir William Herbert, who had helped
to suppress the rising in Wiltshire against enclosures in
May. They wrote about the 10th July, commanding
him to hold himself in " a Redynes " with the men of
Gloucester and Wiltshire, whom he was collecting. On
the 22nd July they sent instructions about " cotes," etc.,
payments and his position under the Lord Privy Seal.
A confused, rough draft of a letter to him indicates that
much was left to Russell's discretion, as they were
ignorant of the size of Sir William's force. He was
authorised to take as many men as he pleased from
Bristol, provided he left enough to furnish the Castle
there. As for Bromham, late the Lord Admiral's
residence, which Herbert wished to occupy, it could be
of no use to him unless he were lying still, and this he
was strictly enjoined not to do. His horsemen, if well
horsed and armed with a lance, were to have 16d. a day,
and other horsemen, either mounted archers or hacque-
butters, 10d., and footmen 6d., while captains were to
be paid the same as those of the Lord Privy Seal's band.
On the 24th, Herbert was instructed to hasten to the
seat of war with all his power, and on the 28th he was
told to take two or three thousand men from Wales and
2000 from Gloucester and Wiltshire.[2]

The Council informed Lord Russell on the 24th that

---

[1] See Grafton's " Proclamations," f. 64.
[2] See S. P. Dom. Ed. VI., VIII. 34.

" Mr. Herbert is of such courage that he saith he is able rather to bring too many than too few, and so ready to do," therefore his Lordship was to instruct Sir William at once how many were required.[1]

Lord Russell, taking their remarks literally, promptly demanded six thousand foot from Herbert, who notified the Council of the same. Such an exorbitant demand drew an indignant letter from the Council to Russell, pointing out the comparative strength of the opposing armies, and adding that if Herbert brought four or five thousand, the best appointed and most willing, they would be better than twenty thousand,

"for the multitude should not only 'pestyre' you and consume your victuals, but of so many some doubtful and hollow-hearted should turn to the rebels' part. Ye should be in more danger of your own company than of the rebels themselves." [2]

From the report of Barbaro, the Venetian ambassador, written in 1551, we can obtain a good idea of the army assembled under the Lord Privy Seal. Of the English soldiers, he writes, some serve on foot, others on horseback. Those who are neither tall nor short but of agile frame, are mounted and are divided into light-horse and men-at-arms, consisting mostly of gentlemen, as they are better able to bear the expense and get good horses. Part of the light cavalry are armed in the Albanian fashion, and the rest with a shirt of mail, a sallet and a light, long spear,and use any sort of horse, as they charge only in flank : these are called demi-lances.

The infantry consists of taller men, divided into four sorts. First, the archers who abound in England, and are very excellent both by nature and practice, so that the archers alone have routed armies of 30,000 men. Second, the bill-men, armed with a short, thick staff with an iron like a peasant's hedging-bill, but much thicker and heavier than the Venetians use. With this they

[1] Pet. MSS. 442, Pk. p. 36.   [2] *Ibid.* 446, Pk. p. 45.

strike so violently that they unhorse the cavalry : it is made short, as they like close quarters. Third, the harquebusiers, who are good for little, as few have had practice south of the Channel, and these, together with the fourth, the pikemen, have been but recently added to the ancient militia of England. The military commanders are : first, the Captain-General ; second, the marshal, who in the general's absence takes his place ; and there is a provost of all the cavalry. There is a treasurer, a master of the militia, a master of the ordnance, a Colonel, and other inferior officers. The infantry is divided into companies of a hundred men, each with its captain, lieutenant, ensign, and serjeant. The cavalry is divided into squadrons of one hundred, and similarly officered. The latter use trumpets, the infantry drums ; and legitimate war is announced by a herald. When the army takes the field the camp is fortified with wagons and barricades, if near the enemy trenches, and earthworks are made and artillery placed in suitable position. There are two sorts of watchmen, the cavalry have scouts and the infantry have sentries. On notice of the enemy's approach, the whole camp cries, " Bows ! Bows ! " which is the nation's last hope, and all rush to a spacious place called the camp square, to await orders.[1]

Soranzo informs us that the English had not much opportunity of providing armour : that the archers, in number and valour excelling all other soldiers, are the sinews of their army, for the English are all by nature expert bowmen, practising archery not only for pleasure, but to serve the King. He also alludes to the harquebusiers and pikemen having little experience with their weapons.[2]

But other matters than the movements of Lord Russell's army and its increase occupied the Council. Following the rumour that Exeter had fallen into the

---

[1] See Ven. S. P. V. 548.   [2] Ibid. 548.

rebels' hands, came a report that the Mayor of Plymouth had traitorously yielded that town, so they promptly ordered a certain Cotton to take his ships and galleys there to attempt to win possession of the Castle, and to get Hawkins and others to apprehend the Mayor and " so give good order for the town." [1] Later Lord Russell contradicted the rumour, but they seem to have doubted the accuracy of his information, for they write—

" For the Mayor of Plymouth, we are glad to hear the matter of the town not to be so evil as we heard, but the end shall show all . . . we like well your device therein." [2]

A possible explanation of these last words is that Lord Russell had suggested that his army might be supported by attacks on the enemy by sea, for later reference is made to a scheme for using pinnaces to cut off the enemies' supplies by sea.[3] But ships were greatly needed at this crisis. Sir Philip Hoby warned them of a threatened descent of the French on the Cornish coast. The rumour ran that the French, encouraged by the rebellion, were sending twelve galleys and other ships in great number to take the Scilly Islands or to land in Cornwall or Devon at a gentleman's house which was on " almost an Isle." [4]

Almost at the same moment they must have received the peremptory demands signed by Arundell and the Captains and Governors of the Camps.

At last, in desperation, the gentlest of the Council felt that strong measures must be taken, so they instructed the Lord Privy Seal, provided he had not already crushed his opponents, to issue a stern proclamation, to the effect that any who should take or hear this letter—i.e. the rebels' Articles—or " Humfrey Arundell's poyson," as

[1] Pet. MS. 441[d], Pk. p. 33.
[2] Ibid. 442, Pk. p. 35.
[3] Ibid. 444[d], Pk. p. 40.
[4] Ibid. 442, Pk. p. 36, and S.P. Dom. Ed. VI., VIII. 6.

they call it elsewhere—or should favour the rebels or aid them with food or otherwise, shall be taken as rebels and suffer forfeiture accordingly, unless immediately, without " participating or opening it to any other," they bring the same to his Lordship, who was to execute the proclamation " straitly with all severity." This they expected could be done, as Lord Grey should have then joined him. He was also to act against such as shall use

" traitorous and rebellious words, moving and tending to sedition or to the disappointing and disfurnishing of you or to not serving the King's Majesty, or shall aid the rebels." [1]

That Lord Russell might be able to enforce these sterner measures a determined effort was made to hasten the advance of the men under Grey and Herbert and of the ordnance under the Knight Marshal.

[1] Pet. MSS. 443, Pk. p. 37. The language and spelling of this letter differ so much from any of the foregoing correspondence that they are a puzzle. It may be that it was penned by one of the Council who urged sterner methods than Somerset had adopted. It is not signed by Warwick, who had signed that of 23rd July, and who did not take command of the forces in the Eastern counties until August. He signed no letter until 10th September.

CHAPTER XVI

THE BATTLE OF FENNY BRIDGES

" Lord ! how hastily the soldiers buckled their helms ! How quickly the
archers bent their bows, and frushed their feathers ! How readily
the billmen shook their bills and proved their staves, ready to approach
and join when the terrible trumpet should sound the bloody blast
to victory or death ! The trumpets blew, and the soldiers shouted
and the King's archers courageously let fly their arrows. The Earl's
bowmen stood not still, but paid them home again : and the terrible
shot once passed, the armies joined, and came to handstrokes, when
neither sword nor bill was spared."—GRAFTON's " Account of Bosworth
Field."

LORD RUSSELL was still impatiently marking time at
Honiton. A " skirmish in the streights," apparently a
small encounter in the narrow lanes, and his attempt to
circumvent the enemy, by way of Ottery St. Mary, had
given no tangible results, if we except the sharp justice
executed upon his captives, including a spy who had
been employed to publish the famous " Articles " from
the pulpits, and who the Council hoped had met with
" dew reward." [1]

Indeed, the Lord Privy Seal was weary of waiting
for Lord Grey with his promised detachment, and for
Sir William Herbert with his fabulous army of Welshmen
and others, so with considerable irritation he wrote to
the Council on the 25th July.[2] He was tired of their
petty dictation, insulting to him as an experienced
soldier, of having horsemen sent when he required foot-

---

[1] Pet. MS. 445, Pk. p. 42.   [2] *Ibid.* 444, Pk. p. 40.

men, of receiving inefficient and ill-advised proclamations instead of men and furniture, of the lack of ammunition, of the delay of reinforcements, and, in fact, of their utter failure to attend to his requests. The " phantasies " of the Council, as they were pleased to style their suggestions, were not to Lord Russell's mind. Money, men, ammunition—men, ammunition, money, was ever his cry—the driblets in the way of funds and their cheese-paring commands liked him not.

This bitter tirade called forth a lengthy defence of the Council's action. They pointed out that they had endeavoured to fulfil his contradictory requests to the best of their ability. He had, they wrote,[1] " made the keeping of Exeter so impossible, and the keeping of them in the straights so full of desperation " that their device was to make him strong with horsemen " to match them on the plain." As for the disinclination of the men of Somerset to serve their King, he must " hang two or three of them, and cause them to be executed like traitors. And that will be the only and the best stay of all those talks." He says proclamations do no great good, while they maintain they do some good, " Hurt they can do none."

They are still confident that they understand the situation, and that he can easily make a mould for his shot, and with " a dice of Iron and lead there " supply his own ammunition. They do not know the calibre of his guns and might send " shot as fit as a shoe for a man's hand." As for arrows, the less he uses them the better, unless he takes greater care, for he only furnishes the enemy with ammunition, as they hear, for in a recent skirmish his own arrows were used against him, while, on the contrary, " the shott of the habirgon pelot is brust, which never returneth." [2]

---

[1] Pet. MS. 444, Pk. p. 40.

[2] This seems to refer to a ball that exploded, scattering its contents and was discharged from a mortar, perhaps shaped like a helmet.

As for the dearth of victuals, if his soldiers cannot live on their wages he must fix a rate of charges for food, and there were doubtless church goods he could raid, as " belike the rebels do," a baseless insinuation against their enemies, but a suggestion carried to the extreme by his Lordship. He is well aware of the low state of the treasury, but, bearing that in mind he may use his discretion as to increasing pay, though they disliked the precedent.

They have written their mind and " phantasies " as they thought best, and he must not imagine that they doubted his wisdom or his experience in war or " reprove your doings when we did ' wright ' unto you our advice." " And how wise and valiant a man is, yet to here counsel of another can do no hurt. And we think us to have some experience in those things." They wind up their letter by urging him to execute sharp justice upon " those sundry traitors which will learn by nothing but by the sword."

Before this letter reached Lord Russell news had been brought in of the advance of the enemy, who, leaving a containing force around Exeter, sent a detachment towards Honiton. Inactivity in their own camp urged them to take the aggressive, and, aware that the Lord Privy Seal's army was weakened by the defection of many gentlemen, and that the efforts to strengthen the force with him were likely soon to be crowned with success, they decided that now was the time to strike, before Lord Grey and Sir William Herbert joined him. It therefore fell out that on or about the 28th July, a breathless messenger brought to Honiton a rumour that a contingent of rebels had advanced as far on the London road as Feniton Bridges, or Fenny Bridges, as the spot is now styled, within two miles of Honiton, evidently meeting some check there on the banks of the Otter, probably a skirmish with Russell's outposts, which would naturally have been placed at this point. This encounter forced them back on their reserves, and gave

Russell opportunity to prepare for an attack in the open, where he could use his horsemen to advantage.

The Lord Privy Seal had despatched hasty messages to accelerate the advance of Grey and Herbert, and then called a Council of war. He trusted much to the advice of the Carews, whose familiarity with the surrounding district was of great service at this juncture. An animated discussion followed, advice of all sorts was tendered, and many speeches were made, ending at last in the decision that it was best to advance to meet the foe and give the onset. All was hurry and excitement that night when the word ran through the camp that the long inactivity was to cease, and that they were to meet these heinous rebels in open combat; stir and bustle reigned in Honiton and its outlying districts, for, the decision once made, " without further delays or much talk it was done out of hand." [1]

The next morning, a holy day, the Royal forces were early astir and probably assembled in some open space to listen to a brief service after the new fashion, conducted by the Lord Privy Seal's chaplain, Coverdale. He may have used, as appropriate to the occasion, the prayer " for men to say entering into battle," which appeared in a recently printed book of prayers, " set forth with the King's most gracious licence." [2]

---

[1] Hoker, 83.

[2] A copy of "The Psalter or Boke of the Psalmes, 1548," is in the British Museum. The prayer runs as follows : " O Almighty kynge and Lord of hosts, which by thi angels, ther vnto appointed, doest minister both war and peace : and whyche diddest geue vnto Dauid both courage and strength, being but a little one, vnarmed, and vnexpert in feates of war, wyth hys slynge to set vpon, and ouer throw the great huge Goliath : owre cause nowe beynge iuste, and beyng inforced to entre into war and battayle, we moste humbly besech the (O Lord god of hostes) so turne y⁰ hartes of our enemies to the desyre of peace, that no Christē blood be spilte : or els graūt (o lorde) that wᵗ smal effusyō of blood, & to the litle hurte and domage of innocētes, we may to thy glory opteine victori : & that y⁰ wars being sone ended, we may al wᵗ one hart & mind, knit together in cōcord & vnitie, laude & praise the, which lyuest & reignest world wᵗ out ende."

But the service ended, amid the scarcely concealed contempt and impatience of the foreign mercenaries, the advance was begun. The steep street of the little town of Honiton was alive with soldiers, with drums beating, flags flying, trumpets sounding, while shouts and laughter broke forth as they splashed through the ford at the bottom of the hill. Out, by way of the old Roman street, past the ancient leper-houses, but recently restored by Bishop Chard, past the Turk's Head Inn, the army pushed in brave array, eager to meet the foe. When they reach the top of the steep pitch above Deer Park they catch a glimpse of the rebels on the river bank below. They see that the bridges across the Otter are strongly held, for their own outposts have been driven back and the meadows between the branches of the river are occupied by the rebel army.[1]

They can see, too, the little chapel at the bridge-foot, dedicated to St. Anne, near which stand the priests, with uplifted host, preparing to bless the soldiers on the eve of battle. The streaming banner of the Five Wounds, the pyx, and other emblems of their holy cause are in evidence to encourage them to fight for their faith. As the religious procession moves forward the soldiers, with a clatter of arms, sink on bended knee to receive this blessing on their enterprise. The royal soldiers watching the scene from above are much impressed; a sharp indrawn breath indicates the tension of mind of the Englishmen, who but recently had been inspired by a similar awe, many a heart retaining its affection for the

---

[1] Leland, writing a few years previously, describes this spot: "There is a Bridge of Stone by the Ford of Tale, from this Ford of Tale I rode about 2 Miles farther to Veniton Bridge, where Oterey water is divided into 4 Armes by Pollicy to serve Grist and Tukking Milles. Apon 3 of these Streames I roode by fair Stone Bridges. The first Arme of the 4 was the leste and had no Bridge that I marked. On the North side of the first Bridge was a Chapelle now prophanid . . . from Veniton Bridge to Honiton a 2 Mile on the Est Ripe of the Oter River " (III. f. 29). Polwhele says this chapel was profaned by a blacksmith, whose son fell dead suddenly in Ottery churchyard (p. 276).

S

ancient forms and ceremonies: the foreign mercenaries openly cross themselves, muttering a prayer for pardon for taking heretic pay to fight their brethren of the faith.

But a warning of Russell's advance reaches the insurgents, who, turning from their pious devotions, make ready for battle. Well entrenched as they are on the wide-spreading meadows, the bridges strongly guarded, the river flowing, though but a tiny thread, between them and the Royal army, they offer no small difficulty to the Lord Privy Seal, who proceeds to use all "the policies" that he can to entice them from their well-chosen position. But there is nothing for it but to detach a strong company under the Carews, ever ready for active service, to capture the bridge: a bold dash, a rattle of harness, a clash of weapons, and the heavy troopers thrust back the guardians of the bridge, who, picked men though they are, give way before the better trained soldiers, but not without making a brave fight with considerable success against the enemy. One well-aimed arrow finds its mark in Sir Gawen's arm, while others of his company lie wounded or dead. Seeing this success of his advance-guard, Russell follows it up " feerselie " and gives the onset with the rest of his troops, who cross the bridge and deploy into the meadow beyond, while the detachment that had held the bridge falls back on its supporters. Here the fight rages hotly, blow for blow at close quarters, the advantage of hand-guns, bills, and pikes in skilled hands over the bows and arrows is evident, so that at length the rebels are forced to give way and retire towards Exeter.

The Royal troops, having for the moment gained the upper hand, think the victory is clearly with them, and that their enemy is clean gone, so, like all mercenaries, the soldiers, and even the serving-men, give themselves to the spoil, and wholly occupy themselves with stripping the dead and wounded of such treasure in money or weapons as they may have possessed.

But evidently the officer in command at Fenny Bridges as soon as he heard of the approach of Russell's army, sent messengers to Exeter for reinforcements. Therefore, as the straggling remnant of his force retreats in confusion to Fairmile and begins the steep climb up Streteway Hill, breathless and panting, they meet a strong detachment of some 250 sturdy Cornish giants swinging down to their aid. Hearing of the defeat, and rallying all he can, Robert Smyth of St. Germans, who is in command, hastens towards the scene of disaster. At the last turn of the road before reaching Fenny Bridges, he calls a halt and sets his little company in order. Creeping close to the fatal meadow, under cover of the hedges, at a given signal they discharge a flight of arrows, following it with fierce yells and cries as they descend precipitately upon the unsuspecting spoilers. Wholly unprepared and thrown into utter confusion, " being in the middle of their game, and they nothing thinking of any more enemies to be coming towards," they are swept clean off the field by the Cornishmen, leaving dead and wounded in their train as they flee for their lives across the river—indeed, they pay dearly for their wares.

But this triumph is short-lived. Lord Russell's " guyder " sounds his trumpet, the forces in reserve come up, and, putting his men in array, the Lord Privy Seal advances to the rescue. It is no easy matter, " the Cornishmen were very lusty and fresh, and fully bent to fight out the matter." For a time the " conflict is very sharp and cruel," and is renewed again and again with fierce resolution until once more the green meadow is red and the Otter is tinged with blood. But in the end the weight and skill of Russell's troops tell, and the insurgents' arrows are spent. Fresh soldiers come up from Honiton, and presently the Royal standard floats victoriously beside the bridge. Smyth, with his broken remnant, is forced to retire towards Exeter, with his comb cut and showing a fair pair of heels, as Hoker ungenerously puts it. The rebels alone are reputed to have lost three hundred men slain here, and if to these are added the loss of the Royal army, the number is sufficient to give foundation for the legend that Bloody Meadow by Fenny Bridges was ankle-deep in blood.

Not permitting his men to loiter again for the spoil, the Lord Privy Seal pushes his advantage, following the rebels in hot pursuit towards Exeter. But not far— Hoker says three miles: this would bring him to Streteway Head, whence he could see that wide stretch of rolling country to the west, full, he believed, of friends of the insurgent. As he pauses to collect his forces, who found the climb up the long hill anything but child's play, clad in heavy armour and weary with the day's work, there comes dashing up the road Joll, Lord Russell's fool, whom he imagines safely ensconced at Honiton, far from the fighting line.

"My lord, my lord," he cries breathlessly, "the country is up behind you. You will be cut off!"

"How now, Joll. What wild tale is this? 'Tis no time for jests," says the Lord Privy Seal, putting a brave face on it, but secretly not so stout of heart, for he is well aware of the disaffection of the gentlemen, the sympathy of the inhabitants for the rebels, and conscious that he is in an enemy's country.

"The bells ring backwards, my lord. They sound the alarm, the people are rising and mean to attack you from the rear!" is his earnest reply, regardless of his professional duties, and forgetful of the fact that it was a saint's day, so that the church bells rang peacefully for even-song.

A hasty consultation with the officers at hand, a recognition of the dangers environing them, the very fact that a fresh contingent had turned up when least expected, the ease with which a force coming from Ottery St. Mary could debouch upon the high-road between him and his base, his men weary with fighting and pursuit, the surrounding hedges forming ambush for the enemy, the dusk of the summer night giving them the advantage—indeed, there are many reasons to imagine that Joll's tale is true, and though the Carews and others urge an advance, a rapid following up of a successful blow, and an unexpected approach to Exeter, scarce ten miles distant, timid counsels prevail, and Lord Russell gives orders for the Guider to sound the retreat, and with all speed they return to Honiton.

Flushed with victory, the Lord Privy Seal writes despatches to the Council, and also sends off a small boy, his usual messenger, to take the good news to the Mayor in Exeter, promising to advance speedily to the relief of the city.

To-night the boy's task is easy on account of the confusion after the long day's fighting and the pre-occupation of the besiegers discussing events around their camp-fires. These letters—

" the city being then but in a doubtful and dismayed state came in very good season and yet in the end scarcely credited by some men because his coming was not so speedy as looked for." [1]

How the news was received in London we know not, as the correspondence with the Council here fails us.

[1] Hoker, p. 85.

CHAPTER XVII

THE FIGHT AT CAREY'S WINDMILL. THE BATTLE OF CLYST HEATH

"Although in battle many should be slain,
Regard not the pleasure of our mortal corse,
But call to our memory where God sayeth thus
Conforamini in bello : nam vobiscum dominus."

ANCIENT BALLAD.

ALTHOUGH Lord Russell retired to Honiton, he was not destined to stay there much longer : before the week ended the promised reinforcements began to arrive. Lord Grey had sufficiently chastised the rebels of Bucks, Berks, and Oxford, hanging recklessly, even suspending clergy from beams projecting from their church steeples, wreaking a terrible vengeance on his path westward ; now he pressed on to Honiton with a force of nearly one thousand men, including Spinola and his "hagbutters," the two hundred men from Reading under William Grey and a large number of "almayn footmen." Probably about the same moment arrived the advanced portion of Sir William Herbert's contingent, the two thousand men from Wiltshire and Gloucester, for his Welshmen put in an appearance only just in time for the spoil at Exeter a week later. Ordnance and munition were also coming to hand.[1]

[1] Forty-six horsemen were brought direct from Gloucester to Honiton. £30 13s. 4d. were paid on 19th August for their expenses, their "coates" at 4s. each and journey money for 160 miles to and from Honiton. Payments were made for ordnance on 29th and 31st July, sent westward under the Knight Marshal. See P. C. Reg.

" My lord being now of a very good comfort and courage as well for the good success which he had over the enemy and that his long looked [for] supply was come : sendeth his other letters to the Mayor comforting him as also (as before) promising him to be with him very shortly, willing him that he should take but a little patience for a little time." [1]

But the " little time " must have seemed a weary while to his Worship, as practically a week elapsed before the Lord Privy Seal was able to enter the city.

The newly arrived soldiers were " in a great chafe," bewailing their evil luck in not arriving in time to take part in the overthrow and spoil at Fenny Bridges. In order to satisfy this restless element and believing himself at last strong enough to take the offensive, Lord Russell summoned his Council of War and perfected his plans.

On Saturday, the 3rd August, all being in readiness, the Lord Privy Seal set forth in good order from Honiton on his march towards Exeter.

Again the old high-road was the scene of motion and gaiety—prancing horses, jingling armour, martial music accompanied the army in which the swarthy Italians and fair, ruddy Germans now predominated over the English element. The muttered curses of the natives, both soldiers and onlookers, would have been returned with interest in strange foreign oaths. Onward they marched until they reached a small village " whence lay two ways towards Exeter," [2] where they found further

---

[1] Hoker, p. 85. Assuming that the Battle of Fenny Bridges was not before 27th July, the date of the letter from Ottery, and that the first letter was received on 28th July, these other letters would not have been sent until the 30th at the earliest, but Hoker refers to Saturday, 3rd August, as " six days after," which would make their despatch as early as Monday. Unfortunately these letters are not to be found in the Exeter Municipal Archives.

[2] Hayward, p. 62. It is difficult to identify this place from the slender data we have, but at Alfington a road turns southward towards Ottery, from which town they could have gone on by a road which rejoins the highway at Streteway Head or, as they seem to have done eventually, by West

progress barred. The insurgents had thrown up entrenchments of earth, which they had manned with
two thousand men, drawn chiefly from the besiegers of
Exeter. This force they had divided into four companies. One they placed behind the bulwark on the
byway, and supported it by another company in ambush
behind a hedge commanding the road. Another detachment held the entrenchment across the highway, and
was supported by the fourth company, which held the
approach to a neighbouring bridge. This point may
have been near Alfington, a hamlet of Ottery St. Mary.

The Royal army was forced to halt. A reconnaissance
disclosed that these places of vantage were so strongly
held that they could only be taken by assault. For this
purpose Captain Travers was selected, with the " arriere
of the King's forces," [1] to attack one of the " forts,"
while the " vauard and Bataille " assailed the other,
apparently under Spinola, who brought his " shot " to
bear on any head that appeared above the bulwark.

At length Travers successfully captured the entrenchment, driving back its defenders upon their supporters
at the bridge, where together they made a desperate
stand, joined presently by the other two companies,
dislodged from their stronghold. Placing a strong
guard on the bridge they formed up in defensive array
on the level ground beyond. But the bridge was soon
won, and, making profit of the fresh terror, the seasoned
soldiers, the footmen firmly ranked and the horse in
good array, descended upon the seditious in the plain,

Hill, over Aylesbeare Common, to Clyst St. Mary, where they could reach
the Topsham road to Exeter. If this surmise is correct, it would have
been Fenny Bridges which was held. Hayward's words are, " In either
of the bulwarks they lodged one, at the bridge, neere the back of one of
the forts, a third company was placed : the fourth was laid in ambush
behind a hedge on the highway, at the back of the other Fortresse."

[1] Hayward calls him Wavers, but the King says that the attack was
" with the rierward of the horsemen of which Travers was captain." He
was probably the Travers who acted as messenger between the Council
and Russell.

who had "' neither weapons, order, nor counsell, but being in all things unprovided, were slain like beasts," [1] while those who managed to escape fell back and joined their companions.

The way thus cleared, Lord Russell's force passed along the by-way to Ottery St. Mary, and, continuing through that town, drew " over the downs towards Woodbury," [2] by no means an easy march, whichever road they chose. The deep-cut, muddy lanes, where the ordnance would easily get "stogged," in local parlance, with high hedges offering ambush for peasant sharpshooters, the abrupt ascent from the Otter valley trying the strength of both horse and man in their heavy accoutrements, would all have tended to delay the advance of the cumbrous army, so the long shadows would have been stretching across the wide-spread landscape before the camp was pitched on the Common for the night. The Lord Privy Seal fixed his headquarters close to the windmill of Gregory Carey, a prominent landmark on the bleak waste. [3]

But before he had fully determined to spend the night here the swarthy Spinola rode up and respectfully asked leave to speak.

" My lord," he said, " my company of seasoned men, accustomed to the heat, is not tired, though the enemy will think that we, like your levies, require rest, so I would suggest that we should feign to pitch our

[1] Hayward, p. 63.

[2] Hoker, p. 85.

[3] It is usually assumed that this stood upon Woodbury Common, but a glance at the map shows that it was more likely to have been on the high ground now known as Aylesbeare Common, as from the Halfway House the road to Clyst St. Mary bears to the right, leaving Woodbury Common proper on the left. Hoker's words are, " leaving his directe heighe waye draweth over the downes towardes Woodburye and there lodged and pytched that nighte at a Wyndemyll apperteyninge to one Gregorye Carye gentleman." This Carey obtained a grant of Grendale in Woodbury Salterton from Thomas Goodwin in 1546, and was said to have resided near Topsham " or thereabouts " in 1554.

headquarters here, and lead the spies to believe that we are going to sleep, and, instead, if your lordship wishes, we can be with them at daybreak, take them unawares, and defeat them easily."

Lord Russell liked this scheme, so ordered a proclamation to the effect that after their exertions they should rest before he gave battle, well aware that spies would spread this story among the insurgents. Secretly he warned his captains to have their men in readiness for an attack at dawn.[1]

But the rebels, wily on their part, construed the opportunity as in their favour, so, creeping up under cover of the night from Clyst St. Mary, they " made amain unto the Downes, thinking to surprise the General before he was ready," [2]   But, owing to Spinola's scheme, they found him as " vigilant as they were forward," and the alarm from the outposts found the troops in readiness for their own advance.

A fierce combat ensued, raging hottest near the windmill.   Their first attack repulsed, the rebels renewed their efforts again and again, but—

" notwithstanding they were of very stout stomachs and very valiantly did stand to their tackles, yet in the end they were overthrown and the most part of them slain." [3]

Lord Russell's trained men and his horsemen, at last of real service in the open field, again proved conquerors, though not without loss, for " to the strength, force, and resolution of these commons (the archers especially) " witness was borne by some that felt them.[4]   At last the insurgents were forced back on Clyst St. Mary, leaving behind many comrades either dead, dying, or prisoners.[5]

---

[1] This story, told by the Spanish Chronicler, p. 181, is so much in accord with what happened later that it may be accepted as fairly accurate.

[2] Speed's "Chronicle," p. 806.

[3] Hoker, p. 85.

[4] Westcote, p. 231.

[5] This must have been in the early hours of Sunday morning.   Hoker

As the insurgents retired from the hill leaving the Royal troops victorious, orders were issued for the assembly to unite in prayer and praise for the God-given victory, and the rough moor became the setting for a strange scene.

Clustering in their companies, their weapons still red with the blood of their opponents, was the mixed multitude : gentlemen with their servants and tenants levied in the surrounding country, recently devout adherents of the faith they were now called upon to exterminate : dark-browed mercenaries, still nominally papists, who later sought absolution for fighting on the behalf of heretics ; heavy-jowled " almayns," countrymen of Luther, whose protestantism varied much from the newly founded English forms ; all these surrounded by the dead and dying of the recent fight. Above the motley congregation, on some elevation, stood Miles Coverdale, formerly an Augustinian monk who apostatised from his order, and was now a licensed itinerant preacher, acting as chaplain to the Royal forces, and trying to convert the insurgents. His sermon was followed by a general thanksgiving, perhaps a special prayer sanctioned by the Protector, for their recent victory—but in its midst his voice was drowned—the alarm sounded, all was bustle and confusion, " every one to horse and harness again," for the enemy was at hand, having crept up unobserved while the heretics were at their devotions.

The stragglers from the fight of the early morning

makes the march from Honiton, the camping at the Windmill, the attack and the repulse, the sermon and the rally all occur on Saturday ; the advance towards Clyst St. Mary, the retreat, the burning of the town, the battle of Clyst Heath, the slaughter of the prisoners, all on Sunday, but says Monday night was spent at Topsham, not accounting for the day ; undoubtedly they reached Exeter on Tuesday. The division of time suggested above is more rational and avoids the confusion of his narrative, due more to carelessness of expression than to ignorance of events which occurred outside his range of vision.

had fled to Clyst St. Mary, and had reported the ill-success of their attack. Fearing that Lord Russell would advance upon their position, those in command summoned their neighbours in all haste, and despatched flying messengers to Arundell at Exeter, asking for aid. Quickly a force, said to amount to 6000 men, was assembled in the district. And now some companies, bolder or more determined to avenge their comrades, ventured up the hill, expecting to find the Royal army occupied in stripping the dead instead of engaged in religious services.

The skirmish which ensued was soon ended by the withdrawal of the insurgents, but the Lord Privy Seal and his men, instead of returning to their devotions, took up a commanding position whence they could watch the assembly of their opponents in the valley beneath.

The rest of the day and night seem to have passed off without further excursions and alarms, but early the next day Lord Russell, determined not to be caught napping, and " minding to follow in his course, commandeth the trumpet to sound, and every man to make ready to march forwards," so about nine o'clock he set out for Clyst St. Mary, dividing his army into three parts in order to attempt each of the three approaches to the village.

But again the insurgents had prepared entrenchments or rampires to block each road and defended them with men " both ready and resolute to fight." After some " bickering," Sir William Francis,[1] one of the West Country gentlemen who had joined the King's forces, was detailed to advance to give the first adventure,

---

[1] Sir William Francis of Combe Flory, Somerset, and of Frauncis Court, near Killerton, was son of Nicholas Francis of Broadclyst, by Cicely, daughter of Sir William Courtenay of Powderham. He married Mary, daughter of Sir Richard Berkeley. His family held property at Talaton, of which place James Francis, probably a brother of Sir William, was rector in 1536.

which he did with such success that he carried the redoubt, driving the rebels back upon Clyst St. Mary, there to join their comrades to " abide the pulse." [1]

Pleased with this victory, Russell advanced in good order towards the town, when suddenly from their rear came the clear note of a trumpet sounding the advance and the roll of a drum, which caused them to halt. Startled, and remembering recent ambuscades which had threatened to cut them off from their base, and recognising the danger of their situation between hedge-rows, swarming with the enemy, which would make them an easy prey to bold assailants, they were, as Hoker mildly puts it, " amazed," [2] " supposing verily that there had been an ambush behind them to have trapped and enclosed them : whereupon they forthwith retire back in all the haste they may." [3]

But amazement became alarm, and alarm panic—in truth, the Royal troops turned and fled incontinently, the inextricable confusion of men, horses, wagons, and guns in the narrow lane degenerated into a *sauve qui peut*, as with yells and a commingling of English and foreign oaths, they made for the more open ground, never resting until they reached the common whence they came, as if the Devil himself, instead of a band of Papists, was at their heels, leaving their " train " behind them, and doubtless losing many men, either trampled under foot in their hasty flight, or slain by their pursuers.

All this rout was caused by Sir Thomas Pomeroy, one

---

[1] Hoker, p. 86. Bickering = skirmishing. Abide the pulse = await the attack.

[2] Hoker, Brice ed. p. 75. In Hoker (p. 87) the word is "dusshed" from a verb meaning to push violently, to move with velocity. Startled or disturbed seems to cover this meaning.

[3] Hoker, p. 87. Observe that these Royal troops are not represented, as Hoker describes their opponents as running all to cover, or " more like slaves than soldiers furiously run away," as Hayward depicts the rebels, but retiring in all the haste they may, although both writers show that the rout and confusion was for the moment as utter as any that accompanied the retreat of the rebels.

of the chief captains of the rebels, who was hidden in a
" furse close " with a single trumpeter and a drum-slade.
When he had watched the army gaily advance beyond
his hiding-place, he commanded the trumpet to be
sounded and the drum to be striken up.

Taking advantage of this confusion, the insurgents
were soon in hot pursuit, never stopping until they came
to the wagons " then being in the high way ; and which
now by fleeing and retiring of the army are the foremost
and next to the Town." [1]

Here they found not only serviceable ordnance, which
they sadly lacked, having heretofore had but one gun,
taken from a ship at Topsham, and certain portable
artillery from captured forts, but also plenty of loot,
" munition, armour and treasure," most acceptable.

Willing hands quickly dragged all this to Clyst St.
Mary, where they placed the guns in convenient positions
and distributed the shot to be used presently against the
Royal forces.

Lord Russell and his officers were not long in dis-
covering the deception, and were soon hurrying hither
and thither distractedly, endeavouring to reduce chaos
to order, trying to induce the terrified soldiers, by all
means in their power, to return to the attack. Some
time must have elasped before they were brought again
into marching order.

In some way the Lord Privy Seal had learnt that the
houses in Clyst St. Mary were strongly garrisoned with
armed men, so that it would not be possible to pass that
way without great peril and danger, so Sir William
Francis was ordered to approach along a by-way and
set the town on fire.[2]

---

[1] Hoker, p. 87.

[2] In the Holinshed-Brice version of Hoker there is an interpolation,
not in the Guildhall or Bodleian MSS., that the town of Clyst St. Mary,
" notwithstanding it was my Lord's own," was to be burnt. As far as
can be traced, Russell owned nothing in this parish, certainly neither
town nor manor, the latter belonging to the Sokespytch family. In the

Advancing by a deep and narrow road, Sir William, " being in the foreward was foremost and leaving the way which he took before," [1] found himself and his men subjected to a heavy shower of stones, hurled by their enemies from the banks above, doing great injury. One, larger than most, fell with such force upon Sir William's moryon that it was driven down, sticking fast to his head, inflicting a mortal wound, and he fell dying by the roadside. But the bulk of his men pressed on and entered the town. A flaming torch was quickly applied first to one building and then to another as they advanced along the village street, till the timbered houses with their thatched roofs were a mass of flame, and the defenders were driven out like rats from their holes. A second time a conflagration maliciously and of set purpose started by the King's supporters, dealt death and destruction to innocent and guilty alike, while, on the contrary, the insurgents' friend stayed the hand of the alien who threatened to burn Exeter.[2]

An open space in the middle of the town offered a foothold for the insurgents, who there made a brave resistance, fighting to the death in most cases. But the onslaught was fierce and cruel, and though their valour made some impression upon the opposing host, they were overborne and compelled to give way, leaving the Lord Privy Seal victor.

" Cruel and bloody was that day : " writes Hoker, " for some were slain with the sword, some burned in the houses,

margin of the Brice edition is " Bishop's Clist Town set on fire & burnt." The episcopal residence and park of Bishop's Clyst had been leased and afterwards granted to Russell, but such cluster of houses as went with it at Sowton could not even in those days have been close enough to form a stronghold or be readily set on fire in mass and were more than a mile away as the crow flies from the road Russell was pursuing. Every one agrees that the site of the fight was Clyst St. Mary, as appears in the MSS. copies.

[1] Hoker, p. 87.

[2] See Chapters IX. and XIII. for the fires and XIX. for the cruel fate of the merciful vicar.

some shifted for themselves were taken prisoners and many thinking to escape over the water were drowned so that there were dead that day by one and other about a thousand men."

However, Lord Russell's day's work was by no means ended. Although he had captured the town and had given the " overthrow " to the insurgents for the time being, they simply retreated to their next stronghold to make an equally stubborn resistance. Until they were again conquered advance to Exeter was impossible. Again a bridge, over which the road to that city lay, offered a point of vantage. The rebels had strongly fortified it, over-laying it with great trees and timber, behind which barricade they placed some of the captured ordnance, probably under the command of that skilful gunner John Hamon, the alien smith of Woodbury, who had threatened such damage on a previous occasion ; [1] for it is recorded that a gunner, with his piece charged, barred the way.

Lord Russell, finding no one ready to volunteer to lead a forlorn hope against this obstacle, made a proclamation offering a reward of four hundred crowns to any one who would adventure and make way over the bridge. As usual, some one was foolhardy enough to run the risk, who " more respecting the gain than forecasting the peril, gave the adventure." But the gunner rewarded him, and not Lord Russell ; a movement of his hand, a flash, a crash, and, as the smoke rolled away, it became evident that the venturesome man had met his doom. [2]

While all eyes were fixed on this exciting scene, a party under the guidance of John Yard, of Treasbeare,

[1] See Chap. IX.
[2] Hoker had, presumably, some cause for assigning pecuniary gain as the reason that actuated this soldier ; otherwise his self-sacrifice, either in trying to capture the bridge or in creating a diversion, would have called forth admiration rather than something like derision.

who must have been familiar with the district, had made its way to a ford. Following the stream a short distance above the bridge, he led them to a mill,[1] near which the Clyst, ever a shallow stream until it meets the inflowing sea near the bridge and swells with every tide, was easily fordable.

Leading his little company to the rear of the brave men who kept the bridge, one crept stealthily up behind the gunner at the critical moment when, after discharging his piece, he was about to reload it, and slew him. With feverish haste, Yard's followers scattered the defenders and cleared the bridge, casting the trees and timber into the marshy land, and the stream, so that a free passage was made to the open heath beyond.[2]

With the way thus clear, the Royal troops hastened forward, flushed with victory, taking with them all the prisoners captured at the Windmill and in Clyst St. Mary, for the Lord Privy Seal did not intend to return to the Common, but to advance towards Exeter.

As Lord Grey rode up to the highest ground near the middle of the Heath, to make a reconnaissance, he looked back towards the high land of the Common, whence they had come. In the evening light, casting long shadows and magnifying unfamiliar objects, he caught the gleam of the setting sun upon weapons, or fancied that he did. Immediately he jumped to the conclusion that a fresh attack was threatened in their rear, so despatched a warning to Lord Russell who was following.

A hasty consultation was held amid great excitement —they had had two weary days of fighting, they had been startled more than once by excursions and alarms,

---

[1] Cotton and Woollacombe (p. 67) say that a mill still marked the spot in recent days.

[2] This place, called Clyst Heath, is the high ground just above Sandiford Turnpike Gate, now cultivated and planted with trees, but a barren heath within living man's memory (*op. cit.*).

T

no wonder that their nerves were racked, and that they were reduced almost to a terrified condition. Here they were, just arriving at nightfall on a new camping ground, ignorant of their immediate surroundings, but sufficiently aware that dangers of all sorts lurked in the deep-cut lanes around. Above all, should another hasty retreat become necessary, they would be burdened with many prisoners, who would not only encumber their flight, but would turn against their captors. Under these conditions a brutal order was hurriedly issued to the effect that every man should kill his prisoners.

Ere darkness fell the cries for mercy and the screams of those being murdered rang through the fields and lanes, as each soldier butchered his victim—nor age nor youth was regarded, and the shambles thus created made a terrible blot upon the scutcheon of the Royal forces, which even their own historians are forced to admit. One of these excuses the crime, saying that the soldiers, " upon disdain " of the unworthy actions of the insurgents, "filled themselves with revenge and blood, and slew above nine hundred, not sparing one," and comments, " this sad blot abated much the courage of the seditious," but he fails to enlighten us as to what was the particular unworthy action of the rebels.[1]

Hoker slurs over this terrible massacre, and reserves his indignation for the brave Vicar of St. Thomas, who had saved Exeter from burning, but had carried out the sentence of execution against a spy. So can writers with partisan bitterness, especially where religion is concerned, not only view events differently, but can perpetuate in history the more or less venial faults of brave opponents and excuse the crimes of their own people.[2]

[1] Hayward, p. 63.

[2] Froude (V. 184), eager to excuse, goes even further. The slaughter, he suggests, was " a precaution which the peril of so small an army might have seemed to justify." He exonerates Lord Russell, indicating that

Meanwhile, the news of the disaster at Clyst St. Mary was carried with all speed by mounted messengers to the besieging force at Exeter. The danger of the further advance of the Royal army was fully recognised, so strong contingents were hurried down the Topsham road to check their approach. Under cover of night, entrenchments were cast up on the lower side of Clyst Heath, towards the high-road, wherein they placed ordnance brought hastily from the siege of Exeter, while every preparation was made to withstand the brunt of Lord Russell's anticipated attack. All night long the sound of stealthily moving men kept the sentries on the alert, and muffled noises disturbed the slumbers of the wearied soldiers.

At break of day a sudden rain of shot fell in the midst of the sleeping camp, seeming to come from all sides, for the rebels had skilfully planted their guns around the Heath. The roused troops were speedily under arms, preparing to attack their opponents. A hasty conference, a hurried arrangement of plans, and the forces were by " policy " divided into three parts in order to approach and attack the rebels from as many different points. The tramp and shouts of the men, and the jingling of harness, indicated that the troops were falling into line in the places and order assigned. While the bulk of the men are engaging the insurgents, estimated to number two thousand, the sappers and miners of the Royal Engineers are busy making a way of escape over the hedges and through the enclosed ground which lay

Lord Grey alone sanctioned the proceeding. In an obscurely worded note, inaccurate in many details (*e.g.* he states that Hoker was an eye-witness of the slaughter though the Chronicler was at that moment suffering the horrors of the siege), he hints that it was the work of mercenaries in revenge for the hostility shown, he asserts, by the rebels to foreigners : a charge for which he produces no grain of evidence beyond a misquotation of Hoker's phrase that the Burgonians escaped not scot-free. Against Froude's unjustifiable suggestion should be put the complaint of the mercenaries that the English ordered prisoners to be killed instead of holding them to ransom.

between Clyst Heath and the Topsham road. Over this route Lord Russell with a detachment advanced, cutting off the insurgents' chief line of communication with Exeter, and falling upon their rearguard.

Thus thrown into confusion, finding themselves entrapped, attacked both in front and rear, confined much between the hedges, the rebels turned at bay. When called upon to yield, they boldly refused : rather would they fight to the death.

"Valiantly and stoutly they stood to their tackle, and would not give over as long as life or limb lasted, yet in the end they were all overthrown and few or none left alive." [1]

Their courage and bravery was such that their opponents were forced to admire them : from Hoker was wrung this tribute—

"Great was the slaughter and cruel was the fight and such was the valour and stoutness of these men that the Lord Grey reported himself that he never in all the wars he had been did know the like."

This was high praise from one who had been in many a terrible encounter, and completely refutes the charges ignorantly made against the insurgents, who are so often represented as an ill-ordered, cowardly rabble.

Long years after—close on three centuries—the virgin soil of the once desolate heath was turned by the plough, disclosing a vast number of bones, which not only bore witness of the terrible carnage on the spot, but, by the enormous size of many, indicated that the men were of no mean stature, and might well have proved formidable opponents to the King's forces. Here lay all that was mortal of many a brave man who fell fighting desperately in defence of his faith, or was a victim of the cruel massacre of the previous day. Let us accept rather the words of admiration wrung from the accomplished

---

[1] Hoker, p. 89.

soldier, Lord Grey, than the partisan account of Hayward, penned less than a century after the event.

" Now the seditious, driven almost to dead despair and supported only by the vehemency of desire, brought forth their forces to Cliston Heath, to whom many of the most vile resorted hourly, which much enlarged their numbers, but nothing their strength. . . . [1] The Lord Grey encouraged his men to set sharply upon the vulgar villains, good neither to live peaceably, nor to fight, and to win at once both quiet to the Realm, and to themselves glory. So he brought the King's forces upon them rather as to a carnage, than to a fight, insomuch as without any great either loss or danger to themselves, the greatest part of the seditious were slain." [2]

And so the evening shadows fell upon the bloody scene, the victors weary with the fight and the victims lying dead. The Royal forces drew off towards Topsham, about a mile distant, bearing in a horse litter the dead body of the brave Sir William Francis.[3] In that town they were quartered for the night, while the news of the terrible encounter at Clyst Heath was brought to the investing army at Exeter.[4]

[1] Holinshed admits that they fought " very stoutlie and gaue it not ouer for a little, and although they were thus driuen to giue place at their first onset yet they got togither againe, and aboad a new charge, defending their ground, & dooing what they could to beat backe and repell those that came to assaile them " (p. 925).

[2] Hayward, p. 63.

[3] He was afterwards interred with honours in Exeter Cathedral.

[4] It is stated in Kelly's Directory that *Sir* William Winslade was hung in a lane near here—perhaps a legend to account for the name of an estate in Clyst St. Mary called Winslade. Both father and son survived this fight.

CHAPTER XVIII

" Learn to be noble by Exeter, whose truth doth not only deserve long
praises, but also great reward."—SIR JOHN CHEKE.

THE news of the awful carnage at Clyst Heath, the loss
of such a vast number of fighting men in one day, struck
consternation to the hearts of Humphrey Arundell and
his host.

Unable to defend the roads from London and from
Bristol, and now with the Topsham road in the hands of
the enemy, he felt himself almost powerless.   By the
London road reinforcements were streaming, more of
Sir William Herbert's 10,000 ; from Bristol way poured
the fierce Welshmen, and now Lord Russell, with the
flower of the army, flushed with victory, was approaching
from the south.   Black despair descended upon Arundell,
his opportunity had slipped through his fingers, it was
useless´ to try to contain Exeter any longer.   The
terrible reduction of his army, the loss at Clyst Heath
of most of the guns he had possessed, combined with the
overwhelming character of the recent disasters and the
hopelessness of retrieving his fortunes, all shook his
determination and left their mark on his haggard face
as he presided over a hastily summoned Council of War.

It needed braver councillors than the mayors of
Cornish towns peasant leaders from Sampford Courtenay,
drawn as they were from a class accustomed to follow the
great landowners of whom they stood in awe, and of

fanatic priests with no experience of warfare, to put courage into even a greater general commanding more skilful troops. Panic entirely ruled the Council, the voices of the gentlemen who advised further resistance were drowned, and all, even Arundell, were forced to admit that discretion was the better part of valour. The western roads still lay open to them, and the majority clamoured for a retreat in that direction—and prevailed.

So the word went forth. Silently, so silently that the watchers within the city were unaware of their movements, they raised their camps and dispersed their companies along the three roads leading west—towards their homes. Before midnight their camp was desolate.

The prisoners confined in St. Sidwell's tower, finding themselves no longer closely guarded, succeeded in escaping from the building. A loud pounding at the East-gate roused the warders, who were inclined to be sceptical, fearing some new ruse of the enemy. But when the gentlemen had convinced the guard, they were led straightway to the Mayor, who forthwith spread the news—

" the joy and comfort whereof was so great and the desire of fresh victuals so much pierced [them] that many not abiding till the daylight gat and shifted themselves out of the gates but more for victual than for spoil," apologises Hoker, " and yet they were glad of both : howbeit, some did not long enjoy the same, for many being more greedy for meat than measureable in feeding did so overcharge themselves in surfeiting that they died thereof." [1]

Amid the excitement and the orgies of the gluttonous, it would seem that no immediate steps were taken to inform the Lord Privy Seal of the insurgents' movements ; it is possible, though not probable, that they were ignorant of his exact whereabouts. Be that as it may,

[1] Hoker, p. 89.

Lord Russell, anticipating possible delay by further
encounters, had determined to be early afoot and to
start on his advance towards Exeter, his scouts probably
reporting that the road was, to all appearances, clear.
So, on the summer morning of Tuesday, the 6th August,
he " commanded the trumpets very early to sound, and
every man to make ready and to prepare a way." [1]

As he advanced unopposed, he would have met
messengers bearing the good news of the raising of the
siege. Pausing only to dress his forces, in order to
present a better appearance, he pushed on rapidly along
the Topsham road. The watching eyes, gleaming from
cavernous hollows in the white faces of the citizens who
were perched on every available point of vantage on that
side of the city, sought eagerly for the advance-guard of
their deliverers, whom those of the new faith and of the
old alike were ready to hail with joy.

The long period of anxiety and suffering was at an
end, the strain on those of the besieged whose sympathies
were with their co-religionists would now be relieved, so
that they were ready to join with their comrades in
acclaiming the Royal host. The arrival of Lord Russell
was—

" to the joy and comfort of the long captivated citizens who were
[no] more glad of their delivery than was his Lo(rdship) and
all good subjects joyful of his.victory." [2]

It was still early, about eight o'clock, when the sounds
of trumpets and drums warned the citizens of the
approach of the Lord Privy Seal's army, and every eye
was strained to see the victors. There rode the gallant
Carews in full armour mounted on their war-horses at
the head of their servants and tenantry, clad in the
heraldic colours of their house, black and yellow ; there
were the Royal infantry, in their brilliant livery, their
coats blue " guarded " with red, their trunk-hose with

[1] Hoker, p. 89.   [2] *Ibid.* 90.

the right leg red and the left blue ; the Almayn soldiers under Jermigny and Sanga, with long bills and staves, the Italian and Spanish arquebusiers under Spinola, with their richly chased, wheel-lock guns a-gleam ; the horsemen under Lord Grey, the men in armour and the heavy steeds almost hidden under housings and trappings ; the captured guns and wagons trailing far behind, all stained and soiled with their recent fights, while in contrast, bright and beautiful, the Royal Standard, bearing the Tudor Red Dragon, fluttered in the summer breeze in their midst, above the Lord Privy Seal, the King's Lord Lieutenant in the West Parts, and his personal retinue.[1]

Lost for a moment in the valley at the bottom of the Hollow-way, the picturesque procession soon turned the corner by the " Valiant Soldier," an inn even at that period, and passed over the waste ground to Southernhay, amid the cheers and sobs of the joyful citizens.

At this moment a messenger from the Mayor advanced in haste to Lord Russell's *aide-de-camp*, a momentary halt was called, and the sharp word of command rang out, passing from front to rear, for the Mayor had besought the Lord Privy Seal not to bring his men inside the city for it " was altogether unfurnished of victuals." So the serried ranks deployed into the open fields outside the walls, and proceeded to pitch their camp. Lord Russell's headquarters were established in St. John's Fields, close to Southernhay, and the Royal Standard was firmly planted upon the walls by the side of the postern-gate of Bedford House.[2]

No sooner had the Lord Privy Seal entered his tent than " the Mayor and all his brethren in most seemly

---

[1] Cf. Cotton and Woollacombe, p. 69.

[2] The Russell residence is given great prominence in the early pictorial maps of Exeter, appearing to be a circular or octagonal building, with a crenelated front containing a large entrance archway. Before this is a walled enclosure, while large open fields stretch behind it to the city walls.

and decent order went unto him," [1] the Mayor in all the gorgeousness of his official robes, the aldermen in murrey gowns with chains of office and all the pomp and panoply of state. Lord Russell most lovingly embraced them, most thankfully accepted them, and most highly commended them for their truth, duty, and service, and promised on his fidelity and honour that these would be well considered by his Majesty.

We could wish that Hoker, now literally " testis oculatus " amid the civic authorities, had given us further details of that scene and the speeches, but we may be sure that Lord Russell was no whit behindhand in his display of robes and insignia befitting the King's representative and the Lieutenant in the West Parts, and that his florid speech of thanks made in this gorgeous setting, had its counterpart in a portentously long and stilted protestation of devotion presented on behalf of the municipal authorities, which those present would have heard with as much patience as they could muster, while they longed to refresh their starved bodies at the banquet which followed, a natural sequence, though no record of it has reached us.

For three days the gates were kept shut, after which there was an official entry of the Royal host in great state, followed by a formal entertainment of Lord Russell, though the latter is unmentioned by Hoker, but reference to the " entrie " and other events occur in certain depositions of Exonians a few years later, indicating that great confusion and disorder existed on that occasion. [2]

Immediately after the Lord Privy Seal's arrival

" Sir William Herbert, then Master of the horses and after the Earl of Pembroke, [3] came with a thousand Welshmen : who,

---

[1] Hoker, p. 90.

[2] See the " Inventories of Church Goods of 1552," Appendix M.

[3] " Master of the King's Horse, and after Earl of Pembroke," according to the Brice edition.

though they came too late to the fray, yet soon enough to the play, and too soon, as some thought, for in spoiling they were so cruel as most insaciable ; [1] how be it in this they were very courteous, for what they could not carry with them they were contented to leave behind them, and what they sold (as they came by it easily) so they sold it cheap and very reasonably.[2] And by their special industry the city within two or three days was fraughted and furnished with cattle and victuals plentifully." [3]

Thus wrote Hoker bitterly, but after the first flush of indignation had passed he modified his statement, and added that the whole country was put to the spoil, and that every soldier fought for his own profit, piously concluding, " A just plague of the Lord upon the rebels and disloyal persons." [4]

But the injury done by the Welshmen was not wholly confined to their opponents. The inventory of St. Stephen's Church preserves a picturesque tale which is here quoted at length. There is mentioned among the missing articles—

" a chalice weighing by estimation xv ounces [which] was taken from the clerk of the said parish in the commotion time after the entering of the right honorable John Earl of Bedford lieutenant of the King's Majesty's army in the West parts by a Welshman, who came into the Church and locked the said clerk in the same Church the same time." [5]

---

[1] Taffy's ancient characteristic is here hinted at. The Brice edition modifies this to, "But the city being as yet altogether destitute of victuals, and the Welshmen at their first coming seeing the same, they did by their special industry and travails fraught and furnish the same within two days with corn, cattle and victuals, very plentifully, to the great relief and comfort of the people therein, and to the benefit of themselves " (p. 81).

[2] " They came soone enough to the spoiles, who in that point were verie cruell & insaciable," according to the Bodleian version (f. 13).

[3] Hoker, p. 90.

[4] Brice ed. p. 81.

[5] Exeter Mun. Arch. Another document in the same place has it, " a chalice weighing by estimation xv oz. or thereabout was taken from the said church in the commotion time after my lord of Bedford came in to the city by a Welshman who went in to the church and locked the clerk in the church . . . and went away with the chalice."

Nor were the depredations committed by Welshmen only ; occasionally plate disappeared from the custody of the parishioners to whom it had been entrusted for safe-keeping. One such person records that he had hidden the treasure in his garden, whence it was stolen at the time of Russell's entry,[1] while two others reported that, having heard that the rebels were shifting the plate and jewels belonging to St. Edmund on the Bridge from house to house, immediately upon the opening of the gates, they sallied out and captured it, dividing the spoil between them.[2] A third party, who, it was said, had received a chalice from the clerk of St. Edmund's, denied it, but admitted that he had found a chalice under his bed at the Commotion time at the coming of the King's army, which he gave to John Cove, of his own parish, St. Thomas beyond Exe Bridge, and the priest there " did mass with it." [3]

But the worst case seems to have been that of St. Sidwell's—

" In the commotion time the Church was spoiled of all things moveable in a manner save only a pix, a paten and two cruets, and four bells whereof one Bernard Duffield took three away which he hath not restored neither can we tell where he have them." [4]

The story, as told by various witnesses and the Churchwardens' records, is that Walter Ralegh, Edward Saintbarbe and John Stowell, with others of their company, perhaps all prisoners in St. Sidwell's tower, had taken possession of a large quantity of the Church-goods, which they proceeded to place in Stowell's house, these included a cross, a chalice, a ship, a censer, etc., of silver, beside two burdens of stuff. William Slocom,

[1] Notes and Gleanings, V. 87. St. Pancras.
[2] *Ibid.* 105.
[3] Exeter Mun. Arch.
[4] *Ibid.*

one of the parishioners, also deposed that he had had possession of a chalice of silver-gilt, weighing twenty ounces, which he handed to Richard Lake, servant to Anthony Hervey, and the " fair foot " of a silver cross weighing forty ounces, which he gave to Thomas Chapel on the day of Lord Russell's entry. This was afterwards taken by John Buller and Richard Wallys, sometime captain and porter respectively of the East-gate, from whom it passed to Sir Roger Bluett. But the parishioners failed to regain it for some time, as they could not " come by " Sir Roger. They also applied to Walter Ralegh for a cloth of tissue, apparently while the Commissioners were sitting in the Cathedral, and were met by the cool reply that they should have it " if it were not cut already for the sparver of a bed." [1] Mr. Anthony Harvey's servant gave a different story of how the chalice came into his possession. As he was destitute at the time of the Commotions he had sallied forth and had captured it from the rebels by virtue of a proclamation.[2]

Other Churchwardens reported that their Church-goods had been sold either for soldiers' wages, for the relief of the poor, or for repairing their buildings, which

---

[1] Sparver = tester. A note, added in a later hand, records that this cloth they "gat out of Mr. Rawley's hands," the foot of the cross from Sir Roger and the bells from Duffield.

[2] No doubt reference is made to the proclamation of 11th July. See Appendix J. Bernard Duffield, beside the three bells of St. Sidwell's, took by force " in the Commotion time a silver cross valued at £27 that had belonged to the parish of Heavitree but which had been deposited with John Coker of Exeter." The hopelessness of its recovery is suggested by the comment that " Duffield remaineth in the King's Majesty's Bench for debt." (Hoker does not quote Duffield's imprisonment as a just judgment as he did that of Richard Taylor. See Chapter XII.) Duffield was also imprisoned in the Fleet, as appears from an order from the Privy Council to the Warden of that prison, written 4th December, 1551, to "deliver Duffyld this night unto the Lord Privie Seal" (P.C. Reg. III. 433). John Stowell, mentioned above, also took away in the Commotion time the best part of the Church-goods of Dawlish. In spite of these ill-gotten gains, he left his wife a " very poor woman," so the recovery of their value was out of the question.

had been damaged in the Commotion time, so it is evident that the stripping of the churches was not done by the rebels, as suggested by the Privy Council.[1]

Lord Russell, as soon as a quiet moment was allowed him, wrote a full description of his doings, having already notified the Council of the successful encounter with the rebels at Carey's Windmill, and having also promptly sent off[2] some brief account of events, as we find the Council writing on the 10th August, of " this success the Almighty God by your travail hath sent the King's Majesty."[3]

But the messenger bearing this communication as he left London for the West must have met Captain Travers, travel-stained and weary, approaching the City bearing his Lordship's despatches of the 7th August, to which the Council sent a reply, also dated the 10th.[4]

In his first letter Russell had told of the capture of Sir Thomas Pomeroy, and had asked for his pardon, which the Council were willing should be granted if Russell thought good, but they suggested that he should prove his loyalty and earn his pardon by capturing the ringleaders of the rebellion. This scheme should, however, be kept a secret, and he must be called upon to abjure publicly his Popish errors so that such as have been seduced in religion by him, he having allured them by blind superstition and papistry, might be brought by his " travail to knowledge " their duties and true

---

[1] The St. David's Churchwardens reported that " at the Commotion time our church was robbed and toke all from us and that (which is) now in the church was brought of a new." This is the only instance where the robbers are unspecified, so they *may* have been rebels.

[2] The Council rewarded Michael Hanis or Hams, [incorrectly printed Michaelmas in Dasents P.C. Reg.] of Cornwall on 6th August, with £20 ; this generosity may indicate their pleasure at this news.

[3] Pet. MSS. 447, Pk. p. 47.

[4] The gallant captain may have had a personal audience of the young King, as in Edward's Journal he refers to Travers's attack on the barricade, and makes other references which suggest that he had heard the story from an eye-witness.

religion. Russell was also particularly instructed to cause inquiry to be made in all places—

" as for papists for mass books of the old superstitious service and cause them to be burnt, [presumably the mass-books, not the papists] giving order that people do use the service appointed by his Majesty and that the gentlemen and Justices of Peace have continually a good eye to see the same executed accordingly." [1]

The rest of their letter was devoted to explaining the urgent necessity of reducing the number of men in his army, not only for economy, but because of the ill news of the threatened French invasion which required their presence elsewhere.

But a different tone—one of elation—pervades their reply to his letter telling of the relief of Exeter, supplemented as it was by Mr. Travers's " credit "—

" by the which, like as we do at good length well understand your wise doings and the good and honorable success it hath pleased God to grant you against those rebels So have we thought good to give your Lordship the King's Majesty's and our most hearty thanks for the same, nothing doubting but as the journey is presently much to your commendation and honor, so shall the remembrance thereof so remain in the King's Majesty as you shall have good cause to rejoice of these your travails and labour employed at this time." [2]

Thanks were also sent to Lord Grey and " sundry other gentlemen," with promises that the King would not fail to minister such " consideration thereof as shall be to all their comforts." Particularly was he to thank

" Mr. Bluet, the gentlemen, Mayor and others within the city of Exeter through whose pains, wisdom, and good courage that city hath very honestly preserved themselves against the said rebels, and thereby declared their good affection to his Majesty, which you may well assure them shall be considered

[1] Pet. MS. 448, Pk. p. 49. [2] Ibid. 449, Pk. p. 50.

towards every of them in any reasonable suits hereafter as shall be to their comforts." [1]

From a further communication of the same date it would seem that Lord Russell had had some difficulty with the multitude of his Councillors, and that he desired explicit instructions as to who should form his official staff. In reply the Council, after commenting on the fact that Sir William Herbert and a great number of gentlemen were with him amongst whom—

" there be many which for their wisdoms experience and other good qualities be worthy to be of his Majesty's council with you for his Highness' affairs there : Yet considering that the having of many councillors shall not only be troublous to them that be called but also may breed a confusion in the affairs "

appointed the following :—Lord Grey, Sir William Herbert, Sir John Paulet, Sir Hugh Paulet, Sir Andrew Dudley, and Sir Thomas Speke.[2]

Another letter, written the following day, by Somerset alone, evidently in reply to a communication from Russell, throws a little further light on events in the West. Among other things, it appears that the Lord Privy Seal had made a proclamation, a copy of which his secretary promised, but failed to enclose. He reported also, that the men about Exeter came in readily to obtain their pardon, that one Drue proposed bringing in his own brother, that Robert Paget had been captured, and he desired instructions as to what should be done with the latter.[3]

As Paget was manifestly known, replied Somerset, to have been " an head Captain of rebellion," in spite of

---

[1] Pet. MS. 450, Pk. p. 51.

[2] Ibid. 450ᵈ, Pk. p. 52.

[3] Ibid. 451. Pocock (p. 53) reads the name in this letter Orme, but it is Drue. There was an Edward Drew, a rather wild young blade, who does not appear in the pedigree of Drew of Killerton, but who seems to have been brother of John Drew of St. Leonard's, Exeter.

the fact that some would think that favour should be shown him for the sake of his brother, Sir William Paget, yet in the case of

" such treason and rebellion as this, it behoveth us most of all to show indifferent justice, and especially considering that we have not spared our own brother in matter concerning the damage of the King's Majesty's person and high treason, as our duty was, it should much import if we should spare any other man's brother. And therefore in no wise we would ye should in this case show any other favour than as direct justice appertaineth, and so proceed to him with the rest."

In a postscript, Somerset endeavours to make his purpose concerning Paget more clear, adding—

" if he be indeed and have declared himself a chieftain leader or captain of sedition, then he is either to have according to justice as reason is. If he have not been a notable stirrer or ringleader, then you to use the thing according to your discretion."

Somerset also writes that he would gladly hear of

" Humphrey Arundell's doings and demeanour, and how ye shall demean yourself with him, whom we trust shortly ye shall have in your hands. Whome and Winceslo and Underhill, (it is for the King's Majesty's honour not to escape due punishment) but that their example should be a terror this great while to all the country and not to attempt such kind of rebellion again."[1]

Russell's execution of some of the ringleaders already captured is praised, and their names and number desired. Unfortunately, no list of these has been discovered. It is also mentioned that Exeter had been requested to supply Russell with money.[2]

---

[1] Pet. MS. 452, Pk. p. 54. It is not quite clear what Somerset meant in this last paragraph. Wynceslo is, of course, intended for Wynslade : Whome may mean Holmes or it may refer back to Arundell, while the brackets spoil the sense.

[2] The city seems to have responded gallantly to this appeal, advancing £1000, as we find this entry, " Mr. Peckham had warrant for m^{li} to the

U

As to men, Somerset was " afraid that the multitude
and number " that he already had would hinder him, and
that he would not be able to provide them with victuals,
therefore he was again admonished to " demysse of "
his number, particularly those of Somerset and Dorset,
who were required for the defence of their counties
against the French.   If Russell could not pay them they
were to leave one or two men for each company to
receive the money due to all.   Instructions for reducing
expenses are given in detail, practically repeating the
Council's orders of the 10th August.

Again the absence of Lord Russell's despatches is to
be deplored, for the names of the captured and executed
ringleaders at this period are not obtainable from any
source, even the municipal records of Exeter.

Mayour of Excester, by him lent to the Lord Privy Seal, Lieutenant of
the army against the rebelles."   It was rather unkind to borrow so large a
sum from the impoverished city before it had recovered from the effects
of the siege.   See P. C. Reg. (Dasent) II. 318.

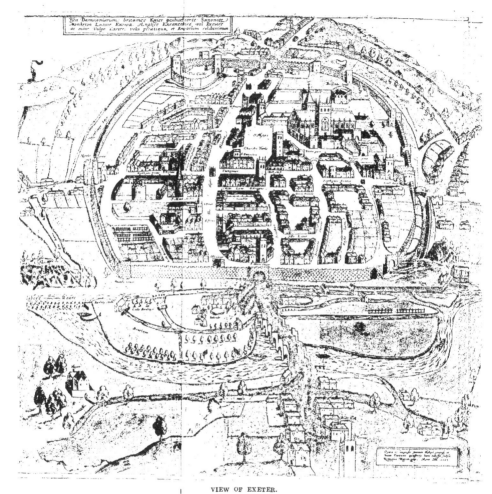

VIEW OF EXETER.

From an Engraving by R. Hogenberg in the British Museum.

CHAPTER XIX

THE BATTLE OF SAMPFORD COURTENAY. THE CAPTURE OF THE RINGLEADERS

" For us it is better in battle for to die,
  and of oure mortal lives make conclusion,
Than heresies extremely to reign with tyranny,
  the nobility of the realm brought to confusion.
                                    ANCIENT BALLAD.

LORD RUSSELL, instead of following up his advantage and dealing a final blow to his enemies, remained in Exeter for ten or twelve days, where he occupied himself in " setting all things in good order rewarding the good and punishing the evil." [1]

He distributed, it is said, the lands of the ringleaders to the two Carews and to William Gibbs, gifts confirmed by the King later by letters patent.

" To many others which had done good services he gave prisoners, both the bodies, goods and lands," which caused complications, ending in a sharp reprimand from the Council.

Nor did he confine himself to acts of generosity with other people's property, for—

" on the other side he commanded forches and gallows to be set up in sundry places as well within the city as also in the country and did command and cause many to be executed and put to death, especially such as were noted to be chief doers and busy ringleaders in this rebellion."

[1] Hoker (p. 91) gives twelve days, but a careful reckoning indicates the former number.

Nor were his actions and those of his deputies in this particular above criticism on Hoker's own evidence, for the chronicler proceeds to give an account of the exceptionally brutal and disgraceful execution of the Vicar of St. Thomas by Exbridge, Robert Welsh, the man who had prevented the destruction of the city by fire, but who had carried out a sentence of a court martial as already described on page 207.

Whether on this occasion the priest was even allowed the form of trial does not appear. His actual execution was entrusted to Bernard Duffield, the turbulent servant of Lord Russell,[1] whose recorded misdemeanours prove him to have been lacking in most virtues. To such a man, probably because he was in the employ of the victorious general, and perhaps that he might wreak some private vengeance, Welsh was committed, and he was " nothing slack to follow his commission."

It is best to quote Hoker's own account at length, that there may be no suspicion that partisanship exaggerates the facts of the case. Bernard Duffield—

" caused a pair of gallows to be made and to be set up upon the top of the Tower of the said vicar's parish church of St. Thomas and all things being ready and the stage perfected for the tragedy the vicar was brought to the place and by a rope about his middle drawn up to the top of the tower and there in chains hanged in his popish apparel and having a holy-water bucket, a sprinkle, a sacring bell, a pair of beads and such other popish trash hanged about him and there he with the same about him remained a long time. He made a very small or no confession but very patiently took his death ; he had been a good member in his commonwealth had not the weeds overgrown the good corn and his foul vices overcomed his virtues." [2]

These " foul vices " are not mentioned, though

---

[1] It was Duffield who had to be locked up to prevent his sallies from the besieged city, who took possession of the bells of St. Sidwells and seized other Church goods and was afterwards imprisoned for debt.

[2] Jenkyns states that the body remained on the gibbet until the restoration of popery in the reign of Mary (Hist, Ex. ed. 1841, p. 119, n.).

Hoker, had he been able to supply any particulars, would have introduced them to palliate the brutality of the execution. Such words could not well be applied to a simple-hearted devotion to the faith in which he had been nurtured, and which he refused to relinquish at the behest of the Councillors who ruled the young King. By insinuation Hoker charges him with ingratitude, but the historian is in error in saying that Welsh was " preferred and presented " to the benefice of St. Thomas by Lord Russell, the patron, as he was presented by the Abbot and Convent of Tavistock, in March, 1537, the then Patrons—Russell did not obtain this advowson until two years later, when he had a grant of the Abbey estates.[1]

There is no reason to suppose that the Lord Privy Seal disapproved of this tragedy enacted by his servant, for to judge by his record, especially the callous brutality displayed at the execution of the Abbot of Glastonbury, he was ever ready to use the sternest and most awe-inspiring methods with those with whom he had to deal. Nor would this execution have made any impression upon Lord Grey and his followers, from whose book Duffield simply took a leaf, as they had just left behind them in Oxfordshire similar grim records of their visit in poor clergymen dangling from beams thrust out from their own church towers.[2]

Hoker comments that Lord Russell—

" was very severe and sharp against such offenders as were chief and principal ringleaders of this rebellion, but against

---

[1] Welsh was born at Penryn, Cornwall, of " good honest parentage." Hoker gives his three chief crimes as : (1) he not only persuaded the people to condemn the reformed religion and to observe the popish religion, but did erect keep and use the same in his parish church ; (2) he was an Arch-captain and prime-mover in the rebellion, and (3) he executed the spy and firebrand Kingwell.

[2] Henry VIII. in 1536 commanded that the chief monks who took part in that rebellion " should be hanged on long pieces of timber out of the steeples."

the common sort who were led and carried, and who did humble themselves, he was pitiful and merciful and did daily pardon infinite numbers."

In so doing he followed out to the letter the Protector's instructions—

" so we pray you that sparing the common and mean men ye execute the head and chief stirrers of the rebellion : And that in so diverse places as ye may to the more terror of the unruly."

But during this period Russell's pen was not idle : he not only undertook to set the district in order, but distributed letters of thanks as well as other favours.   He suggested the knighting of several persons, including the Mayor, he forwarded a petition for the " relief of sheep," and laid before the Council the " Clothiers' case." [1]   He also wrote a letter to the municipal authorities and the gentlemen who had helped them to hold the city, which was calculated to strengthen their hands in levying contributions from recalcitrant citizens.   He had been credibly informed, he writes, that the defence of the city had been very chargeable, and that some of the citizens—

" for some sinister affections they had in this cause, being a great many of them of good wealth and substance, have not only refused to be partakers of the charges, but also have withdrawn themselves from doing service at such times as the same was most needful both for the defence of the city and the safety of themselves,"

so he desired that there should be summoned such as had so demeaned themselves or of whose slackness information had been received, and that orders should be given that they should be compelled to contribute with the rest, those who had failed to serve being more heavily mulcted. [2]

[1] See Pet. MSS. 456 and 461, Pk. p. 61, 67.
[2] Ex. Muni. Let. No. 21

Nor was his correspondence with the Council neglected. Again he asked for more men and money— one thousand men to be sent by sea to " land at the backs of the rebels," and he complained of the difficulty experienced in obtaining provisions, etc. While the Council on their part urged him to dismiss his horsemen, who were the most expensive of the soldiers, and whom they required elsewhere ; as for ships to convey the thousand men, all were employed to prevent the threatened French invasion : as for provisions, the rebels had levied on the country successfully and he ought to do the same in order to punish their sympathisers, forgetting that the district had been clean picked by the former, and that the hungry mouths at Exeter clamoured for food. " All shift possible must be made to furnish yourself there of that ye may," while almost in the next breath they reprove him for not *staying* the soldiers in the King's pay from going to the spoil. He must diminish his forces not only because of the food-question, but because they were urgently wanted elsewhere. The Council enter fully into the troubles in Norfolk, in the North, and with the French, so that he may be aware of the course of events. They also warn him not to issue a proclamation of general pardon, as some ringleaders still uncaptured might benefit thereby ; he should promise to ask the Council for such a proclamation ; so, too, the " relief of sheep " must be deferred, but he should assure the people that he has no authority to deal in the matter, but that he might lay their humble suits before the Council provided " they become again good subjects and leave immediately this their evil lives," and return to their allegiance, in which case he " dare presume so far of the King's Majesty's goodness for them that ye will adventure so much of your own lands as may pay the matter for them if it be not obtained." As for the clothier's case, these men should be held even shorter than other rebels, considering—

" how generally by their ' malignimity ' at the relief putting away of their workmen, yea and privy incensing and encouragement, this spark of rebellion took the kindling to come to so great a flame." [1]

But, above all, they reiterated the importance of following up his success against the rebels by a crushing blow, in spite of the lack of funds urged as his excuse and which they relieved to the extent of £6000, telling him to husband it carefully. They begged him to make some good end to his well-begun victory with speed—

" for if you shall suffer those rebels to breathe, to catch a pride by your somewhat forebearing to follow them, and winning time so to gather strong upon you, you shall not do that with a great number that taken in time you might have done with a much fewer : at the first they were in some dismay, and then one of your men being in array was worth three of the rebels, sythens by some liberty to gather they may take new stomachs, wax desperate and strengthen themselves against you : yea, peradventure they may so take commodity to get some port whereby both to weaken you much and so withal give an entry by their desperation and malice to foreign enemies to hold it, and to force the inhabitants at such ports to take part also expressly against you." [2]

This warning was not unwarranted. Hoker says that Russell believed that all things were now quieted, and the rebels pacified, so he lingered in Exeter,[3] but in reality the insurgents had occupied the intervening days in rallying their forces.

As we have said, they left Exeter by the western roads, either towards Plymouth by the coast, or across the Moor by way of Crediton, or by the Exe valley towards the Bristol Channel.

But a considerable body under Arundell collected at Sampford Courtenay, the scene of the first rising in

[1] See Pet. MSS. 460, Pk. p. 67.
[2] *Ibid.* 453[4], Pk. p. 57.
[3] Hoker, p. 94.

Devon.   News was suddenly brought to the Lord Privy
Seal of this assembly, and that both the men of Devon
and Cornwall were—

"fully bent to maintain their quarrel and to abide the battle.
This news so troubled and tickled my Lord that all business set
apart he commandeth forthwith the trumpet to be sounded
and the drum to be striken up and all his army forthwith to be
mustered which was then the greater by reason of the Welshmen and of the gentlemen of the country and of the commoners
who upon submission had obtained pardon and increased to
the number of eight or ten thousand men and forthwith he
marcheth towards Sampford Courtenay." [1]

This startling information reached him on Friday,
the 16th August, but by the time that his men were
ready to march it was so late in the day that they could
only advance as far as Crediton, seven miles, the way
being "verie comberous," [2] and there bivouacked for
the night.

But on Saturday morning they were early afoot, and
cautiously made their way towards the rebels' camp at
Sampford Courtenay.   In the narrow roads which they
had to traverse Russell's scouts soon encountered the
enemy.   A skirmish ensued, in which the insurgent
leader Maunder was captured.   The noise of the fray
and the return of their comrades gave warning to the
rebels, who were strongly entrenched in a place of vantage
just outside the town.   Lord Grey and Sir William
Herbert, the latter at his own request, having been
granted the "foreward" [3] for that day were thrown
forward by Lord Russell, with a considerable detachment under their command—

---

[1] *Ibid.* Tickled = worried.   In the Bodleian version Hoker says that
with the coming of Sir William Herbert and his Welshmen and the gentlemen who resorted unto him as well as the commoners who had yielded
and received pardon, his army amounted to "above seauen or 8000 persons."

[2] Russell's "Despatch," Galb. B. XII. f. 1136.

[3] Hoker, Brice ed. p. 86.

" for the winning of time and to make with all diligence
possible towards the said camp to perceive and see what
service might be done for the invasion thereof." [1]

Advancing with their guns, these officers engaged the
enemy, firing upon the camp from a safe distance, to
which the insurgents replied with their artillery. Meanwhile the pioneers and miners were engaged in making
a better way of approach over which the main body
soon were able to advance.

A band of footmen were detached to make the assault
on the entrenchment from one side, while the Italian
harquebutters assailed it on the other. The two attacks
were made with such violence that the rebels were forced
to evacuate their position, falling back upon the town,
which they had strongly fortified.

But they had no intention of acting only on the
defensive. The Lord Privy Seal with the rest of his
force, and the heavy train were still far behind when a
sudden attack was made on the rear of the soldiers
engaged in storming the camp. This was executed by
a large contingent of the rebels under Humphrey
Arundell himself.

Surprised by this sudden charge at their backs, the
Royal troops were thrown into confusion. This attack
" wrought such fear in the hearts of our men," writes
Lord Russell, " as we wished our power a great deal
more not without good cause."

Leaving Sir William Herbert to continue the enterprise against the camp, Lord Grey rallied the rearguard,
both horse and foot, turning their faces towards the new
enemy in show of battle, and bringing such ordnance
as they had to bear upon their assailants.

For an hour the battle raged fiercely, the insurgents
not being daunted by the superior numbers of their
opponents, though they were " nothing in order nor in

[1] Galb. B. XII. f. 1136.

company nor in experience to be compared to the Royal forces." [1]

Meanwhile Sir William " followed the first attempt " on the camp, never pausing to take breath until he had driven the defenders of the fortification " to a plain flight." [2]

With these forced back on the town while their opponents were free to help Lord Grey, and with evidence of the approach of reinforcements of the enemy from behind him, Arundell decided to draw off, which he did in fairly good order.

A further desperate stand was made at the town's end, where a chain, according to local tradition, was stretched across the road, for, Hoker says, they were—

" at a point, they would not yield to no persuasions nor did, but most manfully did abide the fight : and never gave over until that both in the town and in the field they were all for the most part taken or slain." [3]

Here fell Ap Owen, a Welsh gentleman, " more boldly than advisedly, giving the adventure to enter the rampire at the town's end," [4] whose body was conveyed afterwards to Exeter, and, after the " manner of wars," honourably buried in the Cathedral Church of St. Peter ; here, too, fell Underhill, who had been in command of the Sampford Courtenay contingent throughout the campaign, apparently a better officer than Hoker's scornful words indicate.

Pursued by horse and foot, in the wild *mêlée*, many a brave man died fighting, and the rebels gave way, leaving five or six hundred of their comrades lying dying or dead.

Arundell, and it is said, Wynslade—perhaps the younger—managed to escape to the high-road, and retired to Okehampton, where they appear to have made a further stand.

[1] Hoker, p. 94.
[2] Galb. B. XII.
[3] Hoker, p. 94.
[4] *Ibid.*, Brice ed. 86.

By the time Lord Russell had effected a junction with his advance-guard, it already " waxed late," and, finding the victory over the Sampford Courtenay defenders complete, and that the ringleaders had again made good their escape, he thought it well to lose no time, but to continue the pursuit, allowing no further ground for the charge of slackness in following up a victory—a charge insinuated by the Council which must have rankled deeply.

To this end he detached Sir William Herbert and Mr. Kingston—presumably Sir Anthony Kingston—with their footmen and horsemen to attack one flank of the fugitives, Lord Grey with his contingent to advance upon the other, while he, the Lord Privy Seal, took the centre ready for a frontal attack. So when they came up to the position held by Arundell this was the order of battle adopted.

Finding themselves hard pressed, their followers weary with fighting against superior numbers, the preponderance of the Royal army being now greatly increased, enfiladed on two sides, confronted by a body of fresh troops eager to distinguish themselves as they had been unable to take part in the earlier combat, the leaders of the rebels saw no chance of victory—the odds were too great. There was nothing to be done but to retreat, or, as Lord Russell picturesquely says, " upon the sight [of his forces] the rebels' stomachs so fell from them as without any blow they fled."

Following up their advantage, the horsemen gave chase, and in the ensuing rout slew seven hundred and captured even more. Greater execution would have taken place had not night fallen. The Royal forces were in an unfriendly country, and before them stretched the open moor, " so all this night we sat on horseback," writes Lord Russell, ready to receive any sudden attack from an enemy whose valour and courage were not to be despised.

But, under cover of the darkness, the feeble remnant of Arundell's army drew off to. Launceston, there to make their final stand.

Of their actions in that ancient town we have only the report of their enemies, and we are not wholly inclined to accept Lord Russell's hearsay evidence : perhaps he repeated the accusation because it might seem to palliate his unjustifiable action in the massacre of prisoners at Clyst Heath. Hoker makes no reference to the event which, if it took place, or even if he had believed a rumour, he would have been eager to record.

The Lord Privy Seal's account runs that Arundell, on his arrival at Launceston—

"immediately began to practice with the townsmen and the keepers of Grenvile and other gentlemen for the [murder] [1] of them that night. The keepers so much abhorred this cruelty as they immediately set the gentlemen at large and gave them their aid with the help of the town for the apprehension of Arundell, who with iiij or v ringleaders they have imprisoned."

No such charge is brought against Arundell in the indictment, but we gather from that document that on the 19th August the leaders were captured, not without a struggle, in the streets of Launceston, nor without treachery, as we learn from another source. Kestell, Arundell's secretary, in the hottest stir, sent secret advertisement of all he knew concerning his master's movements.[2]

His followers, more than decimated, penned in the narrow, steep streets of the town, yet fighting to the death, his trusted secretary a traitor, weary with months of anxiety and days of continual fighting, like a stag at bay, Arundell courageously defended himself. But in vain. By the time Lord Russell arrived, he and his

---

[1] This word in Harl. MSS. 523 is "number"; in Galba. B. XII. it is "numbere," while Strype prints it "murder" (II. ii. 423).

[2] S. P. Dom. Ed. VI., VII. 54.

followers had been overpowered and lodged in the vile
dungeons of the Castle.

The news that several ringleaders had been captured
reached the Lord Privy Seal after his weary vigil on
horseback, and he immediately despatched Sir Gawen
and Sir Peter Carew with a considerable force " to keep
the town in a stay " until he could arrive with his main
army.

Lord Russell thus sums up the gains and losses of
this excursion—

" We have taken fifteen pieces of ordnance, some brass
and some iron. Of our part there were many hurt but not
passing x or xij slain. The Lord Grey and Mr. Herbert have
served notably. Every gentleman and Captain did their part
so well as I wot not well whom first to commend. I have
given order to all the ports that none of the rebels shall pass
that way."

It was not long after this that Arundell and the other
captured leaders were transferred from Launceston to
Exeter gaol. It must have been a terrible journey—
the chief offenders treated with all the ignominy due to
traitors, with feet secured with ropes beneath their
horses' bellies, with hands tied behind them, and every
precaution taken to prevent their escape, they were
escorted across the dreary moorland, where evidence
of their recent encounters was visible, while every
village green presented a grim spectacle of gallows laden
with victims of martial law, then past the church of
St. Thomas by Exebridge, where their late comrade hung
in chains, surrounded by his sacred paraphernalia—
enough to draw tears from the eyes of the most hardened
while to them it was an outward sign of the defeat of
their cause and a symbol of the more awful fate in store
for them at the end of the weary pilgrimage they were
now beginning. With bowed heads and downcast eyes
they moved up the High Street of Exeter, which was lined

by foreign soldiery, keeping back a mob of their late opponents, who jeered unrestrainedly. In more lowly wise than their followers but two short months ago had boasted the insurgent leaders entered the city. They advanced to Rougemont Castle, to be their prison for a few weeks, a station only on their road to the yet more unyielding Tower of London. Here, in Exeter gaol, were incarcerated some of their late comrades, though many had fallen fighting during the last fortnight. Among the captured were Wynslade and his son, Maunder and the Mayor of Bodmin.

Meanwhile Russell's despatch giving these details had reached the Council. They wrote acknowledging—

"with no small joy and pleasure your good proceedings : for the which, as we have given and owe to Almighty God our most bounden thanks from whom all victory and good success doth come, so we do render most hearty thanks unto you as a chief minister of so happy and so well achieved enterprise : And pray you to impart the like to others who under you have painfully travailed in the king's majesty's name and in ours, and chiefly to those that have special letters sent from us." [1]

The Lord Privy Seal was instructed to send to London Arundell, Maunder, the Mayor of Bodmin, " and ij or iij of the most rankest leaders of them here to be examined and after to be determined of as shall appertain." [2]

They urged that more diligent efforts should be made to capture Sir Thomas Pomeroy, who, if taken on a previous occasion, was now, the 19th August, at large, perhaps having been set at liberty that he might help to secure other rebels.[3] They also enclosed a formal letter of thanks, saying—

"whereas it hath pleased God to grant you victory upon those rebels who have so lewdly against their allegiance been in

---

[1] S. P. Dom. Ed. VI., VIII. 47.
[2] Pet. MSS. 458, Pk.¶p. 63.
[3] See Chapter XVIII.

open field : we have thought good by these our special letters
to require you to give hearty thanks in general to all the gentlemen, serving-men and rest of the soldiers who have so valiantly
acquitted themselves in the service of His Majesty, which ye
may assure them shall be considered to their comforts and
benefit as occasion may require accordingly." [1]

But the "fray" at Launceston was not the last
opposition made to the Royal forces by the rebels.
After the raising of the siege of Exeter, a considerable
body of insurgents, said to number a thousand,[2] had
made their way northward towards Somerset, rumour
said they were making for Minehead. To crush these
Sir William Herbert was sent, while Russell himself went
into Cornwall to capture some men reported to be still
in arms at Bodmin, taking with him, apparently, Lord
Grey, who about this time went as far south as Pelynt
in pursuit of rebels or in search of spoil.[3]

Herbert's route is uncertain, but it was probably up
the Exe Valley, by way of Bickleigh,[4] the home of
another member of the Carew family, and then by the
old road along the top of the ridge towards Bampton.
At Cranmore Castle, above Colliprest by Tiverton, he
seems to have overtaken a detachment of the fugitives,
who showed fight, but were eventually driven off the
field, leaving several of their number in the hands of
the enemy : these were promptly hanged and quartered.[5]
Near this point he probably divided his forces, himself

[1] Pet. MSS. 459ᵇ, Pk. p. 65.

[2] Mr. Blake puts the number at fifteen hundred.

[3] John Cory, or Curry, servant to John Wynslade, who was always
in his master's household at Tregarrick, deposed that he had had a chest
in his chamber there containing evidences and "at the commotion time
in Cornwall about the third year of the late King Edward the vjth the
servants of the Lord Grey coming to Tregarrick and rifling the house
brake up the said chest " (Exch. Com. 531, 25, Eliz.).

[4] The Rev. E. S. Chalk has called my attention to a carving now at
Bickleigh Rectory, but formerly at Bickleigh Court, on which is depicted
a besieged city—possibly a memorial of the events of 1549, made for the
Carews.

[5] Lysons' Devon, p. 509.

continuing the pursuit to Minehead, whence, it was reported, the rebels had sailed for Bridgwater. Owing to rumours that other fugitives were to the eastward, he sent the rest of his band, under Sir Peter Carew and Sir Hugh Paulet, the Knight Marshal,[1] to scour the country in that direction.

At Kings Weston in Somerset, they overtook the rebels, and, after a stubborn resistance, conquered them, taking " one Coffin, a gentleman, their captain " a prisoner, whom they brought to Exeter. These insurgents, under the command of John Bury,[2] exhausted by forced marches, lacking ammunition, discouraged by the failure of their comrades, out-numbered and out-manœuvred by the King's men, were in no condition to withstand the onslaught, and after " great slaughter and execution," gave way, leaving at least one hundred and four men prisoners in their enemy's hands.[3] Many of these were executed locally as a terror to others.

So, by this last stand on the 29th August, ended the insurrection after twelve weeks of active opposition to the Council's innovations.[4] On the very same day the first batch of their comrades executed in London were drawn, hanged, and quartered at Tyburn—three unnamed persons of " them that did rise in the West country." [5]

---

[1] Hoker, p. 95.

[2] Hoker makes no mention of Bury in this battle, but from the latter's own confession it appears that he was in command. Collinson gives to Paulet alone the credit of the fight and the capture of Coffin. Kings Weston lies between Somerton and Langport.

[3] The number of prisoners and the date of the battle are obtained from Memoranda Roll, L. T. R., 327, which contains full details of the executions carried out by Sir John Thynne, the sheriff of Somerset and Dorset ; for other quotations from this source, see p. 318. Through a reference given by Prof. Gay these interesting entries have been turned up.

[4] This is counted from the first movement at Bodmin on 6th June.

[5] See Grey Friars Chron. p. 62.

CHAPTER XX

"But though the sword of war was sheathed, there remained work enough
for the sword of justice, in executing many of the rebels, for a terror
to others."—HEYLIN.

AFTER the capture of Arundell—

"the Lord Russell himself minding to make all things sure
taketh his journey and marcheth into Cornwall : and following
his former course causeth execution to be done upon a great
many and especially the chief bell-wethers and ring-leaders." [1]

An absence of dates and a looseness of reference
makes it uncertain how long the Lord Privy Seal remained
in that county or whether he really went beyond
Launceston.

On the 27th August the Council acknowledged a
letter from him dated the 22nd, which by the interval
between these days may hint at his greater distance from
London, but, unfortunately, there is no other letter
from them after this until that of the 10th September,
answering his of the 7th.

But if affairs required his presence elsewhere, he left
a deputy, Sir Anthony Kingston, styled by Grafton
"Provost Marshall in the field," to execute the Cornish
rebels, which was done with sufficient barbarity to carry
terror to the hearts of all men, enough to prevent a

[1] Hoker, p. 95.

recrudescence of rebellion.   To judge from the records preserved, Kingston was not one whit behind, but rather improved upon, Russell's brutality.

Froude, always a special pleader for the Crown, asserts that Hoker states that "care was taken to distinguish the really guilty," [1] but we have failed to trace any phrase of the contemporary historian which can be so understood.

Speed, on the other hand, plainly asserts that "many others were executed without judgment." [2]

Referring to the recorded instances of Kingston's executions, Froude goes out of his way to suggest that they were exaggerated tales, related by the grand-children of the victims, but they are recorded by Grafton, who was a contemporary, and was none too favourable to the insurgents.   It is reasonable to suppose that he received them at first hand from witnesses whose accuracy could be guaranteed.   His version is here quoted at length.[3]

" And among other the offenders in this rebellion I thought it well to note twain for the manner of their execution seemed strange.   The first was one Bowyer who was Mayor of a town in Cornwall called Bodmin.   This Mayor had been busy among the rebels, but some that loved him said that he was forced thereunto, and that if he had not consented to them, they would have destroyed him and his house.   But howsoever it was, this was his end.   On a certain day Sir Anthony Kingston being Provostmarshall in the field wrote his letter unto the said Mayor declaring that he and certain other with him would come and dine with him such a day.   The Mayor seemed to be very joyous thereof and made for him very good preparation.   And at the time appointed, Sir Anthony Kingston with his company came and were right heartily welcomed to the Mayor.   And before they sat down to dinner, Sir Anthony, calling

---

[1] Froude, V. p. 199.
[2] Chron. p. 806.
[3] This is from the edition of 1568, *i.e.* within nineteen years after the date of their occurrence.

the Mayor aside, showed him that there must be execution done in that town, and therefore willed him with speed to cause a pair of gallows to be made, that the same might be ready by the end of dinner. The Mayor went diligently about it, and caused the same to be done. When dinner was ended Sir Anthony called the Mayor unto him and asked him if that were ready that he spake to him of, and he answered it was ready. Then he took the Mayor by the hand and prayed him to bring him to the place where the same was, and so he did. And when Sir Anthony saw them, he said unto the Mayor, ' Think you they be strong enough ? ' ' Yea, Sir,' said he, ' that they are.' ' Well then,' said Sir Anthony, ' get you even up to them for they are provided for you.' The Mayor cried, ' I trust you mean no such thing to me.' ' Sir,' saith he, ' there is no remedy, you have been a busy rebel, and therefore this is appointed for your reward ; ' so that without longer respite or tarrying, there was the Mayor hanged.

" At the same time also and near unto the place, there was a Miller who had been a very busy varlet in that rebellion, whom also Sir Anthony Kingston sought for ; But the Miller had warning, and he having a good tall fellow to his servant called him unto him and said, ' I must go forth, if there come any to ask for me, say that thou art the owner of the mill, and that thou hast kept the same this four years, and in no wise name not me.' The servant promised his Master so to do. Afterwards came Sir Anthony Kingston to the miller's house and called for the miller, the servant answered that he was the miller. Then said Master Kingston, ' How long hast thou kept this mill ? ' and he answered, ' Three years.' Then cried he, ' Come on thou must go with me,' and caused his servants to lay hands on him, and brought him to the next tree, saying ; ' You have been a rebellious knave, and therefore here shall you hang.' Then cried he and said that he was not the miller, but the miller's servant. ' Well then,' said he, ' you are a false knave to be in two tales, therefore hang him up,' said he, and so he was hanged. After he was hanged, one being by, said to Sir Anthony Kingston, ' Surely this was but the miller's man.' ' What then,' said he, ' could he ever have done his master better service than to hang for him.' " [1]

[1] Chron. p. 519.

In the first instance Sir Anthony was particularly brutal and callous in his ghastly jest. The Mayor, who had feared that his connection with the rebels would cause his arraignment, was lulled into a sense of false security by the intimation that the King's representative would be his guest, to find that, not only was he forced to prepare the gallows for his own hanging, but, against all canons of hospitality—respected even by primitive races—the very man who had just eaten his salt and had partaken of his sumptuous banquet, was to be his executioner, and had premeditated this before asking to be his guest. Nicholas Boyer, or Bowyer, as he is styled in local records, seems to have acted as deputy Mayor in the absence of Henry Bray, who was actively engaged with the rebels before Exeter. He had held the office of Mayor in 1536, and his name is bracketed with Henry Bray, in 1549, in the list given by Sir John Maclean.[1]

Another tale, almost exactly the same, lingers as a local legend at St. Ives, concerning John Payne, Mayor or Port-reeve of that place. Matthews, in his history of the parish, repeats the tradition that the Provost Marshal dined with the unsuspecting Port-reeve at the

[1] It is possible that Bowyer really succeeded Bray in office, the mayoral election perhaps taking place before Kingston's visit. It is not clear from Maclean's list that Bowyer's name actually occurs on any Bodmin document as mayor in this year. Another Nicholas Bowyer occurs as burgess in 1563-4, perhaps his son, with another Henry Bray. The "Bodmin Register" (p. 211) contains this note : " In an old list of Mayors of Bodmin is the following entry : Edward the 6th Nicholas Boyer, 1548, Hanged before his own door. A small image of a man, with a rope about his neck, was, a few years since, dug up at the Queen's Head, where it still may be seen." The Rev. W. Iago, B.A., says that far from this being the representation of the executed mayor, he has proved it to be an angel from the tomb of Prior Vivian in St. Petrock's Church, Bodmin, and that he has since had it replaced upon the monument. Tradition states that Bowyer resided where the Queen's Head now stands. Some years ago in the building to the east of this was discovered a finely carved arched doorway with a niche for a saint above. This was gravely suggested as Bowyer's door with the opening in which the beam of the gallows was inserted, but without doubt this archway belonged to the Friary, which formerly stood here.

old house, which was afterwards the George and Dragon inn, and hanged his entertainer immediately after dinner, the gallows being erected in front of the door upon the market-place.[1]

It may be that Kingston, pleased with his grim joke, repeated it on other occasions, or tradition may have attached the Bowyer story to Payne, who Hals simply asserts was hanged on a gallows erected in the middle of the town.

Another victim of Kingston's was William Mayow, of Clevyan, in St. Columb Major, who was hanged at the tavern sign-post in that town. Tradition says that his crime was not capital—

" and therefore his wife was advised by her friends to hasten to the town after the Marshal and his men, who had him in custody, and beg his life. Which accordingly she prepared to do and to render herself a more amiable petitioner before the Marshal's eyes, this dame spent so much time in attiring herself and putting on her French hood, then in fashion, that her husband was put to death before her arrival." [2]

In this manner Kingston pursued his way through the length and breadth of Cornwall, with grisly jests, inhuman sport, and gross breaches of hospitality. Well might Carew, writing within half a century of his visit, have noted that he " hath left his name more memorable

---

[1] "History of St. Ives," p. 122. On seeing a drawing of a bench end in St. Ives' church bearing the name " Ino Peyn," and as Hals wrote that the arms of Payne the Port-reeve, " in a plain field three pine-apples," were upon another bench-end it seemed possible that the name might be Pyne and the arms an incomplete representation of those of Pyne of Ham, " Gu. a chevron Erm. between three pine-apples or.' Thomas Pyne of Ham married Margaret, daughter of Oliver Wyse ; as a widow she married William Kendall, executed at the time of the Exeter conspiracy (see p. 24 n.). If she had had a son John Pyne who became port-reeve, he might have been under suspicion because of his connection with Kendall. But Mr. Matthews is fully satisfied that these arms are " Per pale. I. Three pears. II. A phenon, point in base," i.e. Polpear and Payne, as John Payne married an heiress of Richard Polpear.

[2] Davies Gilbert, II. p. 201.

than commendable amongst the townsmen,"[1] while Hayward, an ardent admirer of the government of that day, writing scarcely a hundred years after the event, admits that Kingston was " deemed by many not only cruel, but uncivil and inhumane in his executions."[2]

If such was the fate of those in the higher walks of life, what must have happened to the common herd, who were executed under martial law ?

Nor was Kingston content with thus dealing with individual rebels : innocent and guilty alike suffered when he gave over most of the country to rapine and desolation, abandoning it " to the spoil of the soldiers, who were not slothful to glean what they could find for the time their liberty lasted."[3] Nor did they trouble themselves to discern between the loyal subject and the rebel, making profit of both indifferently.[4]

Such was the trail of death and terror : with gallows scattered plentifully over the two beautiful counties, putrefying bodies polluting the atmosphere, a veritable shambles on an enormous scale ; the people cowering in hiding-places, the innocent fearing that some spiteful neighbour would accuse them, and the guilty—those who remained true to the faith in which they had been nurtured—seeking refuge in vain. It is no wonder that

---

[1] " Cornwall," p. 292. He adds in justification of Kingston : " Sir Anthony did nothing herein, as a judge, by discretion, but as an officer by direction : and besides, he gave the mayor sufficient watch-word of timely warning, and large space of respite (more than which, in regard of his own peril, he could not afford) to shift for safety, if an uneschewable destiny had not haltered him to that advancement. As for the miller's man, he equalled his master in their common offence of rebellion, and therefore it deserved the praise of mercy, to spare one of the two, and not the blame of cruelty, to hang one for the other."

[2] " Edward the VI." p. 64. Commenting on the stories of the Mayor and of the Miller, Lloyd writes : " Punish the multitude severely once and you oblige them ever : for they love that man only for his good nature, whom they fear for his resolution " (" State Worthies," p. 343).

[3] Holinshed, p. 926.

[4] Hayward, p. 65.

the people dated events from this period as from the Hegira. " After the commotions " and " after the commotion time " became stock phrases in the law courts and elsewhere.[1]

Truly Fabyan's Chronicle puts it well when referring to the rebels and the rising that it " was damage to them and other." [2]

While as to the chosen instrument of this so cruelly wreaked vengeance, what was his fate ? If we accept tradition it was indeed a piece of retributive justice that is seldom seen in real life. Froude describes Kingston as " a young, high-spirited, and, in some respects, a noble sort of person, a friend of Hooper the martyr," [3] but he quotes no authority for his glorification of this wretched man.

The story of his friendship with Hooper rests on these facts. Kingston was cited to appear in that Bishop's court on a charge of adultery, etc. At first he refused to obey, but " in the hope of impunity," it is suggested, he at last consented so to do. When Hooper severely rebuked him he gave the Bishop " a blow on the cheek before all the people, and loaded him with abuse." [4] Kingston, then Sheriff of Gloucester, was appointed by Queen Mary in 1555, to attend Hooper when he was condemned to be burnt in order to persuade him to recant. Finding this impossible, according to Foxe,[5] Kingston thanked the Bishop for having corrected him

[1] One mother, trying to prove the age of her son, testified that she was married " after the commosyon " ; another witness spoke of her daughter's marriage " after the commosyon," while yet another witness stated that the boy was born " after the commosyon in Devon," which was repeated by several others. Johan Pyne, in another case, swore that the legacies mentioned in her husband's will were " spoyled and stolled during the respondent's lyffe-tyme at the last commotion there was now in Devonshire " (See " Old Ways in Olden Days," Reynolds).

[2] Ed. 1559, p. 710.

[3] V. p. 200.

[4] Ab Ulmis's letter, 4th December, 1551. Orig. Let. II. 444.

[5] VI. 651.

on the former occasion, because by his good instructions " God hath brought me to the forsaking and detesting " of such sins. Whereupon both Kingston and the Bishop wept. It is not easy to believe Foxe's story in the face of Kingston's subsequent history.

A few months later, on the 10th December, 1555, Kingston, who is described as Knight Marshal of Parliament, " upon contemptuous behaviour and great disorder by him lately committed in the Parliament House," [1] was imprisoned in the Tower. Among his offences were the use of seditious words and the taking of the keys of the House from the Serjeant. But on his submission, on the 23rd December, he was released, as the Queen, in spite of his intemperate language, believed him to be loyal. But in this she was deceived.

In the following year he was implicated in the Dudley plot, which had for its object the removal, perhaps murder, of Mary, the elevation of Elizabeth to the throne, and the marriage of the latter to Edward Courtenay, Earl of Devon. The chief conspirators were : Dudley, Kingston, Peckham, Uvedale, the Ashtons, Daniel, and the two Tremaynes. Sir Anthony, who resided on his wife's estates at Chudleigh, was appointed to march with the Devonshire men to London, raising the country as he went. The Captain of the Isle of Wight was to receive the English refugees from France, whilst Heneage and others were to raise London and pillage the Tower, where Philip had recently deposited bullion brought from Spain.

The plot was discovered and the plotters fled, though eight of them were captured. On the 4th April a proclamation was issued against the traitors named, who had fled over seas.

---

[1] Harl. MS. 643, f. 68. See also Burnet, Ref. II. 504. The warrant for his arrest contains this curious instruction : " Ye must suffer the said Sir Anthony Kingston to have his men to wayte uppon hym, and his bed, night-gere, and such other things as he shall have need of " (Hist. MSS. Com. 5th Rept. 485).

Such, in brief, is the history of the Dudley Conspiracy, which has received scant notice from historians. Sir Anthony's connection with it is vague, but it is certain that he lay under vehement suspicion. From the confessions of some of those engaged in the plot it seems that great reliance was placed on his assistance, especially as he was " Vice-Admiral of the parts about Severn." They also declared that he had suggested obtaining a copy of Henry VIII.'s will, not openly from the Rolls but by underhand means, for the conspirators relied upon the fact that Mary was breaking her father's will. Peckham did succeed in getting a copy upon which he made marginal notes. There is a letter among the Conway Papers written by Katherine, Countess of Huntingdon, to her uncle, Cardinal Pole, on behalf of " one Kingston, who had accompanied her husband on his late unhappy journey to Cambridge, and had been with him at the time of the capture of the Duke of Suffolk. She says that Kingston had been guilty of harbouring coiners in his house where they had practised their nefarious occupation.[1]

In order to obtain the funds necessary to carry out this conspiracy, it was confessed that skilful coiners had been obtained to deal with the bullion they expected to get out of the Tower, so it seems probable that this letter refers to Sir Anthony.

It is said that Kingston. was arrested in the West Country, where he had estates. This is supported by the fact that two examinations of Sir Anthony were made at Coberley, about five miles from Cheltenham, on the 8th and 9th April, 1556. In these he admits meeting Dudley at Ashton's house during the previous Christmastide, and, though closely examined, he confessed little else incriminating, except that he had rigged up a

---

[1] See S. P. Dom. Mary (Addenda) VIII. 15. This is undated, but it is assigned, for some reason not apparent, to 17th June, 1557, a year and two months after Sir Anthony's death.

pinnace supplied with seven pieces of ordnance, which he declared was for the purpose of preventing forbidden goods from entering the Severn.[1]

The story goes that after his arrest, and on his way to London, Kingston died, some say from a disease of long standing, while others state that he died by his own hand, of poison, in order to escape justice ; but a more picturesque narrative is to be found among the manuscripts of the late Canon Furney in the Bodleian Library. Although it is inaccurate in substituting Elizabeth for Mary, an error perhaps due to the fact that the conspiracy was to place the former on the throne, it may be correct in other particulars—

" 'Tis further recorded that after Queen Elizabeth came to the throne that she sent a pursuivant of arms for to bring Sir Anthony Kingston up to London, who being on the road upon Henley Bridge put spurs to his horse and leapt in Thames where he was drowned and afterwards brought to Painswick and there buried." [2]

Yet there is one thing which tends to discredit this story ; in a list of conspirators committed to prison, some to the Tower, some to the Fleet, and some to Newgate, occurs the name of Sir Anthony Kingston— perhaps he was rescued from the river and carried to London. Still there are no further examinations of him among those of the conspirators. As he died on the 14th April, 1556, according to the Inquisition *post mortem*, he obviously could not be included in the indictment of the others who were tried in the May, June, and July following. Those who were pronounced guilty were executed on the 9th July, 1556. Kingston evidently escaped justice, and to make the stories harmonise, it must be assumed that he was rescued from the river

---

[1] S. P. Dom. Mary (Addenda) VIII. 2 & 3.
[2] Notes on Gloucestershire, by Abel Wantner. Bod. Lib. Top. MS. Glous. C. 2, fol. 149

but died soon after from the immersion and shock aggravating a disease of long standing—a not improbable combination.

Wantner gives further information concerning him with several stories of his cruel disposition. After inserting the tales of the Mayor and of the Miller, he adds—

"Many other cruel things are reported of him amongst the rest let this ensuing report serve to suffice. Sir Anthony Kingston riding one day upon the road saw in a church-yard a great many people, who inquiring what they stood there for, answer was made that they brought a corpse there to be interred ; but the minister would not do his office, before he had the funeral dues paid him. Upon this Sir Anthony sendeth for the parson, and after a little discourse, he caused the minister to be thrown into the grave, and they buried him alive."

As indicative of the local opinion entertained of him the following curious account of a certain form of tenure is quoted from another of Wantner's manuscripts :—

"In the reign of King Edward the Sixth, there was a great rebellion in the western part of the kingdom which being suppressed, the King made Sir Anthony Kingston (who was then Lord of Painswick) Knight Marshal of England, who upon his returning home to Painswick, caused a gallows to be erected in Shipscombe's Green (a tithing of Painswick) with power (within themselves) to draw, hang, and quarter any that should rise in rebellion, and made a prison in Painswick for the keeping and securing such offenders. And withal obliged three estates of his own in the said lordship, for the upholding and maintaining of the said gallows for ever. One of the estates was always for to make good the gallows, and if at any time it fell down or otherwise happened to be destroyed if he that held the estate let it so remain for four and twenty hours he should forfeit his estate and the other two, was, that one of them was perpetually to have two ladders in readiness, and the other to have always halters in readiness, and upon default, or want of either of these upon any time of execution, they were likewise to loose their estates, (called Gallows-land) which they then held, and do still hold, by virtue of keeping up the gallows aforesaid, and that nothing might be wanting when occasion did offer, the tithing-man of Shipscomb successively (to the world's end) should be hangman : And for his service, there is an acre of land bequeathed to him, which is at this day known and called the Hangman's Acre." [1]

It is quite possible that this tenure owes its origin to some other cause, but the fact that tradition in his own county attributed its institution to him goes far to confirm the generally received opinion of his character. Rudder writes—

" he seems to have been a man divested of common humanity, and his name is preserved in history to be execrated for his infamous, sportive cruelty."

Commenting on the executions in Cornwall, he continues—

" This was the behaviour of him to whom the king had intrusted the administration of justice, and for the sake of a joke, he condemned and executed the innocent for the guilty." [2]

But the executions were not confined to the counties of Devon and Cornwall. An interesting light on the way the lesser rebels suffered is obtained from the accounts

---

[1] *Ibid.* C. 3. Wantner dates this second MS. 1714. It is a more finished history of the county. In the first MS. the tithing is called " Pitchcomb's green " ; it is also stated that the gallows was erected for "the speedy execution of all such as should rise against their Prince." The tithing-man is there said to be obliged to provide ladder and halter and that there are several parcels of ground held by the " tenure of the Gallows hold."

[2] " Hist. Glous." p. 554, note. Surely the D.N.B. is wrong in giving the date of Kingston's birth as 1519, and then saying that after he had held many offices he married a widow with children in 1535, *i.e.* at the age of sixteen. There is some doubt as to Cirencester being the place of his death. It is probably so stated because the inquest *post-mortem* was held there, but the inquest concerning property was usually held at the chief town nearest the person's most important estate in the county.

of Sir John Thynne, Sheriff of Somerset and Dorset.[1] He begins with charges for conveying, in a wagon, twelve prisoners, " captains of the Rebells in Devon," from Honiton to Taunton at the commandment of the Lord Privy Seal ; thence they were taken to Ilchester on foot and on to Dorchester " at the commandment of Sir John Paulet, knight, being then authorised by the Lord Privy Seal to hear such matter as appertained to the rebellion." One of these, Thomas Hooper, was sent to Musbury and then to Exeter by Russell's orders. Two men, William Wykes of Bridgwater, and Henry Roberts, *alias* Norman, who was arrested as a pirate, were taken to London.

Then follow particulars of expenses incurred for the Kings Weston prisoners, who, on the 29th August, were taken from Bruton to Wells, bound with cords and watched by four men for eight days under the supervision of two bailiffs. There were one hundred and four of them. Another bailiff, with three men, conveyed two prisoners from Bruton to Bath, where " they suffered as was appointed " ; four shillings and four pence were paid to a poor man to do execution and for irons to hang them with. At Frome, payment was made for the execution, for irons, for " wood for fire to burn the entrails," and a pan and trivet to seeth the limbs. At Mells, Beckington, Shepton Mallet—where a ladder also was used—Wells, and Glastonbury, similar payments were made. At Bridgwater, North Curry, and Mine-head, there were no executions because of pardons, but charges were made for irons prepared " but not occupied." At Milverton, Wiveliscombe, Dunster—where he had a cart to carry the dead man to the gibbet—and Ilminster,

[1] Sir John Thynne was one of the adherents of the Protector and " a principal instrument and councillor that he did use both at this time and otherways, also in the affairs of his ill government " (P. C. Reg., Dasent, II. 343). He was imprisoned with others on 13th October, 1549, released on recognizances the 22nd February following, and discharged from the same 18th May, 1551.

victims suffered. At all of these Sir John attended in person ; but to Thomas Bocher, one of the bailiffs, was entrusted the execution of " John Donne, a notable rebellioner," [1] at Oxford. It would seem that two or more suffered at each of twelve places, while three batches of prisoners were pardoned. The total cost was £26 6s. 10d.[2]

[1] A John Done appears in the list of prisoners still in gaol in Devon or Cornwall on 27th September, 1551. Possibly a son of the above.

[2] See Memoranda Roll, L. T. R. No. 327.

CHAPTER XXI

EVENTS IN LONDON

" Assuredly the vulgar multitude is not unfitly termed a beast with many
   heads, not guided, I will not say, with any proportion of reason ;
   violence and obstinacy, like two untamed horses, draw their desire
   in a blind-fold career."—HAYWARD.

MEANWHILE news of the doings in the West had reached
London. For some time the authorities dreaded that
the rebels would prove successful and march upon the
capital, and to prevent this, one of their earliest precautions was the destruction of Staines bridge on the
main western road.

The first movement in Norfolk occurred unexpectedly
on the 6th July, and the risings in the counties of Oxford
and Buckingham were kept from the public as late as
the 12th July,[1] so it must have been due to the rumours
of the investment of Exeter that on the 3rd July—

" my lord Mayor began to watch at night, riding about the
city to peruse the constables with their watches, and to see
that they keep the hours appointed at the last court of aldermen
holden at the Guildhall, for the preservation and safeguard
of the city because of the rebellion in divers places of this
realm."

and commanded each alderman in his turn to follow
his example.[2]

---

[1] Pet. MS. 437, Pk. p. 26.
[2] Wriothesley, II. 15. " Divers places " might well mean Devon,
Cornwall, and the neighbouring counties.

News of the various risings led to a proclamation of martial law on the 18th July against all rebels and upstirrers, who were to be dealt with without any indictment or arraignment, which was issued with due ceremony. Two days later the city gates were all watched with certain " commoners of the crafts of the city," and precepts were issued to all the authorities to have ready all their " harness, guns, bows, and other weapons for the defence of the same. Divers great pieces of the King's brass ordnance were had from the Tower and set at every gate, and all the walls from Cripplegate to Bevis Markes, by Christ Church were set with ordnance, and gunners appointed for every gate and the walls, having wages at the City's charge." [1]

The authorities were in a state of panic, the danger threatened seemed imminent, and might well have followed had Arundell advanced promptly to London without allowing time for the collection of forces to oppose him. Nor was the terror confined to the City. At Eton, Sir Thomas Smith, one of the Secretaries of State, had been unable to sleep for a week from sheer fright. Writing the day he received the proclamation of martial law, the 19th July, he describes the readiness of his neighbours to defend themselves against the rebels, and loyally support the King. He added his approbation of Lord Grey's sternly brutal treatment of the rebels in this country, which was worth more than ten thousand proclamations and pardons for quieting the people. [2]

At the height of this excitement the Council reopened their correspondence with the Princess Mary, attempting to force her, as they had already tried, to relinquish the celebration of the mass in her house at Kenninghall. They not only complain that she encouraged the rebels by her " obstinate incompliance with the religion and persistence in the use of the old mass,"

[1] Wriothesley, II. 16.
[2] S. P. Dom. Edw. VI., Vol. VIII., No. 33.

Y

but accused certain of her servants of being active agents in the Western rising.[1] In her spirited reply of the 20th July, she denies that any of her servants are implicated, says she has no chaplain at Sampford Courtenay, as suggested, and emphatically declares that " as for Devonshire no indifferent person can lay their doings to my charge." She neatly turns the tables on them with—

" but even as ye urgently without desert charge me so I omitting so fully to answer it as the case doth require do and will pray God that your new alterations & unlawful Liberties be not rather the occasion of these assemblies then my doings, who am (God I take to witnesse) Inquieted therewith." [2]

The panic of the citizens and the promptitude of the execution of martial law without any indictment nor arraignment is illustrated by the story of the bailiff of Romford, Essex, " a man very well beloved." He chanced to be in London early in the morning of St. Mary Magdalen's day, the 22nd July, and meeting the curate of " St. Katherine Christ's Church," one Sir Stephen, was asked—

" What news in the country ? " To which he replied,

" Heavy news. It is said that many men be up in Essex, but, thanks be to God, all is in good quiet about us."

So suspicious and so anxious to show their zeal was every one, that the curate promptly informed against him, and these words were twisted to mean that he was privy to these mutineers. Immediately, by court-martial, he was condemned and hanged upon a gibbet by the well within Aldgate. Upon the ladder he declared that he was no further guilty than that he had said the words mentioned to Sir Stephen. " I heard the words of the prisoner," adds Stowe, " for he was executed

[1] S. P. Dom. Edw. VI., Vol. VIII., No. 30,
[2] Add. MS. 27, 402, f. 40,

upon the pavement of my door where I then kept house."[1]

[1] As was consonant with the Council's aims to enforce the religious innovation at all costs, sermons were made to play a prominent part, although feeling ran so high that during them free fights occurred in church ; as recently as the previous Lent a riot took place in St. Margaret's, Westminster, when Latimer preached.[2] From the pulpit the violent, even foul, language uttered against the religion so recently universally accepted, was unbridled, and served to embitter controversy and kindle indignation, so that some charged the preachers as being instigators and fomenters of rebellion.

In spite of this, the Archbishop thought it convenient " in these commotions round about " to use sermons " to keep those people, that were still and quiet as yet, in their duty." So he ordered special sermons composed for the curates to read in church to their people " to preserve them in their obedience, and to set out the evil and mischief of the present disturbances."[3] A fast day because of the insurrections was appointed when these were to be read.

There is a curious collection of notes made by

---

[1] Stowe's " Survey " (Thoms ed.), p. 55. Cf. Grey Friars Chron. Mon. Fran. ii. 221 and Wriothesley's Chron. ii. 19. The latter calls him a tailor of " Raynesford in Essex." Strype (II. i. 320) styles Sir Stephen " more bold and hot then wise and learned." Stowe (p. 54) also says he objected to the name of St. Andrew Undershaft for a church, as the shaft was made an idol, so he induced the people to destroy it. He wished to alter the names of churches and of the days of the week, to have any day but Friday a fish-day and any other time for Lent. He often forsook his pulpit to preach from a high elm in his churchyard, and would then sing mass at a tomb facing the north.

[2] See Churchwarden's accounts (J. Nichols, " Illus. Manners," p. 13). " For mending of divers pews that were broken when Dr. Latymer did preach." Burcher, writing 29th October, 1548, refers to the catechism translated by Cranmer, and adds : " This little book has occasioned no little discord : so that fightings have frequently taken place among the common people, on account of their diversity of opinion, even during the sermons " (Zur. Let. p. 642).

[3] Strype's " Cranmer," II. 117.

Cranmer described as "An Homily against the Rebellion," which, from internal evidence, must have been
composed about this time, when the Western insurrection
was in full swing and that in Norfolk beginning.[1]

It is suggested that this was the material supplied by
the Archbishop to be expanded by Peter Martyr into a
sermon, prepared in Latin, but translated for the use of
curates. Bucer was similarly employed, while many
contributed to the vast output of sermons on the
subject.[2]

But Cranmer's own sermon demands special notice.
It was delivered with due pomp and ceremony, which
Wriothesley thus describes—

"The one and twentieth day of July, the sixth day after
Trinity Sunday, the Archbishop of Canterbury came to Paul's,
and there in the choir after matins in a cope with an alb
under it, and his cross born afore him with two priests of
Paul's for deacon and sub-deacon with albes and tunicles,
the Dean of Paul's following him in his surplice, came in the
choir, my lord Mayor with most part of the aldermen sitting
there with him. And after certain assembly of the people
gathered into the choir the said Bishop made a certain exhortation to the people to pray to Almighty God for his grace and
mercy to be showed unto us. In the which exhortation he
admonished the people of the great plague of God reigning
over us now in this realm of England for our great sins and
neglecting his word and commandments, which plague is the
commotion of the people in most parts of this realm now
reigning among us specially against God's commandment and
the true obedience to our most Christian King Edward the
sixth, natural, christian, and supreme head of this realm of
England and other his dominions, which plague of sedition and
division among ourselves is the greatest plague, and not like

---

[1] Strype's "Cranmer," II. 362. "And these tumults were excited by
the papists and others which came from the western camp, to the intent by
sowing division among ourselves we should not be able to impeach them."

[2] It is curious to note that on Whitsunday, when the demonstration
occurred at Sampford Courtenay, Miles Coverdale was preaching at Paul's
Cross to the civic authorities, who were present in their scarlets.

heard of since the passion of Christ, which is come on us by the instigation of the Devil for our miserable sins and trespasses in that we have showed us to be the professors and diligent hearers of his word by his true preachers and our lives not amended, which godly exhortation was so godly set forth to the hearers with the true obedience also to our king and superiors and also to the confutation of the rebellors, with also admonition given to the people to fast and pray, putting all pride aside with other sins and vices reigning among us, as delicious and superfluous feedings and sumptuous apparel, that it would have moved and stirred any christian heart to lament their offences and call to Almighty God for mercy and grace." [1]

As a report of the Archbishop's sermon, this can hardly be improved. The sermon itself is given at length by Jenkyns ; the frequent recurrence of the word " plague," as applied to sedition, is alone sufficient to identify this as the one described above, while careful perusal confirms this.[2]

[1] Strype's "Cranmer," II. p. 16. 21st July, 1549, was the 5th Sunday after Trinity, so it is difficult to understand the first sentence. The Grey Friars Chronicle (p. 80) says, " the xxj day of the same monyth, the whyche was sonday, the byshoppe of Caunterbury came sodenly to Powlles, and there shoyd and made a narracyon of thoys that dyd rysse in dyvers places within the realme, and what rebellyous they were and wolde take aponne them to reforme thynges befor the lawe, and to take the kynges powre in honde. And soo was there at procession, and dyd the offess hym selfe in a cope and no vestment, nor mytter, nor crosse, but a crosse staffe : and soo dyd the offes, and hys sattene cappe on hys hede alle the tyme of the offes, and soo gave the communione hym selfe unto viij. persons of the sayd church."

[2] Cranmer's Rem. II. 248. Evidences of identity may be found in such paragraphs as : " The general cause of all these commotions is sin and under Christian profession unchristian living . . . suddenly cometh upon us this scourge of sedition . . . we must needs feel that this plague is the grievous scourge of God for our offences . . . we have rather winked at than punished the contempt both of God and his laws " (p. 250). " We have deserved this plague at God's hands, and much more " (p. 252). " Doth it become the lower sort of people to flock together against their heads and rulers ? and especially now at this time in the King's Majesty's minority, when we be round about environed with other enemies " (p. 255). Of the greed of the gentry, " But yet their fault excuseth not those, which without the commandment and his laws have taken harnes upon their backs and refused to lay it down, when they were by the King's authority

Wriothesley continues—

" This day procession was sung according to the King's book my lord [archbishop] and the choir kneeling, my lord singing the collects and praying and adding one other prayer which he had written for this plague."

No doubt this prayer, which is attached to the sermon—

" And now with humble prayer let us make an end : O Lord, whose goodness far exceedeth our naughtiness, and whose mercy passeth all measure, we confess thy judgment to be most just, and that we worthily have deserved this rod wherewith thou hast beaten us. We have offended the Lord God : we have lived wickedly : we have gone out of the way : we have not heard thy prophets which thou hast sent unto us to teach us thy word, nor have we done as thou hast commanded us ; wherefore we be most worthy to be confounded. But we provoke unto thy goodness : we appeal unto thy mercy : we humble ourselves : we acknowledge our faults. We turn to thee, O Lord, with our whole hearts, in praying, in fasting, in lamenting and sorrowing for our offences. Have mercy upon us, cast us not away according to our deserts, but hear us, and deliver us with speed, and call us to thee again according to thy mercy : that we, with one consent, and one mind, may evermore glorify thee, world without end. Amen." [1]

The Chronicle continues—

" This done he went to the high altar . . . he ministring the sacrament of the bodie of Christ himself to the dean and vij other, the deacons following with the chalice of the blood

commanded so to do " (p. 261). " We should acknowledge and repute all these seditions and troubles, which we now suffer, to be the very plague of God for the rejecting or ungodly abusing of his most holy word. . . ." (p. 267).

[1] Cranmer's Rem. II. p. 267. Strype ("Cranmer," II. 121) says that an office of fasting was composed for this rebellion, giving this prayer with the heading, " The exhortation to penance or the supplication, may end with this or some other like prayer." Jenkins (p. 273) has a note that there are two copies of this prayer in the C. C. C. C. MSS., one at the end of the sermon and the other a draft, corrected by Cranmer, with the above heading.

of Christ. The communion done Mr. Joseph, his chaplain, went to Paul's Cross and made a sermon of the gospel of this Sundaie, briefly and shortly declaring in the same sermon parts of my lord's exhortation to the people, because all heard him not before, and so committed the people to God." [1]

Nor was this the only occasion on which the Archbishop took public notice of the rebels. After the relief of Exeter, that is, on the 10th August,

" being Saturday, the Archbishop of Canterbury made a collation in Paul's choir for the victory that the Lord Russell, Lord Privy Seale had on Monday last past against the rebels in Devonshire, which had besieged Exeter, and lying in camp afore it, by the space of 3 weeks and like to have famished them in the town." [2]

Or, as the " Grey Friars Chronicle " has it, he preached

" in the choir in the bishop's stall that he was wont to be stalled in, for them that [rose] in the West country of the commons of Devonshire and Cornwall, and there he showed that the occasion came of popish priests was the most part of all his sermon." [3]

But, not satisfied with the sermons of himself, his chaplains and the curates, the Archbishop moved the Council to command Bonner, the recalcitrant Bishop of

---

[1] The Gospel for the 5th Sunday after Trinity is St. Luke vi., the parable of the mote and the beam, but the second lesson for 21st July, evensong, was 1 Tim. vi. The heading of this chapter in the A.V. begins, " 1 of the duty of servants, 3 not to have fellowship with new-fangled teachers," and ends, " 20 To keep the purity of the doctrine and to avoid profane janglings." It is difficult to imagine these as appropriate texts. Joseph's sermon may have been that prepared for curates, not a shortened form of Cranmer's. He was of the advanced school of thought. Gardyner, complaining of the public defamation and trifling with Lent, writes, 21st May, 1547 : " I hear that Lent is thus spoken of by Joseph and Tonge, with other new, (whom I know not) as to be one of Christ's miracles, which God ordained not man to imitate and follow " (Foxe, VI. p. 32).

[2] Wriothesley, II. p. 20.

[3] P. 61.

London, a known sympathiser with the rebels, to preach against the insurrection.   As Burnet puts it—

"Bonner fell into new trouble : he continued to oppose everything as long as it was safe for him to do it, while it was under debate, and so kept his interest with the papists : but he complied so obediently with all the laws and orders of the Council, that it was not easy to find any matter against him. He executed every order that was sent him so readily, that there was not so much as ground for complaint." [1]

Therefore, as he gave no opening, they were forced to invent a ground of attack—

"It was known that he was, in his heart, against everything they did, and that he cherished all that were of a contrary mind. The Council being informed, that upon the commotions in England, many in London withdrew from the service and communion, and frequented masses, which was laid to his charge, as being negligent in the execution of the King's laws and injunctions : they writ to him on the 23rd of July,[2] to see to the correcting of these things, and that he should give good example himself.   Upon which, on the 28th following he sent about a charge to execute the order in this letter, which he said, he was most willing and desirous to do.   Yet it was still observed that whatsoever obedience he gave, it was against his heart.   And therefore he was called before the Council the 11th of August.   There was a writing [3] delivered to him complaining of his remissness : and particularly, that whereas he was wont formerly on all high festivals to officiate himself, yet he had seldom or never done it since the new service was set out : as also, that adultery was openly practiced in his diocese, which he took no care to restrain or punish : therfore he was strictly charged to see these things reformed." [4]

[1] Hist. Ref. II. p. 193.

[2] Strype says that the same letter was sent to all the bishops, though the copy he gives is identical with the draft in the P.R.O. (See II. i. 331.)

[3] The draft of this "writing" is dated "ij° August," which might easily be mistaken for 11th.   There is an addendum to it made after the news of the relief of Exeter had been received.

[4] Burnet, Hist. Ref. II. p. 193.

This was " a curious accusation to bring against a bishop," writes Blunt,

" in whose see lived the profligate courtiers of Henry VIII. and Edward VI.'s reigns, including some very far from immaculate members of that body which was lecturing the Bishop." [1]

To this document was added a minatory clause, which appears, with many corrections, at the end of the Record Office draft—

" To the intent ye may [at this most dangerous time] look more nearly [and] better and more diligently [into the charge] to the reformation of this, our pleasure is that ye shall abide and keep residence in your house [at London] there as in the city of state and principal place of your diocese and none other where for a certain time until [the world be in more quiet and until] ye shall be otherwise accused by us."

That is to say, he was to be considered under arrest until some further fault could be discovered in him. He was also commanded to preach at Paul's Cross or in the Cathedral, a sermon on Rebellion, the Council supplying the material for the same, with instructions to preach it on Sunday a week later.

Their idea of an appropriate discourse may be gathered from the headings of this document, which is styled " Articles to be entreated on in your first sermon at Paul's."

" That all such as rebelleth against the prince getteth unto them damnation and those that resisteth the high power

---

[1] Blunt, "Hist. Ref." II. p. 120. Collier quotes from the injunctions given to Bonner, as contained in his episcopal register, which relate to his own conduct as to infrequent preaching, celebration of the Communion, the reparation of glass, buildings and ornaments in his diocese (for which last the courtiers rather than he, were responsible) : the enforcement of laws about attendance at Communion, the punishment of adultery, etc., and the collection of tithes. (See V. p. 345.) He gives 7th August as their date, which tallies better with the P.R.O. draft, for Exeter was relieved on the 6th.

resisteth the ordinance of God and he that dieth therefore in rebellion by the Word of God is utterly damned and so loseth both body and soul. And therefore these rebels in Devonshire and Cornwall [or in Norfolk] who taketh upon them to assemble a power and force against their King and Prince against the laws and statutes of the realm and goeth about to subvert the state and order of the Commonwealth not only doth deserve therefore death as traitors and rebels but do accumulate to themselves eternal damnation Ever to be in the burning fire of hell with Lucifer the father and first author of pride, disobedience and rebellion, what pretence soever they have, and what masses and holy water soever they pretend or go about to make among themself as . . . [here follows reference to ' Chore, Dathan, Abyrom, and Saul '] . . . Better obedience than sacrifices saith Scripture. In disobedience pride disorder and rebellion nothing can please God."

They next dealt with the observation, both with heart and lips, of external rites and ceremonies, which be but exercises of religion, appointable by superior powers, even the magistrate.

" If any man shall use the old rite and thereby disobey the superior power the devotion of his ceremony is made naught by his disobedience so that which else (as long as the law did so stand) might be good by pride and disobedience is made naught."

They contrast the effect of prayer and praise said with or without devotion.[1]

Appended to one of the draft copies is this particularly interesting addition :—

" Further ye shall for example in Sunday come sennight after the foresaid date celebrate Communion at Paul's Church, ye shall also set forth in your sermon that our authority of our Royal person is (as of truth it is) of no less authority and force in this our young age than it is or was of any of our predecessors

---

[1] S. P. Dom. Ed. VI., VIII. 36. The portions in square brackets are erasures and interlineations.

though the same were much elder, as may appear by example of Josias and other young kings in Scripture And therefore all our subjects to be no less bounden to the obedience of our precepts, laws and statutes than if we were of xxx of xl years of age."

"After our hearty commendations to your L[ordship] forasmuch as Almighty God now hath sent to the King's Majesty victory over his highness' most wicked and vile traitors the case being somewhat altered we have thought good to admonish you thereof and to will and require you to declare the same to your audience in your next sermon and to add to your other instructions this clause herein enclosed, praying you not to fail thereof and to exhort the people to give most due thanks therefore to Almighty God as appertaineth. God Almighty of his infinite justice and mercy hath now declared to all men who can or will take example thereby how much he is displeased with disobedience and rebellion so that we shall not now need to read old stories or to hearken what hath been done thousands or hundreds years past for even your eyes and sight in our time in this present year God hath showed his power will and most high justice in punishing of rebellion both in Devonshire and Cornwall where the greatest fountains and well was which is now so punished and subdued that there is none as I am informed of the heads and doers unpunished or unapprehended ready to punishment and also in Norfolk where a most pernicious sort of rebels and traitors were gathered together showing the fruit of rebellion, that is spoil robbery filthiness and to themself and their prince utter destruction and perpetual infamy."

A vast concourse must have assembled at St. Paul's Cross on that September Sunday to hear the sermon.[1] Bonner, when he entered the pulpit, would have looked down upon a sea of faces. He would have glanced at the double balcony to see if the King sat there among the courtiers, and his eye may have caught the colour of

---

[1] Foxe (V. 746) and Micronius (Orig. Let. 557) both give 1st September as the day of the sermon. Wriothesley (II. 24) says 8th September, the same day as that on which the rebels arrived in London. This is the more probable day.

the gowns of the Mayor and aldermen in their appointed places. He may have sought a friendly face among the gentry seated on horseback on the outskirts of the crowd. He would have felt some natural trepidation as he was aware that his audience was to a considerable extent hostile, and that any slip on his part would be eagerly reported, with the result that he might be landed in the Tower. He may have noticed amid the throng William Latimer and John Hooper,[1] who were there for the purpose of watching him. But he bravely met the ordeal.

His text was taken from Luke xviii., and, after discoursing upon the parables of the Unjust Judge and the Publican and Pharisee, he thus fulfilled the Council's requirements :—

" Now for our late rebels yonder in Devonshire and Corn-wall and likewise in Northfolke, I cannot well tell whether I should rather resemble them unto the unjust judge, in that he neither feared God nor man, or unto this proud Pharisee, who reputed himself only good and contemned all other ; or whether I should resemble them unto both. . . . Is it not a marvellous and a strange thing that these men had no fear to rise against their prince ? Is it not a marvellous matter that they feared not the loss of all their goods, the undoing of their wives and their children, the killing of their bodies, the damnation of their souls and the destruction of their own country ? "

Then, pointing out that the Devil moved them to it, he continued :—

" Yet men said that these men in Devonshire and Cornwall had holy water and mass amongst them, and thought through the same to be excused afore God of their disobedience and rebellion. . . . [He quoted various texts to show that holy water and mass, *i.e.* sacrifices cannot excuse it and exhorted his hearers to take example by the end of the late rebels]

---

[1] This Latimer was afterwards Dean of Peterborough and Hooper was afterwards the famous Bishop of Worcester and Gloucester. They were evidently well informed concerning the Council's injunctions.

. . . The King's Majesty and the Council sent unto me yesterday a bill of these news out of Devonshire, Cornwall and Northfolke, willing me to publish the same amongst you here, the which even as I received it, so will I read it unto you."

Thereupon the Bishop, according to an eye-witness—

" took the bill out of his bosom and read the same throughout, the effect whereof was that they should not need to look in no stories to see how God punished disobedience, . . . for they had a sufficient example to beware of rebellion by the end of the late rebels in Devonshire, Cornwall and Northfolk ; and also in the same bill the victories in those places was declared, and how the captains were either taken or slain whose names were there rehersed, exhorting them to give praise and thanks to God for the same." [1]

So did he preach against the evils of rebellion, and declare the victories over the rebels, reading from the very bill of which a draft copy has been quoted above.

But he failed to dwell upon one point which the Council deemed most important—the King's authority during his minority—an omission eagerly noted by the watchers and reported to the Council, with the result that Bonner was immediately summoned before a Commission. Foxe records the remarkable trial which followed, adding marginal notes indicative of his bitter hatred of the bishop. Bonner made a brave fight against fearful odds : he insisted that the tribunal was illegal ; he brought charges against the informers which would have vitiated their evidence ; he disputed over dates and forms, and, at length, stung beyond endurance by his persecutors and judges, he used powerful language —all of which may be read in Foxe. But our chief interest lies in Bonner's final explanation of his omissions ;

[1] See Cecil Papers, 198/34–46. I am greatly indebted to Mr. R. T. Gunton, the Marquis of Salisbury's librarian, for furnishing me with a transcript of these notes of Bonner's sermon. It is more than probable that these were the notes taken by Latimer or Hooper and sent to the Council and which afterwards came into Secretary Cecil's hands.

he had forgotten, he said, the question of the King's age—

"partly by reason of a bill that was delivered to him from the King's Council, to declare the victory then had against the rebels in Norfolk and Devonshire, which being of some length, confounded his memory: and partly also that his book in his sermon time fell away from him: Wherein were divers of his notes which he had collected for that purpose: so that he could not remember what he would, but yet in generality, he persuaded the people to obedience to the king's majesty, whose minority was manifestly known to them and to all others." [1]

Bonner objected particularly to one member of the Commission which tried him, Sir Thomas Smith, who had declared that the Bishop did as thieves, murderers, and traitors were wont to do, being inwardly culpable ; that he was sturdy, wilful, and disobedient, upholding the rebels and their opinions, and that unless he answered by word of mouth, he would be sent to the Tower, "there to sit and be joined with Ket and Humphrey Arundel the rebels "—a statement which Smith even tried to justify when Bonner charged him with the words. He also told the Bishop, when he protested his loyalty, that so had done the rebels of Norfolk, Devonshire, Cornwall, and elsewhere—

" Have they not said this ? We be the king's true subjects : we acknowledge him for our king, and we will obey his laws, with such like : and yet when either commandment, letter or pardon, was brought unto them from his majesty, they believed it not, but said it was forged and made under a hedge, and was gentlemen's doings : so that indeed they neither would nor did obey any thing." [2]

Driven to desperation, Bonner, at bay, turned on his persecuting judges with the famous exclamation—

" Three things I have : to wit, a small portion of goods, a poor carcase, and mine own soul : the two first you may take

[1] See Foxe, V. p. 766,   [2] Ibid. p. 794,

(though unjustly) to you : but as for my soul ye get it not,
' Quia anima mea in manibus meis semper.' " [1]

His trial was prolonged, and he remained shut up in
the Marshalsea, subjected to frequent inquisitions; not
unattended by personal insults, and, on the 1st October,
was deprived of his episcopal office. For some unrecorded
reason, perhaps obscurely connected with the execution of
the rebels, in the following January he was by his jailers
treated particularly harshly, his bed being removed so
that he had to lie on straw for eight days. He remained
imprisoned in the Marshalsea until the 6th August, 1553,
when he was released by the order of Queen Mary.[2]

While sermons of all sorts were used to influence the
people, other means were not neglected. A proclamation, issued on the 6th August, the day the siege of Exeter
was raised, forbade plays and interludes, as they usually
contained matter tending to sedition, and contemned
good order and laws, whence grew such disquiet, divisions,
tumults, and uproars that it was necessary to suppress
them.

Also, in order to reach the public eye and ear,
ballads were composed and sold in the streets. By a
curious accident, some of these have been preserved.
A few years ago, Mr. A. Neale purchased a copy of
Cicero's " Rhetorica," which required repairs to the
binding ; within the covers were found a number of
sheets, evidently proofs, in Black Letter. On examination, they proved to be of ballads relating to the Western
Rebellion. Unfortunately, in binding the book, the
portion across the back was cut off, rendering the ballads
imperfect ; but even in this mutilated condition they
give us an idea of what was expected to appeal to the
people as well as supply a few facts otherwise unknown,

---

[1] See Foxe V. p. 784.
[2] See P. C. Reg. IV. 312. From the evidence of William Seth (see
Appendix H) it appears that Bonner was then in the Marshalsea where
Seth acted as reader until Bonner beat him with his bed-staff.

so their lack of poetical merit may be condoned. The
following transcripts are therefore given here :—

> Whyppet [1] you prestes and tourne you
> Vice and synne they will not rebuke
> Nor come to gods worde to warme you
> Where do you see more Idelnes vsed
> whippet you prestes and tourne you
> Then among you prestes whych shuld be refused
> And come to gods worde to warme you
> Yet they haue an other prety (justy ?) caste
> whypet you prestes and tourne you
> Which they play at the last
> Leaue that you preestes I warne you
> For then they do holde vp a cup
> whippet you prestes and tourne you
> And al the drinke they them selues drynke vp
> Leaue that you prestes I warne you
> Moreouer, they teache theyr god to playe
> Whyppet you prestes and tourne you
> This way and that way
> Leaue that you prestes I warne you
> Now therfore I wyll with it be playne
> Whyppet you prestes and tourne you
> They wyl not stycke to brake their god in twayne

While this ballad refers to religious matters in general,
the following deals with the Cornish Rising particularly:—

> Cornewell was cruel and cam very fast
> They sayde thay wolde thorow w'out any pause
> There hartes ware so roted in the popes lawse
> They begane the laste yere when they slew boldye [2]

> All England reioysethe at ther ouer throwse
> For only the Lorde is oure Kynges victorye.
> They had falce prophetes which brought thīges to passe
> Cleane contrary to ther owne expectasion
> Ther hope was for helpe in ther popishe masse
> They wolde nedes haue hanged vp a reseruacion

---

[1] Whippit = to jump about.   Halliwell.
[2] Possibly this is a printer's error for Body.

The vecare of pomodstoke with his congeraciō
Commanded them to stike to ther Idolatry
They had muche prouicion and great preperacion
Yet God hath gyuen our Kynge the victorye

They did robe and spoule al the Kynges frendes
They called them heritekes with spight & disdayne
They roffled a space lyke tirance and findes
They put some in preson & sume to greate payne
And sume fled a waie or else they had bene slayne
As was Wyllam hilling that marter truly
Whiche they killed at sandford mowre in the playne
Where yet god hath giuen oure Kynge the victory
They came to plumowith the Kinges trusty towne [1]

There is another fragment, evidently of the same ballad, but whether it should be placed before or after the above is uncertain.

" And all this came by confession in the eare
But God hath gyuen ouer Kynge the Victorye

For under confession thes prestes dothe bynd
The simpel people most earnyst of all
On payne of damnacion to follow ther mynde
And then absolucion for that haue they shall
with all good prayer eclesyasticall
And this to upholde ther Idolatry
To most rank treason they caused men to fal
But God hath gyuen oure Kyneg the Victorye

---

[1] These are obviously rough proofs, so " pomodstock " may well be intended for Poundstock, although no other reference to this vicar has been found. The incumbent in 1536 was Simon Moreton. A Gabriel Moreton, vicar of Ewnye next Lelant, was "noted to be a rebel," according to certain Chancery Proceedings (Eliz. Ser. II. 107, 22). Roger Harward paid his First-fruits as Vicar of Poundstoke, 16 January, 1550, so it is probable that Simon Moreton lost his life in the Rebellion. The murder of William Hellyon on the Church House steps at Sampford has been described on p. 135. In placing his martyrdom at Sandford More truth was probably sacrificed for rhyme. For the attack on Plymouth, see p. 130.

The supper of the Lorde ys set forthe truly
to come & receave y^t they do dysdayne
they saye yt ys a thinge that came up but newly
which shall not continew it maye be ceartayne
For we will sure have the masse up agayne
And God of little myght hanged vp on hye
For whiche they haue fowght and manye of them slayne
Because God gyueth oure Kynge the Victorye

And now marke ther madness which here doth ēsewe
The gospell of Christ most sincere and fine
Lyke most cruel tirantes they wolde nedes subdew
They rent and tore the bokes both lefe and line

Another slip is like the above without the first
two lines, and with the following in place of the last
two :—

They wolde nedes contynew ȳ Popes owne wyne
Sclandering the Kinges

The remaining ballad runs as follows :—

" O Lord thy word is our sure touchstone
That leadeth mankynde, to hys saluation
Vyce for to eschewe, and all abomination
Ipocrysie, Idolatry, which is mans perdition
O Lorde is not the merites of thy passion
A sure seale of fre pardone, and remyssion
That once was shed for màns redemption
Upon the crosse was offered, that high oblacion

O Lorde thou dyddest thy fathers wrath pacify
Obedient thou wast unto a shamefull death
For mans lyfe, thou suffredest patiently
Thou yeldest the gost, as the scripture sayth
And rose from death, to lyfe the thyrde daye
And sittest in heauen, with great power & maiestie
Coequall with the father, thys is no naye
Making intercession, for vs synners perpetuallye

O Lorde howe long shall we wepe and crye
For fault of foode, to the soule spirituall
They watchmen are dome, and lie in theyr stye
Their filthy liuying is so abbomynable
To fede they flocke, they take no care nor payne
To teach or preach, thy fathful testament."

Such, then, are the fragments of ballads with other matter contained in the proof sheets picked up probably in Bertelet's office about the year 1549, and used to " stuff " the cover of a book then being rebound.

CHAPTER XXII

THE PRISONERS IN LONDON

> " Down went the Crosses in every country
> God's servants used with such cruelty,
> Dismembered (like beasts) in the open high way.
> Their inwards pluckt out and hearts where they lay,
> In such (most grievous) tyrannical sort
> That too, too shameful were here to report."—
>   FOREST'S " Grysilde the Seconde."

INTO a London wrought up to a high pitch of excitement and full of detestation of the ringleaders of the insurrection, came a sorrowful procession on the 8th September.[1]

After Lord Russell's departure from Exeter, according to his order and appointment, as Hoker says—

" the chief Captains and principal heads of this rebellion whom he left in prison in the King's Gaol at Exeter were carried to London and commanded to the Tower." [2]

Lord Grey was placed in command of their escort and entrusted with the safe-conduct of Arundell and his ten companions. Before he started Russell probably read to him the instructions he had received from the Council—

" When you send up the prisoners we do not doubt but you will send them up strongly enough and if any attempt should

---

[1] Wriothesley, "Chron.," p. 32. The warrant for payment of the expenses incurred in bringing up Arundell and ten other prisoners, given in Aug. Of. Misc. Bk. 258, is dated 22nd September. Naturally some days would elapse before the costs were passed.

[2] Hoker, p. 95.

be [made] to deliver them out of their hands, you will give them that bring the prisoners such charge that rather than that they should be enforced to lose them than make them first sure of escaping that they may give account of them to us quick or dead." [1]

In other words, if any rescue should be attempted, the prisoners were to be killed rather than permitted to escape.

Therefore, heavily guarded, probably securely bound, and with their escort instructed to slay them if the country people tried to rescue them, the company set out for London, issuing by the East Gate on to the high-road. In such manner the conquered leaders passed through the district so recently in their hands, crossing the Otter at Fenny Bridges, where, with bowed heads, they would have murmured a prayer for the souls of their departed comrades, who had fallen bravely fighting there—traces of the battle would have yet remained. At each cross-road they would have been aware of some putrifying corpse dangling from a gallows—a melancholy reminder of their defeat, the adherents whom they had hoped to lead to victory, already thus brutally executed under martial law. So to the confines of the county they made their sad and weary way, broken and van-quished leaders of a ruined cause, with evidence enough on all sides to break the spirits of the most sanguine, and to prepare them for the ordeal they themselves would have to undergo and for the terrible fate which almost certainly awaited them. To add to their discomfiture, they would have heard the jeers and sneers of the multitude, so ready to turn against a fallen hero, and by revilings gain credit with the conqueror. The lowered eyes of the leaders could not have noted the sympathetic glances of those who dared make no open demonstration on their behalf.

We know who composed this melancholy company

---

[1] S. P. Dom. Ed. VI. VIII. 47.

of vanquished men from a letter sent with them, signed by Lord Russell, Lord Grey, and Sir William Herbert. It is endorsed—

> " The names of the prisoners of the West parts. Prisoners sent from the Lord Privy Seal."

The list reads—

> " Sʳ Thomas Pomeroy
> Humfrey Arundell
> Winslade the elder
> Winslade thonger
> Wise
> Harryse
> Coffyn
> Byrry
> Holmes
> ffortescue " [1]

Baldly they are recorded, like so much consigned merchandise; but better so than with some significant paragraph attached as occurs below—

> " Castell,[2] secretary to Arundell by compulsion, sent thither as no prisoner but as the accuser of Arundell and Coffin. To whome for the honesty we have perceived in him in all his declaration we shall heartily pray your Grace to be good Lord accordingly. He came in of himself and in the midst of the hottest stirs he sent his secret advertisement to Mr. Godolphin and other gentlemen of so much as he knew of Arundell his proceedings and the rest."

Other details of his treachery we know not, nor his fate.

On their arrival in London they were placed in close confinement, probably at first together in the Fleet, until further instructions were issued for their disposal. Their

---

[1] This tallies with the number of prisoners given in Aug. Of. Misc. Bk. 258.

[2] This is probably a misspelling of Kestell—a Cornish name—as Mr. Blake suggests in his account of the Rebellion. There was then living a James Kestell of Kestell, whose son John married Jackett, daughter of John Coffin of Porthledge. This John may have been the traitor.

reception in the city that dull September day was doubtless an added trial, for the way would have been lined
with citizens who had for a considerable period dreaded
the advance of the rebels, and who were stirred to violent
hatred by sermons breathing an unchristian spirit, by
ribald ballads, and by distorted tales of the evil conduct
of the insurgents. Such would have actively and vocifer-
ously demonstrated their anger against the ringleaders, as
well as their appreciation of the valour of their conquerors.

Their immediate experience we can only infer from
the documents which have survived. That Somerset
openly or secretly favoured them was believed by many,
and his enemies formulated these charges among others :
That he had entertained the most notablest captains and
chiefest leaders of the said commotions with great gifts
and rewards, and some also with annual livings. That
he had delivered divers persons arrested and committed
to prison for felony, manslaughter, murder, and treason,
contrary to the laws and statutes of the realm. That
against the King and Council's will he had set forth a
proclamation against enclosures, which had caused
dangerous insurrections in the land, wherein divers of the
King's subjects have been spoiled and many a worthy
man slain. That he had suffered rebels and traitors to
assemble and lie in camp and armour against the King,
his nobles and gentlemen without any speedy suppressing them. That by his gifts in money, with promises of
fees, rewards, and services, he had encouraged many of
the said rebels. That in favour of them contrary to law
he had caused a proclamation to be made that none of
the said rebels or traitors should be sued or vexed for
any of their said offences committed in the said rebellion.[1]

But events occurred within a few weeks of the arrival
of the prisoners in London which swept Somerset from

---

[1] It is said by Stowe, but without quoted authority, that Somerset
sought to release the two Arundells, Sir John and Sir Thomas, who were
in the Tower for complicity with the Cornish rebels ("Chron.," p. 810).

power, so that he had little time in which to exercise such leniency. By the 12th October he was himself in custody, and those who usurped authority were so much occupied in securing their own position that they could spare little attention for the rebels, four of whom, Arundell, Bury, Wynslade, and Holmes, at some period prior to the 22nd October, were incarcerated in the Tower, where were also confined their friends, the two clerics, Crispyn and Moreman.

Although the ringleaders had already undergone a thorough examination in the West by Lord Russell, Lord Grey, Sir William Herbert, and the Knight Marshal, who sought information that would implicate others, they had to submit to a further examination at the hands of the Privy Council, who endeavoured to " pick out " matter incriminating persons in high positions, if not the Princess Mary and Somerset, at all events Cardinal Pole and others of the old persuasion. Three members of the Council, Sir Edward North, Sir John Baker, and Sir Richard Southwell, were selected for the task, and obtained nothing to their satisfaction, so further examinations were made, not without suspicion of the use of rack and terror, at the hands of Lord Chancellor Rich,[1] Sir John Mason, and Sir Thomas Smith, the latter being the man who used such coarse brutality towards Bonner, so probably to accused traitors of lower rank he would have shown even less gentleness.

The result of their work as regards the four chief Western rebels is thus recorded in a Memorandum :—

> " A Report of the Prisoners being in the Tower, the 22nd of October, made by Serjeant Mullynax, and the King's Attorney.

[1] Rich is said to have taken part personally in the racking of Anne Askew. Pollard goes so far as to say that under Somerset's rule " the thumbscrew and rack stood idle in the Tower " (" England under Protector," p. 323), but gives no authority for such a statement. In a letter signed by the Protector, Russell is instructed to send up rebels if he thinks they will not confess except " upon the rack or terror " (29th June, 1549).

Humphrey Arundell of Helland in Cornwall esquire confesseth that he and two others fled into a wood for fear of the rebels and there remained two days and after his wife being great with child desired him, this examinant, to come to her and so he did and then a man of Bodmin came to him and procured him to go with him to the rebels and by force carried him to Bodmin and

Justice [1] on the morrow he sent to Sir Hugh Trevanyon to know what he should do and he advised him to tarry with the rebels and to be in their favour to the intent to admittigate their outragious doings And after the commons and rebels made a supplication whereunto this examinant was privy and he after feigned himself sick and went to his house and the rebels did fetch him again and enforced him to go with them again and after this examinant did stay divers of the rebels and after at Launceston this examinant fled from the rebels and override them all and declared all the matter to Sir Richard Grenville and there was he stayed and he hath been examined by the Knight Marshal and at another time by Mr. Smyth.

John Bury of Silverton in Devon, gent. servant to Sir Thomas Denys, knight, came to Exeter to abide there with his harness and this examinant waited upon his said M^r and after returned to his house at which time this examinant was

Justice taken by five hundred rebels and remained with them until the last fray at Kings Weston in the

---

[1] " Justice " is added in a different hand. Tytler, in his note to this document, says : " To Justice—to immediate execution. The order seems to have been given without any trial being thought necessary : at least we have no proof that anything had taken place except an examination of the prisoners " (I. 272 n.). This is not applicable in the cases quoted, as will be seen below. It is probable that Warwick, when he assumed power, ordered this report of the prisoners then in the Tower to be made. It concludes with a separate list of " Prisoners lately committed to the Tower," including the names of Somerset and his supposed confederates, but without confessions.

county of Somerset and this examinant hath
been examined by the Lord Privy Seal and after
by the Lord Chancellor and after by Mr. Smyth.

John " Wyncheland " of Tregarick in Cornwall,
esquire, was sent for by the rebels post upon
pain of burning his house and thereupon he
resorted to them and there remained with them

Justice   four or five weeks, and was continually at Bodmin
and was taken at Bodmin and was at no fray
and was examined by the Lord Privy Seal and
after by my Lord Grey and after by Mr. Mason.

Thomas Holmes of Bliston in Cornwall yeoman,
went forth with the parishioners of Bliston to
Bodmin and continued there among the rebels
unto the end of the matter and was there against
his will and was in the field when the fray was,
about a mile from the fray, and was examined
by Mr. Herbert and after by Mr. North and Mr.
Mason." [1]

Such was their own account of their actions, which
did not implicate others as anticipated.

Of the remaining six out of the ten rebels sent up,
information is obtainable concerning five only. Of
Coffyn no trace has been found; he may have died of
wounds or may have been released without any record
having been discovered of it.

The other five were confined in the Fleet, whence
they were released by an order of the Privy Council on
the 1st November. These were : Sir Thomas Pomeroy,
William Wynslade, William Fortescue, John Wise, and
William Harris. Of these Pomeroy, Wise, and Harrys
had come in voluntarily,[2] and possibly the others had
done the same, and partly for that reason escaped
punishment. It is probable that they were mulcted in

[1] S. P. Dom. Ed. VI. IX. 48.   [2] Galba. B. XII. f. 115.

heavy fines, and gave bonds for good behaviour, though none such have been discovered, but as far as our story is concerned, they vanish.

It was decided that the Western leaders and the Norfolk rebels should be tried together at Westminster, perhaps with the purpose of further confusing the issues and of ignoring the distinctly religious character of the Western rising.

The order for the Special Commission of Oyer and Terminer was issued the 23rd November; the writ to the Sheriff of Middlesex to summon a panel of twenty-four knights and others is dated the 25th, while the trial itself was fixed for the Tuesday next after the Quinzaine of St. Martin. So upon that day Arundell, Wynslade, Bury, and Holmes were conveyed by water in the custody of the Constable of the Tower from their prison to Westminster Hall.

Here, amid solemn and stately surroundings, the trial for treason took place, the people pressing forward eagerly to see the jurors selected, and to hear the reading of the indictment. The charges against the prisoners, as given to the twelve good men and true, amounted in substance to this :—

That not having the fear of God before their eyes, but seduced by diabolical instigation, and not weighing their allegiance, they feloniously and traitorously excited sedition, rebellion, and insurrection against our Lord the King. That for this purpose they assembled at Bodmin, on the 6th June, and during the six weeks ensuing, a large body of men who levied war and compelled the King's lieges to join them: that they threatened to kill certain imprisoned gentlemen, and ravaged and despoiled the country; and also that Humphrey Arundell and John Wynslade, on the 19th August resisted and murdered the King's soldiers under Lord Russell at Launceston, while John Bury, who had been conjoined with them in the other proceedings, had, in various places in

Somerset, issued proclamations, and had otherwise excited the King's subjects to sedition, being finally captured at Kings Weston on the 27th August, and that Thomas Holmes had issued proclamations and had otherwise excited to sedition, and had resisted the King's men at Bodmin on the 1st August.

Not being able to prove these charges false, the indictment was considered by the jury—no depositions nor recorded statements exist because it was a trial for treason, so, according to custom, nothing was put in writing—and, considering the circumstances, it was not surprising that on their return the jury announced that they were all found guilty.

Thereupon the King's Serjeants-at-law and the King's Attorney immediately sought justice and execution upon them ; so the Court condemned them solemnly to be detained in the Tower and afterwards to be drawn through the midst of the City of London to the gallows of Tyburn, and—

" on that gallows suspended and while yet alive to be cast down upon the ground and the entrails of each to be taken out and burnt before their eyes while yet living and their heads cut off and their bodies to be divided into four parts "

to be distributed at the King's pleasure—a sentence which had during the preceding ten years become so common that the Londoners present would have scarcely shuddered, while some would have anticipated, with gruesome glee, joining in the procession that accompanied the victims.

Meanwhile the rebels were removed from Westminster to the waiting barges, and, in the custody of Sir John Gage, Constable of the Tower, returned to their prison, entering by the Traitor's Gate. There they remained for two months before their sentence was carried out.

Records are silent as to how the interim was spent— whether they were tortured in order to make them incriminate others or were left alone ; whether efforts were made to shake their religious convictions for which they had sacrificed all, or whether they were permitted to enjoy the comforting ministrations of their fellow-captives, Moreman and Crispyn.

At length, on the 27th January, 1549–50, the last sad scene of their lives was enacted; brought from their lodgings within the Tower, they were each thrown down upon a hurdle and fastened to it, lying at full length on their backs, and so lying on the hurdle they were dragged at the heels of horses through the city towards Tyburn, by way of Holborn Bars, probably pausing at St. Giles-in-the-Fields, where would have been offered them the customary great bowl of ale, thereof to drink at their pleasure, this to be their last drink in life.[1]

Who can imagine the full misery that they suffered during that terrible journey, three miles long, over the rough and miry way—that Via Dolorosa, as Marks styles it—

"what grievous things, what torture they endured, where one while the road lay over rough and hard, at another wet and muddy places, which exceedingly abounded!"

Mingling in the hostile crowd would have been some friends and servants, like Rowland Jeynens, a youth of nineteen, and Richard Popham, who had faithfully served Wynslade for ten years. With sorrowful, perhaps tearful, eyes they watched the procession, content not to follow to Tyburn, but satisfied that their captains had been executed because they returned not.[2]

[1] See Marks' "Tyburn Tree," p. 134. Here may be quoted Chamberlain's letter to Carleton, 31st October, 1618: "The morning that he (Ralegh) went to execution there was a cup of excellent sack brought him, and being asked how he liked it, 'As the fellow,' saith he, 'that drinking St. Giles's bowl as he went to Tyburn said: "That was a good drink, if a man might tarry by it."'"

[2] See "Court of Requests," Bdle. 86, No. 21. Jeynens said that he saw "when they wente to Execucon by lande," probably having been impressed by seeing them drawn on hurdles by the road after having seen them brought to Westminster by water.

Arrived at Tyburn Tree, the victims were released from the hurdles and led to the place of execution. That they walked bravely to their death we doubt not; has not Sir Thomas Smith, one of those who examined them, written—

" In no place shall you see malefactors go more constantly, more assuredly and with less lamentation to their death than in England. . . . The nature of our nation is free, stout, hault, prodigal of life and blood." [1]

Little recked the Captains of the seething crowd around them. Their minds would have been fixed upon eternity into which they were about to be launched—a touch of pride in their martyrdom for the " old ancient " faith may have mitigated the thought of the awful death awaiting them. Pardoning their executioner, they advanced and climbed the ladder to the gibbet, pausing a moment for silent prayer, for probably spiritual consolation was denied them, they were presently suspended for a brief period, and then, while still living, they were cut down and the rest of their terrible sentence was completed. Their heads and quarters were afterwards set upon the gates of the City of London. [2]

So ended in the horrors of a traitor's death their unsuccessful efforts to maintain the religion in which they had been nurtured, and their attempts to resist the radical changes made by the members of the King's Council.

Their fellow-prisoners, the Rev. John Moreman and the Rev. Richard Crispyn, remained confined in the Tower somewhat longer. The latter is believed to have died there; his will, dated the 9th September, 1551, was proved on the 10th December following; in it he leaves to his companion, Moreman, certain legacies, including a covered silver cup. Although the Doctor was

---

[1] " Commonwealth," p. 204.   [2] Wriothesley, " Chron." p. 32.

Vitæ norma decens pariter mors iunxerit Una,
Hæc duo Thesea pectora nexa fide.

M. bas. f.

AN EXECUTION.

From an Engraving in "The Life and Death of Mr. E. Geninges."

appointed executor, he could not personally prove the will because of his imprisonment, so it was done by two Devonshire colleagues, John Stephyn and Roger Huet. Moreman remained in the Tower until Mary's reign, and formed one of that company that the Queen greeted, with tears in her eyes, exclaiming, " These are my prisoners," as she bent to kiss them.

There were other prisoners in the Tower, among them two whose experiences require some notice, that is, Sir John Arundell of Lanherne and his brother, Sir Thomas Arundell, of Shaftesbury, first cousins of Humphrey Arundell.

At an early date—some time prior to the 8th July— Sir John was suspected of disloyalty and of favouring the ancient forms of religion—in fact, of complicity in the rebellion. Lord Russell wrote that he had com- manded Sir John to appear before him, but that he had failed so to do. Afterwards he was taken, perhaps voluntarily surrendered himself or else was captured. He was sent to Portsmouth, possibly passing through Lord Grey's hands, to which place the Council sent a messenger to fetch him, about the 18th July.[1] After his arrival in London he was kept in custody until the 27th, when he was brought before the Council. He then said that he had received but two messages from Lord Russell, in neither of which he was commanded upon his alle- giance to appear. One came while he was very sick and not able to travel, and the other he was preparing to obey but was prevented by being brought to London. He had been unable to raise men to assist the Lord Privy Seal as he was in a part of the country where he was not well known. He admitted that—

" upon occasion of the light talk of the people at the first rising of rebels in Devonshire he caused two masses to be said which he said he did only to appease the people, and ever since then

[1] Pet. MSS. 438, Pk. p. 28.

he hath heard and caused to be said the service according to the King's Majesty's order. Procession he sayth he caused to be had upon Corpus Christi Day and after procession the Communion according to the laws and no mass." [1]

The Council did not consider the charges against him substantiated, so he was released on recognisances— himself, his brother Sir Thomas, and Thomas Stradling, of Glamorgan, being bound in £4000, on condition that he did not depart from the city or suburbs above a mile without the special licence of the Lord Protector's Grace.[2] Meanwhile letters were sent to Russell for further particulars of the charges against him. It would seem that his complicity in the rebellion was not proved, as he was released from the recognisances on the 1st November.[3]

Just what happened after this is uncertain, but on the 14th December he and Sir William Godolphin were bound in recognisances of £1000 each to keep the peace towards each other until the matter in variance between them was settled.[4]

It is possible that Godolphin brought from the West some evidence against Arundell or made some fresh charge. In any event, Sir John was soon after lodged in the Tower, and his brother, Sir Thomas, was committed to the same prison on the 30th January, 1549–50.[5] The King enters in his Journal, after describing Somerset's submission and Southwell's imprisonment and fine, " Likewise Sir Thomas Arundel and Sir John committed to the Tower for conspiracies in the West partes." [6]

Somerset was released on the 6th February, and was restored to the Council on the 10th April. He appears

[1] Pet. MSS. 443, Pk. p. 38. For misplacing these letters, see Appendix F.
[2] P. C. Reg. 304.
[3] Ibid.
[4] Ibid. 366.
[5] Ibid. 376.
[6] Nichols' " Lit. Rem." II. 247.

to have done his best to obtain lenient treatment of the two Arundells,[1] and so far succeeded as to have permission granted on the 18th to Sir John's wife that she might resort to her husband in the Tower, and a little later the brothers were allowed more liberty within the Tower.[2]

But still the Arundells languished in confinement for some time, availing themselves of the only means of protest—refusal to pay for their " diets." When this payment was demanded they declared that they would not comply " because they be causeless detained in prison," so, on the 14th April, 1551, the Lieutenant of the Tower was commanded to put them " in such straight prison as they were by former letters," in order that " it may somewhat appear to them that their imprisonment was upon just occasion." [3]

On the 4th October, 1551, Sir Thomas Arundell was brought before the Council, the Duke of Somerset presiding, and after being admonished that the King had just cause, considering Arundell's inquiet proceedings contrary to his Majesty's commandment and his own allegiance, to punish him with the uttermost rigour of the law, yet his Highness, being rather inclined to mercy than severity, was pleased to hope that his long imprisonment would be a warning to him from falling into the like fault and an occasion to remember the rather his duty, so he would set him at liberty—upon heavy recognisances.

On the 16th October, not a fortnight later, Somerset and his adherents were again arrested, a story told by Sir Thomas Palmer forming the ground of the charges against the Protector. Among other things, Palmer declared that Sir Thomas Arundell had informed Somerset " that the Tower was safe," and for this Arundell

[1] Pollard's " Protector," p. 283.
[2] See P. C. Reg. II. 432 and III. 27 and 54.
[3] *Ibid.* III. 258.

was arrested on the 18th.[1] The charge finally brought
against him and Sir Ralph Vane was that they had
"feloniously moved and instigated John de Fontunay,
otherwise John Barteville and others at the Tower on
the 20th May previous to murder John, Duke of Northumberland, then Earl of Warwick."[2] Vane's condemnation seems to have been speedily accomplished,[3]
but Arundell "was much pitied and had hard measure
at his trial, which began at seven o'clock in the morning
and continued until noon, then the jury went aside, and
they did not agree on their verdict,"[4] so were "shut up
in a house, together without meat or drink, because they
could not agree all that day and all that night," but
"in the morning they did cast him."[5] Burnet adds that
those who did not consider him guilty "for preserving
their lives, were willing to yield to the fierceness of those
who were resolved to have him found guilty."[6]

[1] Froude says of the conspiracy that "the Duchess of Somerset brought
into it her brother Sir Michael Stanhope and her *half-brother*, Sir Thomas
Arundel" (V. p. 371). The relationship of the Duchess and Sir Thomas
is not apparent.

[2] Barteville had been imprisoned in the Tower for some time. His
name occurs in the list of prisoners there on 22nd October, 1549. He
describes himself as "John Bartylfyld knight, frenchmean," elsewhere
he is called Captain Barteville, and says that "he was retained in the
King's service and has a pension under the Great Seal Cl[h] and he was never
examined but committed to the Tower by Mr. Smythe" (S. P. Dom.
Ed. VI., IX. 48). He was released 1st November, 1551 (P. C. Reg. III.
405), probably that he might give evidence against Arundell. For a time
he was in the charge of two of "the Guard" (*ibid.* 486), then sent to the
Warden of the Fleet, who was to intreat him courteously, and, after the
execution of Arundell, the Knight Marshal was instructed to bestow
Barteville in an honest house where he may be well intreated and his charges
allowed (*ibid.* 491).

[3] Baga de Secretis. Pouch 20, Bdle. 1.

[4] Burnet's Ref. II. 336.   [5] Edward VI.'s Journal.

[6] Burnet says that Sir Thomas Palmer and Sir Thomas Arundell were
not at first sent to the Tower, but kept under guards in their chambers
(II. 329). It seems possible that Somerset's enemies expected Arundell
to confess something to incriminate the Duke, perhaps for that reason they
allowed him to be released from his previous confinement, and that therefore he was treated like the other informer, Palmer. Morysine, commenting
on Arundell's arrest, said he believed him "to be the root of as much
mischief as might have budded out of this practice. He has a head able

Sir Thomas Arundell was beheaded on Tower Hill on the 26th February, 1551-2, and Sir Ralph Vane hanged at the same time.[1] But Sir John Arundell, who was not included in these charges, remained in prison. On the 19th May, 1552, the Lieutenant of the Tower was instructed to speak to Sir John for the payment of his diets, which were due to the present holder of the office and his predecessor. In a list of " suits to be made to the King's Majesty, moved upon Sunday xxix Junij, 1552," is one for his deliverance, " he being bound by recognizance to bide the order of the Lords for his fine and not to depart the city of London or within   miles of the same till he be further licensed by his Majesty." As against this there is a marginal note " granted," it is probable that he was released soon afterwards. In Mary's reign he rose in favour, and held positions of trust.[2]

There must have been many rebels captured and taken to London : some of these were, we learn from the Register of the Privy Council, released upon heavy recognisances, such as Thomas a Leigh, of St. Mary Week, who was a "servant of Humphrey Arundell"; Thomas Dowrish, of Crediton; Richard Roscarrock, into whose family Arundell's niece had married ; John Prideaux, of Tavistock ; and Humphrey Bonville, who had married Wynslade's sister. But in vain do we seek to know the fate of the vast multitude who suffered in the cause of religion.[3]

enough to set them all upon as evil a work as this they had in hand, be it as big as it can be. It seldom happens that a man's head aches for giving good counsel " (S. P. For. Ed. VI. (1547-53), p. 204).

[1] Machyn records that their bodies were placed in coffins and their heads in cases, to be buried in the Tower. The register of the Chapel of St. Peter ad Vincula has an entry of their burial within the Chapel. Poynet is quoted as saying Arundell conspired with Warwick, but it is evident that he has confused Sir Thomas with the Earl of Arundel.

[2] S. P. Dom, Ed. VI., Vol. XIV. No. 45. The number of miles is left blank.

[3] Burnet states that Arundell, the Mayor of Bodmin, Tempson and Barrat, the last two being priests, with six or seven more, were taken and hanged, but gives no further particulars. Perhaps Bray, Thompson, and Barret were the three executed at Tyburn on 27th August. (See Burnet, II, 189, and Grey Friars' Chronicle, p. 62.)

CHAPTER XXIII

LORD RUSSELL'S ACTIONS

" But, alas, most gracious King and godly governors, for the tender mercy
of God, in our Saviour Jesu Christ, take good and diligent heed when
ye be chasing the wily fox of papistical superstition that the greedy
wolf of covetous ambition do not creep in at your backs. For surely
he will do more harm in one week than the fox did in a year."—LEVER.

BUT, turning from the sad scenes in London, let us see
what was happening elsewhere.

Lord Russell's movements after the capture of
Arundell on the 19th August at Launceston are somewhat uncertain. As has been mentioned, Hoker states
that he marched into Cornwall, returned to Exeter, and
" after departed towards London."

It is apparent from one of the Council's letters that
Russell had written to them on the 7th September that
he proposed advancing into Cornwall and disarming the
people there, but perhaps this was a second visit to that
county.[1]

---

[1] See Pet. MS. f. 463, Pk. p. 71. " As for your orders devised for
Cornwall, we have bothe seen them and return tharticles. . . . And yf
you have alredye gone through theis orders " those who were considered
faithful were to receive again their harness for the defence of the coast.
It may have been at this time that Stratton contributed a company of
men and ten horses to ride with the Sheriff to serve the King. Charge
for their horses' ' mett ' and payments to them occur in the Churchwardens' Accounts, 1551 (Add. MS. 32, 244, f. 19ᵇ). One man had xˢ xᵈ
" in part payment for his horse which he lost in thes besynes & the viij
men wer agred that the sayd Nycolas should have xxvˢ for hem & the
rest to hem for his horse vˢ vᵈ ob." After the names of those who served
is a charge for " makyng of the gaylls." This may mean " gallows " as
the next entry is " for helpyng them vp."

He probably remained in Exeter during the greater part of September, endeavouring to settle affairs there, and in the surrounding district—a matter of no little difficulty.[1]

Among his tasks would have been attending to the prisoners in Exeter Gaol, of whom there must have been a considerable number, for we find entered in the City accounts as much as 33^s 4^d received as fees from prisoners at the Gaol Delivery, and 5^s for the sale of a sword taken as deodan from a felon.[2]

Meanwhile his correspondence with the Council continued, though few letters written in this interval are preserved. Such as there are deal chiefly with the question of expense incurred by the army, which he is continually urged to diminish. This had long troubled them ; as early as the 27th July they complained that he required a greater force than the ill-armed rebels possessed, and that a large addition under Herbert would be a source of weakness rather than strength.[3]

But Russell knew the necessity of having a large army when he must take the aggressive against a force working from within the circle and he was aware that the fighting powers of the rebels were not to be despised.

By the 10th August, fearing a French invasion, more urgent orders were given commanding him to diminish his forces further—the Somerset and Dorset men must go to defend their coasts, while the horsemen, who were double charges, and the "strangers," who cost more,

---

[1] There were many claims presented then or later for disbursements made at his order. See Appendix M for entries in local Churchwardens' Accounts.

[2] See Exeter City Muniments, Receiver's Accounts, 2–3 Edw. VI. At the same time he accounted for 16^d for the *cippis de vulnera* (see Chap. XII.) and 30^s for the sale of sixty pounds of gunpowder. No similar entries occur in the previous year nor in the two succeeding years, but in 1–2 Edw. VI. 37^s 6^d was received for "unius vetris bumberd fferror" sold to a smith. Bombard was a kind of cannon.

[3] It was considered necessary to have ten or twelve thousand under Warwick to subdue the Norfolk rebels, who were nearer the Council's own door.

were needed elsewhere. They reminded him that he must prey upon the country, especially as the people had befriended the rebels, ignoring the fact that the district had been despoiled already, and that the arrest of harvesting operations had caused greater scarcity.

To these repeated orders Lord Russell evidently took exception, writing strongly on the subject. He pointed out that he had not enough men to control the disturbed district, and although the rebels daily sued for pardon, they came not in as perfectly as he could desire, so it was unsafe to weaken his power ; indeed, he really required more men and more money.

Still intent on their cheese-paring policy, and ready to sacrifice all so that they might increase the army nearer home, they repeated their former instructions, adding that they required ten or twelve thousand men for Warwick in Norfolk and eight or ten thousand to attend the King, while the North must still be supplied, and the coasts defended. He must, therefore, really send them the stranger-horsemen, but the footmen, whose skill with the hagbut he praised so highly, he might retain. As for sending victuals by sea, he was enough of a seaman to know the uncertainty of that at this season of the year. They insisted that he must not permit the people to deny to the King's forces that which they had readily given to the rebels, at the same time admitting that they knew that Russell's men had already denuded the country of supplies.

But the Lord Privy Seal would not yield, and his replies gave little satisfaction. He again asked for money as well as for men to be sent by sea to be landed at the backs of the rebels, so they sent him £6000, which he was to husband to the uttermost, and they ordered two galleys to collect as many men as possible, but they doubted whether more than two or three hundred could be obtained. He must do what he can locally, and, catching at straws, they suggest that there was a pirate

named Thompson, who haunted the Severn, and Russell
might practise to gain his aid on the promise of pardon
for past offences.[1]

Lord Russell, in his letter, had expressed his opinion
on the much-discussed subject of the " releyfe of shepe,"
that is, the tax on sheep as well as other goods granted
by the Commons for the relief of the King's necessities,
a matter brought to Russell's notice by a letter from Sir
William Godolphin.   He was instructed to reply that if
the rebels would become

"again good subjects and leave immediately their evil life,
which so much displeased God and varieth from their duties
allegiance and subjection, and doing henceforth as becometh
them, ye dare presume so far of the King's majesty's goodness
for them that ye will adventure so much of your own lands
as may pay the matter for them if it be not obtained and they
by their submission and good demeanour henceforth merit it
at your hands." [2]

This question of the relief of sheep crops up again in
another letter in connection with the Clothiers' petition,
and was an important matter in the West.   A relief had

[1] This pirate was brought a prisoner to London on 26th August, just
a week after this letter was written.   The result of this effort to render
help by sea is unrecorded.   But the following notes on the subject may
be interesting.   Immediately after the account of the Western rising in
the King's Journal is entered the loss of the *Black Galley*.   On 5th November
a payment was made to Captain Tyrell of the *Black Galley* sent to "Sylle,"
and £250 3s. 4d. paid to William Hawkins of Plymouth for victuals provided for the King for the seas, which were "spoyled by the rebells"
(see P. C. Reg.).   Perhaps, though, these were stores destroyed when
Plymouth was sacked in the early days of the risings.   There is no indication whatever that sailors *as such* favoured the Government or were then
more Protestant than Romanist in their opinions.

[2] Pet. MS. 456[d], Pk. p. 62.   It might have been a serious risk had
Russell made this promise considering the divisions in the Council ; but
the suggestion was in keeping with their custom of being generous with
other men's goods.   This letter of 19th August reads as if Cranmer had had
a hand in its composition.   He had not signed recent letters as he had been
absent from the Council meetings, but he now returned from his sermonising
to lecture the rebels on their duty to the King.

been granted by the Temporality on the 15th February, 1548-9, for three years, which amounted to 8d. in the pound on cloths and 1d. on each sheep owned by one person beyond their allotted ten " shear shepe." The Clothmakers considered the system of collecting this tax on cloth very " comberous," and so tedious to them " for makinge of their books and accompts thereof by reason of the lacke of Alnegers not always present when tyme requiereth," while as for the sheep tax it was a great charge to the poor Commons who had few sheep and so " cumberouse " to the Commissioners that they could not in a manner tell how to carry out their duties.[1]

It is difficult to tell whether Russell's influence affected the issue, but soon after the opening of the next Parliament, i.e. the 16th November, the House of Commons asked permission to consider the question, and a bill was rapidly passed through both Houses for the discharge of this relief and for the granting of a tax for a year in its place under a different arrangement.[2]

Some friction arose between the Lord Privy Seal and the Council because he had pardoned certain rebels. He, the harsh disciplinarian, had been reproved for not executing justice upon Robert Paget, whose brother was of the Council. A general pardon had been sent to Russell, but the Council wrote immediately afterwards that it should be withheld for a time.

" When these Commotions were over," writes Burnet, " the protector pressed that there ought to be a general and free pardon speedily proclaimed, for quieting the country, and giving their affairs a reputation abroad. This was much opposed by many of the Council who thought it better to accomplish their several ends by keeping the people under the lash, than by so profuse a mercy. But the protector was resolved on it, judging the state of affairs required it. So he gave out a

---

[1] Statutes of the Realme, IV. p. 122.
[2] The Bill was read a third time in the Upper House on 17th January, 1549-50. See Journal of H. of L., Vol. I. p. 318.

general pardon of all that had been done before the twenty-first of August : excepting only those whom they had in their hands, and resolved to make public examples." [1]

As no trace of such a pardon can be found, it has been suggested that the evidence relating to it was destroyed on Somerset's disgrace. That such a general pardon was granted is evident from the instructions to Lord Russell of the 21st August—

" One thing we have thought yet good to admonish you, that for so much as the pardon which ye have is general, if ye should give it soon, ye should peradventure quit at unawares some of the chief authors of these tumults and peradventure of the most obstinate persons, therefore ye shall do well to prolong the time, and with declaring that ye will sue hither for their pardon, and some such fair words acquitting the rest, while ye pick out the most sturdy and obstinate rebels to make example of them by their punishment to the terror of all other, and then with exception of those ye think meet to promulgate, the King's majesty's general pardon to all others." [2]

On the 27th they expressed their intention of personally examining the prisoners sent up in order " to pick out of them further matter," and again they tell Lord Russell to withhold the pardon, because, as it is general, it might include Arundell and others whom he has in hold, but as this delay and doubt may engender worse inconvenience, he should pardon particularly such as he thinks meet, and, to satisfy the people by holding out hope, he may declare that he has already written to the Council for a general pardon, which " shortly ye trust to receive in ample form." Meanwhile, by confessions

[1] It is possible that Burnet bases his statement on the draft of the Council's letter of 21st August, which is at the P. R. O. (S. P. Dom. Edw. VI. VIII., 47). Strype (II. i. 276) gives 4th September as the date of the general pardon. " The King's Free and General Pardon " is noted in the House of Commons Journals on 25th January, 1549–50. Careful search has been made in Privy Seals, Patent Rolls, and elsewhere.

[2] Pet. MS. 458^d (21st August), Pk. p. 63.

or otherwise, he may find out those who have been notable ministers amongst the rebels and apprehend them, so that by the time the pardon is issued the most culpable may have been arrested.[1]

Perhaps the general pardon sent off by Somerset was, on second thought, considered premature ; or that the Council, unaware until later that he had sent it, desired to restrict the effect of his criminal leniency, as they would have styled it ; at all events, one of the charges brought a few weeks later against the Protector was his lenient treatment of the rebels. Already Warwick's influence must have been making itself felt at the Council board.

Between the above-mentioned letter, which differs greatly from all the preceding both in style and spelling, there is a gap extending to the 10th September. From the latter it is evident that the Council had received complaints of some sort of Lord Russell's conduct of affairs. Already there was much dissatisfaction among the people in the West over the transference of the rebels' property. According to the proclamation of the 11th July, any one was at liberty to enter upon and take possession of the property of a "rebellour," especially upon copyholds, a step avowedly taken, according to the letter of the 22nd July, in order to breed variance, and so to cause the people to stay at home to protect their estates from intruders. In some way unknown, Lord Russell had seen fit to alter the wording of this proclamation. But now either those who had been ousted or else such pardoned rebels as found their property occupied, had complained to the authorities who, as

---

[1] It is evident from the following entry that Russell availed himself of this power to pardon. " 23 Feb. 1550(–1). A lettre to the Justices of Assize in Cornwall for the giving of order to staye certain accions waieged agaynst certain persons rebellours in Cornwall, whose pardon were given by the Lord Privie Seal by [sic] Henry Tredennyck, William Tredennyck, William Viell, Robert Whettell, Thomas Calwen, and others." (P, C. Reg. III, p. 222).

usual, sought a scapegoat. They began by administering a reproof to the Lord Privy Seal, to which he made a spirited reply. He justified his alteration of the proclamation, declaring that it would have been impossible to administer it as it was worded ; it would have led to endless confusion. He added that he wished he had known that they did not mean what they said.[1]

In their letter of the 10th September, after ostentatiously praising his actions and protesting that they had not the least intention of impugning his motives, they pointed out that he had misinterpreted their meaning. With much reiteration they explained that the very end and aim of their proclamation was actually what he said it would be—variance and contention among the rebels— so that, rather than leave their lands and copyholds to be taken by their neighbours, they would stay at home and not swell the forces resisting the Lord Privy Seal. But in direct opposition to this statement they proceeded to declare that the proclamation did not " warrantize " Russell's gifts, as it was contrary to the common law of England that the King should dispose of the estate of a subject before he was attainted, and that the proclamation could by no means bear the interpretation which he had put upon it, adding—

" we must say that if no more had been done than that beareth which was sent from us to be proclaimed this matter would be soon answered. . . . And touching our meaning the very words of the proclamation sheweth plainly that it was only to draw back and divide the force of the countries which were coming against you." [2]

Evidently they were determined to have it both ways— whichever he did was wrong.

But in the end the Council, when under Warwick's domination, agreed to repudiate the proclamation entirely, and lay the blame for it upon the Protector.

[1] See Pet. MS. 462ᵈ, Pk. p. 70.   [2] See Pet. MS. 463, Pk. p. 70.

One of the charges so soon after formulated against him was " that in favour of them [the rebels] contrary to law he had caused a proclamation to be made, that none of the said Rebels, or Traitors, should be sued or vexed for any of their offences committed in the said Rebellion." [1]

Russell had protested that if they repudiated the proclamation as issued by him it would bring all proclamations into disrepute. They agreed with him except so far in as the one under discussion was concerned. They remind him that he had made gifts to some of his own followers which, no doubt, he meant for the best " for the encouragement of your soldiors and chastment of the disobedient subjects " ; still, others would grudge not only in Devon but elsewhere when they heard that men's goods were taken away without order of law.

Another cause of complaint had been brought to the notice of the Council by the Exonians—the conduct of the wild Welsh soldiers. They write that the men " being in the King's wages, and under your government, might have been well stayed from going to the spoil." [2] This, with the dispossession of owners, might well make the people desperate, " and much the more stirred to follow their devilish enterprise."

Complaints of the lack of restraint of the soldiers came with ill-grace from those who had long been urging Russell to force the inhabitants of the district to provide victuals for his men by fear of burning, and who had so reluctantly paid the necessary funds for these soldiers' wages in driblets. The payments made to him were scanty enough. On the 20th June, £2,000 ; on the 10th July, £500 ; on the 19th July, £2,000 ; on the 30th July, £1,000 ; on the 14th August, £4,000 ; and on the 21st August, £2,000. Besides these are £1,000 borrowed from the Mayor of Exeter ; £693 6s. from the town of Totnes,

---

[1] See Speed, p. 810. [2] Pet. MS. 464³, Pk. p. 71.

and £30 paid for the Gloucestershire men. Lord Grey received £500, while Jermigny and Sanga had £3,464, with several disbursements for Almayne soldiers, some of whom served in the West : so the cost, as gleaned from the Council's Register, exceeded £17,000. But these payments, dragged with the greatest difficulty out of the Council in small instalments by Lord Russell, should be compared with the liberal treatment of Lord Warwick, who received £5,000 in one payment. In the above-quoted letter, the Council complain of the inaccuracy of a " scedule " of expenses enclosed in response to their request, and insisted that he should further reduce his forces.

Two letters from the Protector are also preserved, dated the 18th and 25th September. The first is brief, reproving the Lord Privy Seal for not seeing to it that due execution had been done on Robert Paget " for his worthie deserts." He cannot understand Russell's reluctance, for there are those who cast it up against Somerset that he had consented to the death of his own brother, but would wink at Paget's misdoings—a matter that touched his honour. The other deals with the much-talked-of relief of sheep, for which the rebels were to taste his Majesty's goodness, and, after expressing sorrow for their late disorders and obtaining pardon, were to be treated as all others were. Reference is also made to certain rewards which Russell had suggested should be given.[1]

It must have been shortly after the 25th September that the Lord Privy Seal left Exeter. Just before his departure for London he wrote a letter to those in authority within the city, appointing five gentlemen of the neighbourhood to assist them in the task of maintaining order in the district, and to attend to the removal of

---

[1] See Pet. MS. 465ᵈ and 466. Pocock (p. 74) heads the latter letter, " The Protector's Letter to Lord Russell recommending merciful dealing with the rebels," which is not a very apt description.

the clappers of the church bells—a subject discussed elsewhere.[1]

Meanwhile events of moment were occurring in London. The Protector's days of power were running short. On the 27th August, Warwick had broken the strength of the Norfolk rebels with terrible slaughter at Dussindale, and soon afterwards returned to London, counting the time ripe for his own rise to power by causing the downfall of his rival, Somerset. There may be some truth in the story given by the Spanish Chronicler, which, at least, is a picturesque version of a rumour. Warwick, accompanied by many English and foreign captains, who had served in the late rebellions, went to the Protector and demanded rewards for their services. " They have been paid their wages, and the King is not in a position to give rewards," was the reply. Warwick insisted that as they had done so much when the whole kingdom was in revolt they must be rewarded, and when again told nothing could be done for them, angrily exclaimed—

" What ! my lord Protector, do you think to excuse yourself by saying there is no money ? Well, it shall be so. I do not wonder that the King is poor, my lord Duke, seeing the sums of money you are squandering in buildings. You think much more of that than what is good for the King and his kingdom. God knows, and we all know, that if you had made proper provision, the King would not have lost the forts near Boulogne which he has lost. If you keep in power much longer you will end by losing everything." [2]

This sentiment would have been applauded by the

---

[1] The date attributed to this letter in the Calendar at the Guildhall in Exeter, where the original is preserved, is inaccurate—August, 1549. In the first place the Council's order concerning the church bells is dated 12th September, and besides, Russell's letter is addressed to the " right worshipfulles Mr. John Tuckfilde Mayor, &c."; and this gentlemen was not elected to that office until Michaelmas, 1549. This contains his instructions for the safe keeping of the city which, on his departure, Russell transferred to the civic authorities and others appointed in place of the military officers who had attended to it under his orders hitherto.

[2] Spanish Chronicle, p. 185.

captains with much rattling of swords and jingling of spurs, and it was followed by wrangling between the Duke and Earl, the former attributing Warwick's insolence to his own forbearance, while the Earl blamed the Lords for allowing Somerset to usurp power.[1]

Even in his letter to Lord Russell it seems possible to read between the lines indications of Somerset's waning power and his dread of approaching trouble. Was it premonition of evil, or secret warnings of Warwick's intentions, or his own schemes against the Earl that caused him to add this postscript to his letter of the 25th September ?

" We do look for you and Sir William Herbert, at the furthest about the viij[th] day of the next month, about which time we would gladly have you here for matters of importance." [2]

Some suspicion may have led Warwick to strike his blow a couple of days earlier. On the 5th October, Somerset sent out hasty messengers calling upon all loving subjects to repair to Hampton Court to defend the King and his uncle. Then followed that rapid sequence of events which brought Somerset to the Tower with the headsman's axe hovering over him, averted for the moment, but to fall before very long.

The general question of his fall is beyond our scope, but some reference to events which immediately ensued is needed.

When Somerset sent copies of " the message to loving subjects," to Russell and Herbert, he added a hasty letter urging them to come to his aid. Following on the heels of his first messenger—on the very next day—he despatched his son, Lord Edward Seymour, to declare and

---

[1] Perhaps in consequence of this armed demonstration Sir Thomas Chaloner was given, on 3rd September, £2,000 to pay " according to thorder to him geven to the bandes of Jermigny and Petro Sanga, togeyther with the full contentation of the ij ensigns of Almaynes for all former demands until the present day " (P. C. Reg.).

[2] Pet. MS. 466[d], Pk. p. 76.

communicate to them certain things touching the King's Majesty, taking with him a letter in the King's name, "Letting you understand that such a heinous and grievous conspiracy as never was is attempted against us, and our entirely beloved uncle the lord protector. The which they are constrained to maintain with most untrue and false surmises," and untrue tales. He declared that " by the rest of the Council's confession nothing to have been done by our said uncle but that the rest of our Council did agree to." [1]

Somerset also sent a letter to Russell in his own name, saying that such charges were made against him, and calling upon him to " shew the part of a true gentleman, and of a very friend the which thing we trust God shall reward and the King's majesty in time to come." He expected his opponents would also write to Russell, so he added a postscript, " They are not ashamed to send post abroad to tell that we are already committed to the Tower, and that we would deliver the bishops of Winchester and London out of prison, and bring in again the old mass." [2]

Somerset's despairing epistles caused Russell and Herbert to advance with such company as they had " for surety of his Highness as appertained," but, on reaching Andover, on the 7th October, they " understood many things," as they informed the Lords of the Council in a letter. The country was everywhere in a " rore," the gentlemen had received identical letters to those sent to them and among the Commons had been sown abroad bills to raise them in the King's name. They piously declare that God was the guide of their journey, for instead of raising " v or vj^{ml} men at the least to have gone to Windsor," and permitting the " uncertain rage that the commons might have taken . . . as God would, the gentlemen of these parts hearing of our being here have stayed upon our setting forwards," and

[1] S. P. Dom. Edw. VI. IX. 9.　　　[2] Pet. MS. 467, Pk. p. 83.

sought their opinion. Weighing well the state of affairs, including the " tyckelnesse " of the country, they sent by Lord Edward Seymour their reply to the Protector.[1] Their decision was against him ; they wrote lamenting the " civil dissension which is happened between your Grace and the nobility," and expressed their conviction that " this great extremity proceedeth only upon private causes between your Grace and them : " consequently they decided " in the heat of this broil to levy as great power " as they might for the security of the King and the realm, which they thought to be in peril and danger during these factions. As for the Protector's opponents

" out of doubt the Devil hath not so enchanted nor abused their wits as they would consent to anything prejudicial and hurtful to the King's most royal person, upon whose surety and preservation, as they well know, the state of the realm doth depend."

They agree so entirely with the other lords that no other argument may dissuade them to the contrary, and they beg Somerset to conform himself so that

" these private causes redound not to an universal displeasure of the whole realm. Would God all means were used rather than any blood be shed : which if be once attempted and the case brought to that misery that the hands of the nobility be once polluted each with other's blood, the quarrel once begun will never end till the realm be descended to that woeful calamity that all your posterity shall lament the chance."

They misliked very much the proclamations and billets which he had put abroad among the Commons. Evil and wickedly disposed persons would stir as well as faithful subjects, and—

" we and these other gentlemen, who have served and others of worship in the country where the same have been published do incur by this means much infamy, slander and discredit.

[1] S. P. Dom. Edw. VI. IX. 31.

Thus we end, beseeching Almighty God, the matter may be so used, as no effusion of blood may flow." [1]

Having despatched this discouraging letter the two noblemen retired to Wilton to await the assembly of those whom they had summoned to join them, that they might advance with force, having obtained from Bristol ordnance and money. They wrote of their movements to the Lords who opposed Somerset, and said that they could not believe that the Protector would stand to violence, his quarrel being private, and that if he did he could get no help in their direction, as they held the district in control, and he had few followers there. [2]

The tragedy of those succeeding days need not detain us ; they are described graphically, perhaps inaccurately, but at all events with partisanship, by Froude, commented upon sympathetically by Tytler, and summed up by Pollard. Suffice it to say that the lack of enthusiasm of the people, whose favour he had consistently sought at such sacrifice, combined with Russell's defection, which deprived him of the support of the army in the West, was enough to turn the scale, and Somerset yielded to the opposing party, promising to relinquish all his offices, and begging for his life. Even his own secretary urged this course on the plea, among others, that the realm be not made in one year " a double tragedy and a lamentable spoil and a scorning stock of the world." [3]

Having decided to submit, he wrote again to Russell and Herbert, informing them of the fact. They received this letter while at Wilton, and thence wrote their reply on the 11th October. [4] They expressed their approval

---

[1] Pet. MS. 468, Pk. p. 92.
[2] S. P. Dom. Edw. VI. IX. 31.   [3] Tytler, 1, 223.
[4] Although both their names are attached to the proclamation about Somerset, and Russell's is in the Council's Register on 8th October, these were probably added later, for they most likely remained at Wilton from the 9th to the 11th.

of this line of action, and offered their services to promote a reconciliation between him and his opponents, so that—

" some good conclusions may ensue of these terrible tumults : the mischief whereof we doubt and fear so much as in all our lives we have never been more troubled and disquieted."

They had been in constant communication with the Lords on his behalf, and they promised to continue their suit, as they hoped some tranquillity would follow. They were taking the necessary precautions for the safety of the King and the realm against foreign invasion. They conclude—

" And thus we wish again some speedy end of this miserable desolation and beseech Almighty God to extend his merciful hand for the surety of the King's majesty and the comfort of the realm." [1]

The very day they wrote, Somerset was arrested and lodged in the Tower.

[1] Pet. MS. 470, Pk. p. 112.

CHAPTER XXIV

REWARDS AND MEMORIALS

" Insomuch as thereupon tumbled such tempest of sedition . . . that
ye Honor and safety of the whole Realm was therby endangered,
multitudes of people were made a Carnage : So many were Slayn,
so many Hanged, Drawn and Quartered, and soe many Innocents
as Nocents perished by Martiall Law : as that England became ye
spectacle of misery, and a Prey to her Enemys."—" Prevarication
of the Church's Liberties."

THE victory having been won, and the rebels either
executed or pardoned, the distribution of the spoil, in
the shape of rewards, claims attention. Under the
proclamation of the 11th July, as has been seen, those
who were faithful to the King were given the right of
entry upon the possessions of recalcitrant owners, with
the object of causing dissensions and divisions. It
would seem that it was Lord Russell's effort to legalise
their holdings that called forth the Council's able exposition of their original meaning, and how diametrically
opposed to the laws of the realm was any grant of
estates before the attainder of a subject.

Hoker refers to Russell's presentation of the estates
and bodies of rebels to those who fought under him ; the
bodies were, of course, to be held to ransom.

Before describing the individual rewards and punish-
ments, it is best to deal with two of a more general
character.

On the 12th September, 1549, the Council wrote
commanding Lord Russell to give orders for the bells

in all the churches in the two counties to be taken down—

"leaving in every church one bell, the least of the ring that now is in the same, which may serve to call the parishioners together to the sermons and divine service." [1]

That they anticipated resentment on the part of the people is evident, as they add—

"in the doing hereof we require your lordship to cause such moderation to be used, as the same may be done with as much quietness and as little offence of the common people as may be."

Such a punishment for rebels was recognised in some countries. The bells having been used to call together the insurgents, their absence would make this less easy in future. Moreover, in later years, in France at all events, the bells were considered the perquisites of the bombardiers, for if the inhabitants of a besieged place failed to ransom them the gunners could make use of the bell-metal. [2]

A recent precedent for such confiscation had occurred in the same country. A salt tax imposed in 1547 led to an insurrection, which was eventually suppressed. Severe retribution was inflicted ; among other things—

"the man who had first sounded the Tocsin was condemned to be hanged from the clapper of the bell. All bells which had been used to rouse the people to rebellion were destroyed, and the others were carried to different châteaux." [3]

But the Council's instructions appear to have been

[1] See Pet. MSS. f. 465, Pk. p. 73.

[2] J. Tavenor Perry gives an interesting account in the Antiquary of January, 1909, of the ransom of the Abbey bells of Noyon in 1591, claimed by the victorious bombardiers. He states : "The custom which the bombardiers invoked had gradually grown up in warfare, and it gave not only the bells but the metal-work of any place which had been captured by the aid of guns to the *grand maître* of the artillery and his officers, but with the abolition of the office the custom fell into desuetude. It was, however, revived by Napoleon at the siege of Dantzic."

[3] Ellacombe's "Bells of the Church," p. 255.

modified by Russell. In his letter to the Exeter civic authorities and the gentlemen of the district, written at the end of September, he orders that—

" forasmuch as the rebels of the county of Devon have used the bells in every parish as an instrument to stir the multitude and call them together, thinking good to have this occasion of attempting the like hereafter taken from them. The said commissioners appointed for the government of the shire and their assistants shall cause all the bells in every parish or chapel within their said limits to be taken down (the least bell of every ring in every church or chapel only excepted) and taking away the clappers of the said bells from the place, shall leave the same bells in the custody and charge of some honest men of the parish or near neighbours thereunto to be safely kept unto the King's Majesty's use until his grace's pleasure shall be further signified for order or disposing of the same otherwise at his most gracious pleasure. And in the practice hereof to use such discreet moderation and honest persuasion as it may be done with as much quietness and as little offence to the common people as may be." [1]

It would seem that in their discretion, to accomplish the King's object with little offence, the Commissioners further modified their instructions, and, instead of taking away the bells from the church towers, they only removed the clappers, and, in some instances, commanded that one bell alone should be rung. If this theory is correct, it accounts for the fact that when the returns of church goods were made under the commission of 1551–2, the full complement of bells is recorded in almost every instance as among the church goods,[2] although there is one

---

[1] See Exeter Municipal Archives, No. 20.

[2] The lists of church goods in Exeter, returned by Coverdale, Prestwood, Hurst, and Midwinter in 1552, contain a curious entry. Each list begins with the bells and their weights, then follow the ornaments, vestments, etc. At the bottom is a note that " over and beside " the articles mentioned above the Commissioners have left, inter alia, one bell (the least of the ring as appears from its weight) " in the stepull there." This emphasis on its situation may be intentional or it may not, but at all events it suggests that the bells of the first list, with the exception of this particular

striking exception, that of St. Sidwell's by Exeter, whence three bells were actually taken away by Russell's servant, the terrible Bernard Duffield, the fourth alone being left.

In the event the King's most gracious pleasure was to grant these clappers to two Devonians by letters patent, entered on the roll of 4 Edward VI. After reciting the order given in the King's name by Lord Russell to take down all bells, except one required to warn the people to attend divine service, the grant continues—

"in consideration of the good and acceptable service unto us done by our trusty and well-beloved servants Sir Arthur Champernon, knight and John Chichester, esquire," the King grants to them "all the clappers of the said bells so commanded to be taken down within our counties and city aforesaid with all the iron and other furniture to the said bells appertaining," which were to be given up to them by "the nowe or late Sheriffs, Escheators, Bailiffs, Churchwardens or other Officers of our counties and city aforesaid." [1]

This grant is undated on the Patent Roll, but all uncertainty on the point has been removed by the discovery of an entry in what is styled a "Council Warrant Book," but which is better described as a "Register of Signed Bills," showing that the King signed the grant on the 2nd December, 1550. [2]

Champernoun and Chichester must have received a large sum under this grant. They appointed as their

one, had been removed from the steeple, but, while placed in the custody of honest men, were allowed to remain within the church building; indeed, it is difficult to imagine where else they could have stored so many heavy objects. In the Cornish inventories the phrase " in the tower there " was almost always inserted, which may indicate that the bells were taken down and stored in the tower.

[1] Sir Arthur Champernoun of Dartington was a minor in 1545, so was a youth when this was granted. He married the widow of Sir George Carew, who was drowned in the *Mary Rose* in 1545, and he was Sheriff of Devon in 1561. It is uncertain which of four John Chichesters was the grantee ; those of Arlington and Hall were minors at this date. Sir John of Youlston was born about 1521, and John of Widworthy about 1531 ; the latter was probably the one named in the grant.

[2] Royal MSS. 18, C. XXIV. f. 17.

agents John Courtenay and Edward Ford,[1] who per-
ambulated the country selling the clappers and other
iron of the bells, in most instances to the parishioners of
each place. As early as the 27th June, 1551, they sold
the clappers and whole furniture appertaining to the
bells of Morebath to three parishioners for 26s. 8d., to
the use of "Sir Arture Chapman knyzth & John Che-
chester Esquyre to them given by the King's majesty's
letters patent." [2] In the same year Ford sold the
clappers of the bells and the frames with the iron work
of Woodbury to the parishioners for 40s.[3] In 1553, the
High Cross wardens of Stratton account for money
received for "three score and two pounds of the old bell-
clappers," [4] and as late as 1554 the Barnstaple people

---

[1] Probably John Courtenay of Ottery St. Mary, who was in Exeter
at the time of the siege, and Edward Ford of Fordmore in Plymtree.

[2] See "Morebath Wardens' Accounts," p. 168. The receipt given at
length in this instance ends with "We gave Rumbelow x[s] in y[e] byeng of
them for hys fader in law ys sake." Although the receipt is made out to
John Norman, Thomas Myll, and Edward Rumbelow, the money was
advanced by John Norman at Court, otherwise John at Court, and Thomas
Borrage, who may have been Thomas Borrage at Mill, as no other reference
to Thomas Myll has been traced. These two paid Edward Rumbelow the
full amount and collected it themselves from the parishioners, charging
it as 31s. 4d., or 15s. 8d. each, not a large interest considering that they
were not wholly repaid until 1553, but when the account was then settled
John at Court demanded, and received, 16[d] "for expenssis ij tymys to
M[r] Ford to have a byll of hys owne hande what there was payd for y[e]
clappers" (p. 177). Until the debt was paid off part of the iron work is
described as " q[d] pertenet to Court & Borrage " (p. 173).

[3] See Brushfield's "Church of East Budleigh," p. 285. In this connection the writer calls attention to Froude's statement that "some few
peals of bells were spared for a time, but only under condition of silence.
A sweep as complete cleared the parish churches throughout the country,"
and to his marginal note, "bells . . . are carried off from parish churches"
(V. 459); and Dr. Brushfield adds: "In striking contrast to this is the
assertion of Mr. Ellacombe that "in nearly all our (Devonshire church)
towers the peals were complete at the time of the death of Edward VI.,
July 6, 1553." But even this is subject to correction, as Mr. Ellacombe
failed to notice the distinction between bells in the steeple and in the church.
(See note 2, p. 374.) His suggestion that the grant was obtained "for the
express purpose of keeping the bells in their places " is most improbable.

[4] See Add. MSS. 32, 243, f. 54. It is not clear why the High Cross wardens'
account for this sum, unless they had advanced the money from their store.

bought their bell clappers and other furniture for
£2 13s. 4d.[1]

Though the clappers were repossessed by the
parishioners, it does not appear that they were used.
There is reason to believe that, excepting the one bell
rung to call the people to Divine Service, they remained
silent in obedience to a command thus noted in the Woodbury Churchwardens' Accounts for 2 & 3 Edward VI.—

"M[d] that the Commotion was at Clyst at Lammas this same
year, and then after the parishers were commanded to ring
but one bell."

In the same accounts for the year 1552–3 (1 Mary) the
charge of viij[d] is made for bell ropes with this significant entry following—

"Also to James Myllward for mending of the bawders
for the bells to ring againe when my Lady Mary was proclaimed Queen, which was the xxiij day of July."

Evidently in their enthusiasm on that occasion they
injured the bells, for in the following year there is entered,
"For mending of the great bell clapper paid to Hamon
two times, once for the stemen, and again in the bell
being broken."[2]

A cursory glance through several churchwardens' accounts suggests that the bells elsewhere were disused in
this interval, the usual entry for the keeping and the oiling
of the bells between 1550 and 1553 has not been found.
At the latter date the interdict would have been removed.[3]

[1] See Chanter's "Barnstaple," p. 75.

[2] See transcripts of accounts in Ex. Dioc. Arch. Soc. Tran. 2nd Ser.,
I. p. 391. This must surely have been Hammon, the smith, who levelled
the great piece at Sir Peter Carew at St. Mary Clyst bridge. See Chap. IX.
"Stem" is used in Devon for the handle of a tool.

[3] Ever finding excuses for obtaining funds, Edward's Council mulcted
the Western men by making them account for all the church goods, charging
for deficiencies, while profiting by the sale of the parish possessions. The
money paid for missing articles was, of course, not spent in replacing them
nor even for the purchase of the Bibles, Service-books, and Paraphrases.
Truly the wardens and parishioners were unfortunate in those days!

Although the whole district was punished by being deprived of the use of their bells, the city of Exeter alone was rewarded for its faithfulness. As early as the 15th August, the Lord Privy Seal not only suggested the knighting of the mayor, John Blackaller, but made suit "that by the discharge of the fee ferm, Annuity or otherwise The towne might be benefitted as for a memory of the service." Among the correspondence relating to this is a letter, dated the 7th December, 1550, containing the King's instructions as to the way his intentions were to be executed.[1]

He, "having good zeal to the city of Exeter the rather in recompence for their good service in the last rebellion," proposed to bestow on it the manor of Exe Island, which had fallen to the Crown on the Marquis of Exeter's attainder, so he commanded that the grant should be drawn for that and should include also the ancient right to cut timber in Cotley and Pirage Woods for the repair of the mills and weirs, and the Corporation should be licensed to purchase £100 worth of land. "In the ende," wrote the Lords of the Council, who convey the instructions—

"we pray you that this book may have and contain certain sufficient considerations for the services done in the said Rebellion to the intent the same may be a memory to the posterity of the City to cause them (to) retain the ancient faith and duty to their sovereign lord."[2]

Such a "book" or document was drawn up, and it received the King's signature on the 21st December, 1550. In the Register of Signed Bills this is described as—

"A confirmation to the Mayor and Commonalty of the City of Exeter and their successors of all their old customs,

[1] Ex. Mun. Arch. Let. XXVI. In Mr. Stuart Moore's calendar this is incorrectly described as addressed " To the Attorney General," but in the P. C. Reg. (III. 177) it is " to the Chauncellor of thaugmentations."

[2] See Exeter Mun. Arch., quoted in "Notes and Gleanings," II. p. 76.

liberties, privileges, franchised &c. and jurisdictions contained in any charter of letters patents of the King's majesty or his progenitors with a gift to them in fee simple of all the manor of Exisland in Devonshire with divers other lands, tenements, &c. To the yearly value of xxix^h xviij^s x^d over and above the reprises to be holden by fealty only in socage &c. with a licence to purchase C^{li} a year lands over and above all reprises." [1]

In compliance with the orders given, this charter contained a reference to events which is here translated—

" Whereas our well-beloved and faithful subjects, the Mayor, Bailiffs, Commonalty and citizens of our city of Exeter, of whose fidelity and circumspection we are assured not only by the report of our noble peers and subjects but also of our own certain and royal knowledge, in the time of the commotions, insurrections and rebellions of our ungrateful and unfaithful subjects in divers parts of our kingdom, especially in the western parts of our realm of England, in the counties of Devon and Cornwall, they, most faithful adherents to us, most valiantly resisted these rebels and defended our city of Exeter aforesaid and our Chamber against their most fierce assaults and siege, with a great number of people in warlike manner besieging and surrounding it continuously for the space of six weeks and more, not only to the intolerable costs, expenses and burdens of the aforesaid Mayor, Bailiffs and commonalty of our said City but also with great trials, losses and famine by reason of the lack of victuals, before we with our army and troops were able to raise the said siege, which we ought not and will not, nor is it worthy of our royal dignity to pass over or fail to reward worthily. . . ." [2]

The grant of the Manor of Exe Island settled a dispute which had existed for centuries between the City

---

[1] See Royal MSS. 18 C. XXIV. f. 26^b.

[2] Mr. T. Lloyd-Parry, Town Clerk of Exeter, kindly supplied me with a copy of the original of the above.

and the Earls of Devon. In that manor these noble-men—

"had their own rule, their own laws, and their own guards, and laughed to scorn the authority of the Corporation. It was a thorn in the side of civic dignity, besides being a scandal and a nuisance. Fearing lest it should be restored to the Courtenays, the Chamber used the greatest efforts to purchase the manor of the King, but without success. They employed Burgesses of Parliament, on their behalf, to offer an extravagant price, and volunteered a handsome douceur to any one who should succeed in obtaining for them the coveted property. What money could not purchase for the city, the fidelity of her governors did. . . . It remains to the corporation a lasting monument of the courage and loyalty of John Blackaller and his brethren." [1]

Besides this generous grant there were other rewards given. All the estates of the ringleaders were promptly distributed to those who had done good service in the recent rising.

Sir Gawen Carew received most of Humphrey Arundell's lands, subject to his widow's dower rights,[2] and he even obtained the services of one of Arundell's men, Thomas Aleigh.[3] Wynslade's lands were divided, part to Sir Peter Carew, and the rest, which had been transferred to trustees for his wife's benefit, were granted to Reginald Mohun, because he was "spoiled in the commotions by Arundell and Wynslade and for his faithful and chargeable service at that time." [4] William Gibbs received Bury's estates.

---

[1] Cotton and Woollacombe, p. 70.

[2] See Pat. Roll, 4 Ed. VI. pt. 6. A portion of these estates were after-wards claimed by Arundell's children.

[3] Court of Requests, 78, 33. Aleigh deposed that he had been Arundell's servant for many years, and that at the time of the commotions a chest containing his master's evidences, which had been left in Exeter, passed into Sir Gawen's hands.

[4] Court of Requests, 86, 21. The profits of this estate were divided at first between Mohun and the guardians of Giles Arundell, to whom a lease had been made.

Richard Reynell, of East Ogwell, was also rewarded because—

"in the western rebellion, an. 6 Edw. 6, he having charge of a troop of horsemen, did special good services ; when in suppressing and confounding those traitors, he being sorely wounded and hurt, it pleased the King's Majesty of his princely bounty, to grant his warrant to the Earl of Bedford then general in those wars, for the rewarding of the said Richard Reynell with the demesne of Weston Peverell and house called Pennicross in Devon, near Plymouth." [1]

To Russell, Herbert, Lord Grey, and others of importance, large grants were made, chiefly of estates in Devon, and titles conferred, while the foreign soldiers of fortune in some instances obtained annuities.

Payments were made to loyal citizens and corporations for the sums advanced to pay the soldiers, for the repair of bridges and other damages sustained.[2]

Hoker states that "to many others which had done good services he (Russell) gave prisoners both their bodies goods and lands." [3] One curious instance of this will be sufficient, especially as it indicates that danger attended those who were known to have been connected with the late Marquis of Exeter.

John Furse, of Crediton, was a man of wealth and position, having been at one time under-sheriff of Devon, and having held such offices as that of steward of the

---

[1] Prince's "Worthies," p. 693. It is, of course, a slip to give the date as 6 Ed. VI. instead of 3 Ed. VI.

[2] Among such may be mentioned £693 6s. 8d. paid to William Bogan for the townsmen of Totnes, from whom the Lord Privy Seal had "emprest" that amount (P. C. Reg. II. p. 347); £433 paid to Thomas and John Harrys of Crediton, "by reason that thei were spoiled in the last commotions by the rebels" (ibid. III. p. 231); The goods of the attainted vicar of Sutton to John Malorie for his services in the West (ibid. III. p. 48) ; £400 to William Grey of Reading (ibid. p. 153) ; £79 1s. 8d. to the Mayor and Commons of Plymouth for gunners' wages (ibid. 292), and the presentation to the living of Ewnye next Lelant to Sir Anthony Kingston (Chan. Proc. Eliz. Ser. II. 107, 22).

[3] Hoker, p. 91.

Stannaries and of the Duchy of Lancaster, as well as head-steward " of all the Abbots' Courts of Tavistock and Buckland." [1]

"In his youth . . . for his manhood and good qualities Mr. Shilston had him in service and after him he served a worthy knight one Sir Thomas Denys, he was with him in Scotland and last of all he was in service with the Right Honorable Henry Courtenay, Earl of Devon and Marquis of Exeter and in great favour and credit with him."

It was no doubt because of his connection with the latter that he was accused of high treason by a "noftye pryste." He had incurred the hatred of Sir Hugh Pollard through his refusal to pay rent for certain lands claimed to belong to Kingsnympton, of which Pollard was lord of the manor. It was by the "enticement" of Sir Hugh and one Hanford, his man, that the naughty priest brought the accusation ; but Furse—

"most honestly did acquit himself to be a good subject to their great shame and reproof. God be therefore praised. Sir Hugh for the recompense of this wicked enterprise made the priest presently parson of Okeford : this wicked priest was after Bishop of Exeter and long after John Furse was dead he by chance did lie at Marches (Furse's residence) where he did confess to one Christian Remond, John Furse's daughter, that he had falsely accused her father."

This priest was, undoubtedly, William Alley, who was instituted to Okeford on the 29th May, 1544, on the presentation of Sir Hugh Pollard,[2] which living he held until 1549, when he became rector of Croscombe, Somerset.[3]

[1] See " Furse of Moreshead " in Devon Ass. Trans. XXVI. 177. The MS. history of the family there quoted was written by Furse's grandson at the close of the sixteenth century.

[2] Mr. W. H. Bowers of the Diocesan Registry has kindly furnished me with this information from the Episcopal Registers, and the Rev. F. G. Buller, the present rector, has also communicated with me on the subject.

[3] Hoker describes him as an earnest preacher, much inveighing against false doctrine, consequently he was so " despitefully dealt withal in the

But this was not the last of Furse's misfortunes. No doubt because of the previous accusation, he was readily suspected in the later rising. His grandson records that—

" this John was also greatly spoiled in the commotion in King Edward the VI. tyme, for he was then given body and goods like a rebel and yet during all the time of that rebellion he was continually in his bed sick and not able to travel. That trouble cost him seven score pounds, but his wife Margaret after his decease, by verdict in the Castle of Exeter tried her husband a good subject and by that means she was released of some charge which otherwise she had paid."

His death took place very soon after the close of the insurrection, on the 14th February, 1549–50.

The City, with a devoutness to be admired, instituted a memorial of their deliverance from the besiegers. They appointed the 6th August, called " Jesus Day," [1] as a day of thanksgiving to Almighty God. Annually for three centuries or more, the " Mayor, Chamber, and Corporate Trades " walked in solemn procession on that day, clad in their official robes, to the Cathedral, where a sermon, suitable to the occasion, was preached by one of the Mayor's chaplains, and the Cathedral bells were rung. [2]

Three such sermons have been found. One, delivered on Jesus Day, 1594, by John Charldon, D.D., is on the text : " Hear, O heavens, and hearken, O earth, for the Lord hath said, I have nourished and brought up children, but they have rebelled against me." It deals

church, that he durst not to adventure to come again into his pulpit," but the Carews guarded him, and at sundry times brought him into his pulpit and countenanced and supported him against his adversaries (" Life of Sir P. Carew " (Maclean), p. 111).

[1] 7th August in the calendar of our present Prayer-book is noted as dedicated to " The Name of Jesus," just as it was in the Elizabethan Calendar of 1561. It seems strange that Charldon (see below) should have been ignorant of this as early as 1591.

[2] Jenkins' " Exeter," ed. 1841, p. 118, note,

largely with the condition of the Church at that date, and has but few references to the rebellion. After mentioning the storms that disturbed the happy rest in the days of Her Majesty's dear brother, Charldon continues—

" For the Lord in our City's distress, in the time of the Commotion, (as we call it) or insurrection, awaked as one out of sleep and as a Giant refreshed with wine, Psal. 7, 8, 65. He smote his enemies and ours in the hinder parts and put them to shame. . . . This is the day which you call *Jesus day*, whether because it is so fixed in the Calendar I know not; but sure I am it was Jesus day unto you, a day of salvation. For if *Jesus* the Lord had not been on our side when men rose up against us, they had swallowed us up quick (so unable were we to resist) when their wrath was kindled against us."

In his peroration, he says :—

" so shalt thou be called merciful . . . specially for that (as upon this day) thou diddest deliver us and our City out of the hands of our wicked enemies and hateful foes ; which said that they would burn our dwelling places, and kill our young men with the sword, & dash our sucking children against the ground, and make our infants a prey, & our virgins a spoil ; which also said, we will divide the booty, our lust shall be satisfied upon them, and then we will draw the weapon and our hand shall destroy them . . . thou diddest over-throw them . . . and by the blast of thy nostrils the waters came which ran mightily through the channels of our streets & so drowned the labours of their hands [1] . . . for which and all other thy blessings . . . we shall from age to age re-member thy goodness : this shall be a feast day unto us and our posterity." [2]

---

[1] He probably refers to the thunderstorm which is said to have assisted the drowning of the mine. See Chapter XII.

[2] This sermon is entitled " Fulford et Fulfordæ," and is dedicated to Thomas Fulford, Esq. It contains some Latin verses on the marriage of a Fulford. Davidson mentions two editions of 1594 and 1595. The B.M. copy (C. 12, d. 17) was printed by John Dauter in 1595. The above quota-tions are on p. 39 and p. 76 of that edition. John Charldon or Chardon was Canon of Exeter, and became Bishop of Down and Connor in 1596.

The other sermons are both by John Fisher, B.A. The first was preached—

" before the Right Worshipful the Mayor and Chamber. On August the 6th, 1723 : Being the Anniversary of the Deliverance of the City from the Cornish Insurrection, in the Reign of King Edward the VIth."

He thus refers to the reason for this customary sermon—

" A very remarkable instance of the Mercy of God, may be seen, in the Deliverance he was pleased to vouchsafe to this City, from the Hands of its cruel and malicious Enemies, which we are now met together to commemorate with the joyful Tribute of Praise and Thanksgiving. God was pleased (for Reasons best known to himself) to suffer it to be Besieged by barbarous and restless Men, whose Religion naturally leads them into Faction, and not only persuades, but commands them to Rebel : yet if we consider how soon they were routed and dispersed, and by how small a Number of Men, we must confess that the Stars in their Courses fought against them, and God was not unmindful of his Promise which he made to our Forefathers. Five of you shall chase an Hundred, and an Hundred shall put Ten Thousand to flight, and your enemies shall fall before you by the Sword."

Elsewhere he adds :

" There is no People, since the Jews were a flourishing Nation, that have received more Blessings than we of this Island : and This, among the rest, which we now commemorate, ought to be Treasur'd up in the Breasts of all True Englishmen : since their Lives, Liberties and Religion depended upon the Issue of this Barbarous and Cruel Insurrection, which was contriv'd to overthrow the Government and Laws, and every Thing else that was Dear and Valuable. I should trespass too much upon you, should I describe the dreadful Consequences that would have attended their Success (had they gotten the Victory :) you are already too well acquainted with such Descriptions and are too sensible of the dismal Effects of Arbitrary Power both in Church and State. What Honour our Ancestors have by their Loyalty procured to this City, whom

2 c

Death, in all its frightful and horrid shapes, would not prevail upon to Surrender, will never be forgotten : and as the present Loyal Body have inherited the Semper Fidelis * of their Forefathers so may it descend to their Posterity for ever.

"* The Honourable Motto, which was given to this City by Queen Elizabeth." [1]

The second sermon has a similar heading, with the date 1725, only the preacher is now " John Fisher, M.A., Vicar of S. Uryan in Cornwall." [2] The text is, " Except the Lord keep the City, the Watchmen waketh but in vain." There are two passages dealing with our subject—

" When we see Cities and Countries in an extraordinary manner protected from imminent Dangers : as was the Case of this City in particular, when the Sword was without, and Famine within then God was pleased to preserve us from both : which blessing we are now met together to commemorate." " Yet if we refuse to give God the Glory, by whose Assistance it is that we enjoy these Blessings [3] . . . we may soon be reduced to the like dismal Circumstances, from which we are now met to commemorate our Deliverance this Day : When, if the Lord himself had not been on our side. . . . For a Multitude of fiery Zealots, unwilling to part with their Idolatry and Superstition, gather'd themselves in a mutinous Body and besieged the City, in such a manner that the Inhabitants were reduced to Famine and the utmost extremities till they were relieved by the King's Forces."

[1] This sermon was printed for Edward Score and Nathaniel Thorn, booksellers in Exon, 1723. The quotations are from the B. M. copy (225, h. 27), p. 9 and p. 22.

[2] This sermon was published at the request of the Mayor of Exeter and printed by Andrew Brice in that city. It was sold by the local booksellers for 6d. The quotations are from the B. M. copy (226, g. 14), p. 13 and p. 29.

[3] " These Blessings " were, among other things, a well governed city

CHAPTER XXV

CONTEMPORARY ACCOUNTS

"Put away contention, and read with discretion:
 Try only by the touchstone: judge without affection." [1]

OUR story of the Western Rebellion is practically completed—the cause, the early movement, the insurrection itself have all been passed in review; now must be added the opinions of contemporaries upon the whole matter; first, upon its real aim and object—whether religious or agrarian: secondly, upon its dimensions—the numbers involved on both sides, and its connection with risings in other parts of the realm.

Beside the regular "Chronicles" dealing with the period and the published accounts written by contemporaries and by persons of the next generation, there are many references in printed books, sermons, manuscripts, and letters from all of which we are able to glean impressions of how events appeared to men of the day.

It has been said that it is impossible for any one to write a wholly unprejudiced history of his own times, therefore, not only in these scattered references, but in the printed stories, we notice a distinct tinge given to the statements by the sentiments of the writer.

But first let us deal with the opinions expressed by the Council, or members thereof, upon the causes of the Rebellion.

From their correspondence with Lord Russell, it is

[1] J. Clement (temp. Edw. VI.).

evident that they were not in any doubt upon this point. Even before the Lord Privy Seal was sent West we find Somerset warning the Marquis of Dorset and the Earl of Huntingdon, on the 11th June—probably the very day he heard of the trouble at Sampford Courtenay—that the assemblies which at first sought the redress of enclosures, now, in some places, through the instigation of seditious priests and other evil-disposed persons, desire the " restitution of the old bloody laws." [1]

On the 23rd June, the Council licensed Mr. Gregory to preach in the West parts, as by such means the people are best brought into order, quiet and due obedience,[2] as if by such means they could easily overcome the complaints of the people which were obviously of a religious character.

On the 29th June they write, in a letter to Lord Russell,[3] that the Commons are abused by popish priests, who wish to subdue the people to the Pope, and they require that Mr. Blackston, the Ecclesiastical Commissary who had spoken seditious words, should preach the contrary in order to revoke the people to more quiet.[4]

On the 10th July they say that the rebels in other counties have declared themselves so well persuaded for religion that they desire to " dye " against the Devonshire men on that account.[5]

On the 12th, they warn Russell not to trust any country gentlemen unless he knows that they are " fully persuaded for the matter in controversy of religion," and add that there is a stir in Bucks and Oxfordshire by instigation of sundry priests " for these matters of religion." [6]

On the 22nd, they mention the disturbances in the counties nearer London, " though their articles be not

---

[1] S. P. Com. Edw. VI., VII. 31.
[2] Pet. MSS. f. 431, Pk. p. 6.
[3] *Ibid.* f. 433, Pk. p. 16.
[4] *Ibid.* f. 434, Pk. p. 18.
[5] *Ibid.* f. 435ᵈ, Pk. p. 24.
[6] *Ibid.* 436, Pk. p. 26.

such as your matters," but of "raves, and spoiling of Towns, &c." [1] and they urge that the people of Dorset and Somerset should be persuaded to fight "against those rank rebells and papists of Devon as becometh good subjects." [2]

On the 10th August they refer to the people who have been allured to blind superstition and popery by Sir Thomas Pomeroy, and they give orders for the burning of mass books "of the old superstitious service," apparently as one means of suppressing the rising.[3]

The Council do not seem to have furnished their representatives abroad with any account of affairs at first, probably expecting the insurrection to be quickly ended.

Paget, who was at the Emperor's Court, had evidently heard only vague rumours when he wrote his lengthy epistle of warning and advice to the Protector on the 7th July, and he seems to think then—that is, nearly a month after the famous Whitsunday at Sampford Courtenay, and, though he did not know it, the day after the gates of Exeter were closed—that the rising could not have reached serious proportions. The next day he writes anxiously to Peter of the "brutes" of the doings at home, which are in the mouths of both Englishmen and Frenchmen, and which he feels sure must be true, so he cannot parry the questions addressed to him.[4] Five days later he implores Peter to tell his secretary to send particulars, and to instruct him what to reply to the Emperor, who says that he has heard that "your commons at home *font grand barbula*." [5]

That very day, the 13th July, the Council were engaged in writing to Paget, minimising the whole affair. Some "light persons" and "a multitude of simple persons" before Paget's departure had thrown

---

[1] Pet. MSS. 440[d], Pk. p. 32.   [2] *Ibid.* 441, p. 32.
[3] *Ibid.* 448, Pk. p. 49.   [4] S. P. Dom. Edw. VI., IV. 185.
[5] *Ibid.* 189.

open enclosures ; since he left there have been similar stirs in Essex, Kent, Hampshire, and Devon, which are partly already appeased and the rest " in good towardness "—

" so as there is no likelihood of any great matter to ensue hereof, and yet having experienced how slanderously these small tumults shall be divulged and spread by the Frenchmen we have thought good to advertise you by these letter of the truth of their malice." [1]

But when the insurrection is almost suppressed, and they enclose Lord Russell's account of the Battle of Sampford Courtenay to Sir Philip Hoby, another ambassador, they describe the victory that it has pleased Almighty God to give the Lord Privy Seal over the rebels of Devon and Cornwall in order that he may spread the news abroad,[2] and add that the assembly of light persons in the hither part of Yorkshire " for the matter of commons," has been suppressed by the gentlemen of the district without much difficulty, leaving it to be inferred that the rising for other matters, religion, was not so easily overcome.[3]   In a letter of the following day they write, " The Devonshire men are well chastised and appeased," three of their captains, Pomeroy, Wise, and Harrys, have voluntarily submitted.   Hundreds and thousands daily crave pardon.   Bury and his companions, who have fled to Somersetshire, have by now, they hoped, got their deserts. . Then follows the revised version of the causes of the risings, which they, on due consideration, thought wise to put forth for public consumption, as likely to redound most to their advantage, grouping all the insurrections together in order to confuse the issue and to represent the rising in the West as having the same object as the others—a version not in consonance with their previous letters, but one which has been carefully copied by most historians.

[1] S. P. Dom. Edw. VI., IV. 180.   [2] See Galba, G. XII. f. 113ᵇ.
[3] *Ibid.* f. 115.

" The causes and pretences of their uproars and Risings are divers and uncertain and so full of variety almost in every Camp, as they call them, that it is hard to write what it is, as ye know is like to be of people without heads, and rule, and that would have they wot not what.[1] Some crieth, pluck downe enclosures and parks, Some for their comons. Others pretend religion. A number would rule and direct things as gentlemen have done And indeed all have conceived a wonderful hate against gentlemen and taketh them all as their enemies. The Ruffians among them and soldiers cashiered, which be chief doers, look for the spoil. So that it seemeth no other thing but a plague and fury among the vilest and worst sort of men, for except only Devon and Cornwall, and there not past ij or iij, in all other places not a gentleman or man of reputation was ever among them but against their wills as prisoners." [2]

To both Wotton and Hoby, on succeeding days—the 31st August and the 1st September—they sent practically identical reports of the whole affair—

" After our right hearty commendations, we have heretofore advertised you of the troublesome business, uproars and tumults practised in sundry places of the realm by a number of lewd, seditious and evil disposed persons to the great disquietness both of the King's majesty and all other his highness's quiet and loving subjects, which tumults and commotions albeit at the beginning there were spread in many parts of the realm yet in the end all places were well pacified and quieted saving Devon and Cornwall and Norfolk, where they continued their rebellions so stubbornly as the King's majesty was forced to send the King's highness's Lieutenant with a power both ways the sooner to repress them and bring them to their duties : viz. my Lord Privy Seal for Devonshire and Cornwall and the Earl of Warwick into Norfolk. And alike as we have heretofore signified unto you the proceedings of my Lord Privy Seal in his journey with his politic and wise handling of the matter after the slaughter of more than one thousand of the rebels and execution of some of the ringleaders, he hath (thanks be

[1] This is a favourite expression with Cranmer in his " Answer to the Articles of the Rebels."
[2] See Galba, B. XII. f. 115.

to God) so honorably achieved and finished as not only the country remains presently in good order, but also the multitude so repent of their former detestable and naughty doings as they abhor to hear themselves spoken of, so you shall understand that in Norfolk [here follows the story of Kett's rebellion.] . . . Thus are those vile wretches that have now of a long time troubled the realm, and, as much as in them lay, gone about to destroy and utterly undo the same, come to confusion. So that we trust verily that these traitors, mutineers, and rebellious have now an end, lauded bey God." [1]

To sum up, it is evident that the Privy Council, almost to the last, differentiated between the Western Rebellion and the tumults elsewhere, which, except in Norfolk, had no prominent leader.

Meanwhile the Papal and the Venetian Courts received the news of the insurrection. Letters of the 3rd July informed the Doge that the English people have rebelled in several parts of the kingdom, " not choosing to conform to the new religion." [2] By the 10th the Pope had heard that there was a great insurrection against the Government, that the King had retired to a strong castle outside of London, that the cause was the " grasslands," but the insurgents also required the Mass, or, at least, that it, together with the religion, should remain as left by the late King. The Government, wishing to apply a remedy, put upwards of five thousand persons to the sword, sparing neither women nor children, so that it gained strength, and was increasing. [3]

The opposite point of view is taken in a letter to the Protestant leaders on the Continent. Ab Ulmis, writing the day after Exeter was relieved, the 7th August, from Oxford to Bullinger, says—

" The countrymen are everywhere in rebellion and have already committed some murders. The enemies of religion are rampant, neither submitting to God nor the king. They

[1] See Galba, B. XII. f. 125[d].   [2] Venetian S. P. V. 568.
[3] *Ibid.* 567.

· would give a good deal to renew and confirm the Six Articles. . . . The king is now sending a large army against them. But all these things will not continue long : for all of us expect that they will be put an end to by the next month. The Oxfordshire papists are at last reduced to order, many of them having been apprehended, and some gibbetted, and their heads fastened to the walls. But king Edward six days ago (I mention only what is whispered about) having sent the better part of the popish camp a book (the liturgical Mass they call it) is grievously slandered, though not consenting to annul the smallest part of his own laws about such things." [1]

Elsewhere he refers to the rebels as papists.

Bucer writes from London on the 14th August that Satan is stirring up the people and the French.[2]

Burcher, residing at Strasburg, on the 25th August, relates what he hears has occurred in England—that in June and July some 16,000 armed men assembled, that the leaders first proclaimed the deliverance of the people from the oppression by landlords, but they were everywhere immediately pacified by the King's proclamations and promises, except in Devonshire and Cornwall.

" In those parts two Roman priests,[3] who were the authors of the sedition, warned the people that their religion was in danger, and that it was the duty of all Christians to be prepared for its defence and re-establishment. They assembled therefore, a large number of papists in the name and authority of Christ and the king. The king wrote to them, admonishing them as a father to desist from the rebellion they had begun. They disregarded his admonition, and began openly to declare their intention of setting up another king, another council and another religion, as appears by their articles. . . . The

---

[1] Zurich Letters, p. 391.

[2] *Ibid.* p. 539.

[3] It is a curious fact that Dandolo mentions in a letter to the Signory on 20th July that Cardinal Pole had sent two of his confidential servants, both English, with a safe conduct, to exhort the Government to return to the Catholic religion, and that they had had audience of the Protector who dismissed them rather harshly (Ven. S.P. V. 573). Is it possible that they then went westward as emissaries from Pole ?

king, being now compelled to it, attacked them as enemies with a regular force, destroyed three or four thousand of them, and delivered the city of Exeter, which they had besieged : whereupon some of the leaders of the rebellion were taken prisoners, and all the rest dispersed in divers quarters." [1]

In a later letter he says that the rebellion is entirely ended and the principal perpetrators punished, " especially those impure mass priests, who stirred up the people." [2]

That it was long, however, before quiet was fully restored is evident from Hooper's letter, written as late as the 5th February, 1550, wherein he says that he has not been able to visit his parents who lived in the West—

" by reason of the frequent and dangerous commotions stirred up in those parts on account of religion, and which indeed are not yet calmly and quietly settled. . . . The people, that manyheaded monster, is still wincing : partly through ignorance, and partly fascinated by the inveiglements of the bishops, and the malice and impiety of the mass-priests." [3]

Such letters as these may be taken as voicing the opinions of the " man in the street " when he happened to be fairly well informed.

In connection with the above, it is worth while to read the lengthy correspondence which passed between Cardinal Pole and the Protector. The latter sat " in the seats of the mighty," and talked down in a patronising manner to the exiled member of the Royal house, while the Cardinal on his part warned him at an early date— before June, in fact—of the probability of an insurrection caused by the discontent with religious matters among the people. He had long feared that " some great tumult might easily arise in the kingdom, as was, in fact, demonstrated by some recent acts of rebellion." Here he probably refers to the Cornish commotion of 1548, as further on in the letter he says that he has just

---

[1] Zurich Letter, p. 654.   [2] *Ibid.* p. 658.   [3] *Ibid.* p. 74.

heard of the "popular insurrection." He points out that matters of religion are the most important and of the most difficult possible adjustment. In the middle of his letter he breaks off, saying that as he was in the act of writing news of the rising was brought to him. He deals at length with the cause, which he distinctly asserts to be religious. He expresses his willingness to return as they wish " provided they contain themselves in the limits of their just and religious demands, as I see they have done hitherto," his purpose being to bring concord to the parties concerned. In his mind there was no question as to the cause of the disturbances in the West Country.

The impression received by the foreign ambassadors then resident in London is best conveyed by Barbaro's report to the Signory, written in 1551, reviewing the events during his embassage, and, as an opinion fearlessly expressed and not intended for publication, it is well worth notice.

" Religion is as it were the heart of man on which life depends, an excellent principle, as seen in all republics and governments (especially in monarchies), whereby to regulate men's minds, and make them acknowledge God as the giver of kingdoms and victories. This is not the case with the English, amongst whom there is nothing more fickle than religious opinion, for to-day they do one thing and to-morrow another ; and now those who have accepted the new creed as well as the others are dissatisfied, as shown by the insurrection of '49 ; and in fact, had they now a leader, although they have been grievously chastised, they would rise again." [1]

In certain of the sermons of the succeeding year reference is made to the insurrection of the previous summer, but they are of little interest beyond indicating that many held that the priests were at the bottom of this rising, while some followed the Court lead and

---

[1] Venetian S. P., Vol. V. p. 345.

confused the commotions together. Yet, in passing attention may be called to Cranmer's sermon, described in Chapter XXL, from which it is clear that he considered this insurrection due to religious discontent.[1]

Having dealt with these various expressions of opinion, written chiefly in the midst of the strife and turmoil, let us now see what form the story took at first. Historians present us, as it were, with an authorised version which inevitably bore marks of those contemporaries who held more or less partisan views, but eventually this " fluid " history crystalised into an account accepted by such standard writers as considered this rebellion of sufficient moment to be mentioned.

HOKER, who was in Exeter at the time of the siege, wrote his first account of events while many of the prime movers still lived, probably less than a quarter of a century after the insurrection—for it passed through several mutations before it was appended to the edition of Holinshed's Chronicle, which Hoker issued in 1586.[2] It is perfectly evident that Hoker firmly believed that religious discontent worked up by the priests and *nothing else* was in reality the true origin of the Commotion. He writes—

" The cause thereof as by the sequel it did appear was only concerning religion which then by act of parliament was reformed. . . . And here doth appear what great detriments come and ensue to the Church of God and what great troubles to the public and commonweal when learned preachers do want [*i.e.* are lacking] to teach and instruct the people and well persuaded magistrates to govern the common State, for these people lacking the one and not stored with the other were left to themselves and to their own dispositions and thereby, partly of ignorance but more of a froward and a rebellious disposition they do now utterly refuse to accept and resist to

[1] In the preceding chapter we find Fisher attributing the Siege of Exeter to " fiery Zealots, unwilling to part with their Idolatry and Superstition."

[2] See Appendix D.

receive the reformed religion now put and to be put in ure and execution." [1]

Again, he dwells upon the fact that the chief citizens were well affected to the Romish religion, and as for the rebels—

" the principle and chief captains in Devon being fully resolved by their own power and authority to maintain and continue the religion according to the Romish Church and utterly to impugne the reformation thereof established by act of parliament and to support the Idol of Rome . . . sent their messengers unto the Mayor." [2]

After describing the considerable party in the city who would not hear of any religion but that in which they were first " noselled," he adds, they were " wholly of the opinion of the rebels and would have no reformation of religion." [3]

In his " Life of Sir Peter Carew," he writes of the rebellion— [4]

" But such was the obstinacy of the people, and so much addicted to the popish religion, then to be reformed, and wherin they had the countenance of some such of the best as who did both favour their course, and secretly encourage them herein : that they were thoroughly bent to maintain their quarrel."

That the cause of the rising was purely religious was emphatically the opinion of the man on the spot, and it should be noted that he, at all events, makes no reference to agrarian discontent being connected with the insurrection.

WRIOTHESLEY—also writing at the time events were taking place—was more dependent on hearsay, but he may have obtained his information from persons who had taken part in the suppression of the rising. After

---

[1] Hoker, p. 56.   [2] *Ibid.* p. 67.   [3] *Ibid.* p. 71,
[4] Maclean ed. p. 48.

reference to the Commons of Essex, Kent, Suffolk, and Norfolk making insurrection against enclosures, he adds—

" Also in Devonshire about Exeter the Devonshire men and Cornish men made insurrection against the King's proceedings to maintain the masses and other ceremonies of the Pope's law." [1]

Neither does he suggest that these rebels had any complaint against enclosures.

THE CHRONICLER OF THE GREY FRIARS, under the 18th July, 1549,[2] alludes to the " Commyns of Cornwall and Devynshire," with " all the other parts of the realm who rose and pulled down enclosures," but under the 10th August he says that the " Bishop " of Canterbury preached—

" for them that (rose) in the West contry of the Commons of Devonshire and Cornwall, and there he showed that the occasion came of popish priests." [3]

CHEKE, whose " Hurt of Sedition " contains some reference to this rebellion, exclaims—

" Ye rise for religion. What religion taught you that ? . . . Thus for religion, ye keep no religion. Do you prefer the Bishop of Rome afore Christ ? men's inventions afore God's laws ? . . . Ye seek no religion. Ye are deceived. Ye seek traditions. . . . Why rise ye for religion ? . . . And thus much for religious rebels. The other rable of Norfolk rebels, ye pretend a common wealth ∴ . ." [4]

BALE, in his Introduction to Leland's " New Year's

---

[1] Maclean ed. p. 15.

[2] P. 60.

[3] Cranmer's Sermon on the Rebellion as given in the Parker Society publication, reads : " We be round about environed with other enemies : outward with Scots and Frenchmen, and among ourselves with subtle papists, who have persuaded the simple and ignorant Devonshire men, under pretence and colour of religion, to withstand all godly reformation " (p. 93).

[4] Edition 1549, Sig. A. iiij.

Gift," says that the priests and others have led the people—

"in a palpable kind of darkness by their masses, and other sorcerous witchcraft, as lately appeared in the last commotion in Cornwall and Devonshire, to reduce them again to the old obedience of the great Pharus of Rome, in the stinking kingdom of idolatry." [1]

Elsewhere he reproves the people because they—

"were able to conspire, rise, and rebel with the danger of your bodies, goods and souls against your godly and lawful king and that chiefly to defend the devilish mass, and all the puddles of popery with the caterpillars and rabble of all unclean spirits as Cardinals, Bishops, Priests, monks, Friars, nuns, etc."

There seems to be no question with him as to the origin of the rebellion.

CROWLEY, in his " Way to Welthe," [2] points out that the ignorant curates have been the stirrers up of strife, which is evident from the fact that where the people had been better instructed by learned and godly preachers there had been greater quietness.

THE SPANISH CHRONICLER [3] gives as the cause of the rising in the West that " commissions had been sent thither to remove the sacrament from the churches, and the people, resenting this, rose to resist it."

SLEIDAN [4] writes : " for though the Devonshire men were also against Enclosures, yet their chief quarrel was for the alteration made in religion."

In the TROUBLES AT FRANKFORT [5] reference is made to the Earl of Bedford, who had been sent to " subdue the popish rebels in the West."

COOPER, in his " Epitome of Chronicles," [6] refers to

---

[1] See edition 1550, p. 9.
[2] Edition 1550.
[3] P. 181.   Believed to have been written 1551-2.
[4] Date before 1556, in which year he died.
[5] Date 1554.
[6] Ed. 1560.

the insurgents in Norfolk not mentioning religion, while those of Devon not only required enclosures to be thrown open " but also their old religion and the Act of Six Articles to be restored."

STOWE varies this phrase but little : he says that they—

" rose against the noble and Gentlemen and required not only that the enclosures might be disparked, but also to have their old Religion, & act of six articles restored." [1]

JEWEL, a Devonian, born near Berry Narbor, in 1522, although at the time of the commotions absent at Oxford, where he was " professor of divinity," was sure to be well informed concerning the cause of the rising in the West. In 1567, in his reply to his Roman Catholic opponent, Harding, he wrote—

" What rebellion has been moved in England by some of your side in the late reign of king Henry the eighth and king Edward the sixth, in defence of your religion ye may well remember." [2]

FOXE, in his edition of 1563, makes a very brief reference to this rebellion, although he gives the fifteen Articles and the King's Message in full. But he states that the Devonshire men,

" who for the misliking of the order of religion then set forth, being stirred up by some whispering Papists, conspired and flocked together in a rank rebellion." [3]

But in the edition of 1570 he gives a much fuller account, with the set of nine Articles, and says that the rising was against the King's Proceedings—

" through the pernicious instigation . . . of certain Popish Priests, who grudging and disdaining against the Injunctions

---

[1] Annals, ed. 1566, p. 596.
[2] " Defence of the Apology," Works, Parker Soc. ed. III. 171.
[3] See Acts and Monuments, ed. 1563, p. 885.

. . . and especially mourning to see their old Popish Church of Rome to decay, ceased not . . . under colour of Religion to persuade the people then to . . . assemble in companies." [1]

After giving some account of the persons connected with the insurrection, he states that the object of those who rose in other counties was " only about plucking down of enclosures and enlarging of commons," and was, therefore, divided from that of the Western rebels.

GRAFTON writes—

" These rebels (of Devon and Cornwall) demanded not only the enlarging of Commons and disparking of Parks as is above-said : But they were chiefly offended by the alteration of religion." [2]

In the " HOMILY AGAINST REBELLION," we read, after several references to rebels who pretend reformation of religion—

" And to join unto the reports of history, matters of later memory, could the bishop of Rome have raised the late rebellion in the North and West countries in the times of king Henry and king Edward our gracious Sovereign's father and brother, but by abusing of the ignorant people." [3]

HOLINSHED states that in Somersetshire they broke up parks, and there and elsewhere the rebels were appeased and quieted. He continues—

" But shortly after, the commons of Devonshire and Corn-wall rose by way of rebellion, demanding not only to have enclosures laid open and parks disparked ; but also through the instigation and pricking forward of certain popish priests, ceased not by all sinister and subtle means, first under God's name and the King's, and under colour of religion, to persuade the people to assemble. . . . At the first they were in great

---

[1] See Acts and Monuments, ed. 1570, p. 1268.

[2] "Chronicles," ed. 1568, p. 46.

[3] "Homily against Rebellion," published in the time of Elizabeth probably 1571.

hope that the other disordered persons, which stirred in other parts of the realm, would have joined them, by force to have disappointed and undone that which the prince had ordained and established. But afterwards perceiving how in most places such mischievous mutinies and devilish attempts . . . were appeased, or that their cause being only about plucking down of enclosures, and enlarging of commons, was divided from theirs, so that either they would not or could not join with them in their religious quarrel, they began somewhat to doubt of their wicked begun enterprise." [1]

JOHN WOOLTON, afterwards Bishop of Exeter, but an incumbent in the diocese as early as 1561, and who therefore knew the opinion prevalent among the residents of Exeter and the vicinity during the siege, writes, in his " Castell of Christians," published in 1577—

" For whereunto can we impute the sundry rebellions within this our region and country, in our own memory, but only to the blind and malicious ignorance of popish priests." [2]

NORDEN, whose tour in Cornwall is assigned to 1584, writes—

" Another rebellion began in this country under the pretence of religion, upon which occasion Arundell, Wydeslade, Rogeson, and others, became conductors and leaders of a rebellious troup, near 6,000 men, who assailing the City of Exeter, they were repelled by the lord Russell." [3]

CROMPTON, in his " Short Declaration of the end of Traitors," after inveighing much against the wickedness of a subject rebelling against his sovereign, even in

---

[1] Ed. 1577, p. 916. The wording of this paragraph varies but little from Foxe's 1570 account.

[2] Sig. E. iiii⁴. Woolton was instituted to Sampford Peverell in 1561 ; he held Whimple, Braunton, and Kenn before 1577, and was appointed Canon of Exeter in 1565, so he had exceptional opportunities of forming an opinion of the cause of the Western Rebellion.

[3] "Speculi Britanniæ," p. 33.

defence of his faith, refers to the great number in Edward VI.'s reign who

"rebelled in the West parts of this realm, whose pretence was to have the religion then (which is now professed) to have been suppressed." [1]

WESTCOTE, writing about 1600, attributed the rising wholly to religious feeling.

CAREW, in his "History of Cornwall," speaks distinctly of this commotion as having been begun "upon account of religion." [2]

SPEED, after telling how images were cast down and Body killed, adds—

"which fact was so favoured among the rural Commons of Cornwall and Devonshire (who ever gave voice for the papal continuance) that in a rebellious manner they combined together against the King . . . (they) all sought to undo those points of religion, which the King by law and act of Parliament had ordained to be observed." [3]

All the above accounts were written practically within half a century of the events, and may be assumed to be based upon facts coming within the cognisance of the writers or else learned from persons living at the time that the events took place.

These twenty-two, with five exceptions, attribute the movement wholly to dissatisfaction with religious changes, while the exceptions, Sleidan, Cooper, Stowe, Grafton, and Holinshed, say that beside this source of discontent the Western men desired the redress of enclosures—that is to say that less than one-fourth of those who may be classed as contemporary and almost contemporary writers give enclosures as a subsidiary reason.

In the next half-century we have—

GODWIN, speaking of the various rebellions, "especially Devon and Somerset," says that beside the

---

[1] Ed. 1587, sig. B. iiii^d. [2] Written about 1602, p. 376.
[3] Ed. 1611, p. 805.

question of enclosures they " stretched their complaints to a higher strain," and he gives a list of reasons urged, including " Holy Rites established by antiquity, are abolished, new ones are authorised, and a new form of Religion obtruded," and adds, " This was a common complaint and resolution, especially of the Devonshire Rebels." [1]

HAYWARD classes the Western counties with the others who rose on account of enclosures, describes their confused demands, and then prefaces the account of the Devon and Cornwall rising with a reference to the " Religious Mutineers." [2]

HEYLIN distinctly states that the Devonshire in-surrection was begun " under the pretence of throwing open the enclosures, but shortly found to have been raised in maintenance of the old religion." [3]

FULLER declares that, in contradistinction to those of Norfolk, " the Devonshire rebels did openly avouch the advancing of popery." [4]

BURNET describes the risings for enclosures and then deals with the insurrection in Devon, which was better formed because that county " was generally inclined to the former superstition, and many of the old priests ran in among them." [5]

Elsewhere he has—

" I have nothing to add concerning the tumults of the year 1549, but that the popish clergy were generally at the head of the rebels. Many of these were priests who had complied and subscribed the new book : some of them were

---

[1] Godwin's " Rerum Anglicanum " was printed in 1616–26, and the translation by his son, from which the above is quoted, appeared in 1630 (see p. 230). Godwin was born in 1652, and became Canon of Exeter in 1586. He married a daughter of John Woolton, Bishop of Exeter mentioned on p. 402.

[2] Date 1630, p. 56.

[3] Date 1660, p. 75.

[4] Date 1660, II. p. 326.

[5] Date 1679, II. i. p. 236.

killed in every skirmish, and very few of the clergy shewed much zeal against them, so that the Earl of Bedford could have none but Miles Coverdale to go along with the force that he carried into Devonshire to subdue them." [1]

This brings us down nearly to the close of the seventeenth century, when the idea began to creep in that, though the priests were largely responsible for the insurrection, the question of enclosures formed a large item in the grievances even of the Western rebels, though no evidence is produced in support of the theory. [2]

STRYPE gives no decided opinion upon this insurrection, which he does not describe very fully. In dealing with the various risings of the year, he says— "Some were Papists and required the restoration of their old religion," [3] and he mentions that preachers were sent to help quell these stirs, [4] and that the leaders were "inflamed with an ignorant zeal for religion." [5] So it is evident that even at this date a difference was recognised between the Western rebellion and the other risings.

The more recent histories which do condescend to deal with the insurrection—for it was permitted to sink into comparative obscurity—are based upon the statements of the books above quoted, but there is always a tendency to emphasise, one way or the other, the cause of the rising. As we have seen, scarcely any doubt was entertained by the earlier writers as to the question of religion forming the chief reason for the insurrection. But while some modern writers, notably Froude and Dixon, lay stress on this point, others—like Pollard— strive to turn the current of opinion the other way. The latter has it that the movement of discontent with

---

[1] III. 326.

[2] It does not seem worth while to quote here the earlier Roman Catholic writers who dwelt almost wholly on the religious character of the rising.

[3] Date 1721, II. i. p. 260.

[4] *Ibid.* p. 262.

[5] *Ibid.* p. 281.

enclosures was captured by the priests,[1] and even goes so far as to say it is not clear—

" that the various risings of 1549 had any close connection with the Book of Common Prayer. There had been many disturbances . . . due to the enclosure of common lands. . . . But popular discontent was turned to account by priests of the old persuasion, and even by emissaries from France." [2]

He supports this latter statement by a note to the effect that the " Response " to the King's Message was not, as Pocock thought, a translation from English, but probably emanated from the French Ambassador. This point is fully discussed in Appendix G.[3]

[1] " Protector," p. 239.

[2] " Cranmer," p. 247. His opinion on this point is ably controverted by Mr. Gay (Trans. Roy. Hist. Soc. XVIII. p. 195) and Mr. Blake (Journal Roy. Inst. Cornwall, LVI. & LVII.).

[3] Pollard, in his chapter on the Edwardian Reformation in the Cambridge Modern History," has the following paragraph : " The rising in the west, for which religion had furnished a pretext and enclosures the material, died away after the fight at the Barns of Crediton, and the Relief of Exeter by Russell on August 9." The error of the date, 9 for 6, is of minor importance, but the confusion of the two events, one at the very beginning and the other at the end of the rising, is hardly excusable. From the foregoing account it is evident that the rebels began their active resistance to royal authority at Crediton, and this steadily increased until it culminated in the Siege of Exeter. After the relief of that city the rising died away. Furthermore, in dealing with the events of 1550, he writes : " Two Cornish divines, Crispin and Moreman, who had been implicated in the Cornish rebellion, were confined in the Tower." Cornish for Devonian may be overlooked. From the context it is to be inferred that they had been incarcerated in consequence of active participation in the rising of the previous year, but we know their imprisonment preceded the rebellion and probably began in 1547.

His more recent reference to the rebellion in the sixth volume of the " Political History of England " is more extended and more in accordance with facts, but exception must be taken to two statements on p. 26, that the rector of Sampford Courtenay was chaplain to the Lady Mary—the reader is referred to Appendix D for all the information we can find—and the bold statement that " the seafaring folk fought for the new religion." The only instance quoted is the rescue of Walter Ralegh near Topsham by mariners, who may have been actually in his own employ. So far no evidence has been forthcoming even of any expression of sympathy with the new religion made by sailors individually or as a class at so early a period as this. In Elizabeth's reign, as a body, having come in contact with

Miss Lamond, in her Introduction to " The Common Weal of this Realm," attributes even the first rising in Cornwall, when Body was killed, to the enclosing of pasture land, and uses this statement to support her argument.   From the foregoing pages it is evident that the earlier movement was due to a combination of personal hatred and aversion to religious innovations. A close connection is traced between this almost accidental murder of an individual and the more formidable rising of the following year.   Through it all we find that the cause of religion was indelibly stamped upon the movement, so much so that the man on the spot—Hoker —does not even hint that any other cause underlay the discontent of the people.

A study of the history of the period shows that there was an " epidemic of distemper of rebellion " in 1549, and that the risings against enclosures in various counties, with one exception,[1] were practically suppressed before the movement took shape in Cornwall and Devon in June.   The only trace of actual sympathy with the aims of the Western men appear to have been in the Buckingham and Oxfordshire risings of the same summer, suppressed by Lord Grey, who captured two hundred rebels and ruthlessly executed priests, hanging them from their church towers,[2] and also in an insignificant movement in Winchester, which came to nothing.[3]

the Spaniards, they may be considered to have been averse to Romanism, but they certainly did not fight for the new religion in Edward's reign.

[1] That is Kett's, although it cannot, strictly speaking, be counted with the others, as it began after the Western Rebellion.

[2] It should be emphasised that there is no reference to the execution of laymen in this rebellion.

[3] On 6th August, 1549, several men met at the Crown in Winchester when a rising was planned ; money was to be supplied by certain members of the Cathedral body, and the plotters were to take possession of five pieces of ordnance at Selsey.   A banner was ordered to be made " of the fyve woundes & w^t a chales and an oyst (host) & a priest kneling to yt vpon the same banner."   As Flynt, their leader, did not turn up at the appointed trysting place the whole conspiracy fell through (S. P. Dom. Edw. VI. VIII. 41).

Concerning the number engaged and how many were killed we have but the vaguest information—indeed, nothing at all reliable. Excluding the earlier movement, that of 1548, when many lives must have been lost, we find reference to individuals who fell—Hellyons, Underhill, Sir William Francis, Ap Owen, etc.—as well as some rough estimates. The number engaged is not approximately known. Ten thousand stout Cornish men are reported to have advanced to Exeter. Hoker says that six thousand assembled at Clyst St. Mary, while at the same time there remained a considerable force—two thousand, some say—encircling Exeter. Hoker puts the loss at Fenny Bridges alone at three hundred rebels, ignoring the number of royal troops slain. The King doubles that number, but probably includes another engagement. The Spanish Chronicler, who is untrustworthy, says six hundred were killed at Carey's Windmill. Hoker and others say that one thousand fell in the encounter at Clyst St. Mary, apparently including the massacre at Clyst Heath, though Hayward implies that nine hundred were murdered on that occasion alone. Lord Russell reports that between five and six hundred of the rebels were left dead on the field at Sampford Courtenay.

From these figures one might safely infer that of the rebels two thousand were killed in action in three days, and to these should be added about as many more killed in smaller encounters, as well as within and without the city of Exeter and in the flight westward. Another thousand would perhaps be accounted for by executions under martial law, and there would still remain others who died of their wounds to be included. It would be a low computation to fix five thousand as the number of rebels who died for their faith.

As regards the loss on the part of the Royal forces and their supporters, we have even less data. Hoker, writing on this point, says—

"but what number was of the contrary side despatched nothing is reported albeit it be well known that they escaped not scot-free and especially the Burgonians, who were abhorred of the one party and nothing favoured of the other." [1]

"Not above ten or twelve slain," reports Lord Russell of the last encounter at Sampford Courtenay, evidently counting this small in comparison with the losses of his opponents. It might not be wide of the mark to make their total five hundred.

Considering the entire population of England at that period, five thousand five hundred was no insignificant number.

Information as to the amount expended is even more difficult to obtain—we have only the sums mentioned as paid by the Privy Council, recorded in their Register, and a paper preserved at the British Museum, containing detailed expenses incurred in suppressing the various rebellions of the year, which amounted to £28,122 7s. 7d., [2] and when we consider that Devon and Cornwall were the most remote districts—soldiers were partly paid according to the distance traversed—and that this rebellion lasted longer than any other, a fairly large proportion of this sum must be allotted to this rising. Indeed, as has been pointed out elsewhere, over £15,000 was disbursed in this connection according to the Privy Council Register. This alone, considering the enhanced value of money at the present day, is a considerable sum. To this must be added the financial loss sustained by Exeter, by the spoiling of the country and the loss of the crops in the following season. Altogether, the total cost of the insurrection was no small matter. [3]

Therefore, in conclusion, taking one thing with

---

[1] P. 96.

[2] Harl. MS. 353, f. 102.

[3] Froude (V. p. 183, note) gives a list of moneys paid into the Mint by noblemen, but there is no evidence that these were loans to the Crown, as he suggests.

another, it cannot but be admitted that the Western Rebellion was no insignificant affair. But when we come to consider the consequences which would have ensued if the rebels had advanced to London and had been joined by the disaffected from other parts of the realm, as would not have been improbable, it is not too much to say that the almost forgotten victory of Fenny Bridges was a decisive battle in English history. That the success of the rebels would have wholly prevented the Reformation, as we style it, is more than can be claimed, but there can be little doubt that it would have given its progress a serious, though momentary, check.

APPENDIX A

THE Insignia of the Five Wounds played such a prominent part in all the risings of this period that it requires more than a passing reference.

The selection of the emblem of the Five Wounds of Christ by the insurgents was intended to suggest the sufferings inflicted upon His Church on earth and was particularly appropriate especially as the Mass of the Five Wounds was celebrated in order to remove afflictions from individuals and, no doubt, would be applicable to the whole corporate body.

In the Sarum Missal is an account of the origin of this service, and it is said that—among other benefits—" in whatsoever tribulation a man may be in this world, if he shall procure from a priest this office to be celebrated five times without doubt he shall be delivered." [1]

---

[1] The late Dr. Brownlow, Roman Catholic bishop of Clifton, in a description of a copy of the Sarum Missal, given in the Transactions of the Devonshire Association, etc. (Vol. XXVI. p. 92), quotes the following account of the origin of the Mass of the Five Wounds : " Saint Boniface (Pope) was sick even unto death, and earnestly begged of God that his life might be prolonged in this world. The Lord sent to him St. Raphael the archangel, with the Office of the Mass of the Five Wounds, and saying, ' (Holy Pope) arise and take this Office, and say it five times, and thou shalt at once recover thy health. And whatsoever priest shall devoutly say this Office five times for himself or for another sick person, he shall receive health and grace, and in time to come he shall possess life eternal, if he persevere in good even to the end. And in whatsoever tribulation a man be in this world, if he shall procure from a priest this Office to be celebrated five times, without doubt he shall be delivered. And if it shall be read for the soul of one departed, as soon as the said five times shall have been completed, the soul shall be loosed from pains. Saint Boniface (Pope) then hearing these things, forthwith rose up in the place where he lay sick, and

This emblem was therefore chosen to be painted upon a banner and to be embroidered as a badge used in the Pilgrimage of Grace.[1] It formed part of a design on a banner ordered by certain Cornishmen about the time of the Marquis of Exeter's conspiracy. It was embroidered upon a tunic produced as evidence against the Countess of Salisbury. It was displayed on the chief banner borne before the walls of Exeter as well as upon another prepared for a proposed rising at Winchester. Indeed, its use in all these insurrections forms a link in the chain, which shows how closely connected they were in origin and purpose.

In exactly what form the Insignia were represented, or whether always in the same form in all these instances, is uncertain. But that used in the Pilgrimage of Grace is known from the badge worn then by Sir Robert Constable, a reproduction of which forms our frontispiece.[2]

The emblem of the Five Wounds is frequently to be found at the present day upon the ancient carved bench-ends in West-Country churches. The most usual design consists

conjured the same (spirit) by Almighty God, that without danger to him, he should depart from him (recederet), and at once make known to him who he was, and for what purpose he had come. At once he said that he was the archangel Raphael sent by God, and *quae superius pronunciata sine dubio fore rata*, what was declared above shall doubtless be fulfilled. . . ." Dr. Brownlow adds, "The Devotion to the Five Wounds was very popular in England, and it was adopted as the banner of the Catholic rising called 'The Pilgrimage of Grace,' in the time of Henry VIII. Hence numbers of legends gathered about it, and obtained credence. This story is scored out with a pen, as superstitious; but the word 'papa, or pp.' is erased from the parchment."

[1] When Lord Darcy was examined he was asked, "Was not that badge of v woundes your badge, my Lorde Darcey, when ye were in Spain?" Had he not kept these by him, or how were they so quickly made, and why? Were they not told that "they were Christes Souldiours, and that when they looked vppon their badges of v woundes of Christ, they should think that their cause was for the defence of Christes faith and his Churche?" Aske, however, explained that this insignia had been adopted because a member of the Pilgrimage had killed a comrade on one occasion through mistaking his black cross of St. Cuthbert for the enemy's device, so they agreed to wear the badge of I.H.S., or the Five Wounds, both before and behind.

[2] This badge belongs to one of his descendants, the Duchess of Norfolk, who has most kindly supplied a photograph of it with permission for its reproduction.

of a wounded Heart in the centre, with two pierced Hands above and two pierced Feet below it. Sometimes a Chalice is added into which drops of blood are falling.

That this was the recognised emblem of the insurgents of that period is evident from the following quotations.

Among the Salley Papers [1] are some verses, supposed to have been sung by members of the Pilgrimage of Grace, beginning—

> " Crist crucified
> for thy wounds wide
> vs comons guyde
> which pilgrimes be
> through gods grace
> for to purchase
> old welthe & peace
> of the spiritualitie."

Latimer, in a sermon, rebuked the rebels for using it. " They arm themselves with the sign of the Cross and of the wounds, and go clean contrary to him that bare the cross and suffered those wounds." [2]

Bishop Jewell wrote : " They paint their banner with the cross and five wounds. Why bring they those arms against us ? Do not we rejoice and comfort our hearts by the remembrance of his wounds ? Do not we read and show forth to the people the story of his passion ? " [3]

In the " Homily against Rebellion," written in the time of Elizabeth, we read : " The rebels display and bear about ensignes, and banners, which are acceptable vnto the rude ignorant common people, great multitudes of whom by suche false pretences and shews they do deceaue, and drawe vnto them . . . Let no good and discrete subiectes therefore folowe the flagge or banner displayed to rebellion and borne by rebels, though it haue the image of the plough painted therein, with God speed the plough, wryten under in great letters, knowyng that none hynder the plough more than the rebels, who will neither go to the plough them selues, nor suffer other that would go vnto it. And though some rebelles beare the picture

---

[1] L. P. XI. 786³.   [2] Sermons, Parker Soc. p. 29.
[3] Works, Parker Soc. II. 883.

of the fiue woundes paynted agaynst those who put theyr
onlye hope of saluation in the woundes of Christ, not those
woundes whiche are painted in a clout by some leude paynter,
but in those woundes whiche Chryste hym selfe bare in his
precious bodye, though they little knowyng what the cross of
Christe meaneth, which neither caruer nor paynter can make,
do beare the image of the crosse paynted in a ragge, against
those that haue the crosse of Christ painted in their hartes,
yet though they paynt withal in their flagges, Hoc signo vinces,
By this signe thou shalt get the victory, by a most fond imita-
tion of the posie of Constantinus magnus, that noble Christian
Emperor, and great conqueror of God's enemies, a most vnmeete
ensigne for rebels, the enemies of God, theyr prince and countrey:
or what other manner so euer they shall beare, yet let no good
subiect vpon any hope of victorie or good successe, folowe
such standarde bearers of rebellion." [1]

[1] See Sig. F. iiiiᵈ and G. iiᵈ.

APPENDIX B

IN the search for information concerning William Body it has become apparent that the list of Archdeacons of Cornwall hitherto accepted [1] is incomplete, so a more accurate list is here given with a fuller history of the holders of the office between the years 1534 and 1616.

THOMAS BEDYLL admitted Archdeacon 11th June, 1534 ; [2] died September, 1537. [3]

THOMAS WYNTER, clerk, collated 8th October, 1537 ; [4] installed 10th October ; leased Archdeaconry to William Body 9th November, 1537. Resigned 22nd May, 1543.

JOHN POLLARD, clerk, collated 25th May, 1543. [5] On 16th June, 1544, he was collated to the Archdeaconry of Barnstaple.

HUGH WESTON, S.T.P., collated 17th October, 1545. [6]

JOHN GERVES, clerk, compounded for the First Fruits of the Archdeaconry 26th December, 1545. [7]

ROWLAND TAYLOR, LL.D., obtained Letters Patent granting the Archdeaconry dated 3rd May, 1552. [8] He was martyred at Hadley, 8th February, 1554–5.

---

[1] See Oliver's " Bishops of Exeter," p. 289. I am very deeply indebted to the late Mr. W. E. Mugford for his assistance, especially in examining the records at Exeter, and I am grateful for the time and labour he so generously expended in attempting to make this list complete.

[2] Chapter Act Book, Exeter, 3551, f. 91.

[3] L. & P. XII. ii. 700.

[4] Veysey's Reg. i. 90ᵃ·

[5] *Ibid.* 110ᵇ.

[6] *Ibid.* 118ᵃ.

[7] Composition Books.

[8] Pat. Roll. 6 Edw. VI. pt. 5.

JOHN RIXMAN, B.D., instituted 23rd September, 1554.[1] Resigned 1555. Died December, 1557.

GEORGE HARVIE installed 2nd March, 1555–6. Died 1563.

ROGER ALLEY, scholar, instituted on Harvie's resignation, 13th October, 1563. Deprived 1574.

THOMAS SOMASTER, D.D., instituted 3rd July, 1570. Died 1603.

NICHOLAS MARSTON, B.D., instituted 10th June, 1574.[2]

WILLIAM HUTCHINSON, S.T.P., instituted 5th September, 1603.[3]

So much for the succession of the Archdeacons of Cornwall, but the list contains some curious overlapping which in some measure is due to the complications of the patronage.

Bedyll and Wynter, considering what has been written already, may be passed over, merely adding one fact. On the 17th September, 1537, Sir William Kingston wrote to Cromwell in reply to a letter from the Vicar-General concerning the Archdeaconry, stating that he understood that the Bishop of Exeter had given this advowson to Mr. Rowsewell—" on condition if he had any other promotion it should be void, and Rowsewell has had a prebend of my lord a year past." [3]

Thomas Rowsewell was one of the Prebendaries of Ottery St. Mary in 1536. From this letter it would seem that the appointment of the Archdeacon lay with the Bishop of Exeter, as it does to-day.

From the account given in Chapter IV. it is apparent that Wynter parted with his rights in the Archdeaconry to William Body, and as we find that the latter was objected to because he was " purely a layman," it seems that the grant was believed, at first at all events, to carry with it spiritual jurisdiction. But in the end Body was forced to content himself with the profits and with the presentation, which he claimed and exercised although his right so to do was contested.

After Wynter resigned, which seems to have been by arrangement, John Pollard was collated on the 25th May, 1543, having compounded for his First Fruits three days previously.[4]

[1] Veysey's Reg. ii. 29ᵃ.

[2] *Ibid.* 11, 18ᵇ.

[3] L. &. P. XII. ii. 700. By advowson he probably meant the next presentation.

[4] Composition Books, Vol. II. His sureties were John Rudgeway of the Middle Temple and Thomas Williams of the Inner Temple.

As no reference to the appointment of William Horsey to the Archdeaconry has been discovered it is very much to be doubted whether he ever held the office. The only authority for his having done so is Hoker, who may have been mistaken.

According to an entry in the Augmentation Office Miscellaneous Book, No. 105 [1] John Pollard, clerk, Archdeacon of the Archdeaconry of Cornwall, did grant, demise, betaken and to farm let by Indenture, dated xiij day of April, 1544, to William Body of London, gentleman, all his said archdeaconry, his Prebend in Glasney, etc., etc., for thirty-four years thence next ensuing and Body was to pay therefor £10 of lawful money on the day of the Nativity of St. John the Baptist "in the Chappell called Busshop Oldames Chappell in the Cathedral Church of Saynt Peter in Excetter betwene the houres of eight and eleven of the cloke before none of the same day." [2]

About the 29th May, 1544, Brerewood died in prison, and thereupon the Archdeaconry of Barnstaple became vacant and to this John Pollard was collated on the 16th June following. He compounded for his First Fruits a week later.[3]

In the ordinary course this made the Archdeaconry of Cornwall vacant, but no appointment immediately followed. Indeed, for some reason it remained vacant for more than a year. On the 17th October, 1545, Hugh Weston was collated to the Archdeaconry, "certo modo jam vacantem," [4] just sixteen months after Pollard's promotion. Against this entry in the Episcopal Register is a marginal note,[5] faintly written, to the effect that this collation was made because Body who claimed to be patron, had neglected to present.

But evidently Body soon became aware of the lapse, for on the 26th December, 1545, it is recorded that John Gerves

[1] Fol. 144. See also in Auditor's Patent Book, No. 4, f. 64.

[2] In the Exchequer of Accounts of the First Fruits and Tenths there is record of a Process against William Body, farmer of the Archdeaconry of Cornwall for the Tenths and Subsidy for the year " xxxvj° " (Henry VIII.), which had not been paid.

[3] Comp. Bk. II. His sureties this time were George Pollard of the Royal Household and Nicholas Prideaux.

[4] Veysey's Reg. I. 118ᵃ.

[5] It is not clear whether this marginal note was made at the time by the same hand or was added afterwards.

compounded for the First Fruits of the Archdeaconry : [1] so it would seem that the Bishop made one appointment and that Body made another.

Body was killed at Helston on the 5th April, 1548, and his will was proved by his widow, Anne, on the 23rd May following. Who was actually in possession of the Archdeaconry at this time is not clear, but the patronage must have been a matter of dispute, as in February, 1550–1 a decree was obtained in favour of John Tusser in the Court of Augmentations.[2] He was to be recompensed for his Prebend of Glasney and to have the synodals, etc., of several specified churches in Cornwall. This John Tusser had married Anne, widow of William Body and made this claim in her right.

On the 26th March following depositions were taken concerning the rights to the house, garden, etc., belonging to the Glasney prebend.[3] But the dispute between the Bishop and Tusser was by no means at an end, for the former appealed for the support of the Privy Council, as he alleged that Tusser did "interrupt him in the execucion of his office of Bysshop within the sayd countie of Cornwall" under the pretext of a lease of the Archdeaconry to Body.[4] But which Bishop of Exeter this was is not certain, for Veysey resigned, and Coverdale was consecrated in August, 1551, and the exact date of the commencement of the appeal is not known, still it was probably the latter, as Coverdale must have been the one to carry it on. The Privy Council already had had the matter under consideration when, on the 17th November, 1551, they referred it to Mr. Justice Hales and Doctor May, Dean of St. Paul's. On the 2nd January the business was again before the Council, who wrote to the Dean of Exeter to find out how the lease of the Archdeaconry was granted to Body, by whose procurement, and who signed it, so that they might end the controversy between the Bishop and Tusser. His reply is not forthcoming, but it seems to have been favourable to the Bishop, as on the last day of February, 1551–2, Tusser appeared

---

[1] Comp. Bk. III. His sureties were Mathew Broke, clerk, Rector of St. Tudy in Cornwall, and William Body of St. Mylor, in the same county, gentleman.

[2] Aug. Of. Decrees, 15, 127, and 146.

[3] Aug. Of. Misc. Bk. 132, f. 32.

[4] Privy Council Reg. Vol. III. 419.

before the lords of the Council, and upon examination of "long matter" it was commanded that "neither he nor any of his should intermeddle with any part of the Archdeaconry of Cornwall, without further lycence from the Lordes here, because he had very ungodly [1] and unlawfully used the office of the same." He was also bound in recognisances of 1000 marks not to meddle in the same.[2]

Almost immediately after this, that is on the 3rd May, 1552, Letters Patent were made granting the Archdeaconry to Rowland Taylor. This was that Rowland Taylor, who had been domestic chaplain to Cranmer and who was afterwards martyred at Hadley. For particulars of his martyrdom the reader is referred to Foxe's volumes.[3] This appointment may well have been due to Coverdale's influence.

Taylor was not allowed to remain in undisturbed possession, for Tusser almost immediately attacked him. According to the Privy Council Register a letter was written on the 26th September, 1552, commanding Tusser's attendance " to aunswer to certeyn slanderous reportes which he hath raysed uppon Doctour Taylour, Archdeacon of Excester." [4] This is evidently a mistake for the Archdeacon of Cornwall of the diocese of Exeter, for it was to Cornwall that Taylor was appointed both according to the Patent Roll and the Land Revenue Enrolment record. At this time Adam Travers still held the Archdeaconry of Exeter.

In the end Tusser was committed to the Fleet on the 12th November, 1552.[5]

Edward VI. died on the 6th July, 1553, and almost at once Dr. Taylor was cited before Bishop Gardyner, according to Foxe, and was burnt at Hadley on the 8th February, 1554–5.

Meanwhile John Rixman had been instituted to the Archdeaconry, "jam certo modo vacantem," on the 23rd September, 1554,[6] with all its rights and appurtenances by the right, title,

---

[1] From this expression it looks as if he had undertaken to exercise some spiritual jurisdiction.

[2] Privy Council Reg. III. 494.

[3] He was probably the same as the one of the name who was one of the suppressors of the monasteries.

[4] P. C. Reg. IV. 131.

[5] *Ibid.* 167.

[6] Veysey's Reg. II. 29ᵃ.

and interest of John Tusser and Anne his wife in the said archdeaconry to the jurisdiction and rights, fruits, income and
emoluments, etc., by the concession and confirmation by *us*
made, etc., which is an unusual form to be used by the Bishop.

Rixman did not die until 1557, but he appears to have
resigned the Archdeaconry a little earlier than this date. He
was succeeded by George Harvie, who was installed 2nd March,
1555-6 and of whom we have the scantiest information. He
resigned the Archdeaconry in 1563.

Roger Alley, son of the Bishop of that name, was instituted
13th October, 1563, on the presentation of John Tusser, gent,
Patron for that turn,[1] but another dispute about the Archdeaconry arose through his appointment. Thomas Somaster was
presented to it by the Crown on the 3rd July, 1570, the previous
appointment of Alley seeming to be ignored. The whole
question of the Archdeaconry was eventually referred to the
Archbishop, who on the 22nd May, 1574, gave his decision in
favour of Somaster.[2] Le Neve says Alley was deprived because
of his youth, being only 23 years old.[3]

Within a month of the Archbishop's decision Nicholas
Marston was instituted to the Archdeaconry, "certo modo
vacantem," on the presentation of Thomas Marston of the
City of London, *Farmer* of the Archdeaconry, true patron for
that turn.[4] It would seem that the "farm" had been transferred by Tusser to Marston and that this institution was made
for asserting his claim. Yet the matter must have remained
in dispute, as we find that William Hutchinson, S.T.D., was
instituted 5th September, 1603, on the *death of Somaster*, on
the presentation of Ralph Hutchinson, S.T.B., patron for
that turn only, "by Advocacio," by the then Bishop of Exeter,
(William Cotton) to John (Whitgift) Archbishop of Canterbury,
and by him assigned to the said Ralph Hutchinson.[5]

Of Tusser we may add that he held an office in the Duchy

[1] Alley's Reg. 84ᵃ.
[2] Archbp. Parker's Reg. 212.
[3] Fasti Eccl. I. 399. It is to be presumed that he was only twenty-
three when he was instituted, for he seems to have held the benefice for
seven years before Somaster's appointment.
[4] Bradbridge's Reg. 18ᵇ.
[5] Cotton's Reg. 78ᵃ. This Ralph Hutchinson was one of those who
translated the present Bible.

of Cornwall, of which his brother William was a clerk. His will is dated 9th March, 1574,[1] and was proved 5th May, 1578. He is therein described as of Truro ; in an action in the Court of Requests he is styled " of Saincte Mabin in Cornwall, gentilman," and in an inventory of his goods among the Duchy papers he is said to be of St. Columb the Lower.[2]

[1] P. C. C. 19 Langley. [2] Bdle. 127, No 10.

APPENDIX C

THE Proclamation of Pardon for the murdering of William Body here given is copied from the original among the Privy Seals. It varies in some minor particulars from the transcript in the British Museum (Titus, B. II. fol. 15), which may have been made from a printed proclamation, of which I have been unable to find a copy. It is here given without any attempt at pointing as in the original, but spaces have been left between the names of those exempted so that the number of persons may be seen more clearly.

Privy Seal. Series 3. File 884. May 2. Edw. VI.

To the kings ma^tie our Soueraigne lorde Memorandm xvij^mo die May Anno RR Ed^w sc^do ista billa delibat fuit dño Cāncellar' Anglie apud Westm exequend

Please it yor highnes of yor most noble and aboundaunte grace to graunte yor gracious l~res patents vnder yor great seale of Englande in due forme to be made according to the teno^r herafter ensuing and that this bill signed w^t yor most gracious hands may be sufficient and imediate warrañte vnto the Lord Chaūcelor for thensealing and delyu'ie

(The signature " Edward " appears at the top.)

Edwardus Sextus, &c. Rx Vic. Cornub, Saltm̄. Precipim̃ tibi q^d immediate poste recepcōem p̃sentm̃ in Anglis locis infra balliam tuam tam infra libtates q^um extra vbi magis expedire videris ex parte nrã publicas pclamacōes fieri facias in hoc verba.

Albeyt that many of you the Kings Hyghnes Subiects &
comons dwellynge & inhabitinge in the Shyre of Cornewall
Aswell wythin lyꝗtyes ffraᵘnches as wythout wythin the sayd
Shyre or in any other place or yle beyng reputyd or taken
for any part ꝑpcell or membre of the same Shyre and suche
other the Kings sayd Subiects inhabyted in other places/
Haue nowe of late Attemptyd and comytted manyfest & open
Rebellyon agaynst hys most royall maiestye wythin the sayd
Shyre or the lymytts of the same/   Whereby was lyke to haue
ensued the vtter ruyne & destruccon of that whole Shyre/
& to the hyghe dyspleasure of Almyghtye god/ who strayghtly
comaundyth you to obey your souaygne lorde & kyng in all
thyngs & not wyth vyolence to resyst hys wyll & commaunde-
ment for any cause whatsoeu ytt be Neutheles the kynges
moste royall maiestye ꝑceyuynge by Credable reports that
your sayd offences ꝑcedyd of ignoraunce and yll intysemente &
by occasyon of sundrye false tales neu ꝑposed mynded nor
entended by hys hyghnes nor of any of hys counsayll but
moste craftely contryved & most spytefully sett Abrode
Amonge you by certen malycyous & sedycyous ꝑsons/   And
therapon hys hyghnes enclyned to extend hys moste gracious
pyttye and mercye towards you/ hauynge the chyeffe charge
of you under god bothe of your soules & bodyes & desyryng
rather the ꝑseruacoñ of the same and your reconsylyacon by
hys ḿcyfull meanes then by thordre of rygor of Justice/ to
punyshe you Accordynge to your demeryts/   Of hys inestym-
able goodnes replenyshed wyth most godly ḿcye & pytye &
att your moste humble petycons & submyssyons made vnto
hys hyghnes is contented & pleased to gyue & graunt and by
thys ꝑsent ꝑclamacoñ dothe gyue & graunt and by thys
ꝑsent ꝑclamacoñ dothe gyue & graunt vnto you all &
to all & euy your confederats whersoeu they dwell of what
estate degree or condycyon so eu you or they be or by what
name or names so eu you or they be called hys geñall & free
pdon for all mañ of treasons Rebellyons Insurreccons mes-
prysons of treasons murdres Roꝗyes felonyes & of all mañ
of Accessaryes of or to the same & of & to euy of them & of &
for all mañ of vnlawffull Assemblyes vnlawffull conventycles
vnlawffull speakings of words confederacyes conspyracyes
Ryotts routs & all other offences trespaces & contemptes done

and comytted by you or any of you wythin & from the tyme
of the begynnynge of the sayd Rebellyon whensoeu yt was/
vntill the ffyrst day of May last past & of all paynes Judge-
mentes & execucons of deathe & all other penaltyes fynes &
forfeytures of londes tentes heredytamentes goodes & catalles
by any of you incurred by reason of the ꝑmisses or any of them/
Whyche fynes forfeytures londes tentes heredytementes goodes
& cattalles the kynges sayd hyghnes of his especyall grace &
mere mocon by theys ꝑsents gyueth to suche of you as should
haue forfeyted or loste the same by occasyon of the ꝑmisses
or any of them/ And also hys hyghnes ys pleasyd & contentyd
that you and euy of you from tyme to tyme shall & may haue
uppon your suytes to be made hereafter in the kyngs chauncerye
hys sayd moste gracyous & free pdon under hys gret seale
specyally to be made for any of you concernynge the ꝑmisses
Wythout any further byll or warraunte to be obteyned for
the same/ & wythout payyng any thynge for the grett Seale
therof And that you & euy of you from tyme to tyme may
freely and lybally sue for hys sayd pdon When & as often as
yt shall lyke you Wythout any trouble vexacon or ympechement
of the p'misses or any of them by hys hyghnes or by any hys
officers mynysters or Subiects by any mañ of meanes or in
any mañ of Wyse/ ffurthemore the kings most Royall maiestye
strayghtly chargeth & commᵃandeth that you & all and euy
of you shall from hensforth lyke trew & faythefull subiectes
vse your selfes in goddes peax & hys Accordinge to your duetyes
of Allegyaunce/ And that ye shall in nowyse hereafter Attempt
to make or ꝑcure any suche Rebellyon vnlawfull Assembles
Ryottes Routes & conspyricyes/ nor att the comᵃndment nor
by the Aucthoryte of anie ꝑson of what estate or degree or for
what cause so eu yt be/ shall arryse comotte or styrre warre
in any forcyble mañ & Array/ Onlesse yt be at the specyall
commᵃndement of the kynges hyghnes or suche as hys hyghnes
shall Auctoryse for the same/ ꝑuydyd alwayes that thys
geñall & free ꝑdon shall not extende or In any wyse be beny-
fycyall vnto John Wyllyams Wyllyam̃ Kylter John Kylter
John Kelyan Rychard Trewela Wyllam̃ Amys John Chykose
Alen Raw lawrence Breton Mychaell Vian Briton Olyver Rise
John Tregena Rychard Raw Pasco Trevian Martin Resse
Jamys Robert Henry Tyrlever John Trybo thelder Thomas

Terlan vien Mychaell John Moryce Tryball/ Syr Martyn Gefferye priest John Pierse maryner Willyam̃ Thomas Alias Nenys Richard Hodge Tribo theyonger Edmonde Iryshe & Hew mason alias Wavers alias Parker [1] In wytnes wherof the kinges moste Royall maiesty hathe caused thys hys pclamacon to be made patente & sealed with hys gret seale at Westm'

E Somerset
 W Seant John J Russell
   Willm Petre sr. A Denny R Saldeyr

[1] Among the uncalendared documents at the Public Record Office is a letter, dated 21st April, with signature erased, asking for the release of Hew Mason, who had been arrested at Exeter on suspicion of being " one of the stirrers of the villains of St. Keverne's." It is stated that he forsook their company at the first proceedings, and came to Pendennis Castle for safeguard of his life, as he had been threatened with hanging and burning of his house. The writer had advised him to "get hence eastwards until such time as the villain creatures were subdued." The recipient was desired to be his good master and release him " unless ye have heard any further credible report of his demeanour than I have declared for surely I found him like a true man to his prince in all points in this broil."

On the back of this is a draft of another letter giving further particulars; that he was from Grade, had left the rebels on the 5th April, had been transferred from the west to the east castle of Falmouth, and thence for safety conveyed to Exeter by his son-in-law, William Leye.

Probably it was in consequence of these letters that Mason's name was erased from the "True Bill" as mentioned in the note on page 85.

APPENDIX D

HOKER'S DESCRIPTIONS OF THE REBELLION

THERE are several descriptions of the events of this period written by John Hoker alias Vowell.

Judging from internal evidence the earliest written is that preserved in manuscript in the Bodleian Library, for it mentions the fact that some of those who took part " are yet liuuinge but beinge sorrie and ashamed of their follye I doe suppresse their names " (f. 5).

It is difficult to say which comes next in chronological order, but it is most likely that the " Guildhall " MS. follows—this is in process of being printed by the Devon and Cornwall Record Society.

After this we would place the description embodied in Holinshed's Chronicle, which chronicle was revised and extended by Hoker in 1587. This contains more names and additional information, with many new anecdotes, not given in the Guildhall MS. The small volume printed by Brice in 1786 is the same as this, and appears to have been lifted bodily from Holinshed without acknowledgment.

Another description is to be found in Hoker's " Life of Sir Peter Carewe," the MS. of which is in the Lambeth Palace Library. This has been printed by Sir John Maclean and also in the " Archeologia." The story is here given from the point of view of the biographer in connection with Sir Peter's life.

There is also a condensed account in Hoker's History of Exeter, dated 1559, which is in manuscript in the British Museum. (Titus, F. VI. fol. 78).

APPENDIX E

THE advowson of Sampford Courtenay came into the hands of the Crown on the attainder of the Marquis of Exeter and in course of time it was granted to Henry VIII.'s queen, Katherine Parr, who presented to it William Harper, her Clerk of the Closet. He was instituted on the 18th October, 1549 and in the entry in the Episcopal Register is described as " Regine Sacellanum." [1]

Foster's " Alumni Oxoniensis " gives two of this name at this period : the first was " secular chaplain, fellow of New Coll. 1503–27, from Axbridge, Somerset, B.C.L. (disp. 6th July), 1521, B. Can. L. (disp. 9th April), 1522 ; one of these names rector of Sampford Courtenay, Devon, 1546." This man held the New College living of Writtle, Essex, from 1526 to 1553 and in 1551 was accused of illegal practices. On the 29th April of that year an inquest was held at Chelmsford, when it was found that, contrary to the Statute which commanded the use of the services according to the Book of Common Prayer and the administration of the Sacraments, etc., William Harper, rector of Writtle did elevate the sacred body of our Lord Jesus Christ and had shown the said body to the people and did invoke saints.[2] It is quite possible that this was the William Harper, rector of Sampford Courtenay. The other of the name given by Foster as B.A., 27th June, 1522, he suggests was rector of

---

[1] Veysey's Reg. I. 121. Sacellanum, from Sacellum, a reliquary, is given by Du Cange as equivalent to Capellanus. It is possible that it was used in a more restricted sense than chaplain, and may have been the term particularly applied to a Clerk of the Closet.

[2] Baga de Secretis, Pouch, XVIII.

North Buckenham, Norfolk, 1542, prebendary of collegiate church of Stoke-juxta-Clare, Suffolk, 1547.

As Clerk of the Queen's Closet Harper had many duties : he had the care of the Closet and its appurtenances, he supplied it with books, he acted as confidential messenger and accompanied the Queen upon her journey, celebrating mass for her. From the bills rendered by him found among the private accounts of Katherine Parr [1] it is possible to obtain an idea of his duties. There is an entry, constantly occurring, for " half a cart " at a penny a mile, this being required to transport the " furniture of the Closet," and was probably shared with some other officer of the Household. The furniture of the Closet was not always adequate as he enters 4d. " gyven in rewarde to the clerke and sexton at buckyngham [2] for bryngyng of theyr church stuffe to serue the quene." Once he charges for the " caryage of the plate for the Closet." He paid the " launder " five shillings quarterly for washing the linen, which included " albes, awter clothes and other lynnen." There were, probably, also altar frontals, vestments of tissue or velvet and " balkyns " or canopies, such as George Wolfet, Clerk of the King's Closet, enumerates in an inventory. [3]

Harper also supplied herbs and flowers and " Syngyng breads." [4] He asks allowance for the following curious items : a perfuming panne to the closet. iiij yardes whyte caddas for gyrdles, a basket lyned w^t ledd^r to cary coles to the grett closett, a fyer sufill (elsewhere called a showyll), iiij yards of silke lace for hangyng the pycks, a skeyne of whyte thrydde, iiij^c teynter hokes, a hamer, sylke laces for regesters for the portuas occupied in the quene ys closet and thryd for Reparyng vestments and Removyng Albes.

Among the books supplied for the Queen's use were " two great halfe portuas for the queyns Closet," " a prymar for her grace in laten and englyshe w^t epistyles and gospeles vnbounden," with a charge for " Rewlyng and Coleryng of the letteres

---

[1] Aug. Of. Misc. Bk. 161.

[2] This seems to identify the Clerk of the Closet with the Rector of North Buckenham. See above.

[3] L. &. P. XII. i. 329.

[4] Halliwell gives Singing Bread as sacramental wafers, but it is more probable that this was the *pain benit* distributed on high festivals during a sung mass.

of the seyd p'mar," "her graces testement in frenche," and for "gyldyng coveryng and byndyng of the two seyd bokes." He also received from Berthelet, the King's Printer, for the Queen's grace " a boke of psalme praiers [1] couered in white and gilt on the leather, a boke of the .x. cōmaundementes, couered in white and gilt on the Leather, and Enchiridion of Erasmus in englishe and the boke called the preparacion to dethe."

Harper's position as Clerk of the Queen's Closet was one of honour, the corresponding office in the King's Household was usually held by a clergyman of importance. The wages paid to both officers was the same, £6 16s. 10½d. per annum.[2]

After Henry VIII.'s death and the marriage of Katherine Parr to the Lord Admiral her household was much reduced and then, or else on her death in 1548, William Harper would have been free to attend to his duties as parish priest at Sampford Courtenay. It seems probable that he took refuge in this remote district as he was out of sympathy with the changes at Court. During his residence in the Queen's Household he must have known the Princess Mary [3] and may have been on friendly terms with her, sympathising with her in the persecution to which she was subjected. He may even have resided in her household after the Queen's marriage. The fact that he was known to be her friend may have given rise to the charge made against the Princess that one of her chaplains at Sampford Courtenay was a prime-mover in the insurrection.

He held the living of Sampford Courtenay until the end of Mary's reign, his successor being instituted on the 10th January, 1558-9 on the resignation of " Mr. Wᵐ Harper." [4]

[1] This was most likely Katherine Parr's " Prayers or Meditations," commonly called the " Queen's Prayers."

[2] The above information has been printed in the *Library* for January, 1911.

[3] A visit to the " More " is entered in his accounts.

[4] Turberville's Reg., f. 44.

APPENDIX F

THE Petyt manuscript, which has furnished so much information for this book, is No. 538, volume 46, and is preserved in the Petyt collection in the library of the Middle Temple. Through the courtesy of its custodians I have been able to compare Pocock's printed copy with the original and have found many errors in his transcript.

It is stated in Foro Juliensis that this and the succeeding volume, No. 47, are supposed to have belonged to Sir Thomas Smith and according to an entry on fol. 29a of this volume the documents from fol. 431 onward were manuscripts "out of Fox's study."

Pocock's transcript must have been done for him by a careless scribe. The spelling, which is extraordinary in the original, has been varied without any apparent reason, while the punctuation of the printed copy is arbitrary, frequently altering the sense. Three of the letters are misplaced without any obvious reason. Omitting the slips as to spelling, capitals and punctuation there remains a formidable list of errors of a more or less serious nature : perhaps the most glaring are the numerals on page 21, and the substitution of the name Orne for Drue, and the omission of " not " on page 91.

Because of the many mistakes the originals have been quoted in the foregoing pages. For the benefit of others I subjoin a list of errors, with reference to page and line.

P. 15, l. 19, For " serve " *read* " seem."

P. 15, l. 24, *For* " tarying " *read* " carying."

P. 17, l. 7, *For* " complying " *read* " compayng."

P. 17, l. 8, *Insert* " in " *after* " man."

P. 18, l. 17, *For* ' Commyssion^r " *read* " Comyssarry."

P. 24, l. 7, *For* " thus " *read* " this."

P. 24, l. 12, *Insert* " to " *between* " mynde " *and* " send."

P. 24, l. 23, *For* " herein closed " *read* " here inclosed."

P. 25, l. 13, *Insert* " for " *between* " furnyshed " *and* " eight."

P. 25, l. 17, *For* " tauld " *read* " could."

P. 25, I. 21, *For* " m^l vj^c " *read* " m^{l}m^l (2000) *and for* " m^l vij^c " *read* " iiij^{ml} " (4000).

P. 25, l. 25, *For* " present " *read* " paie."

P. 27, l. 6, *Insert* " most " *between* " footmen " *and* " necessarie."

P. 27, l. 12, *Insert* " of " *between* " accompt " *and* " service"

P. 28, l. 9, *Insert* " Northfolk " *between* " at " *and* " and."

P. 28, l. 22, *Insert* " with " *between* " wyshing " *and* " you."

P. 29, l. 13, *For* " in " *read* " on."

P. 31, l. 9, *Insert* " have " *between* " wold " *and* " els."

P. 31, l. 13, *For* " out " *read* " cut."

P. 32, l. 11, *For* " which " *read* " while."

P. 32, l. 16, *For* " the awe " *read* " they avow."

P. 33, l. 6, *For* " execute " *read* " execucon."

P. 33, l. 11, *For* " face " *read* " force."

P. 35, l. 9, *For* " Aleurg " *read* " A Leury " (? O'Leary ?)

P. 35, l. 13, *For* " That we " *read* " That ye."

P. 37, l. 13, *For* " see " *read* " here."

P. 37, l. 17, *For* " bendyng " *read* " tendyng."

P. 41, l. 9, *For* " will " *read* " wile."

P. 41, l. 20, *For* " ermatytie " *read* " quantitie."

P. 42, l. 8, *Insert* " yor L loving frends."

P. 44, l. 18, *For* " harmes " *read* " harnes."

P. 48, l. 5, *Insert* " after " *between* " ferthest " *and* " theyr."

P. 48, l. 7, *For* " provyded " *read* " payed."

P. 46 (This letter should follow that ending on p. 49).

P. 46, l. 16, *For* " destroy " *read* " do stay."

P. 50, l. 13, *For* " (same) " *read* " iorney."

P. 53, l. 13, *For* " Orne " *read* " Drue."

P. 54, l. 14, *Place phrase* " Yt is . . . ponyshment " in ( ).

P. 56, l. 18, *Insert* " forren " *between* " the " *and* " enymies."

P. 6, l. 30, *For* " an " *read* " oon."

P. 7, l. 11, *For* " staie " *read* " servis."

P. 7, l. 17, *Insert* " end " *between* " good " *and* " and."

P. 59, l. 8, *For* " compamy " *read* " companys."

P. 59, l. 11, *For* " D " *read* " C."
P. 59, l. 14, *For* " therin " *read* " them."
P. 60, l. 26, *For* " xi^{th} " *read* " xv^{th} "
P. 61, l. 13, *For* " muster " *read* " amass."
P. 61, l. 24, *For* " admice " *read* " adunce " (for advance).
P. 64, l. 10, *For* " Devshire " *read* " Denshire."
P. 65, l. 6, *For* " my " *read* " our."
P. 65, l. 27, *For* " this " *read* " theis."
P. 66, l. 13, *For* " desertion " *read* " detēcon " (detention).
P. 66, l. 20, *For* " always " *read* " alredye."
P. 66, l. 25, *For* " lykewise apprehendid " *read* " lykewise to
        (be) apprehendid."
P. 67, l. 21, *For* " incōvenyence " *read* " incōvenyences."
P. 69, l. 33, *For* " the meanynge " *read* " our meanynge."
P. 72, l. 6, *For* " certification " *read* " certificatye."
P. 73, l. 20, *For* " force " *read* " offence."
P. 89, l. 1, *Insert* " by us " *between* " advised " *and* " and."
P. 89, l. 3, *For* " no herme " *read* " therebie."
P. 91 (This letter follows that ending on page 83).
P. 91, l. 30, *For* " redounde unto " *read* " redounde not to."
P. 92, l. 1, *Insert* " to be " *between* " bludd " *and* " shedde."
P. 112, l. 14, *For* " miserable " *read* " terable."
P. 112, l. 20, *For* " plye " *read* " folleye "
P. 112, l. 21, *For* " servts " *read* " sewts."
P. 112, l. 24, *Insert* " the " *between* " for " *and* " sewerty."

A misunderstanding of dates requires special notice. On page twenty-seven is a letter from the Protector to the Lord Privy Seal, dated at the head " xvij^{th} of Julij," and at the end " xxvij^{th} of Julij." Pocock says that the later date is a mistake of the writer, but, on the contrary, the 27th July is correct. Sir John Arundell's recognisances are entered in the Privy Council Register under the 27th July, and it is also obvious, from the Council's letter of the 18th July, on page twenty-nine, that Sir John had not then arrived in London, while their report of his examination, in a letter dated the 27th July, on page thirty-eight, confirms the Register. On the other hand, the Council's letter on page twenty-nine, headed " xviij^{th} of Julii," and " xxviij^{th} " at the end, must have been written at the earlier date, as orders had just been given to have Sir John sent to London.

APPENDIX G

SOMERSET'S REPLY TO THE REBELS.

(S. P. Dom. Ed. VI. 1549. Vol. VIII. No. 6.)

The kinges Ma^{tes} answer to the supplicaĉon made in the name of his highnes subiectes of Devon and Cornewall.

Yғ ye our subiectes who by goddes ordinãnce and your owne othe do owe to vs obedience, wolde here vs as redely according to your dewties, As we of our princelie clemencie haue taken and pervsed your Supplicaĉon we do not doubt, but ye wolde easely returne to your olde quiet and good ordre. And ye shulde playnely pceive what difference there were betwixt the harte and wordes of a king enoincted that ruleth by counsell and kepeth his Realme in defence and quyetnes, And suche blinde guides of Sediĉon and vprore, who nowe takes vppon them to rule yo^w o^r subiectes and people to leade yo^w agenst vs your naturall lorde and king and to bring bothe yo^w and themselfes w^t all haste to Destruccon.

Ye do require thinges of vs by a bill o^r supplicaĉon, and as we are aduertised ye send a gentilman w^t your requestes to our trustie and welbiloued Counsello^r and lieuten^ant the lorde privie seale. But after what sorte do ye come to your king to demand ? w^t sworde in hande ? And in battaill arraye ? What manner is that to come to yor Prince ? What other order wolde ye keape if the frenche or scottℓ shulde invade yo^w. Content, content yo^rselfes, good people, see o^r Shires of Deuon-shire and Cornewall well in order. see the corne and the fructℓ of the earthe, which god hath sent of his most greate clemencie gathered now in tyme wherby ye shulde be susteyned in winter./ Do not w^t this rage and furie drive your self to

2 ғ

the swerde, your wiffꝭ and chyldren to famyn and honger/
Yf any thing be to be reformed in oᵣ Lawes, the parliament is
nere at hand a place and tyme where men ought and euer
hitherto haue ben wonnte to common of such maters where
the wise heades and the three estatꝭ of the Realme be congregate together for that purpose deliberately to consyder and
wisely to debate what lawes or statutꝭ are to be made or re-
voked/ We haue aunswered to a greate parte of your suppli-
cacõn by a message sent to oᵣ people of Devonshire, the whiche
to thintent it might be more common and seen we haue caused
to be put in printe./ There ye shall·lern how moche ye be
deceyved in many poinctꝭ, and how they abuse youe wᵗ lies
that wolde haue yoʷ thus in this confusion./

ffurst of Baptysme ye are put in feare that your children
shulde not be christened by vppon the holie daye/ There is
no daye tyme nor howre but by our order the Priest may
christen the childe if it be brought vnto him even as he might
before this tyme.

Thorder of confirmacon ye seme not to mislike but yoʷ
thinke your children shall not learne it except they go to scole/
The curate is appointed to teache it them wᵗoute going to schole,
And it is not so long and agin it is so godlie, that one childe
ones having learned it will sone teache it twenty

How did ye all lerne before the pater Nr̃, Ave, and Crede in
Laten whiche was a strainge language, and which ye did not
vnderstand? And cannot yoᵣ children learn so moch in Englishe
which is no more but the belief in effect and ten comãunde-
mentes, the whiche all men must knowe vppon pein of
dampnacõn? And herin the bishop and curate must haue
dyscrecon if such impediment be in the childe that he cannot
aunswer distinctly if it do not cõme of Malyce but of infirmitie
of witte or nature he shall not therfore denye the childe of
full aege either confirmacõn or the holey sacrament. Ever
heretofore and eu' herafter discrecon in suche cases must rule
and not straight lawes and so to do according to Wise discrecon
is not ageinst the lawe but wᵗ it/.

The vjᵗʰ articles and the statutꝭ that made wordes treason
and other suche severe lawes ye seme to require ageine the
wᶜʰ all our hole parliament almost on their knees required vs
tabolish and put awaye And when we condiscended thereto wᵗ

an hole voice gave us most humeble thank℄. ffor they thought
before that no man was sure of his lief landes or goodes, when
for eu'y light worde or gesture he was in dangier of death, and
w'in peine of the laws. And wolde youe haue those lawes
again ? will yoᵂ that we shall resume the scourge agein and
hard snaffle for your mouthes ? Yf all the Realme consent
and ye require to haue our sworde agein awake and more nerer
yoʳ heades ye maye sone haue it by vs and by parliament
restored to his olde power/ But we feare vs they that most
desire it will sonest and sorest repent yᵗ When we are content
to rule like a father wᵗ all mercy and clemency do yoᵂ call for
the bridell and Whippe ? Ah oʳ loueng subiectes, who be
these that put this into yoʳ heades ? Do ye knowe what ye
demaunde and what thend wolde be of that request.

Where ye complaine of the blindnes and vnwillingnes of
yoʳ curates to the setting forthe of our proceedines we do not
thinke your complaintes moch vntrew in that behalf and do
fear that a greate parte of this daungerous stirre cometh of
them But what blind heades they be, howe vngodly and
vntowarde your owne applicacõn dothe declare

Dothe receiving of the Cõion either make matrimony or
give authoritie and Lycence to horedome ?/ Did not men and
wymen alwaies hertofore go to goddes borde and receyve
togither and all at one tyme as they do nowe ? And did euer men
think then that thei that did so shulde be in cõmon ? Theye
did then eate all of one breade as they do nowe and in sacrament
receive one bodie whiche is the bodie of Christ as they do nowe
and so that bodie is made common vnto them and therfore
it is called the cõion/ But this they did tencrease puritie
clenes and holines of lif, not to licence fylthines or horedome, to
their saluacõn and gostley comforte they ought to take it, and
not to dampnacõn Where the same curates abuse Baptisme
and refuse buriall contrary to our orders, and will do no divine
s'uice in church for frowardnes and voluntary laking of bookes
These be iust causes whie they des've ponishment, not whie
ye shulde rise ageinst vs/ We colde haue sene this reformed
w'oute any suche enormitie cõmitted vppon yoʳ pties

And where ye saie certein Cornishmen be offended because
they haue not their s'uice in Cornish for somuch as thei vnderstand no English. Whie shulde they nowe be offended more

when they vnderstand it not in English then when they had it
in Latin and vnderstode it not ?/   And whie shulde not yo^w
all the rest than be gladde and well pleased that haue it in
English, that ye do vnderstand.   Yf they haue just cause to
be greved that haue it in the tongue the which they do not
vnderstand   But we are enformed to be veray fewe or no
townes in Cornewall but ye shall find more in them that vnderstand English then that vnderstand Laten.   And therefore
they be yet in better case nowe then the(y) were bifore

Ye obiect vnto vs as though theis thinges were done vs not
knowing/   But we do declare vnto yo^w that there was nothing
but at o^r consent and knowledge, nor nothing passeth in
parliament but our consent is at it.   And for that our booke of
orders of the churche We knowe nothing is in it but according
to the scripture and the worde of god and that we our self
in parson altho as yet yong in aage are able to iustifie and
proue.   We trust by scriptures and good lernyng against who
so eu' will defend the contrary

Lastlie of all ye require to haue the relief graunted vnto vs
by pliament of clothe and Shore shepe to be remitted vnto
yo^w affirmyng that we haue no nede therof.   And ye do reckon
up all suche thinges as o^r derely biloued father had graunted
vnto him for the mainten^ance of his warres and otherwise for
the keping and defence of the state of the Realme.   And ye do
not consyder what infinite charge it is to keape such warres
as hathe ben bothe towardnes ffraunce and Scotland now
contynued almost these eight yeres.   What Suℳ of money an
armie doth consume in shorte space   And our said most dere
father and we haue ben constrayned to kepe diuers Armies
bothe by land and by sea/   Yo^w do not reken how many
thowsand pound℥ Bulloign doth stand vs in monethely beside
the other pec℥ Whiche be ther/   Nor how many thowsand
pound℥ we are faine monethly to send Northwardes to maintein
o^r guarrisons agenst the scottes and ffrenchmen/   And we do
knowe o^r father was at no less charge, whome yo^w do accompt
to haue lefte vs so ryche   We do moche marvell what occaĉon
yo^w haue to thinke so seing he was constrayned to take so many
lones subsidies and benevolences and also sell his land which
were no tokens of Abundant Ryches.   And how riche so eu^ll
yo^w thinke he lefte vs we knowe he left vs aboue thre hundrethe

thowsand pound℮ in debt. Now gesse yo^w whether we haue
nede of relief or no And where ye mistrust our officers and
magistrat℮ and those whome ye saie were apoincted to rule by
our said most dere fathers will Do yo^w not feare but if anything
were to be had that waies we could call our officers welenoughe
to accompt w^{t}oute yo^w, and also do as tyme is, and loke as
narely vnto them as nede or reason is. And thoughe some of
them shulde be riche and welthie whiche is the gifte of god and
reioyse of Princ℮ to haue welthie subiectes so they haue it by
trueth and do vs no wronge, what cause haue we agenst them ?
We do wishe yo^w all riche and welthie and do what lieth in vs
to kepe your Ennimies ffrom yo^w and yo^w in quiet that ye
might be so/ Altho warre and your defence dothe consume
and waste o^r treas^r/ And yo^w on your pties to these warres
that we haue alredy, and be to vs so chargeable adioyne this
your Insurrecōon and comocōn that ye make in our Realme
the whiche to redresse & to defend our ryall Ma^{te} against this
your Rebellion and lewdnes must nede be a wasting of our money
& causeth vs to spend twise so moch as is given vs in the
Relief to bring yo^w our naturall & vnkinde Subiect℮ in obeience./
The whiche we do not doubt we shall shortly do, and will do
thoughe we spend all the treaso^r we haue yea & o^r lyf vppon
it And who shall beare o^r Losses. Youe will not se your
prince lacke, or if youe wolde, the rest of our subiectes whiche
be true and faithfull vnto vs will not suffer that there prince
and king shulde be nedy for if he shulde how sholde he maintein
his garrisons paie his souldio^{rs} susteyn warres defend and kepe
oute thememies whiche on every side are readie to assaile
them Wherfore this waye that ye go aboute is not the waye
to make vs haue no nede of this relif but rather make us call
for a doble relif/ And we do mervaill that yo^w do not vnderstand and that those heades whiche teache yo^w howe litle
we do neade and what thing℮ we haue so vntrewlie do not tell
yo^w also that which they might truelie do, that for this relief
of Shepe and clothes at the peticōn of our comōons in the parliament we did remit and forgeve for the space of these thre
yeres fee farmes of Townes and divers other thing℮ we did
graunt and remitte vnto them the which as we be enformed
dothe come to moch more than this relief will make. And is
it reason we shulde lose that and not haue this ? And yet

seth the said parliament at their humeble sute and peticon/
We haue given to all oʳ other loving Subiectₑ two easis in
this relief, that none shall this yere paye of shepe but he that
hath aboue one hundreth/ And that clothiers shall give but
notₑ of the nomƀr and contentₑ of their clothe wᵗoute valuacon
or praysing of them till our most deare vncle and our counsell
hathe taken further order in it, this is all that eny other Subiect
of ours durst euer demand & We more lyberallie haue graunted
it vnto them then they did aske it not constrayned of there
force but moved of our naturall pitie and love to our subiectₑ.
Altho at this tyme we haue most nede & mych the more by
yoʳ vnrulynes/ ffor when all scotland was in mannʳ redy to
obey vnto vs, The french durst not aid them as thei gladlie
wolde, Now the french at this pñt taking courage of your
rebellion hathe made oute xij gallies and other shippis in grete
nomƀr ageinst our Realme and entendyth to take the Iland
of Sylly if they may or elles as they brute to land in Cornwall
or Devonshire and there as oʳ espīall sheweth vs take a gentyl-
mans howse which is almost an Ile and more then half environed
in the Sea. Yoʷ that shulde defend it where so eů it be and
kepe foren powre from our Realme are now against vs/ and
most vnnaturally kepith vs from the defence of yoʷ and yoʳself from the aide of yoʳ owne contrey.

But thinke yoʷ if the french or eny oʳ enemies shall take
aduᵃntage of this yoʳ misrule and decende & take place in eny
of our domynion that we shall not aske accompte of yoʷ for
the losse/ And howe wolde they handell yoʷ thinke yoʷ
straungers and Enemyes to the realme & nacon. Yf they
shulde descend and take place wolde not they then rob and
spoile pill and subdue yoʷ/ And yet what so eů parte or
pece ye shulde lose howe vnnaturall vnloving and disobedient
ye are vnto vs the same we must reken losse to our self/ for
we esteme oʳ wealth to consist in the wealth of our subiectₑ and
our losse in their losse and dam͂age/ And for that we & our
most entirely beloued vncle & all our counsell sendith day and
night and taketh care to preserue yoʷ who haue no regarde
of your self as it apeareth and all the rest of our Realme from
thenemye that yoʷ might not feale the losse and distrucͨon
that other nac͂ons fealith/ And yoʷ put yoʳself and our
Realme in hasarde by yoʳ owne foly and sturdines/ Ye haue

enfected all our Realme w^t yor wicked exaumple but they are all retorned and acknowledged their dutye & humebly desired and obteyned o^r mercy saving onely yo^w/ What sprite of myschief and disobedience constrayneth yo^w to tary for our sworde when ye may haue mercy/ Wherfore repent yo^w by tymes and so many of yo^w as do acknowledge vs for yor Princes superio^r and soueraign lorde, and haue regarde of yor owne welthes depte yo^w in peace home to yor howses. We can be content and had rather vse clemency and pdon than the sworde and ponishment ageinst yo^w/ But how shall we recon those rebellℓ and traito^{rs} that thus stobbornly contynueth ageinst o^r Ma^{ti} to be o^r subiectℓ. Or howe dare ye that do so call vs yor prince or yor selfℓ o^r obedyent subiectes, Which in nothing will obeye vs but as ye liste yor selfes/ but excepte ye spedy depte we shall so poneshe yor stobbernes that ye shall be example to all the rest of England and appetuall memorite to yor posteritie

Ye complayne of Darth of vittailℓ and other thingℓ/ And is this the way thinke yo^w to make plentie ? What a wast and spoile do ye make of grasse Corne Haye and all other thingℓ where ye co$\tilde{m}$e ? And o^r po^r that shall mete w^t yo^w must nedes spend grete quantity of vitayll bothe whereby they pas and where they shall lie. And ye bring w^t youe those that sholde mowe down yor grasse and carie in yor corne and kepe them Idle that sholde make yor cloth and gather yor tynne whereby ye shall live all the yere And some nom$\tilde{b}$r also shall co$\tilde{m}$e w^t vs that shulde be so occupied. So that by this meanes the olde stores are wasted and consumed and the new not saued nor kept as it shulde be. Whereto dothe this tend thinke yo^w to a plenty or a dearth ? to abundance or to scarcite ? This last yere ye said there was death of cataill emonges yo^w And nowe ye spoile them and wast them as thoughe there were an host of enemyes in the cuntry. Shall we haue more by this think ye or the fewer ? Will rebellion against yor naturall and lie$\tilde{g}$ lorde make yo^w welthier Na god will se it reuenged, if we shulde not god who is the autho^r well and fountain of obedyence and humilitie will see this pride and disobedience well chastised. And we are sorie that in our tender aege we shulde as we feare we shalbe con-strayned by yor stubbernes to teach yo^w howe greate a mischief it is to subiectes ageinst their Prince to make an insurrec͠con.

(Endorsed)
  The Ans^r to the Supplicac͠on
  of ye Comons of Devon
  & Cornwall.

APPENDIX H

I am greatly indebted to Mr. A. F. Pollard for calling my attention to certain documents relating to this tract. At the same time I cannot admit his contentions concerning the rebellion and this book.

In his " Cranmer " he writes : " It is not, however, clear that the various risings of 1549 had any close connection with the Book of Common Prayer." He then refers to the risings against enclosures and adds : " But popular discontent was turned to account by priests of the old persuasion, and even by emisarries from France, then on the eve of war with England." To this is appended a lengthy note which may be thus summarised : A defence of the insurgents, written in French and not published until 1550 is considered by Pocock to be a translation of a lost English original. " It is more probably an original emanating from the French ambassador or one of his agents." Henry II sought on a former occasion to embroil England in civil war. The statement of grievances, which were no doubt drawn up by priests, laid more emphasis upon religious matters than the mass of the insurgents would naturally have done themselves. Mention is made of the almost justifiable objection of the Cornishmen to the use of English and also to Cranmer's reply. Mr. Pollard refers to " the compulsory worship of the Sacrament and the execution of all recusants as heretics—a ferocious requisition which deprived its authors of all title to mercy," and to the 7th, 8th, 13th, and 14th Articles " as the only ones which can be supposed to represent a really popular sentiment." [1]

With the foregoing description of the Rebellion before us it is not necessary to enter into the question of the connection of the Prayer Book therewith or with the fact that its moving cause was religion. Attention should be called, however, to the reference to a single set of Articles—probably No. III.

[1] P. 247.

There is no good reason for doubting that a reply based on the same lines as "La Responce" was compiled by some persons, very likely priests, and accepted by the leaders of the insurrection. A careful scrutiny of the tract tends to the conclusion that the writer had in his hands such a reply and used it as the basis for this book, but there does not seem to be sufficient evidence to show that it was written at the instigation of the French ambassador for political purposes : indeed, it is difficult to understand how it could have furthered that object.

The history of this "Responce" is curious. At the end of the book is printed a statement to the effect that an application had been made to the Provost of Paris by Jehan Riviere for permission to print this response of the English People to their King on certain articles touching religion and that it had the approval of " Monsieur l'Inquisiteur de la Foy " as worthy to be printed. He desired the exclusive rights for it and these were granted for a year on 25th October, 1550. It was for sale by Robert Masselin, printer, living opposite the cemetery of " St. Etienne du Mont," in Paris, at the sign of the Three Red Trenchers.[1]

Scarcely six weeks after this licence was granted Sir John Mason, then ambassador in France, sent a copy of the book to the Council. In his letter of the 4th December, accompanying it he says that " some Scot was either author or at least a helper." He promised that he would declare the lewdness of the device to the Constable of France immediately and would have search made for the author. On the 15th January following the Council reminded him of the subject and on the 7th February he wrote that in the Constable's absence from Blois he had laid the matter before the French Council. The Chancellor, after complaining of a book by " Mr. Smyth at my Lorde of Somersett's going into Skotelande," promised to send letters to Paris to remedy this business. Mason added that before despatching these letters he had received another book to the same effect " made in more ample sort and dedicated to the Queen of Scots."[2] On his return the Constable seemed displeased with the matter,

---

[1] The title-page gives the address as opposite St. Genevieve du Mont. These churches were close together.

[2] The question of Scotland occupies many pages, out of all proportion to the subject.

so sént straight to the Provost of Paris, first to see that the printer was forthcoming and then to do his best to suppress the book and make diligent search for the author. This was done so promptly that Mason was able to enclose in a letter of the 18th March the report of John Watson, from which we learn that Masselin, besides being inhibited from printing and selling the book, had lost all the copies he had, which had been removed by a gentleman of the Court.

As the result of Mason's own investigations he was convinced that the author of the book was one Peter Hogue, "who hath long served in all practices of dissension between the subjects and the prince, against whom this King [of France] hath meant hostilitie. He was first secretary to Rincon and sithen to Poullin and lastly he was joined with Monluc in Scotland and Ireland and was at the Commotion time in habit dissembled in England. But finally being sent to the Emperor's Countries to make some stir there he was taken and lieth by the feet in Riplemond like to have that he hath long since deserved. This Peter penned the book but it was set forth as far as I can learn by the said malicious Monluc, the prothonotary, who in time of wars had commission in Ireland." [1]

Meanwhile the Council were busy attempting to prevent the circulation of the book and in trying to discover how it had been imported. On the 7th March, 1550-1, a man named William Seth was examined by certain great Court officials, including the Lord Privy Seal, because he was accused of bringing from France certain seditious books, among them "yll bookes made by Doctour Smythe in Fraunce agaynst the Busshop of Cantorburies and Peter Marter's bookes." Among the rest were two copies of "La Responce," one destined for Bishop Bonner. He confesses : "I have also ij lytle bokes yn french of thanswere of the Comons to the kinges Maiestie, the one I brought w^t me yn my chest at Kyghtleys, the other unbownd yn ye baryll the which Mr. Baynes dyd send to my late Master." His late master was Bishop Bonner, who had employed Seth to read to him while imprisoned in the Marshall-sea, until the Bishop, in a fit of temper, beat him with his bed-staff, driving him from the room. In consequence of this Seth

---

[1] Hogue appears to have left France some time previous to the publication of the tract.

left his service and crossed to France to learn the language. In order to obtain funds to enable him to apprentice himself to a printer in Paris named Nicholas le Jeune, he returned to England to beg of friends. He also brought books, some of which were to be sold on commission and others to be distributed to friends of the exiles.[1]

The day after Seth's first examination the Council, considering the matter divulged important, appointed a committee to examine into it—" Doctour Poynet, now named Busshop of Winchester, Mr. Gosnall —— and John Throgmorton."

Among those mentioned in Seth's confession was John White, then Warden of Winchester College, to whom letters had been brought from " T. Martyn, a student at Paris, touching books which he could not provide for the said White, according to his request, which books were to be delivered to White of London to be sent to White of Winchester." [2]   On the 25th March White appeared before the Council and confessed that he had received divers books and letters from beyond sea, from one Martin, " a scoller there, who repugneth the Kinges Majesties proceedings vtterlie : and being manifest that he hath consented to things of that sorte, in such wise that greater practises are thought to be in him that waies, he was committed to the Tower." [3]   There he remained until the 14th June following when, upon knowledge of some better conformity in matters of religion he was committed to the custody of the Archbishop " till such time as he may reclayme him, which done to commaunde him agayne to the Tower until the Kinges Majesties further pleasour

---

[1] See P. C. Reg. III. p. 232, and Cecil MSS. I., No. 346 et seq. I am greatly indebted to the Marquis of Salisbury for permission to examine the original documents and to Mr. R. T. Gunton, the librarian at Hatfield, for his assistance. Seth also brought messages, among them one to Bonner from Dr. Baynes, who " willed the bishop to receive his persecution patiently, for he was neither the first that suffered persecution nor should be the last." Seth stuck to his story though threatened with the rack. He wrote a pathetic letter to " Master Frogmorton " (Throgmorton), headed, " Jhus help me," in which he declared that though he might be forced to tell lies under the rack he would afterwards declare the truth.

[2] White of London was no doubt John White, brother of the Warden, also named John, who was Lord Mayor of London in 1563. Warden White was in great favour under Mary, becoming first Bishop of Lincoln and afterwards of Winchester.

[3] P. C. Reg. III. p. 242.

be knowen uppon his Lordship's certificat of his proceedings with him." [1]

Strenuous efforts were evidently made to implicate persons of high position, and if any evidence had been forthcoming indicating that "La Responce" emanated from the French authorities it is strange that it is unmentioned in any records or letters of the day which have been preserved.

It seems quite possible that a genuine "Responce" was made by the Commons of Devonshire to the King's Message, and that a copy came into the hands of Peter Hogue while he was in England at the time of the Commotions. He may have given this, or a translation of it, to Monluc before his departure for the "Emperor's Countries." Perhaps Monluc published this under an assumed name at the instigation of the French Ambassador, though it is not obvious how he could use it as a political weapon.

If such were the case it would in no wise vitiate the claims of the Response as an exposition of the Commons' opinions on the King's Message. [2]

Brit. Mus. Grenville Library. 11,906.

(Title page.)

LA RESPONCE DU PEUPLE
ANGLOIS À LEUR ROY EDOUARD,
SUR CERTAINS ARTICLES QUI EN
SON NOM LEUR ONT ESTÉ
ENUOYEZ TOUCHANT
LA RELIGIŌ CHRE
STIENNE.

Auecques priuilege.

A Paris
Par Robert masselin Imprimeur de-
mourant aux trois trenchoirs rou-
ges deuant saincte Geneuief-
ue du mont
1550.

[1] P. C. Reg. III. p. 302.

[2] Only one copy of this book has been traced in England, this is in the Brit. Mus. (G. 11,906). M. B. Minssen informs me that there is a copy in the Bibliothèque Nationale of Paris (8° Nf. 129).

LA RESPONCE DU PEUPLE ANGLOIS

a ii

A honnorables Seigneurs maistre Pierre Cheua-
lier Seigneur Desprune, & Secretaire du Roy
notre Sire en sa chãbre des comptes: &
Jacques Paillart Seigneur de Iumeauuille,
Recteurs de la maison du Sainct Esprit à Pàris,
Jehan Riuiere prebstre humble Salut.

LES philosophes anciens (spectable seigneurs) auec
longue experience nous ont delaissé ceste sentēce
qui a esté tournée en prouerbe comun, touteffois
tresueritable. Quand le chef se deult, tous les
membres sont dolens. Ce qu'est entendu non
seulment ny particulierement au corps de l'home,
qui par les Grecz est appelle μικρόκοσμος petit
monde, mais & par l'vniuersel, par tous siecles,
degrez, regnes, & dignitez, En ceulx qui sont veuz
hauoir la préeminence sur les autres Car quãd
ailleurs ilz ne diuertissent leur office fors selon le
droict des gēs, & l'ordonnance premierement de
Dieu qui ainsi les cõstitue Chefz du peuple par le

1 Reg. 15
Rom. 9
Prou. 20

tesmoinoges de sainct Paul portans le glayue
en le vengeance des malfaicteurs & louenge des
bons, *dissipant omne malum intuitu suo.* Comme
au contraire si pour les pechez du peuple Dieu
est tant irrité, qu'il tourne leur cœur a hypo-

Job 34

chrisie (ce que iamais n'a aduienne) hauront leur
peuples, ministres & subiectez d'autant plus
impietable, & tellemēt que les vns d'iceulx
s'efforceront estre promeuz en honneurs, biens,
offices, & dignitez: Les autres qui ineffablement
sont plus pernicieux comme en ce trouuãs voye
plus facile s'estudirōt seulement a faire courir
l'opinion de leur bruit & nom: Generalement
tous les reuererōt & craindront comme qui
seulz en auant peuuent poulser oultre leurs

Gen. 10
(?) Para 1.

effortz. Les exemples de ce premierement nous
ont esté dõnez en Nemroth, lequel en ses entreprinses a esté ensuyuy par grande multitude de

Exod. 14.

2 Reg. 12

Eccl. 47

a iii

2 Cor. IV.

Mat. vlt.

Rom. (?)

peuple. Pharaon consenté par les Magiciens Dieu endurcissant son cœur auec son peuple a persecuté en sa perdition les enfans d'Israel. Les enfans d'Israel long temps apres auec leur Roy Hieroboam ont ensuyuy les Dieux etranges. Arrian, Sabellian, Nestore, Mahomet, & autres faulx docteurs iamais n'ont peu trouuer les moyens de faire courir leur doctrine pestifere, que premierement n'ayent gaigné les Magistratz & recteurs du peuple. Et sans vagues ailleurs presentment sont veuz en diuers lieux petitz vestiges de l'anciēne & premiere maniere de viure estre demourez par la faulse persuasion de Sathan se transffigurant en l'Ange de lumiere en hypocrisie mere de toute iniquite parlant mesonge par ses prophetes & empeschant & detenant la cœur mesmes d'iceulx, qui auec nous au parauant tant sainctement tout au contraire auoient conuersé, faict, presché & escript, qu'ilz sont veuz en grande compassion de tous bien zelez se mettre hors des bornes des louables institutions de tous Chrestiens. Toute-ffois le bon Dieu qui aux siens a promis assister iusque a la consummation de siecles uncores entre iceulx s'est reserue plus de septāte mille hommes qui n'ont flechy le genou deuāt Baal, selon qui nous est referé de ce bon & catholicque peuple Angloys, lequel ces iours passez ensemble s'est congregé a vny en Dieu pour pourueoir à telle absurdité : & à leur Roy Edouard sur quatre articles que aulcuns non bien entendans les mysteres de la religion en son nom leur auoient mandé, ont faict responce si treschrestienne, qu'ilz se sont appareillez iusque a prendre les armes, pour maintenir iusque au peril de leur vie ce qu'ilz ont receu par l'Euāgile, escriptz des Apostres, & leur successeurs, & en tout ce semblablement pour cōseruer leur Roy, entent qu'ilz pourroient, qu'en son ieune aage ny iamais il ne puisse estre tiré à erreur. Mais venerable

seigneurs mieulz vous verres tout le discours
ioyeux & consolatif pas leur dicte respōce, la
quelle en ces liens comme pour consolation m'a
esté enuoyée. Car c'est la querelle laquelle
autreffois ailleurs i'ay soustenu, & icy ie soustiens,
& iusques à la mort soustiendray Iesus Christ
nostre seigneur me confortant. Et apres en
diligence ladicte responce auoir transcript i'ay
voulu la presenter à voz Seigneur. Non pas pour
vouloir vser de l'office de vous exhorter a garder
tousiours, ce qu'auec louenge nous tenons. Mais
pource que ie vostre treshumble suys de l'ordre
du Sainct Esprit, le moindre : Et qu'en ceste
ville de Paris ou plus specialement fleurist la
Christienne religion, vous estes les maistres, &
gouerneurs de la maison du Sainct Esprit, comme

iiii bons peres, nourissiers, tuteurs, deffeseurs,
Et m'asseurant sur tout vostre singuliere humanité,
que ne me reputeres temeraire, ainçois gratieuse-
mēt me recepueres en cest escript. Car par
vostre moyen, ayde, faueur, turelle & protection
ceste responce du peuple Anglois tant catholicque
de tous autres sera receue, embrassé, aymée,
enuoyās leur humbles prieres vers Dieu, qui
ne de laisee iamais les siens estre tentez plus

Cor. 10 qu'ilz ne puissent porter, pour iceulx Anglois, à
fin que grace force, & main leur soit octroyée, a
maintenir en tout honneur, fidelite, & obeissance
leur Roy, pareillemēt la religion Chrestien—
ne, a l'augmentation de l'honneur
d'iceluy qui en est l'autheur
nostre souuerain Seigneur
& createur Iesus Christ,
Lequel, venerables,
Seigneurs, incessam-
ment ie prie vous
donner en santé
bonne vie
& lon
gue.

La Responce Dv Pevple Anglois à leur Roy Edouard sur certains articles qui en son nom leurs ont esté enuoyez touchant le religion Chrestienne.

GRANDE a esté & telle sera tousiours par nous estimée l'humanité dont il a pleu à vostre Sacrée Maieste vser enuers nous qui sommes (quelque chose qui il aduienne) voz treshumbles seruiteurs, tresobeissans & fideles subiectz, nous ayans faict escripte vne lettre en responce des articles qui pour le bien publicq & conseruation de la religion nous furēt de vostre part presentez laquelle touteffois encores que par vostre commandement ait esté escript, nous sommes assurez n'auoir esté dictée par vous, ne selō vostre esprit et bonté : mais plus tost par ceulx qui non contens d'auoir quelque temps abusé de vostre nom & conuerty vostre authorité & puissance à l'effusion du sang de voz subiectz, à la desolatiō & ruine du pais, oppression du pauure peuple, et, si possible eust esté, dimunition en partie de vostre reputation mettent peine voꝗ mouuoir en leur affections sanguinnaires, engendrer en vostre cœur vne hayne contre ceulx que debuez naturellement aymer, induire vostre ieune aage à violences, cruaultez & vengeances. Et qui plus nous deplaist, vous donner à entendre que nul mal ne sçauroit nous aduenir que ne l'ayons trop plus grand merité. Comme certes ne pourrions nier, si par quelque occasion que ce soit estions telz que par leur dictes letres il nous baptisent, c'est a sçauoir seditieux, traitres, rebelles, hereticques, & scismaticques, vsans en cest endroict, & à nostre grand deplaisir de la caultelle des ignorans & malicieux medecins, lesquelz pour s'excuser des erreurs dont ilz pourroient estre notez, apres auoir tué ceulx qu'ilz ont heu en charge, les dissament : & alleg-uent l'intemperance & desobeissance auoir esté cause de leur mort. En ceste façon & matiere nous qui en fidelité & obeissance auons satisfaict au debuoir & obligation de voz subiectz, sommes à present traictez & gouuernez par ceulx, qui apres auoir espan du nostre sang, suffé nostre substance, & appauury nostre

b.

pauure famille, reduict noz corps & noz biens à vne
extreme seruitude : & s'estre efforcez de contraindre
noz ames a prendre le chemin de damnation, que voluntairement & pour eulx mesmes ils ont voulu choisir,
nous accusent de crime de lese Maiesté diuine & humaine,
N'estans de rien tāt offencez sinon que sommes encores
en vie, & que parmy si grande seruitude, ayons peu
reseruer quelque peu de liberté en nostre lāgue pour
nous douloir, pour nous plaindre, pour appeller celuy
qui d'enhault a promis estre nostre protecteur : &
presenter à vous, qui estes nostre naturel Seigneur,
nostre Roy, pere & protecteur, noz iustes & treshumbles
prieres. Lequelles touteffois ne nous ont apporté
autres fruictez qu'vne letre digne d'estre par nous auec
tout honneur receue, & auec reuerence estimée pour y
estre le nom de vostre Maiesté lascript.   Mais en reste
soubz correction ne tenant rien de vostre Esprit, d'autant
qu'elle est pleine de parolles semblables on si pres,
c'est a sçauoir, haultes & infructueuses, par foys reiet-
tant noz yeulz la force, l'authorité, puissance & espée
tranchant de vostre Maiesté, par fois nous rappellant
auec doulces & gratieuses. Sans touteffois mettre en
cōsideration quelque priere, doleāce, & plaincte qui
par nous ait este presentée à vostre Sacrée Maiesté, puys
que pour la punition de noz pechez, ou (peult estre)
b ii   pour quelque aultre cause plus preiudiciable au bien de
ce royaume Dieu a permis que ne soyons escoutez :
Nous vous supplions treshumblemet ne trouuer mauluais, si pour le defence de nostre honneur, estans la
vie & les biēs abandonnez au benefice de la fortune;
& qui pis est au vouloir a ire de voz gouuerneurs, nous
vous respondons à quatre principaulx articles dont est
par vostredicte letre faict mention.

Quant au premier article, ou nous sommes notez de
rebellion pour nous estre vniz & assemblez, et auoir
abusé du nom de vostre Maiesté, et ce que sensuyt.

TROIS choses Sacrée Maiesté selon le dict anciēs &
l'experiēce qu'en plusiers endroictz en a esté veue, hont

puissance decomouuoir le cœur du subiect ēuers son
maistre, mais non pas l'excuser qu'il n'en soit punissable.
Et sont la crainte, l'iniure, et le mepris, pour les quelles
causes encores que plusieurs occasions à diuerses fois
nous aient esté données : il n'y a personne d'entre
nous qui ait voulu penser, non plus que tuer soymesme,
de s'esloinger d'vn seul poinct de l'obeissance, que
par ordonnance de Dieu vous debuons par le droict
des gens & consentement de vostre peuple. Ne se pourra
dire que nostre assemblée soit faicte pour commettre
chose preiudiciable á vostre personne, á vostre authoritè
& puissance. Ains seulement pour restraindre & re-
primer la dissolue liberté dont voz gouuerneurs ont
parcy deuant vse sur noz biens, sur noz vies, & qui pis
est sur noz ames. En quoy certainement ilz ont
excessiuement passé les bornes d'administrateurs de
ce royaume, faisans l'office qui seulement est reserué à
Dieu ou son vicaire, Euesques & aultres ministres de
l'Eglise. Et si pour induire & precipiter vostre Maiesté
en ce ieune aage à semblable erreur, ils vous proposent
en cecy & nō en plusieurs chose vertueuse & louables
l'exemple du feu Roy Henry huictiesme vostre pere, qui
pour certaines occasions deuant sa mort chāgea quelque
institutiō de l'Eglise. Nous voꝗ supplions treshumblement les vouloir cognoistre pour imitateurs de mauluais
& ignorans painctes, lesquelz, s'il leur aduient ne pouuoir
b iii   viuement exprimer la beaulté d'un personnage, se con-
tentent de representer verrues & cicatrices & autre
imperfections de la face. Et comme veoyons le nez s'il
est de sa droicture & forme detourné a estre Aquilain ou
camus, on peut pourtāt l'estimer laid ny difforme, mais
pourroit il bien estre tiré à si grande & demesurée
longeur qu'il ꝑdra la forme & nō de nez. Tout ainsi
ce peut il dire que la religion fut par le feu Roy vostre
pere en quelque partie touchée. Mais à present à nostre
grād desplaisir, grande infamie de nostre nation, mespris
de Dieu & hayne de la Chrestienté le nom desia est
parmy nous perdu, l'vsage & l'effect reietté & aboly sur
la peine de crime de lese Maiesté. Ce n'est pas doncque
la persuasion du diable, ce n'est pas la ligerté du peuple,

la simplicité des ignorās, ny la temerité des seditieux, qui
a esté cause de nous assembler.   Ains plus tost le soing
particulier que chascun de nous doibt hauoir de son
ame, le desplaisir commun de veoir la religion que
noz antecesseurs auec si grande reuerence ont gardé
l'espace de douze centz ans, à l'appetit de deux ou trois
à present tellement chāgee & reduict en nouuelle façon,
que les vieulx d'entre nous ce pendant mourrōt, & les
ieunes viendront à vne extreme viellesse auant que bien
ententre ce qu'on leur commande pour leur salut.   Et
à la plus part restera vn scruple & telle defiance, que
si tout ce que nous faisons sans Foy, est peché comme
dict l'escripture, toutes œuvres qu'ilz feront seront à
Dieu inutiles & infructueuse, comme à ceulx qui pour
asseurer leur consciences n'entendront autre raison de
l'institution nouuelle que la seule authorité & commandement de vostre Maiesté, lequel commandement
oultre qu'il sera tousiours vne force & violence ne
pourra persuader ceulx, qui deuant leur yeulx repre-
senterōt la memoire de tous voz predecesseurs Chrestiēs ; tant de gens de bien & de grande doctrine & vie
exemplaire en ce royaume, qui n'ont iamais publié ne
gardé autreffois que celle qu'on veult presentement
changer & destruire.   Et si pour corriger la superstition des simples, or l'auarice des gens d'Eglise
vne reformation estoit necessaire, c'estoit à vous Sacrée
Maiesté d'assembler les Euesque & non les intimider,
les prier, & non leur donner la loy ny les contraindre,
ains leur assister a l'exemple d'vn Cōstantin, d'vn
Constance, d'vn Theodose, & autres bons Empereurs.
Et a l'exemple d'vn Iuas & Helphe, Henry premier,
second & troisieme, & autres voz predecesseurs, dont
les vns se sont contentez de la charge qu'ilz hauoient
d'administrer la police exterieur enuers tous les subiectz de l'empire, Remettans les affairs qui concernoient
le salut des ames aux prelatz qui par commandement
de Dieu sont chargez d'en rendre compte.   Les autres
c'est a sçauoir lesdictz voz predecesseurs non contens
de l'obedience que chascun Chrestien rendoit en ce
temps là au chef membres de la Chrestiēté ont voluntaire-

ment rendu leurs royaume & peuple subiectz à l'Eglise
Romaine. Et si les inuenteurs de nouuelles loy pour
seduyre vostre ieune aage vous donnent a entendre que
l'exemple de tant de gens de bien ne doibt hauoir quelque
authorité & puissance en vostre endroict, ilz se contente-
ront au moins de vous laisser reigler selon l'intelligence
de l'escripture Saincte : laquelle nous trouuons bien
Sacrée Maiesté vous donner puissance de prendre
seruice de noz corps de noz vies, & vser de noz biens.
Nous trouuons bien que sainct Pierre nous commãde
d'obeir au Roy, & le craindre comme le plus excellent
dans tretous, & ministre deputé a cognoistre les bons
& chastier les mauluais. Nous trouuons bien que
Sainct Paul nous recommende l'obeissance qui est deue
aux Magistratz, qui sont ministres ordonnez de Dieu
pour conseruer la police & iustice exterieure. Mais
nous trouuõs biẽ, que le mesme sainct Paul parlant de
ce que appartient au salut des ames nous dict que Dieu
en son Eglise a premiermẽt ordonné les Apostres, seconde-
ment les Prophetes, tiercement les Docteurs. Nous
trouuons bien qu'il nous cõmande d'obeir aux Euesque,
aux prebstres qu'il dict estre complables deuant Dieu
de la perte de noz ames. Et n'est en telle matiere
faicte aulcune mention des Roys. Et est a craindre
que tout Prince qui s'empeche de ce qui reserué aux
prelatz de l'eglise, ne tombe en l'erreur dont Magabises
fut mocqué, auquel s'essayant de parler des lignes, vmbres,
& autres termes de paincture, Appelles dist. Ses enfans
& mon disciple ont longuement regardé le principe &
l'ont heu auec grande admiration : mais depuis qu'ilz
ont cogneu par tes propos que tu parle de chose que
tu n'as apprinse & qui n'appertiene a tõ estat, ilz se
mocquent de toy. Telle mocquerie Sacrée Maiesté
c.   pourroit estre faicte de vous, si vous vsurpez plus auant
que ne porte la puissance Royalle. Mais elle seroit
de trop plus grãde importance, que celle de Magabises,
par ce qu'ils s'en ensuyuroit la perpetuelle damnatiõ
de tous les subiectz de vostre Royaume, & le nõ s'escuser
sur l'assistance & conseruation des prelatz, par ce que
les vns accorderõt tout ce que l'on vouldra pour iouir de

la liberté & nouuelle façō de viure, & les autres pour
n'encourir vostre male grace auront vsé de la prudence
de Fauorin, lequel estant reprint qu'il eust contre la
verité celé à l'Empereur Adrian disputāt auec luy
d'vne parolle si elle estoit Latine ou non, respōdit.
Vous verres si vous m'estimez meilleur grammairien
que ie ne suys : ou celuy qui a traicté legione armée.
Ainsi n'aurōt failly lesdictz prelatz d'estimer tresbons
theologiens qui hont la force & main. Mais Dieu scet,
s'il y en qui nuict & iour crient de cœur, *vim patior.*
Petmettez dōque Sacrée Maieste, que vostre pauure
peuple, pour satisfaire à ce qu'ilz doibuēt vous offrēt
corps & les biēs : mais endurez, qu'ilz recognoissent
tenir les ames de Dieu & non de vous, & laissez les
conduire & guider a ceulx qui comme dessus est dict en
sont cōptables. N'estimez qu'il y ait aucun d'entre nous
qui de soy mesme ne vueille recognoistre, honorer & auec
la perte de noz propres vies maintenir & accroistre vostre
authorité, sachans tres biē ce dequoy vous nous asseurez
que vous estes nostre Roy, Edouard, filz du Roy Henry
huictiesme : qui nous faict d'autāt plus croire que le
droict, que vous hauez sur nous, ne peut estre plus
grand ne moindre, mais du tout pareil à celuy de voz
predecesseurs qui vous laissé le Royaume.

> *Quant au second article, contenant cinq pointz de la
> Foy, c'est a scauoir, du Baptesme, de la messe, du
> Sacrement, du Seruice qui se faict en l'Eglise, et de la
> Confirmation.*

Nous ne voyons Sacrée Maiesté, q̄ ce qui este si longuemēt, & auec si grande reuerence obserué, par tāt de
Roys, tāt de paiz tant de gens, se puisse ne doibue
chāger que par vne ordonnance & vniuersel consentement de toute Chrestienité. Et seroit plus conuenable
à vostre reputation & grādeur de nous laisser l'honest
eté & louable ambitiō de noz predecesseurs qui en toutes
chose vertuese, ont mis peine d'estre dictz singuliers
parmy les autres nations, que de faire qu'en chose si
perilleuse soyons notez seulz & separez de tout le reste

c ii

des Chrestiēs Et permettez s'il vous plaist, que ceulx
qui sont si legers & faciles à faire nouuelles constitutiōs
nous respōdent, s'il a esté riens par eulx changé de la
substance des susdictz pointz, ou seulement des circonstances. Si ce a esté de la substance pour le moins
fauldroit il qu'ilz nous monstrassent quel Sainct Esprit
ilz ont apporté auec eulx, qu'ilz puissent destruire ce
que par l'Euangile, escriptz des Apostres, & traditions
de leur successeurs nous a esté delaissé. Si ce est aux
circonstances, quel inconuenient y auoit il d'en remettre
l'abolitiō à vne vniuerselle determinatiō de la Christienté
& endurer par chascun entendre à prouuier son salut
& recueillir le fruict des susdicte Sacremens en la facō que
tant de gens de bien ont estimé bōne & louable, s'ilz
ne veulent dire q̄ tous Chrestiens auant leur venue,
soient (pour n'auoir esté si biē inspirez) damnez parmy
les mauluais. Et commençant par le Baptesme, quel
besoing estoit il adstraindre a baptiset nos enfans à
certains iours. Et combien que par vostre Maiesté, il
nous soit mandé qu'en cas de necessité pourrōs baptiser
nos enfās en quelque iour que ce soit de la sepmaine.
Quand ainsi seroit, encores en aduiendroiēt ilz trois
inconueniens.

Le premier est vne seruitude grande & insuportable
aux peres & meres de prēdre garde tous les ious & a
tous les momēs des heures si á leur enfans, comme
souuent en tel aage aduiennent soubdaines maladies,
suruiendra quelque accident, qui cōtraigne les baptiser.
Et n'y sçauroient estre si diligens qu'il n'en moure
tousiours quelqu'vn sans Baptesme. Et quand il n'en
mourroit qu'vn en cētz ans, encores seroit plus grand le
dommage d'vne seule ame, que le proffit si aucun y en
auoit, en ladicte institution.

Le second qu'auec le tēps, le menu peuple, qui tousiours
par ignorāce a esté facile à mesler la superstition parmy
la religiō, estimera quelque vertu secrette estre en vn
iour plus qu'en autre, & cuydera qu'il y ait difference
d'vn iour à autre cōtre la sētēce de l'Apostre.

Le tiers est, que si le pauure people n'ha tousiours auec
soy les tesmoingz & notaires pour faire preuue de la

c iii   necessité aduenne à leur enfans ce sera vne occasiō d'en
cōdamner plusiers à peines corporelles & pecuniaires
comme infracteurs de vostre loy & ordonnance.

*Et quant au Sacrement du corps de nostre Seigneur
Iesus Christ.*

Ce qu'ē vostre nō, Sacrée Maiesté, sur ce passage nous
esté escript, Nous n'hauons l'entendemēt de pouuoir
comprēdre qu'il soit possible, q̄ du pain que vous appellez
Sainct & benoist, nostre ame prenne aucun nourrisse-
ment spirituel, si le corps de nostre Seigneur n'y est
par miraculeuse conuersion de pain en iceluy. Et pour
estre matiere, si haulte, & telle que bien petit erreur,
amene auec foy vne grande heresie, & pourroit engendres
plusiers scruples au plus sçauant du monde, qui de son
propre esprit en vouldroit deffinir, il nous semble debuoir en cela recommender nostre ignorance & simplicité
à celuy qui faict reluyre sa prudēce en l'esprit des
simples. Et ne pensons faillir : mais (f)aire tresbien,
si a l'exemple cōtinué quinze centz ans a, adorons Iesus
Christ en ce ou nous hauons vraye foy que veritablement
il y est, & que realement il y assiste, par diuine transubstantiation.
Et quand à la Confirmation, pour laquelle il plaist à
vostre Maiesté nous demander si nous n'estimons point
q̄ noz enfans sont par baptesme & non par la Confirmation sauluez. Nous sommes grandemēt obligez, Sacree
Maiesté, à Dieu premierement qui a enuoyé planter les
premieres racines de sa foy en ce Royaume, qui depuis
ont produit grādz & notables personnages, pour biē
instruire noz antecesseurs. Et a esté parmy nous la foy
Chrestienne si bien espandue & publiée, & si voluntiers
receue & estimée, qu'il n'y a personne entre voz subiectz
qui puisse ny doibue ignorer que le salut de noz enfans &
l'absolution de la peine qu'apporte auec soy le peché
originel, despēde que de l'effusiō du sang de nostre
Seigneur Iesus Christ duquel ilz se rendent auec le
Baptisme institué à l'Euangile, participans. Mais ce n'est
c iiii   pourtant raison suffisante de cōclure qu'autres choses qui

par bons respectz & grandes considerations ont esté ordon-
nées doibuent estre cessées pour superflues & inutile, &
encores moins changées ny applicquées en autre temps
ny vsage, cōme dessus auons dict. Et pour n'estre
tant fondez aux subtilitez & façons de disputer comme
sommes voluntaires & enclins a doner obeissance telle
que debuons & premierrmet à Dieu, secondemēt a vostre
Maiesté, il nous semble ne debouir vous respondre à
l'article de la Messe, & du Seruice de l'Eglise, & à tout
ce que cōcerne la Foy, qu'en la façon que desia auons
dict. Et quand bien les ordonnances faictes par voz
gouuerneurs soubz le nom de vostre Maiesté soyant
accompaignées de quelquez apparence de raison. Toutte-
ffois pour estre faictes contre les institutions de tant
grandz personnages, contre la coustume vniuerselle de
la Chrestiēté & par celuy qui n'ha authorité ne puissance
de disposer de semblables matieres, meritēt, soubz
correction, qu'elles soient comme scandaleuse & curieuse
caseés & aboliés.

Pour le troisiesme et quatriesme articles. Nous
sommes notez d'ignorance et rebellion. D'ignorance
par ce que demandons le statut de six articles estre
reueu, lequel vostre Maiesté dict auoir faict casser et
adnuller comme trop violent, sanguiniaire et grande-
ment preiudiciable à la liberté et repoz de voz subiectz.
De rebellion en ce que demandons les loix anciennes
demourer en leur force et qu'autres qui sont faictes
soïēt suspendues iusque au temps que par la grace de
Dieu soyez en l'aage de discretion et cognoissance.

Il n'y a personne d'entre noꝰ, Sacrée Maiesté, qui voluntiers & sans replic q̄ ne vous accorde qu'en beaucoup de
chose se pourroit descouurir la nostre & assez notoire
ignorance : mais elle n'est toute ffois en cest endroict
sì grande, qu'elle nous puisse n'y doibue empecher a
cognoistre ce que nous a par cy deuant endommagé
Et si lesdictes loix estans par trop rigoreuse, & cōme
vous dictes, vray stimule & aguillon de crualté enuers
nous, cela voꝰ doibt seruir d'vn clair & euident tesmoinage

de nostre sincerité, & que noz demandes ont esté plus
sur le biē vniuersel de vostre Royaume, que pour nostre
proffit, soulagement & affection particuliere.   Et encores
d.   que l'abolition qui a esté faicte soit authoriseé par
l'approbation & cōsentement de Parlemēt, ne trouuez
s'il vous plaist mauluais si à cela nous respondons
qu'elles furent pareillement inutiles & priuilegieés par
le feu Roy vostre pere, receues & obserueés par l'vniuerselle consentemen de voz subiectz.   Et si telle raison
n'a esté par voz gouuerneurs estimée : au moins doibuent
ilz considerer que toutes cruaultez & mutatiōs de loix
& statuz en quelque royaume que ce soit, mais en cestuy
cy plus qu'en nul autre, sont perilleuse : & souuent ont
esté causes de susciter grandes seditions. Mais si
l'experience des inconueniens, qui pour semblables
occasions sont aduenues, ne leur faict cognoistre la faulte
qu'ilz ont faicte : pour le moins, s'ilz ne veulent contre-
dire à l'opinion de tous les sages anciens, qui ont escript
à l'institution & obligation des loix, police & conser-
viatiō de tous royaumes & republicques, ilz ne pourroient ne sçauroient nier que la mutation desdictes loix
ne soit cause de les mespriser & à toutes occasions qui
se presentent les faire moderer, amplier, & du tout
adnuller.   Et d'autant que la force de la loy consiste
en obseruation & coustume auctorisée de longeur de
temps, il est aisé a cognoistre que la changement ne
sçauroit profitter, que l'accoustumance de ne les garder
& de n'y obeir pourroit estre preiudiciable.   Et ores
q̄ toutes ses raisons ne fussent digne d'estre acceptées,
ny entendues, pour le moins ainsi que nous auons
demandé, deburoit lon laisser les loix anciennes en leur
force & vigueur iusque à vostre aage legitime, pour
reseruer l'honeur & le degré de voz subiectz, & remettre
à vostre bon iugemēt la cognoissance de ce que seroit le
bien, repoz & tranquilité de vostre royaume.   Pour la
quel demande, qui ne peut estre dicte que iuste &
raisonnable, ne debuons estre sans aucune apparence de
verité, calumniez d'auoir heu intention de ruiner vostre
royaume, mescognoistre nostre Prince, diminuer sa
valeur & differer sa grandeur a certaines années.   Ny

sommes si ignorans ou malicieux & temeraire de vouloir
dire ny penser que ne soyez nostre souuerain Seigneur :
& monstrer autant en l'aage de douze ans, que de vīgt
& deux ans.   Entendens tresbien que le bas aage n'em-
pesche le Sacre & courounement des Roys & des Princes.
Comme lon pourroit dire d'vn Pierre, qui depuis fut
grand renommé & victorieux.   Nous lisons qu'en France
qui est plus prochain du nostre, Loys neufiesme & Charles
huitiesme ne laisserēt pour leur bas aage a regner.   En
ce propre royaume Henry sixiesme & Richard second
n'estans sortiz de minorité furent Roys Sacrez & courou-
née.   Ne voulans pareillemēt ignorer qu'aux Princes de
vostre aage Sacrée Maiesté, doibuent assister quelzques
grandz & notables personnages faisans l'office de gouuerneurs de vostre personne & de tuteurs & administrateurs
de vostre royaume.   Auxquelz si biē s'acquittent de
leur charge lon doibt obeir, & recognoistre la peine
qu'ilz ont prins pour le biē publicq soustenir.   Mais
pourroit estre friandise de commander & gouuerner si
grande, que les anciens l'ont estimée digne de faire
commetre vne iniustice & les hommes plus tost enclins
à mal qu'à bien.   Il est a craindre comme dict le Iuris-
consulte que les tuteurs ne tendent plus à diminuer
qu'à conseruer les biens, l'honneur & les mœurs de leur
pupille.   Ainsi cōme il aduint de Ruffin, & de Stillico
tuteurs d'Arcadio & Honorio.   Lesquelz pour auoir si
longuemēt & si librement regné, par leur malice &
meschanceté furent cause de l'euersion & ruine de
l'Empire de Rome.   Et pour ne cercher ailleurs ce que
parmy nous a esté, Richard second en la grand ruine
& misere peut tesmoigner le peu de foy qu'il trouua en
ses oncles & tuteurs, les Ducz de Clocestre, Lanclastre
& Yort.
Par telz exemples & plusiers autre que on vous pourroit
mettre en auant, & par les sentences des Iurisconsultes
& des Philosophes peut lon facilement comprendre que
durant la minorité d'vn Prince, l'administration &
gouuernment des royaumes, pour quelque occasiō que
ce soit ne doibuēt estre baillez à personne tant soit sage
& bō en apparence, que la liberté de les sandicquer &

d ii

cōtraindre pour leur mauluaise administration ne soit à ceulx qui sont interessez tousiours reseruées pour empecher que telz incōueniens n'aduiennent. Que s'il estoit enduré & comporté, peu de dommage apres seroit irreparable. Ce que nous a induict Sacrée Maiesté, à nous assembler contre ceulx qui presentemente en portons la peine sur noz corps, noz biens & noz ames, ont mis vostre hōneur, vostre reputatiō & vostre royaume en hazard de la fortune, comme plus amplement nous esperōs vous faire cognoistre si les affaires selō qu'ilz ont proietté ne leurs succedent. Il est certain que la paour qu'ilz hauront de rendre compte auec la perte de leur vie, les conuiera à conspirer contre vostre personne & l'estat de vostre royaume. Et par vostre ruine, s'ilz peuuēt le faire, mettrōt peine d'eschapper de cela qu'ilz auront merité. Et pour vous monstrer qu'en noz parolles n'y a menterie aucune, & qu'on ne puisse dire que contrefaisans les bons & loyaulx subiectz, aions enuie de malicieusement faire l'estat de calumniateurs encores qu'aions par plusieurs fois & particuliermēt par ceste letre remonstré les causes de noz plainctes & doleances. Nous vous supplions treshumblement ne trouuer mauluais, & puis que cela procede de nostre bon zele, prendre à bōne parte si par le discours de ce qui est depuys la morte de vostre pere aduenu, sans touteffois mentionner ce qui est secret, & qui doibt estre diuulgué par les nations estrāges, nous faisons cognoistre que l'Angleterre, ni est si grande prosperité, n'estre si craincte & redoubtée que voz voysins & tous autres Princes, comme les gouuerneurs de vostre conseil nous veulent par nostre letre donner a entendre. Le feu roy Henry vostre pere, Sacrée Maiesté auāt sa mort comme si par inspiration de Dieu il eust cogneu que sa fin s'approchoit, s'asseura & renouuella l'amytie qu'il hauoit auec l'Empereur, & par vn traicté de bonne & louable paix s'accorda auec le Roy de France. Auquel traicté expressement consentit la comprehension du royaume d' Ecosse comme amyz, alliez de l'vn & de l'autre, monstrant que pourla plus grande richesse & forteresse ne vous pouuoit il laisser, comme paix asseurée

auec tous Princes Chrestiens, qu'vn repoz & vne tranquilité à voz subiectz, pour les laisser refaire des grādes
charges & dommages encouruz aux guerres passées, qui
estoit vn bien, & s'il eust pleu à Monsieur le Protecteur
& autre devostre conseil de le vouloir continuer, vostre
Maieste premierement eust heu grande occasion de les
estimer à iamais comme bons & loyaulx seruiteurs, vostre
pauure peuple se ressentant de leur prudence, eust esté
redeuable a prier Dieu pour leur prosperité & grandeur.
Mais tout le contraire à nostre grand deplaisir & ruine
pouuons dire estre aduenue, parceque lesdictz gouuerneurs
abusans de la desmesurée licence d'administrer le bien
d'altruy. Tout ainsi que si le temps de vostre legitime
aage ne deust iamais aduenir, commancerent contre
Dieu & le droict des Gens, la raison & l'equité de vostre
particulier proffit, la guerre au royaume de la veufue
& petite Royne d'Escosse. Contre Dieu disons nous
Sacrée Maiesté, d'autant qu'il est iuge de veufues pere
& protecteur des orphelins. Et pour estre la source de
verité qui ne peut iamais mentir, promet en l'escripture
faire vengeace des tortz & iniures que par les grādz &
autres leur serōt faictes. Contre le droict des Gens
disons nous Sacrée Maiesté, d'autt que ledit royaume
de-Escosse estoit expressemēt comprīs comme dessus
auons dict au traicté de paix, accordé receu, & iuré sur
les Euangiles par le feu roy vostre pere.
Contre la raison & equité disons nous Sacrée Maiesté,
parce q̄ oultre le scruple qu'il y a d'vsurper le bien d'autry,
ledict royaume estant desolé & pour lors destitué de tous
aydes. Ce que debuoit estre mis en quelque cōsideration
par voz gouuerneurs pour ne irriter Dieu a mander
semblable persecution à vostre royaume, & debuoit lon
vser de quelque bonne & louable equité à l'exēple d'vn
Isdegery roy de Perse, lequel ap̄s auoir entēdu que
Arcaduis Empereur son grand ennemy en mourant luy
auoir particulierement recōmendé son filz Theodose
q̣ encores estoit au berseau. Cōbien qu'il ne fust
chrestien, mais gardé seulmēt & cōduict du droict
naturel, & de la grandeur de cœur & bonté, que les
Prince doibuent hauoir les vns enuers les autres, non

seulement ne voulut par expres faire aucun moment de guerre contre ledict Theodose pupil. Mais auec son conseil, auec ses forces print la protection : & le deffendit contre tous iusque ad ce qu'il fust hors de l'aage de minorité.

Pourra doncques auec bonne occasion dire la pupille d'Escosse, que plus d'honnesteté, plus de misericorde trouua Theodose pupil en vn Prince barbare & infidele qu'elle n'a faicte en vous qui estes son propre cousin germain. En vous qui estes roy, comme elle est royne, Chrestien comme elle est chrestiëne, pupil comme elle est pupille.

Pourra auec bonne occasion appeler son garend & ayde, celuy qui d'enhault a promis d'estre son pere & ptecteur. Pourroit la veufue & pupile se plaindre à Dieu des violences qui leurs ont esté faictes au temps que l'vne estoit au berceau, les auoir desolées & distituées de la presence du mary & de pere & dire. *Quoniam quem to purcussisti persecuti sunt : et super dolorem vulnerum meorum addiderunt.*

e

Et si nous sommes chrestiens debuons certainemēt craindre que la fin de la dicte guerre n'apporte auec soy vne grāde calamité & ruine en vostre royaume. Et desia si la verité ne vous a esté desguisée plusiers de voz subiectz y ont esté comme par miracle de Dieu rompuz & diffaictz. Et encores q̄ les aduersaires & deffenseurs dudict royaume d'Escosse ne soient pareilz à nous en vertu, en force, en experience de guerre, ilz hont grande occasiō de bien esperer estans auec Dieu leur deffenseur, & de l'orpheline & portant leur enseigne contre ceulx qu'ilz estimēt peruers & infracteurs de paix. A l'exemple de Belsede lequel estant sur le poinct de cōbattre contre les Persiens, dont il rapport vne grande & heureuse victorye, feit attacher au hault des enseignes les traictz de paix que lesdictes Persiens luy auoient violez & rompuz. Mais pour ne passer en cecy ny en autre chose, le debuoir de bons & loyaulx subiectz nous remettons le cognoissance de la iustice ou iniustice de la querelles de vostre Maiesté, quand elle sera parvenue à l'aage parfaicte cognoissance. Ne voulans touteffois cependāt differet à .vous faire cognoistre le proffit ou dommage, que le Protecteur & autres de vostre conseil, ont apporté en ce royaume. Et en premier lieu, Sacrée Maiesté, n'y a personne en ce royaume qui ose ny pense nier, que si les traictz de paix accordez par le feu roy vostre pere, eustent esté maintenuz iusque a vostre aage legitime, lō eust peu mettre sans greuer vostre peuple, quatre ou cinq milions d'or en reserue, qui vous eust faict aymer ou rendre formidable á tous les Princes de la chrestienté, Vostre pais qui est à present pauure apres vn long repoz & soulagement eust esté riche de biens, d'argēt & d'honneur, de sorte, que si pour quelque occasion il vous eust semblé mouuoir la guerre, Dieu q pour vous eust esté en aucune sorte irrité vostre prudence, l'argent accumulé, l'obeissance de voz subiectz riches, & obligez d'auoir esté si doulcement traictz eussent faict heureusement succeder toutes voz entreprinses. Cepēdant estoit il facile de gāgner les seigneurs & peuple d'Ecosse, les vns par dons & presens, les autres par conuersation, amité & licence de librement contracter & traffiquer. Lesquelz eussent en peu de temps oublie l'ancienne & cruelle hayne d'entre nous & la petite Royne, apres l'aage de sa minorité, par les moyens que chascun ignorant pourroit facilement inuenter, eust este voluntiers plus que contente de mariage & vnion de ces deux royaumes.

Le contraire de tout ce que dessus a esté faict Sacrée Maiesté, & n'a este riens obmis en ce que peut amener auec foy & desobeissance de vostre royaume.

Premierement l'Ecosse qui auec bonnes parolles & sage negation ne pouuoit faillir a estre vostre, a esté indiscretement hors de temps & cōtre Dieu assaillie & bruslée auec si grande effusion de sang & cruaulté, que pour ne se laisser si oultrageusement destruire, a esté contraincte de se despoueiller de sa petite Royne & l'enuoyer au Roy de France lequel pour son honneur ne voulant abandonner le royaume qui fust mis soubz sa tutelle & protection ne pourra faire de moins q̄ d'y tenir tousiours vn bō nōbre de gens de guerre & d'estre sinon en parolles

e ii

au moins affectuelles enuers iceluy. Et par ainsi vostre royaume sera d'icy en auant contrainct auec grāde perte, dommage & occasion d'hōmes, redoubler les gardes & garnisons de la frontiere, sans en raporter autre fruict, que d'auoir fortifie vn vilaige qui iusque à ceste heure couste vn milion d'or.

D'autre costé à fin que la force de deux royaume à present vniz ensemble puissent s'ilz veulent plus facilemēt assaillir voz gouuerneurs expressemēt comme il semble ont cassé les vielles loix, & en ont faict d'autres nouuelles & insuportables. Ont abatu & aboly du tout la Religion, qui si longuement auoit esté gardée pour irriter & commuuoir vostre peuple, si faire se pouuoir, à desobeissance & rebellion, & par mesme conuier l'Empereur de la contraindre a prendre les armes contre vostre personne. & à la destruction de vostre royaume. Lequel Empereur, combien qu'en ce temps pour quelque sien desseing particulier, sache dissimuler ses pensées, vous ne debuez faire doute, & qui voꝗ dict autrement vous trompe, que bien tost ne soit pour vous entamer la guerre. Et si ne se responde de l'honneur & victoyre que dieu pour mesme occasion luy a donée sur les Alemans, vous contraindre auec vne grande honte & dommage de reprendre la religion delaissée. Ce pendant Sacrée Maieste voz pauures subiectz sont auec detestable violence tirez par force de leur mestier, labeur, & commodité de gangner leur pauure vie, pour seruir de souldarz & pionniers : & qui pis est de valletz aux estrangers. Les Alemans, les Espaignolz & Italiens emportēt le fruict de noz labeurs, mengent le pain & la substāce de noz pauures enfans. Et nō sans grande admiration de beaucoup de gens de honneur, de bien & de foy : qui trouuent fort mauluais, que la natiō Angloise qui de tout temps a esté honnorée, estimée & redoubtée sur toutes les autres nations, à present soit par vne poignée de estrangers despouillée, pillée & en ses biens & honneur endommagée & gourmandée. Et qui plus est, non sans cause, plusiers notables personnages, commancent a dire que tel & mesme inconuenient, nous adiuendra il par la multiplicatiō des estrāgers, que autrefois aduint aux Bretons,

e iij

premiers possesseurs de ce royaume. Oultre plus claire voyons, & auec meilleure raison estimeront que ladicte assemblée se fa ce pour fortifier quelqu'vn de mauluais volunté, contre la personne de vostre Maiesté. Voyla doncques, Sacrée Maiesté, les fruictz des conseilliers, qui sont à l'entour de vous. Voyla le soulagement & repoz qui par eulx a esté donné a voz subiectz. Voyla le pondāt & sage conseil dont ilz ont vsé à fortifier vostre royaume, lequel de riche ilz ont faict pauure, de Chretiē, payen, faulx, Ethnicque sans aucune religion : d'estimé & aymé l'ont rendu hay & deprisé. Habandōné à vne infinité d'estrangers barbares qu'ilz font venir tous les iours. Pourrions nous doncque estimer Sacrée Maiesté, telz conseilliers & gouuerneurs dignes de l'obeissance que nous vous debuons, qui malicieusemēt ont desarmée ce royaume de l'aliance des Princes que le feu roy vostre pere auoit laissé. Pouriōs nous & encores que par vous vous soit commādé, aymer ny estimer ceulx qui pour se retenir quelque moyen de consumer les forces de ce royaume à petit feu ne voulurēt mettre fin à la guerre indiscretement commēcée contre l'Ecosse. Ains apres la bataille ou toute la noblesse du pais fut ou prins ou morte, n'ouserent ou pour myeulx dire, ne voulurent poursuiure la victoire & seulmēt manderent vn herault à la vefue Royne luy commandant de se render à la bonté du protecteur qui en foy de Prince promettoit la bien faire traicter.

A quoy comme nous auons entendu, fu auec grande mocquerie repondu que vne Royne & née Princesse ne se debuoit cōmettre ne fier à vn qui naturellemēt ne pouuoit vser de foy de Prince. Et tout a vn moment n'eust ou sceu iuger & cognoistre quelle estoit la plus grande diligēce ou celle dudict Protecteur à son retourner, ou de ladicte Royne de s'esloigner du danger & pourueoir à le seurté de la pupille sa fille. Et à present Sacrée Maiesté ilz vous donent a entendre, que sans nostre assemblée eussent ceste année gaigné ledict pays. Eñ quoy il se monstrent aussi ignorās de vouloir vaincre les forces de deux royaumes vniz ensemble France & Escosse, cōme ilz furent malicieux de ne le vouloir accepter au

2 H

temps qu'apres la bataille elle estoit entirement diminuée
de ses forces, & distituée de celle de ses amyz. Pourrions
nous estimer telz gouuerneurs estre dignes d'assister a la
ₚsonne d'vn Prince, d'administrer vn royaume, de
gouuerner vn peuple ? lesquelz à vostre iuene aage ne
vous monstrent qu'à estre sanguiniare, & mespriser la
Religion, destruire & abolir les loix, s'armer des estrangers
& mespriser voz subiectz, piller, deserter & ruiner vostre
Royaume.

¶ Souuienne à vostre Maiesté que la premiere institution de
Roy a esté faicte pour la deffence des bons contre l'iniure
des mauluais. Et que le nom de Roy apporte quelque
fois necessité d'estre pl' verteux que les autres : plus
constant obseruateur de la Religion : plus audacieux
contre les ennemis : plus vigilant aux occasions qui se
presentent : sur tout plus enclin a fauoriser & aymer
ses subiectz desquelz il se doibt estimer Roy, Seigneur
& Maistre. Et auec son grand hōneur & reputation
doibt il prendre aussi le nom & auec les effectz se monstrer
leur pere.

¶ Souuienne a vostre Maieste qu'ilz n'y a chose si perilleuse
apportant auec soy plus grād dommage à vn Prince que
prester l'oreille & donner foy à ceulx qui du peuple sont
haiz. Et qui, comme dessus est dict, vsurpent auec trop
grande licence, l'authorité & nom de leur maistre. Et pour
ceste cause disoit ce Sage, que moins de biēs doibt esperer
le Royaume qui est gouuerné par vn bō & sage Prince,
que si les ministres sont de mauluais volunté. Que s'il
aduenoit que les ministres fussent bons & le Roy mauluais, inutile & peu experimenté, pour autant que s'ilz
f estoyent de mauluais nature ilz corrumptōt les mains
de leur maistres. Et auant qu'entrer en sa chambre ilz
s'accoderont, luy desguiser les affaires, pour le diuertir
& detourner de sa bonne volunté. Qui nous donne
occasion Sacrée Maiesté d'entrer en vn extreme despoir,
se plus longuement ceulx qui en tant d'affaires ont faict
essay à nostre grande ruine de leur ignorance ou malice
demeurent à l'entour de vostre Maiesté, Et de celle
supplions treshumblement vueille mettre en consideration la bōne fidelité & obeissance de voz subiectz, plus

que à la coniunction de sang & affectiō particuliere
qu'elle pourroit hauoir à lendroict de ceulx qui con-
seillent vostre Maiesté, pour l'amour & reuerence qu'elle
porte au Seigneur Dieu, ne nous reffuse à l'appetit de
psonne. Ce que p l'escripture vous est expressement
cōmande nous donner, sachant comme il est dict au
mesme lieu, que vous mesme hauez vn Seigneur au
Ciel. ¶ Plus iuste ne plus recepuable demāde ne
pourrions faire Sacrée Maiesté qu'auec le peril de noz
propres vies, mais qui pis est auec le peril & d'anger
d'encourir vostre male grace interrompre le cours de la
mauluaise volunté de ceulx, qui mettent peine a precipiter
vous & nous en quelque grande ruine. ¶ Plus iuste ne
plus recepuable demande ne sçaurions nous faire, que
vous supplier treshumblement comme plus que nulz
interessez, ne vouloir plus longuement q̄ ceulx qui ne
font qu'a seruir s'accoustument par trop, & a noz despens
commander ¶ Plus iuste, ne plus recepuable demande,
ne pourroit estre la nostre Sacrée Maiesté, que vous
supplier treshumblemēt, de donner plus de foy aux loix,
aux ordonnance & à la religiō de tant de gens de biē
voz predecesseurs, qui à l'ignorance des vns & expresse
malice des autres, qui pour leur particulier desseing, ne
se sont espargnez a faire chose qui ait esté preiudiciable
à vostre grandeur, honneur, & reuerēce : Lesquelz
cōfessons & voluntairement accordons auoir offence.
Mais nō pas comme ilz disent à vostre Maiesté, qui nous
a faict prendre ceste hardiesse de vous dire touteffois
auec l'honneur & reputation que nous vous debuons,
qu'il n'est besoign nous presenter ou enuoyer aucun
pardon. Car autrement que n'auons en riens qui soit
offencé, ne faict chose qui doibue tourner au desplaisir
de vostre Maiesté. L'exēple de la cruaulté vsée par
les ministres du feu roy vostre pere enuers quelquez vns
de voz subiectz, cōtre la foy & promesse dōnée & iurée,
f ii   nous a faict ressouldre de mourir en gens de bien, les
armes en la main, & Angloys, qui n'estimerent oncques
la vie, ou l'occasion de mourir a esté presentée. ¶ Plus
grande occasion de bien mourir, ne nous pourroit il
aduenir Sacrée Maiesté, que ceste cy ou il nous conuiēdra

cōbattre pour l'honneur reputation & salut de vostre
personne ¶ Plus grande occasion ne sçauriōs nous
hauoir de faire cognoistre à tous les voisins que l'ancienne
vertu des Angloys, espandue partout le mōde, n'est
encores ny sera qu'auec la perte de noz vies estaincte,
¶ Plus grande occasion ne sçaurions nous hauoir de
bien & honnestement mourir, qu'en faisant sacrifice de
noz corps au temps que lon veult eloigner noz ames
de la bomme Chrestienté voye de salut ¶ Trop
mieulx vault il auec vne mort honorable mettre fin
à noz trauaulx, qu'auec la vie honteuse d'entrer d'vne
honneste liberté en vne grande & miserable seruitude.

¶ Trop mieulx vault il mourir laissant gloyre à noz
enfans, d'estre descenduz de ceulx qui sont mortz, pour
ne laisser seduire leur Prince & destruyre la religion, que
d'estre en viuant, notez par le reste des Chrestiës comme
schismaticques & hereticques, & cōtinuellement estre
menassez de la mort, par ceulx q desirent estre bourreaux
de noz corps & de noz ames. ¶ Ne permettez doncques
Sacrée Maiesté, que pour complaire á la malice de trois
ou quatre, soit auec les armes à noz iustes recepuable
& treshumbles prieres respondu. ¶ Ne permettez Sacrée
Maiesté, que voz gouuerneurs faisant semblant de vouloir
vsurper les autres Royaumes, abusent plus de vostre
nom & authorité pour plus tiranniser & reduire en l'extreme seruitude.

¶ Ne permettez Sacreé Maiesté que leur heresie sinistre &
malheureuse opiniō de la Foy nous contraigne de changer
la Religion qui si sainctement & heureusemēt a esté par
voz predecesseurs gardée. Et acceptez voz treshumbles
& tresobeissans subiectz, qui desirons estre les chiens
deputez a garder vostre maison & vostre royaume, & les
bœufz a cultiuer voz terres, les asnes a porter les charges
qui pour la deffense de vostre personne & ce que vous
appartient, seront par vostre commandement ordonées.
Prierons au Seigneur Dieu, qui tiēt & tourne les cœurs
des Roys ou bon luy semble, veuille garder & conduire
vostre ieune aage à telle perfection de sens de sçauoir
& de vertu que soit pour la salut de vostre ame, pour le

soulagement & tranquillité de voz subiectz, l'accroisse-
ment & reputation de la gloyre de Dieu, le bien de la
Chrestienté.

FIN

On les vende chez Robert Massellin
Imprimeur, demeurrant deuant
le cymetiere sainct Etienne
du mont, a l'enseigne
des trois trenchoirs
rouge.

¶ A Monsievr Le Prevost de Paris, ou son Lieutenant.
Supplie humblement Iehan Riuiere prebestre comme
ledict suppliant ait recouuré & transcript vne copie
intitulée. La responce du peuple Anglois à leur Roy
Edouard sur certains articles touchant la Religion
Chrestienne, qui en son nom leurs ont esté enuoyez.
Et que Monsieur l'inquisiteur de la Foy ait approue
l'œuure, & iugé pour seruir a grande edificatiō du
peuple, & digne d'estre imprimée ainsi qu'il appert par
certification cy attachée. Neantmoins à raison qu'autres Imprimeurs, Libraires ou autres pourroient imprimer ou faire imprimer ladicte copie, & en ce faisant
frustreroient ledict suppliant des labeurs qu'il a employé
a recouurer ladicte copie & icelle trãscripte. Ce con-
sideré mondict Seigneur, & attendu que ledict suppliant
ha vouloir tousiours de s'employer & proffiter pour le
bien public, il vous plaise de vostre benigne grace per-
mettre audict suppliant faire imprimer par tel qu'il
aduisera, ladicto copie, & ordonner defenses estre
faictes à tous Libraires & Imprimeurs & autres qu'il
appartiendra de non imprimer vendre, ny distribue
ladicte copie apres l'impression d'icelle, fors iceulx
liures qui par la permission, congé & licence dudict
suppliant en auront esté imprimez Et ce iusque à vn
an continuel & consecutif commançant du iour de
paracheuement de ladicte impression, sur peine de

confiscation desdictes liures qui seroient imprimez, vendez, & distribuez, & d'amende arbitraire. Et vous ferez bien.

Soit faict ainsi qu'il est requis auec lesdictes deffences iusques à vn an. Faict le vingtcinquiesme iour d'Octobre, mil cinq centz cinquante.

Ainsi signé   DES ESSARS.

APPENDIX I

THE WELSH CHRONICLE

Mr. John Hobson Matthews has kindly furnished me with the following transcript and translation of extracts from a document in the Cardiff Free Library (Phillips MSS.), being a chronicle in Welsh of the sixteenth century, which formerly belonged to the Wynne family, and is contained in a quarto paper book. Notes with his initials are appended.[1]

I.H.S.

Pan oedd oedran krist 1532 y hysgarwyd y brenin a brenhines gatrin Ag achos na chytton y Pab ar anghyfreithlon ysgar hwnnw Evo ai bower a nakawyd yn y dernas Ag ni bv ddim gwelliant ir ynys hynny.

Pan oedd oed krist 1533 y 23 o harri 8ed y llosged yr holy maed o gent [2] A dav vynach A dav ffrier Ag yffeirad A groged ag a dorred y ben am dresson A blasphemy ag ypokrisye ag y Kaeth yn heddwch Rrwng lloegr ag ysgotlont.

Mys Myhevin y tored penne Esgob Rochester a Sr Thomas more Am wrthnebv nei Nakav y brenin yn ben ar yr eglwys loegr A thri mynach or Siartr-hous am yr vn achos a varnwyd y veirw. Mis Tachwedd y vlwyddyn hon (1539) [3] y tored pen abad Reading a glassonbry a cholchestr.

[Regn. E. 6.]

Ye ail vlwyddyn y gorchmynwyd kymryd y kominiwn mywn bodd kynds.[3]

Pan oedd oedran krist 1548 y gorchmynwyd bwrw r delwe ir llawr ymhob eglwys (ac)y gnaeth-bwyd yn gyfreithlon yr yffeirid briodi Trwy act o barlment.

Pan oedd oed oedran krist 1549 y kyfododd yn erbyn y brenin
ddefnsir a chornwel [4] yn ghylch kanol y vlwyddyn ai kaptenied
a ddalwyd ag a roed yngharchar yn y twr yn llonden ar xxvj
o vis Jonor gwedi hynny y llusgwyd y kwarterwyd ag y kroged.

llyma r kweryl ar pynke
I Roedd wyr kornwel
a defnsir yn I gofyn

Yn gyntaf Ni a vynnwn gael y gyfraith yn gyffredin megis y
kafas yn henafied A chadw ai chynnal Ar gyfreth eglwys yn
vnwedig.

Hefyd Ni a vynem gael kyfreth Ag acts brenin harri wythved
am y 6 articl ai harver megis y Roedd id yn [ei] amser Ef.

Hefyd yr yfferen yn llading mal y Roedd yn y blaen yn amser
yn henafied Achos nid ym y yn koelo bod yn vn or ysgolheigon
kystal ar Rrai a vv veirw a chymryd korff krist Ehonan heb y
llygion gidac ef.

Hefyd bod yn wastad y Sakrament yn wastad vchben yr allor
megis y bv arveredig.

Hefyd kael korff krist y pasg ir llygion Ar amsar hwnnw yn yn
nathirieth.

Hefyd ir Egwysswyr vedyddio ganol wythnos kystal ag amser
arall or gwyle.

Hefyd bēdigo dwr a bara yfferen bob Sul ar blode ar llvdw
megis or blaen Ar Rroi r delwe yn yr Eglwysi y ddwyn kof
am verthyrdod krist ai Saint Aphob pregeth [5] gyfreithlon yn
yr Eglwys lan gatholig megis y bv arveredig yn amser yr hen
bobl.

Hefyd Ni vynwn Ni ddim or gwyssaneth Saesson newydd nar
hware barrs nei gristmas gam y maen hwy Achos nyni a
wyddom Na bydd abl yboludd y kristynogion y ymdaro ar
Yddewon. [6]

Hefyd Ni a vynnwn ddoktor moor A doktor kryspyn y Sydd vn
piniwn a ninnav yn Rrydd ai danvon yn gadwedig attom megis
y kaffom hwynt y bregethv geire duw yn yn mysg.

Hefyd Ni a vynnem y Ras y brenin ddanvon yn ol kardnal pool
y gar Ef Ehon Ag nid yn vnig Rroi i bardwn iddo ond hefyd y
wnnevthur yn gyntaf nei yn ail oi gynghoried vchaf.

Hefyd Ni welen gymwys Na bai ond vn gwyssnaethwr y wr dan
gan mork Rent tir Ag am Kan mork vn gwr.

Hefyd Ni ddisyfiem ar Ras y brenin Rroi hanner tiroedd y tai

o grefydd vddon drychefn y gynnal gwyssaneth dnw yndon yn
vnwedig y ddav dy o hanon ymhob Sir y weddis dros y Ras Ef
a thros vnw a meirw.

Hefyd am a wnaethbwyd o gam Ar gwledydd yma Ni a vynnwn
gael llywodreth a barn hwmffre arudel a henry bray mayr yn
Rre vodnam.

A chael Seou'did dan Seall vawr y brenin y vyned a dyfod A
dyfod a myned A herof of arms y mywn ag allan.[7]

Hefyd ar gynnal achadw a chwplav pob pwynt o hyn Ni a
vynnwn yngwystl iiij arglwydd Ag viij marchog A xij ysgwier
A xxiiij o yomā gida Nyni A hyn trwy barlament gwedi gania-
dhav.

Kaptenied yn ghent A chornwel

humffrey Arndel John burry
Scoyman Thomas vnd^r hyll
A Willm̄ Segar
John Tompson pryst
henry bray mayr bodnā
henry ley mayr toriton
Rogyar bared yffeirad
llywodraethwyr
y kamp oedd
y iiij hyn.

LITERAL TRANSLATION.

When the year of Christ was 1532, the King and Queen
Catherine were divorced ; and because the Pope did not allow
of that unlawful divorce, he and his power were denied in the
realm ; and this was no bettering to the island.

When the year of Christ was 1533, the 23rd of Henry 8th,
the Holy Maid of Kent was burned, and two friars ; and a
priest was hanged and his head cut off for treason and blasphemy
and hypocrisy ; and our peace was obtained between England
and Scotland.

In the month of June, the heads of the Bishop of Rochester
and Sir Thomas More were cut off, for opposing or denying the
King to be head over the Church of England ; and three monks
of the Charterhouse for the same cause were condemned to
death.

In the month of November this year (1539) was cut off the head of the Abbot of Reading, and Glastonbury, and Colchester.

[Regn. E. 6.]

The second year it was commanded to take the Communion in both kinds.

When the year of Christ was 1548, it was commanded to throw the images down in every church ; and it was made lawful for priests to marry, through Act of Parliament.

When the year of Christ was 1549, there arose against the King Devonshire and Cornwall, about the middle of the year ; and their captains were taken and put in prison in the Tower in London ; and, on the 26th of the month of January after that, they were drawn and quartered and hanged.

These be the complaints and points
which the men of Cornwall
and Devonshire asked.

Firstly, we will have the law in general as our ancestors had, and to be kept and maintained, and the law of the Church especially.

Also we will have the law and Acts of King Henry the Eighth about the 6 Articles and their use as they were given in his time.

Also the Mass in Latin, as before in the time of our ancestors ; because we do not believe that there is one of the scholars equal to those who have died ; and the Body of Christ Himself to be taken without the laity with him.

Also the Sacrament to be always over the altar, as was accustomed.

Also to have the Body of Christ at Easter for the laity, and at that time in one species.

Also the churchmen to baptize in the middle of the week as well as another time of the festivals.

Also water and mass-bread to be blessed every Sunday, and the palms and the ashes, as before ; and images to be put in the churches to bear remembrance concerning the martyrdom of Christ and His saints. And every lawful sermon in the Holy Catholic Church, as was accustomed in the time of the old people.

Also we will have none of the new English Service, nor the

playing at barrs or a Christmas game are they; because we know the Christians will not easily be able to contend with the Jews.

Also we will have Doctor Moor and Doctor Crispyn, who are of one opinion with us, free and to be sent safely to us, so that we may have them to preach the words of God in our midst.

Also we will the King's Grace to send back Cardinal Pole, his own cousin; and not only to give him pardon, but to make him the first or second of his highest councillors.

Also we see fit that there be but one servingman to a man under a hundred marks' rent of land, and for a hundred marks one man.

Also we would desire the King's Grace to give half the lands of the houses of religion to them again, to maintain God's service in them; especially two houses of them in every shire, to pray for his Grace and for the living and the dead.

Also, for what has been done of wrong on these lands, we will have the government and judgment of Humphrey Arundel, and Henry Bray, Mayor in the town of Bodmin.

And to have a surety, under the King's Great Seal, to go and come, and to come and go; and a Herald of Arms in and out.

Also, to maintain and keep and finish every point hereof, we will have as hostage 4 lords and 8 knights and 12 esquires and 24 yeomen with us; and this through Parliament after granting.

Captains in Kent and Cornwall

Humphrey Arundel, John Bury,
Sloman, Thomas Underhill,
and William Segar

John Thompson, priest
Henry Bray, Mayor of Bodmin
Henry Ley, Mayor of Toriton
Roger Barret, priest
Governors of the camp were these 4.

NOTES BY J. H. M.

(1) The handwriting of this MS. shows it to have been written in the third quarter of the sixteenth century; and the sacred

monogram heading each page strongly suggests that the writer
was a " Marian priest." The Chronicle ends with the date 1557.
There is ample internal evidence that the matter is a translation from an English original. The English is sometimes
embodied in the Welsh in a curious fashion.

(2) " yr holy maed o gent " would be in Welsh " y ferch
sant o Gent." " Ffreir would " be " frawd," " Dresson " would
be " fradwriaeth." The Welsh spelling is far removed from
the present method, though it is less irregular than in some
writings of the same period.

(3) " bodd kynds " gives the phonetical spelling of *both,*
but *kynds* does not represent the sound in Welsh spelling. The
equivalent Welsh phrase would be " dan y ddau rywiogaeth."
And for " kominiwn " we should have " Cymmun."

(4) " ddefnsir a chornwel " in good Welsh should be " Ddyf-
naint a Chernyw."

(5) " Pregeth " (sermon) is obviously a clerical error, the
translator having read the original as " sermon " instead of
" ceremony."

(6) " Christmas game " in Welsh would be " chware Na-
dolig." The reference to the Jews is baffling.[1]

(7) " Seou'did " is a curious rendering of the English word
" surety." " Hereof " is a clerical error for " herot-heraut."

[1] This refers to the clergy confounding heretics. See p. 221.

APPENDIX J

PROCLAMATIONS

FROM TUDOR PROCLAMATIONS

A Proclamacion, set furth by the kynges Maiestie, with thassent of his derest vncle, Edward Duke of Somerset, Gouernor of his moste royall person, and of his Realmes Dominions and subiectes Protector, and others of his moste honourable Counsaill, concernyng certain Riotes and vnlawfull assembles, for the breakyng up of enclosures.

WHEREAS of late, the kynges maiestie moued of a Godly zeale and loue to the common wealthe of the realme, by the aduise of his derest vncle, Edward Duke of Somerset, Gouernor of his hignes persone, and Protector of all his Realmes, Dominions, and Subiectes and the rest of his maiesties priuie counsail, did by Proclamacion will and commaūd all maner of persones, who had offended against the good and wholesome lawes heretofore prouided against the decaye of houses and vnlawfull enclosures, to amende their suche offences, and to redresse all faultes by theim committed, against the saied actes and statutes, and against the benefite of the common wealthe, vpon pein to encurre the daungiers and paines, in thesame actes and statutes prouided. And for the better performaunce thereof, by thaduise afore-saied, willed and commaunded all his highnes officers and ministers, to whom it did appertein, to see thesame redressed, to receiue informacions, make enquiries, and with all spede and earnest endeuour, se to the redresse and punishement, of all suche offendors, as by the lawes and statutes of the realme, thei might and ought to do. Upon this moste Godly warnyng, admonishement and Proclamacion, whiche was to kepe ordre and lawes, his highnes is aduertised, that a greate nombre of rude and ignoraunt people, in certain Shires of Englande, hath taken occasion, or at the least pretended to take occasion, of

doyng greate and most perilous and heinous disordre, and
contrary to all good lawes and statutes, and thordre of this
realme, haue riotously with routes and campaignes, with
force, strength, and violence, of their owne hed and aucthoritie,
assembled theimselfes, plucked doune mennes Hedges, disparked their Parkes, and beeyng led by furious and light guydes
of uprore taken vpon theim the direccion of thynges, the
Kynges royall power and sworde, and committed thereby suche
enormitie and offence, as thei haue iustly, therefore, deserued
to lose life, landes and goodes, and to bee made example to all
other. But forsomuche as thei haue humbly sūbmitted theimselfes, and demaunded pardon, beeyng sory for their former
offences, the kynges highnes of a most high clemencie, and
tendre loue to his Subiectes, is content not to looke vpon his
iustice herein to bee executed, but muche more of naturall
mercie and clemencie, and so for this tyme, acceptyng that
this outrage was dooen, rather of foly and of mistakyng thesaid
Proclamacion, and at thinstigation and mocion of certain leude
and sedicious persones, than of malice or any euill will, that his
said subiectes did beare, either to his highnės or to the quiet
of this realme, of his maiesties moste aboundant clemencie, and
tendre pitie, by the aduise of the saied Lorde Protector, and the
rest of his highnes priuie counsaill, is contented and pleased,
to remit and pardon all thesaied outragies, misbehaviours,
riotes, and conspricies, to all and synguler his said subiectes,
other than to suche as bee alredy apprehended and in prison,
as heddes and stirrers of thesaid outrage and Riottes, and
therefore willeth and commaundeth, all Justices of Peace,
Maiors, Sheriefes Bailifes, and all other his hignes officers and
ministers, not tenterrupt, vexe, or trouble, for and in his
Maiesties behalfe, any maner persones, other than is specified
before, of, or for any offence, iniurie contēpt, or conspiracie, doen
at thesaied stirre or riottes lately made, about the breakyng
of enclosures, so that thei do not attempt, or go aboute any
suche thyng hereafter. But if so bee there be any iust cause
to complain, for default of iustice, or lacke of redresse, in any
suche enclosure, or default made against thesaied actes and
statutes before specified, in this case provided thei who finde
theimself iustly greued or iniuried, maie geue informacion,
make sute or complaint to the kynges Maiestie, or other his

highnes officers, deputed to the redresse of all suche offences, accordyng to the lawes of the realme, and the good and lawfull ordre of the same.

But if any man shall at any tyme hereafter, attempt, or go aboute to make any suche riot, or vnlawfull assembly, for any suche cause before rehersed : his maiesties will and pleasure is, by the aduise aforesaied, that all suche offenders, shall immediately be apprehended, by the next Justice or Justices of Peace, and lose the benefite of this moste gracious pardon, and suffre suche peines of death, losse of landes, goodes and cattalles as by the lawes of the realme in suche case is prouided, any thyng in this present Proclamacion, heretofore mencioned notwithstandyng.

Geuen the xiii day of June, 1549 and in the third yere of his Maiesties moste gracious reigne.

God saue the Kyng

excusum Londini in aedibus Richardi Graftoni

Regii impressoris

Cum priuilegio ad imprimendum solum.

From GRAFTON'S PROCLAMATIONS, fol. 59.

The XI daie of July.

A Proclamacion, for the punishment of rebelles of Devonshire and Cornwall.

WHEREAS diuerse euill disposed persones are at this present rebelliously and trayterously assembled in sundery companies, within these, the Kinges Maiesties Counties of Devon, and Cornwall, shewyng themselfes, not onely to contempne and disobeye his most royall maiestie, his lawes, ordinaunces, and most godly procedyings but also to leuie warre against his highness, to the great displeasure of almightie God, his maiestie moste graciously waiyng, and consideryng what appertaineth to the good order and quiet reformacion of his good and louyng subiectes, by thaduise of his most entierly beloued vncle, the lorde Protector, and the rest of his priue counsaill, is pleased and contented, and by this present Proclamacion willeth it to be notified and knowen, to all and singuler his louyng subiectes, that all and euery of his saied subiectes, whiche, at the time of the publishyng of this present proclamacion, do continue in their vnlawfull, and disobedient assembles, within the said Counties, and within daies, next after this Proclamacion, shal not willyngly and obediently submit, and yelde themselfes, vnto the right honorable lorde Russell, his highnes Lieutenant in those partes, shal be demed, accepted and take, for rebelles and traitors, against his highnes most royall persone, his Imperiall croune and dignitie. For more terror and exaple, of whose punishement, and for the good incouragyng and aduancyng, of suche his true, louyng, and obedient subiectes, as shall withdraw themselfes, from the saied rebellious traitors and of suche others as shall aide and assist his highnes saied Lieutenant, to suppresse and subdue the said rebelles and traitours. For so muche as the forfaicture of all maner of goodes, cattals, offices, pencions, landes, tenemetes, farmes, copie holdes, and other heredimentes, of al and euery traitors and traitor, within his Maiesties realme and dominions, onely and most iustly apperteineth, and belongeth to his Maiestie. The same is further pleased and contented, that al and singuler, the forfaictures of al the gooddes, cattales, offices, pencions, manours, landes, tenementes, farmes, copie holdes, and other hereditamentes, of the said rebelles and traitors which shal perseuer and continue, theire rebellion and treason, shall growe, com, and bee vnto all and euery suche persone and persones, as shall first haue, take, possede, and attain to the said goodes and cattalles, or shall firste entre into the saied manours, lands tenementes and hereditamentes, and the same shal haue, holde, possede, and enioye, to his and their owne proper vse, commoditie and behalfe, in as large and ample sort, as his highnes, by meanes and right of the said forfaicture, and confiscacion ought and may dispose of the same, and shall haue thereof suche assurance, from his Maiestie by his Letters patentes, or otherwise, as thei or any of them can or shall best imagin or deuise.

From TUDOR PROCLAMATIONS.

Concerning theffect of his maiesties pardon graunted to certain of his subiects, lately hauyng made vnlawfull riottes and assembles.

A Proclamation, set furthe by the Kynges Maiestie, with the assent of his derest vncle, Edward Duke of Somerset;

Gouernor of his moste royall persone, and of his realmes dominions and subiectes Protector, and others of his moste honorable priuey Counsaill, concernyng theffect of his maiesties pardon graunted to certain of his subiectes, lately hauyng made vnlawfull riottes and assemblies.

THE Kynges Maiestie, by the aduise of his entirely beloued uncle Edward Duke of Somerset, Gouernor of his persone and Protector of all his Maiesties Realmes, Dominions, and Subiectes, and the rest of his priuy counsaill considereth, that as it is the fruite of his mercy, to receiue his humble, repentant, and sorrowfull subiectes, knowlegyng their offences, to the benefite and grace of his mercie. So also is it the reputacion of his Maiesties mercie, to defende, and saue harmeless, all suche whiche submitted themselfes to his mercie, and to let them fele his protection, with their quiet, as thei haue sought it, with their deuoute repentance, and so to saue his repentaunt people with mercie, as his Maiestie ought to punishe, his obstinate subiectes with iustice. In consideration whereof, his Maiestie by thaduise aforesaid, willeth, admonisheth, and commaundeth, first all maner of his subiectes, whiche of late, by their humble submission, and sorrowfull repentaunce, of their offences committed, in sundry vnlawfull, and riotous assembles : that thei from hencefurthe, be of such good behauiour, in the peace of God, and the Kynges Maiestie, and in all their actes and deedes, bee so quiet, peaceable, and well ordered, that the Kynges Maiestie, may thynke his grace and pardon bestowed vpon them with effecte.

And likewise his Maiestie willeth, and straightly commaundeth, all maner his other subiectes, of what degree soeuer he bee, hauyng suffered any maner of grief, damag, or losse, by the acte of any of the aboue saied, the Kynges subiectes, whilest thei offended, and before thei receiued the Pardon from his Maiestie, that thei shall not by action, sute, violence, or compulsion, force, punish, auenge or correct, any maner of offence, trespasse, or vnlawfull acte, committed by the same offendors, and pardoned by thesame acte : but shall suffre and permit them to enioye and take the benefite of the Kynges Maiesties pardon, in the like intent and purpose, as the same hath been ment and intended by the Kynges Maiestie. Geuen at

2 I

Richmount the xii of July, the third yere of his highnes reigne.

God saue the Kyng
Excusum Londini in edibus Richardi Graftoni
Regii impressoris
MDXLIX
Cum priuilegio ad imprimendum solum.

16 July 1549.

From TUDOR PROCLAMATIONS.

For executyng of a lawe Martiall.

A Proclamacion, set furth by the Kynges Maiestie, with thassent of his derest vncle Edward Duke of Somerset, Gouernor of his most royall persone, and of his realmes, dominions and subiectes protector, and others of his most honorable Counsayle, for the executyng of a lawe Martiall for payne against rebellors and their vpstyrrors.

FORASMUCHE as the Kynges Maiestie hath of late for the redresse of vnlawfull enclosures, and suche like enormities directed his seueral Commissions with large instrucciones for the same into euery his coūties not only aucthorisyng his Commissioners to redresse and reforme al maner of thynges so farfurth as the lawes, could anywise be construed or expounded, but also by special his Maiesties letters missive, hath charged the same Commissioners vpon great payne in thesame letters contained to redresse and amēde their own proper faults : whiche cōmissiōs be now part in execucion, and part redy to be executed, and delayed onely by the folly of the people, sekyng their oune redresse vnlawfully : so that no subiect can any more require of any prince, than by his Maiesties sayd vncle and counsail hath been deuised, ordered and cōmaunded. Yet neuerthelesse his Maiestie vnderstādeth, that diuers of his subiects, neither consideryng how they be ordained by God to be subiectes and obey, neither reguardyng their souereigne lordes most ernest good will and zeale, whiche he beareth and dayly declareth to his cōmonwelth, neither hauyng in remembraunce what distruccion it is to themselfes, to truble and disquiet this state of his cōmon welthe thereby impouerishyng themselfes, weakenyng ye realme and bredyng sedicious and continuall cōtencion betwixt one subiect and another, do attempt and trauail, frō tyme to tyme and from place to place, to make assembles, riotes, conuencions, stirres, and vprores, and by theim so vnlawfully made, presume to doo and attempt, that whiche oughte only to bee done, by the aucthoritie of the kyng and his maiesties lawes : yea and in many pointes accordyng to the euil disposicion of their assembles, attempt with violence and fury, suche vnlawful thinges as be extremely forbidden by all iustice and lawe, and to be abhorred of any good Christian. For the whiche causes his Maiestie neither of good iustice and honor, neither for the estate and saueguard of his hignes royalme wil or may endure his subiectes, so to offēd without presēt punishmēt and correctiō, But as a prince reignyng by almighty goddes prouidence, most mighty, and in iustice terrible, by the aduise of his sayd dere vncle and lord Protector and the rest of his maiesties priuey counsayl, straightly chargeth, and with the thretnyng of his sword, cōmaundeth al maner his subiectes of what degre, condiciō, kinde or estate soeuer he or thei be to departe, returne and cease furthwith vpon this proclamacion proclaymed from al maner their vnlawful assembles, ryotts, and uprores, and quietly and in peace, to take and receaue his Maiesties ordre and directiō, in redresse of their wronges whatsoeuer thei be. And that also no maner of subiect, of what degre, condicion, kynde he or thei be, shall from hence-furth by dromme, tabret, pype, or any other instrument, strykyng and soundyng, bell or belles ryngyng, open criyng, postyng, rydyng, runnyng or by any newes, rumors and tales inuētyng, diuulgyng, and spredyng, or by any other meanes, diuise, or tokens whatsoeuer thesame shal happē to be, call, gather, assemble, congregate and muster, or attempte and practise to gather, assemble, congregate and muster, any nombre of people whatsoeuer thei be, either to plucke doune any hedge, pale, fence, wal, or any maner of enclosure, or to hurt, wast, spoyle, desolate or deface any parke, chase, warrē, hedge, ponds, waters or any other vnlawfull act, which is forbiddē, or to redresse any thyng, whiche shal and maie be, by the force of the kynges maiesties Commission, reformed, re-dressed, and amended, upon payne of death, presently to be suffered and executed by the aucthoritie and ordre of Lawe

Martiall, wherein no delay or differyng of tyme, shal be permitted or suffred, as in other cases, beyng in dede of lesse importaunce it is accustomed : And therefore, his maiestie most straightly chargeth and commaundeth, all maner of his, Sherifes, Justices ministers, and officers, vpon the knowlege of any offendor, against the tenour of this proclamacion, furthwith withall expedicion and with suche power as thereto shallbe requysite, to apprehend and attache thesame offendor, and him to committe to a saue gayle, and thervpon indelayedly to certefy the lord Protector and the rest of the Counsaill, or any of them, to thintent most spedy ordre may be geuen for thexecucion of the offendor, with suche hast and expedicion as is aboue mencioned.

Dated at Richemoūt the xvi day of July, the third yere of the reigne of kyng Edward the vi.

God saue the Kyng.

excusum Londini in edibus Ricardi Graftoni
Regii impressoris
Cum priulegio ad imprimendum solum.

APPENDIX K

Of this rare tract, to which reference has been made on page 246, only three printed copies are known to have survived; these are respectively in Lambeth Library, in the Library at Stevenstone, North Devon, belonging to Lord Clinton, and in the Library of Corpus Christi, Oxford.[1]

The copy in the Lambeth Palace Library is here transcribed at length.

It is headed " A Copye of a letter contayning certayn newes, and the Articles or requestes of the Deuonshyre and Cornyshe rebelles."

" Since my laste letter sēt vnto you, of the newes in these parties (Because I wyll kepe my fyrst promes, for enter-chaūge of lettres) I haue chaūsed of matter worthye aduertisement & some leasure to aduertyse the same, so that I could not with honestye, but satisfye your desyre, to knowe our newes, as I myself am verie desirouse of yours. By my former letters you vnderstode the dysordre and dysloyall, vprores of the Deuonshyremen, whyche at the begynnyng semyng to me, to haue proceded but of some wyldenes of theyre braynes, or of some ignorance lackynge teachynge, I thought wolde sone haue bynne tamed wyth authoryte, and reformed wyth instruction, as I vnder-stande the lyke ende hath wel happened of al the disquiet assemblyes, in the other partes of the Realme. But the matters of Deuonshyre nowe shewes furthe the rotes of

[1] I am indebted to the Archbishop of Canterbury, the authorities of Corpus Christi College, especially to the librarian, Mr. R. W. Livingstone, and the late Hon. Mark Rolle, for permitting me to examine and copy these tracts.

treason; the buddes of rebellion, and the fructe of fylthye poperye, leauyng now pretenses of treason and auowynge hyghe treason, leauynge nowe colour of Relygion and reiectyng all trewe religion, nowe come to verye madnes, whyche before were but droncke, and cared not, for the name of rebelles, whych before were angry to be called trespassers, thys crafte hath the deuyll to encrease hys swarme. He taughte the Priestes and theyr Captaynes to cal the people together to defende theyre olde fayth, and therin vsed the name and aucthoryte of the kynges mayestye, hauyng no waye so ready, to assemble them together, whyche vsuallye is the trompet, that good subiectes followeth, two good begynninges, Ye see the deuil vsed the name of God, and of the Kyng, and in dede, dyrectlye agaynst God and the Kynge. Wel, now was it tyme for hym to worke, he sawe the assemblye dayly encrease. One part was assured his owne, the Romysh priestes and the sturdy vacabundes. Wyth them he neded not vse craft but rather taught them howe to vse it with others. The other parte were symple ignoraunt people, easelye disceyued, and quicklye made the partakers of euyll. Thus the deuyl hauyng made hys bandes (parte of hys owne olde seruantes, parte of a newe retynewe) beganne to send forthe hys embassages (the same beyng certen requestes, as he termed them) to remedye the grieffes of the Deuonshiremen, to the which the Kynges maiesty made a verye princely and reasonable answere. Of the whych I receyued syxe Copies in printe from you, by M. Mohan, at his last comming frō the Court to my Lord pryuey seale. And for the same I thanke you, praying you, yf any suche lyke thynges come fourth in printe, I may haue some sent me wyth the fyrst, & yf you wyll speake to the Kynges Prynter in my name, I dare say, he wyll not denye you. But nowe to my matter. by these embassages of his he thought to haue encreased hys power, thynkyng in dede ẏ all they (whyche gathered them selues together in other partes of the Realme, for pluckynge downe enclosures & enlargyng of commēs) would haue entered in to hys seruice and taken hys quarell : but after hys articles were confounded by the kynge, and certen knowledge came in to Deuonshyre, by theyr currours abroad, that the Kentish Essex, Suffolke, and speciallye Hampshire, hauing byene within the iurisdicyon of the stoute Prelate of Wynchester, vtterly dyffyed and abhorred the Deuonshyremē, protestyng euen in theyre moste disorder, that they wolde spende thyr lyues agaīst all suche rancke rebelles traytours & papistes. It was maruell to se the newe deuyses and inuencyons of the pryestes and vagabunde Captaynes, for the furtherance of theyr first purposes. Then begāne they to perswade theyr people, that they had all gone to farre to shrinke, and that nothinge now shoulde helpe them, but stoutnes & courage, eyther wolde they now be Lordes, or els haue nothynge, eyther rule, or els not lyue, eyther make a kynge, or haue no Kynge, no meane thynge might content them. Theyr fyrst botye (they thought) shoulde be the cytye of Excetter, the next, ẙ spoyle of theyr owne countrye, and so consequently all other partes of the Realme, for Excetter they gape, but they catche nothynge sauing gonne shot, whereof God geues them pletye. Theyr owne countrey they haue so spoyled, & so disordered, that it is myserable to heare. The sonne robbeth the father, the doughter is rauished before the mother, he hathe nothing at night, that had most in ẙ morninge, & he hath moste, whiche ought to haue nothing : And howe longe he shal haue it, there is noo warrant. Two maner of men go to wrack amōgest thē. Good true subiectes, & welthie. And other two, be daile promoted, traitours and vile vagaboundes. The viler mā, of more aucthorite ; the honester, of more seruitude. Byeng and selling seaseth amonges them, in place wherof is come Robbynge, and reauynge. If hell be in earth, it is amōges them. And the pristes there, be the deuils. And the traytours be the tormētours, & the reste of the people forgetting of their King, be as it were soules tormented. Alas howe shall I be wayle them ? shall I pray to God that they may perishe ? or that they may amend ? The one they haue deserued, the other me thinkes I dare not aske of god. For settīg a syde their robberies, their murders, theyr raueshynges, their spoyle of the countrey, and the losse of it for many yeres, howe haue

they offended their Kyng & soueraigne Lorde ?   How haue
they dispysed hys name and aucthorite. And (as much as
lyeth in thē) deminyshed his credit and renoume. Shal I
say merely ? Euery honest man amōges them, may repēt
him self of his good lyuing And euery euil mā (I thinke) is
sory : he was no more wretched, & yet no euilnes nor
wretchednes, alloweth any mā (yf he wyl not be a ranck
traytour) onely that profession maketh rulers. And
because they vnderstād that seruynge men be comenly
brought up in such ciuylite that hardely they be made
traytours, Yt is a comon Prouerbe, that trust seruynge
man, trust gentyll man, & now no place is left but for
traytours, all other sciences goeth a beggyng with them,
and yet I doubt not, but theyr facultye wyll haue the price
of the market whiche is a halter and a tre. Thus farre
after my accustomed maner I haue entreated generallytees,
and yet such as my harte is ful of, and where myght I
better discharge my sorowe then wyth one, which wyll
take parte thereof, I coulde not tell ? But you wyl say,
ye can lamente the thynges as much as I, but for the
matter of my Letter, you wolde desyre some particular
newes, or at the leaste my Iudgement, what I thoughte
wold folowe. For newes, as I promysed in my former
letters to sende you theyr Articles, so I do nowe here
include them, the whiche I coulde not well performe before,
because they chaunged them so often, and deuysed so
many, sometyme hauing some reasonable, an other tyme,
not one tollerable, suche diuersites of hedes there were
amonges them, that for euery kynde of brayne there was
one maner of Article, the priestes, they harped all upon a
playne songe of Rome, certē traytours woulde halow home
Cardinall pole, a nombre of vagabondes wolde haue no
Iustice, a bande of theues, wolde haue no State of anye
Gentlemen and yet to put al in one bagge, a sorte of
traytours wolde haue nother king nor good subiectes.
And so euery varlet (abounded in hys owne sense) At
the laste they concluded vpon these Articles, and set to
their names as ye shal see in the copie therof. As for
other newes (vntil my Lord Priuey seale shal haue ẙ power
come to him, which he daily loketh for) I cā not haue to

write. For my Lord lieth wyth the kinges power, here at a place called Honnyton. Who (I assure you) hath so gouerned these parties here, by hys contynuall labour, and wisdome, that hyther to, the ennemyes dare not come forth out of their dennes (for so wold ye cal them) yf ye saw the lanes, the hilles, the woodes & straight passages, betwixt vs and them. They lye still nere Exceter as I wrote in my last Letters. And not ẘstandynge, the twyse burnyng of the gates, yet hyther to can they not preuayll. A greate part of thē cōtinueth with their fyrst Captain called vnderhyl, a taylour of Sāpforde courteney. I thinke they kepe hym styl, because they can not fynde hys match, a Captaine wel chosen by the deuil at the first. This is for the newes. For my opiniō, I dare be bolde wyth you and yet therin I wyll vse few woordes, because yf I erre, I wil not erre to long a time, I assure you, nothyng more encouraged them, then that they loked all other people being sturred vp in other parties for enclosures and such lyke grieffe wolde haue taken theyr quarell in hande, so nowe nothynge hath so muche decayed theyr courage as that they heare and knowe the contrarye. Theyr boldenes beyng nowe of theyr owne stoore, without hope of partakyng, more desperate then myghtye and lesse for theyr purpose, then for theyr nombre, very many beyng there assembled with them, by force against theyr wyll, and manye dayle by repentaunce, reacknoweledgīge theyr dutyes and Subieccyon. And in dede, the very ordre and maner of quyetyng of all other countreys putteth them clerelye from hope to styrre agayne, for they be not ignoraunt that the more parte of the requestes of them were such, as bycause they could not reasonable be reiected, being for reformacion of diuers abuses in the comūe wealth (not for the brīging in of the Roman auctoryte agaynst the Kyng, and hys Royall Croune,) they be for the most parte graunted, in such sorte as the people haue receyued mercye, and be departed home wyth good contentacyon, lyke good Subiectes. The Kinges Maiestye sustayned no dishonoure, hauyng ruled his people, bothe wyth Iustyce & mercy, proporcyonallye, and finally the thynges whiche were euyll vsed in the comon wealthe, very lyke to be reformed, part presētly by Commission, parte, by Parliament, to the comen profyte of the whole Realme, of so good an ende oure rebelles here haue bē moste sorye, wisshing that the other people had leaped frō hedge breakinge, to house robbing, frō dere hunting, to horse huntyng, from wantonnes to starke madnes, as they haue here frō robberies to rape, frō rape to murder, frō murder to treason & popery, & so to the deuil, whereas I fear they wil cōtinue, and in dede yf I maye presume (as I dare do much w̃ you my friend) to alow the Coūsels dede, me thinketh ȳ matters haue byne very wel ordered (as it is reported here amogēs vs) for although by Iustice euery mā deserueth death, which ryseth against his prince, yea though he haue moche griefe, & that the Kinges Maiesty might of Iustice make slaughter of his people, yet yf there be any place for mercy, it was in this case, for the Kinge to shewe it, vpon hys owne people, vpō people forgetfull, not obstynate traytours by construccyon of Law, not by offence of harte, where the fault of the moste parte of them was in dede vnlawfull Assemblyes, but withoute open robberyes, murder or spoyles, referrynge theyr grieffes as Sutours, not Orderars, cryeng for mercye as offendours, not Challengers. And on the other syde, the Iustice shewed, was ryght necessarye, beyng extēded, vpon such as eyther lacked cause to cōplayne, or lacked grace to seke for ȳ kinges mercy, and to say my mynde as one nether of Court nor Coūsayle yf the Kynges sworde lyghte shorte vpon anye, it was vpon the two kinde of people, rāke Popish priestes, repynynge agaynst the kynges holsome doctrine, or vpon the cōmen runnegates, seedmē of sedicion, of the which we haue plentye here, agaynst whome. If the martiall law were executed, and were currante quoyne in euery shyre, as I here say, there is a Proclamation for the same (which I haue not yet sene, but by youre nexte letters trust to receiue) I thinke there wolde be as fewe runners abrode, as now there be many. You must geue me leaue to talk a litle more after my wounted maner, which is to sai my mynd frākly vnto you without offēce, howe me thinketh the ende is such of your matters there, as euery state of people wilbe content therwith, and so the moste trouble wil rest with these

traytours. For with you, the kinges people which deserued death, be by mercy preserued, & the thyngs euell
vsed (as in dede disceases there be in the cōmō wealth)
shalbe now wel ordered by Parliamēt. And if the cōmon
people shalbe eased of their griefes, the gentelmen shall be
relieued of them, for se how much the fermour crieth oute
of hys rent, so may the gentelman wel crye out of the
market, the one as muche greued as the other, & one
remedye I trust shal serue both. For me thinketh it is no
more difference for me, to haue xx pound, spēdyng xx
pound, then to haue xx marke spendinge xx marke, so that
my estate be kept like w both, you wyll thynke I wryte
now at my wyl, because yf ye remēber the last yere in the
parke at Wynsour when the Court was there, thys question
made great argument betwyxte you and me, whether for
the amendement of thinges in the common wealth the
fermour should fyrst abate hys pryce, and then the Landed
man his rent, or in contrary order, at whyche tyme, I re-
membre you stode vpon one poynte, which I could not
denye, that the Gentylman by deere byeng, was dryuen to
let deere, and I vpon the other poynte (not al vntrewe) that
the deere hyrynge made a deere sellynge. But where the
fault fyrst beganne, neyther of vs woulde graunt to the
other, neuerthelesse, so wayghty a matter it is, as no wayes
to be discussed but by Parliament. Where when the argument is at an ende, it may be establyshed by a lawe, wherof
there was neuer more lykelyhood, because the amendement therof, wyl helpe so many as well Lordes and Gentilmē,
as al other Commoners, no man hauyng cause to repyne
agaynst it, but suche as gather, not to spende and improue
their lyuinges not for their charges, as many Gentilmen
haue done, but for their coffers. So that to conclude,
improuemēt alone maketh no man ryche, but improuement
and sparynge. But what medle I wyth thys matter, and
yet what dare I not to you my fryende, by Sayncte George
I saye to you merely out of bourde, no one thinge maketh
me more angry with these rebelles then one article, which
toucheth me on the quicke, and I belieue, there be few in
the realme but it will make them smart, to forgoe his
Abbey & Chauntrye landes wherin I for my part am so

heated, that if I should fight wyth those traitours, I wold
for euery two strokes to be stricken for treason strike on
to kepe my lāds, the which I bought to suerlye, to deliuer
it at a papistes appoyntement. Thus I haue exceded in
woordes, & yet you shal counte it littel, because the matter
is large, & therby you muste measure me, & not by my
lynes. One thing I wil ye shal marke and then I ende, the
matter of Cardynal Pole (as in this case) of greate importaunce, lyke as I am sure my Lord Protectour is aduertised, for emonges these rebelles, the chiefe Captayne of
all, sauinge one, was the Marques of Excetters man, and
setteth forth the matter of the Cardinall so much, as in
dede, he maketh no other matter. Hys name is Berry,
one of them which subscrybed to the Articles. Yf ye can
conuientlye sende me a Dagg when the Kynges Maiestyes
ordynance commeth doune. Ye shall receyue moneye for
the same of my Brother Henry. Ye shall take payne to
do my humble commendacyons to myne olde Mayster
(good Syr Anthonye Dennye Knyght) and especyally to my
Coosyn Mayster John Peres of the Garde, who I woulde were
here with one or two hūdreth of ẏ Garde, to knocke these
knaues wyth theyr Halbertes. Thus fare ye, moste hartelye
wel, and praye you, as I do, that we maye mete merelye.

The Articles of vs the Commoners of Deuonshyre and
Cornewall in diuers Campes by East and West of Excettor.

❡ Fyrst we wyll haue all the general counsell & holy decrees of
our forfathers obserued, kept and performed, and who so euer
shal agayne saye them, we holde them as Heretikes.
❡ Itē we will haue the Lawes of our Souerayne Lord Kyng
Henry the.viii. concernynge the syxe articles, to be in vse
again, as in hys tyme they were.
❡ Item we will haue the masse in Latten, as was before, &
celebrated by the Pryest wythoute any man or woman
cōmunycatyng wyth hym.
❡ Item we wyll haue the Sacrament hange ouer the hyeghe
aulter, and there to be worshypped as it was wount to
be, and they whiche will not therto consent, we wyl haue
them dye lyke heretykes agaynst the holy Catholyque fayth.

❡ Item we wyll haue the Sacramet of y̆ aulter but at Easter delyuered to the lay people, and then but in one kynde.

❡ Item we wil that our Curattes shal minister the Sacramēt of Baptisme at all tymes aswel in the weke daye as on the holy daye.

❡ Item we wyl haue holy bread and holy water made euery sondaye, Palmes and asshes at the tymes accustomed, Images to be set vp again in euery church, and all other auncient olde Ceremonyes vsed heretofore, by our mother the holy Church.

❡ Item we wil not receyue the newe seruyce because it is but lyke a Christmas gāme, but we wyll haue oure olde seruice of Mattens, masse, Euensong and procession in Latten as it was before. And so we the Cornyshe men (wherof certen of vs vnderstāde no Englysh) vtterly refuse thys newe Englysh.

❡ Item we wyll haue euerye preacher in his sermon, & euery Pryest at hys masse, praye specially by name for the soules in purgatory, as oure forefathers dyd.

❡ Item we wyll haue the Byble and al bokes of scripture in Englysh to be called in agayn, for we be enformed that otherwise the Clergye, shal not of lōg time confound the heretykes.

❡ Item we wyll haue Doctor Moreman and Doctor Crispin which holde our opinions to be sauely sent vnto vs and to them we requyre the Kinges maiesty, to geue some certain liuinges, to preach amonges vs our Catholycke fayth.

❡ Item we thinke it very mete because the lord Cardinal Pole is of the kynges bloode, should not only haue hys pardon, but also sent for to Rome & promoted to be of the kinges coūsayle.

❡ Item we wyll that no Gentylman shall haue anye mo seruantes then one to wayte vpō hym excepte he maye dispende one hundreth marke land and for euerye hundreth marke we thynke it reasonable, he should haue a man.

❡ Item we wyll that the halfe parte of the Abbey landes and Chauntrye landes, in euerye mans possessyons, how so euer he cam by them, be geuen again to two places, where two of the chief Abbeis was with in euery Countye, where suche half part shalbe taken out, and there to be establyshed a place for devout persons, whych shall pray for the Kyng and the common wealth, and to the same we wyll haue al the almes of the Church boxe geuen for these seuen yeres.

⁋ Itē for the particular grieffes of our Countrye. We wyll haue them so ordered, as Humfreye Arundell, & Henry Braye the Kynges Maior of Bodmā, shall enforme the Kynges Maiestye, yf they maye haue saluecōduct vnder the Kynges great Seale, to passe and repasse, with an Heroalde at Armes.

By vs

HUMFREY ARUNDELL
BERRY
THOMAS UNDERHYLL
JOHN SLOEMAN
WILLIAM SEGAR
Chiefe Captaynes.

JOHN TOMPSON Pryeste
HENRY BRAY Maior of Bodmā
HENRY LEE Maior of Torriton
ROGER BARRET Prieste
The foure Gouernours of the Campes.

This tract is bound up with a number of others, the one immediately after it being " The King's Message," which differs in type and in size of the printed matter on the page. The volume measures 5 × 3½ inches and the printed matter of the " Letter," including the catch-word, 3⅞ × 2⅛ inches. It consists of sixteen leaves with signatures running from Aij to Aiiij and Bi to Biij. Its title page reads :

A CO
pye of a Let
ter contayning cer-
tayne newes, & the
Articles or reque-
stes of the De
vonshyre &
Cornyshe
rebelles
x
x   x
M.D.XLIX.

This is surrounded by an elaborate frame, which agrees exactly with a compartment used by Wayland thus described by Ames : "with this coat of arms at the top ; Parted per fess, sable and argent, two curtlaxes in saltire points upward : terminusses of Mars and Venus, on the sides ; and a bass-relief of Judith with Holofernes's head at bottom." [1]

On the dorse is an elaborate design identical with one used by Grafton which Herbert describes in his edition of Ames : " the king's arms crowned, supported by angels ; over which are the rose, the flower de luce, and the pomegranate ; beneath are the portcullis, the feather and the castle ; the royal motto, ' Dieu et Mon Droyt,' on a ribbon flying over all." [2]

The copy at Stevenstone is identical with this as far as can be discovered, even to the fact that it has the King's Message bound with it. [3]

The third copy, at Corpus Christi College, Oxford, differs essentially from the others, and bears every appearance of being a later and revised edition, although its title-page and its dorse are the same. The chief point is that at the end of the letter is added : " From a village, nygh sainct Mary Oterye, the .xxvii of Julie. Yours euer sure R. L."

It also has a revised set of the Articles at the end. Each one has prefixed a small Roman numeral and beside some slight verbal changes, the VIII., X., XII., and XIV. articles have words added, and there is an entirely new Article, XVI., at the end. For particulars the reader is referred to Chapter XIV. There are also a number of verbal alterations, such as *Ddeuon shire* for Deuonshire, fol. 2^d ; *bene* for byne, fol. 8^d ; *Coyne* for quoyne, fol. 9^d, and *some* for many Gentilmen, fol. 11, in this last instance the line is re-spaced to make the single word fit in.

It has not been possible to identify the " R. L." who signs the letter.

Beside these three printed versions of the " Letter," there

---

[1] Typo. Antiq. p. 563.

[2] P. 522.

[3] On its title-page is the autograph of the famous antiquary, Humphrey Dyson, who died about 1632. See *The Library* of April, 1910, for an article about him by R. L. Steele.

is in the Bodleian Library [1] a manuscript which appears to be a copy of another manuscript transcript of the tract, unless it is from the original draft of the letter. This is headed " ffrom a gentilmā of devonshier to Mr. C. concerninge newes of the doings of the devonshier and Cornyshe rebelles." A number of the documents copied into the same volume are connected with Secretary Cecil, which suggests that "Mr. C." might be identified with him.

As to the printer of this tract, which bears no printer's name, Ames attributes it to the press of Edward Whitchurch, but gives no reason for so doing, while he describes, as has been said, the same ornamental frame to the title-page among Wayland's publications and the design on the dorse among Grafton's. A careful search has revealed that these two designs do not occur together in any volume examined of those issued by Grafton, Whitchurch, or Wayland, but do occur, the title in at least ten books and the arms in one, in books issued by Day or Day and Seres. Of these ten, six were issued in 1548, one in 1549 and three in 1550. The arms appear in one of 1548. Moreover, there are several minor resemblances in type, spacing, etc., between these and the " Copy of a Letter." [2] In no other book discovered do both the title-page frame and the arms occur together. It is therefore, at least, probable that this tract was from the press of Day and Seres.

[1] Rawlinson MSS. D. 1087. The theory that this is a copy of another MS. is based on the fact that certain words were evidently left out by the transcriber and afterwards inserted in the spaces left in slightly different ink—as if he had been unable to decipher them, and had returned to the task later.

[2] The following have the ornamental frame: A Notable Sermon by Latimer. 1548. The names of Herbes by William Turner. 1548. A most Godly Instruction by Richard Tracie. 1548. The Sū of Diuinitie by Robert Hutton. 1548. Certeyn Meditacions by T. Broke. 1548. Copie of a Letter to Chrispyne by Philip Nicholles. 1548. Fyrst Sermon by Latimer. 1549. Sermon xiiii December, 1550, by Lever. 1550. An ouersight . . . of the . . . Prophet Jonas by Hoper. 1550. The Image of God by Roger Hutchynson. 1550. The arms of the dorse are found in The minde and judgement of Frances Lambert of Auenna Englished by N. L. 1548.

APPENDIX L

THE names of those who are known to have been implicated in this Rebellion are here given, with such information as has been obtainable. The source whence this is gleaned is added.

Aishreidge, ——, of Sampford Courtenay, a fish-driver. Hoker, p. 67.

A Leigh, Thomas, of Week St. Mary, servant to Humphrey Arundell. Son of Thomas Aleigh alias Leigh. Released on recognisances 2 Sept., 1549. (P. C. Reg.)

Alsa, William, priest (Holinshed, p. 916), Vicar of Gulval als Lanistey, in 1536. (Ol. Eccl. Antiq. II. 188.)

Arundell, Humphrey. See Chap. VI.

Arundell, Sir John & Sir Thomas. See Chap. XXII.

Ballamey, Peter. In prison in the West, 27 Sept., 1551. Examined and confessed much matter. (P. C. Reg. III. 386.)

Baret, Roger, priest. Signed Articles. See Chap. XIV. Philippa, sister of John Wynslade, married Nicholas Barret.

Barrow, John, priest (Holinshed).

Benet, Richard, priest (Holinshed), Vicar of St. Vepe (Ol. Eccl. Antiq. II. 185) and St. Neots. Is said to have died in 1549, being succeeded in the latter living by Thomas John, who was inst. 9 Dec., 1549, on the presentation of the King.

Bochym, John, of Bochym (Davies Gilbert). Polwhele says his land was granted to Reginald Mohun (Cornwall IV. 61); but the manor of Bochym belonged to Wynslade and passed with the rest of his estate to Mohun.

Bochym, Robert, priest (Holinshed), brother of the above.

2 K

Bonville, Humphrey, of Ivybridge. Released on recognisances 13 Apr., 1550 (P. C. Reg. II. 428). He married Johanna, sister of John Wynslade.

Bowyer (or Boyer) Nicholas, Mayor of Bodmin. Signed Articles. See Chap. XX.

Bray, Henry, Mayor of Bodmin. Signed Articles. See Chaps. XIV. and XX.

Bury, John, of Silverton. See Chap. VI.

Calwen, Thomas. Pardoned by the Lord Privy Seal. (P. C. Reg. III. 222.)

Coffin, ——. See Chap. VI.

Crispyn, Richard, Canon of Exeter. See Chap. VI.

Crocker, John. In prison in the West 27 Sept., 1551. (P. C. Reg. III. 368.)

Done, John. In prison in the West 27 Sept., 1551. (*Ibid.*)

Donne, John. Executed at Exford. See Chap. XX.

Dowrish, Thomas, of Crediton. Released on recognisances 14 Dec., 1549. (P. C. Reg. II. 366.) Son of Richard Dowrish. He died 7 Dec., 1552. (Vivian's Visit, Dev. 289.)

Drewe, ——. (Pet. MS. 451.) See Chap. VI.

Foole, Stephen. In prison in the West 27 Sept., 1551. (P. C. Reg. III. 368.) Probably a misreading of Poole.

Fortescue, William. See Chap. VI.

Furse, John, of Morshead. See p. 381.

Geste, William. In prison in the West 27 Sept. 1551. (P. C. Reg. III. 368.)

Harris, William. Sent to London with Humphrey Arundell, released from the Fleet 2 Nov., 1549. (P. C. Reg. II. 354.) Perhaps son of Phillipa Grenville, who married Francis Harrys and had a son, William Harris of Radford. She married secondly Humphrey Arundell, uncle of the Leader.

Hamon, John, an alien and a smith of Woodbury. See Chap. IX.

Hayes, Robert. In prison in the West 27 Sept.; 1551. (P. C. Reg. III. 368.)

Hayman, Richard. Same as preceding.

Holmes, Thomas. See Chap. VI.

Hooper, Thomas. See Chap. XX.

Hore, Stephen. In prison in the West 27 Sept.; 1551. (P. C. Reg. III. 368).

Hore, William. Same as preceding.

James, Edward. Same as preceding.

Lee, Henry, Mayor of Torrington. Signed Articles. See Chap. XIV.

Lethbridge, ——, of Sampford Courtenay. (Hoker 93.) Killed William Hillions.

Martin, George. In prison in the West 27 Sept., 1551. (P. C. Reg. III. 368.)

Maunder, ——, a shoemaker of Sampford Courtenay. (Hoker 67.) Captured at the Battle of Sampford Courtenay.

Mayow, William of Clevyan, in St. Columb Major. See Chap. XX.

Moreman, John, Canon of Exeter. See Chap. VI.

Mourton Gabriel, priest. Vicar of St. Uny next Lelant. Mr. J. H. Matthews has kindly furnished me with an extract from Chanc. Proc. Eliz. Ser. II. B. 107, No. 22, in which Nicholas Kemishe, clerk, vicar of Ewnye next Lelant, says that Gabriel Mourton, clerk, late vicar and complainant's predecessor in the said benefice in the time of the late wicked commotion and rebellion in the said county of Cornwall, in the third year of the late King Edward VI., of famous memory, was suspected and noted to be a rebel and therefore, as an offender, given by the right honorable the late Earl of Bedford (then Lord Lieutenant) unto the King's Majesty's (*sic*) of the counties of Devon and Cornwall, unto Sir Anthony Kyngeston, knight. By reason whereof the said Sir Anthony gave the occupation, profits and tithes, unto the same benefice belonging, unto one John Tewennecke, of Botreaux Castell ... yeoman ; who received the same during all the time of the said Gabriel Morton, that is to say, by the space of seven years. . . ." Gabriel Mourton compounded for the First Fruits of the vicariate of Lelant and St. Ives in 1549. (Matthew's "St. Ives," p. 132.)

Mourton, James, priest (Holinshed). Perhaps same as the above.

Mourton, Simon, priest. Vicar of Poundstock. See Ballads. Chap. XXI.

Osborne, Thomas. Imprisoned in the West 27 Sept.; 1551. (P. C. Reg. III. 368.)

Payne, John, Reeve of St. Ives. See Chap. XX.

Paget, Robert, brother of Sir William. See Chap. VI.

Parker, Edward. In prison in the West 27 Sept., 1551. (P. C. Reg. III. 368.)

Paw, Anthony. As above.

Perin, Robert. As above. There was a Vicar of Cullompton named Robert Peryns. On his *death*, according to Oliver (Ec. An. I. 114), in 1549, William, bishop of Hippo, succeeded.

Pomeroy, Sir Thomas. See Chap. VI.

Prideaux, John, of Tavistock. Released on recognisances 11 Dec., 1549. (P. C. Reg. II. 365.) John Prideaux, son of John Prideaux of Orcharton, married Agnes, daughter of William Honeychurch of Tavistock, and had a son John, probably the John above-mentioned. In Dasent's P. C. Reg. his place of residence is given as Lestock—in the original it is Tastock and Vivian, in Prideaux pedigree (Vis. Dev. 617), gives Honeychurch of Daystock, but on p. 478 has Tavistock.

Quarme, Roger. Polwhele ("Cornwall," IV. p. 61) says that the manor of Nancarn was sold 1 Ed. VI. (*sic*) to the Earl of Oxford in order to purchase a pardon of Roger Quarme, who was engaged with the discontented Papist that then rose in arms in Cornwall and Devon and besieged Exeter.

Reve, Nicholas, a brewer of Exeter (C. & W., p. 60).

Roscarrock, Richard. Released on recognisances 12 Nov., 1549. (P. C. Reg. II. 356.) Probably son of John Roscarrock of Roscarrock.

Rosogan, James (Holinshed and Carewe). One of this name was buried at St. Columb Major 25 Aug., 1549.

Rosogan, John (Holinshed).

Rosogan, Richard, priest. Rector of Crede. (Ol. Ec. An. II. 186.)

Royse, Robert, priest. Vicar of St. Clere. He was admitted on 4 Mar., 1546–7, and George Luxton was admitted on 15 Mar. 1549–50, " per actinctura ultim : incumb." on the presentation of the King.

Segar, William. Signed the Articles. A labourer of Sampford Courtenay. See Chap. VIII.

Sharke, John, a resident in Exeter. (Hoker, 75.)
Shere, John. In prison in the West 27 Sept., 1551. (P. C. Reg. III. 368.) One of this name had been Prior of Launceston.
Sloeman, John. Signed the Articles. See Chap. XIV.
Smyth, Robert, of Tregonack in St. Germans. See Chap. VI.
Taylor, Richard, a clothier of Exeter. (Hoker, 73.)
Tompson, John, priest. Signed the Articles. See Chap. XIV. Burnet says he was executed.
Tredynnyck, Henry. Pardoned by the Lord Privy Seal. (P. C. Reg. III. 222.)
Tredynnyck, William. As above.
Underhill, Thomas. Signed the Articles. See Chap. XIV. Hoker (p. 66) says he was a tailor at Sampford Courtenay. He was killed at the Battle of Sampford Courtenay.
Viell, William. Pardoned by the Lord Privy Seal. (P. C. Reg. III. 222.)
Vincent, John, a resident in Exeter. (Hoker, 75.)
Whettell, Robert. Pardoned by the Lord Privy Seal. (P. C. Reg. III. 222.)
Wolcot, John, a merchant of Exeter. (Hoker, 72.)
Wykes, William, of Bridgewater. See Chap. XX.

The following churches in Devon and Cornwall had new incumbents instituted shortly after the insurrection, some of their predecessors *may* have been rebels. The notes are chiefly taken from the Episcopal Registers as I glanced through them.

Brampford Speke. Richard Harris was admitted 14 July, 1540, on the presentation of Dr. Thomas Brerewood. William Mogrigge was admitted 26 April, 1550, on the presentation of the King.
Clyst St. George. Nicholas Smale who was rector in 1536 died about this time : his Inq. p. m. is 4 Edw. VI.
Eggesford. Walter Williams was admitted in 1548 : he was succeeded by Bartholomew Cowd in 1549.
High Bray. Walter Bowen was admitted in 1539, on the presentation of John Moreman and others. Robert Derche was admitted 29 July, 1550, to the living then vacant.

St. Austell and St. Blazey. Michael Nichols was admitted on 29 Oct., 1547. John Bridgewater was admitted on 2 Apr., 1550, to the vicarage now vacant, on the presentation of the King.

St. Wennap. Thomas Bosythyow was admitted in 1538. John Kendall was admitted 27 Apr., 1550, on the presentation of the Dean and Chapter.

There were also changes in 1550 at St. Columb Major (where an important branch of the Arundells lived), Brent, and Withiel.

APPENDIX M

The references to the " Commotion Time " in local contemporary records are very numerous, so that only brief extracts can be given here. The first group is from the Lists of Church Goods made in 1552 and still preserved in the Guildhall of Exeter and refer to certain churches in that city. The letter enclosing copies sent to London by Sir Peter Carew, Sir Gawen Carew, and Anthony Harvey concludes with these words : " And thus not thinking it vnmet to give yo^u inteligence that in thexaminaçon of this commission we haue founde the people vearie quyet and conformable and ioyfull that thei haue wherwith to encrease the Kings ^{M}a^{ties} Treasure, we leave any farder to trouble yo^u .... ffrom Execeter the xvj^{ti} of June, 1553." [1]

St. Kerian. Thomas Grigg and Thomas Stonye . . . depose y^t of their church goods y^r is nothing remoued save onelie a pyx of silu and gilt which was sold by the parishioners for reṗaçon of the church in ye comocion tyme.

St. Lawrence. William Pety deposeth y^t afore ye late comocion Richard Hert & Sr Spring curate of the same parishe and Thomas Walter wardeyn caried out of ye church to ye said Ric. Herts house being wardeyn, and delyuered the jewels to Michael Germayn, Save onelie S. George on horseback of silu masse two Apostles a pyxe of silu, all togeth weyeng by estmaçon vj uncs wch remayned at ye said Ric herts. . . .

St. Mary Arches. Thomas Grau and Harry Anderson .. saie .. y^t a shipp, a censo^r and a spone of silu was sold

[1] Stowe MSS. No. 141, f. 54.

in ye coṁcion tyme for relief of ye poore whan ye citie
was besieged.

St. Olave. (S. Tooley & S. Tolows) M^d John Thoker warden
in a° iij° Edwardi vj° soled by the consent of the ᵱisshe
a sence & a shippe of silũ wayenge xxxvij^to vnces at
iiij^s vij^d the vnce sum viij^li xj^s x^d. The wch was sollde
for the Relyve of the power in ye cõmotion tyme.

St. Davids Downe. . . At the cõmossyng tyme ou^r church was
robyd, & toke all frome vs & that y^s now yn the Church
was bofft of a newe.

. . . before ye comocun tyme all the foure alter clothes
two payre of Vestiments Surples, etc, were stollen from
them & els nothing & now have thei no more but one
chalice as is aforesaide.

St. Edmunds . . . Nicholas Cove toke awaye ffrom the [church
in the] commocyon [tyme] a cross of Silũ weyng by
estymãcon xxx^ti ounces. Itm̄ one chalyce wayeng cij
vnces. It. A shipp a Censo^r & a payr of cruetts & a
spone & a paxe all Sylũ wayng by estymãcon xx^ti vnces.

Thomas Westcote . . . deposeth y^t ye saide Inventory
was taken awai out of his house in the comocion tyme
while he served with the Citie.

. . . . The saide Thomas Westcote and Nicholas Cove
. . . depose that immediatelie upon y^e openyng of y^e
gates of y^e Citie the same two deponents hearing y^t the
saide plate was shifted from house to house by the Rebells
went thither and toke it and devyded the same betwene
them ech one having xliiij unces for thei confesse y^t y^e_r
whole weight of the said plate was lxxxviij unces, moreo^
y^t as thei have allwai pro [   ] for y^e saide plate even
so do thei offer [   ] to y^e determynacon of y^e Kings
ma^tie and (honor)able counsaill concernyng y^e saide plate
. . . . one Harry Wyat of y^e Parishe of St. Thomas
beyonde Exbridge . . . deposeth y^t whereas he is
reported to have rec^d of the clark of St. Edmunds a
chalice, the said deponent never received chalice of y^e
said clark or of anye o^r man. Nevertheless this deponent affirmeth y^t he himself found a chalice under his
owne bed at the comocion tyme at ye comyng of ye King's
Armie wh^ch chalice he delyvered to Jhon Cove of ye saide

parishe of St. Thomas and Robert Tuckfielde Priest dyd masse with ye saide chalice which priest can tell where we sett it. And whether the saide chalice belonged to ye church of St. Edmunds or no this deponent canot tell but y^t he supposeth it belonged to St. Thomas parishe.

St. George. Thomas Hancock and John .... Churchwardeyns ... depose .. that at ye Comocion tyme and ye besieging of ye citie, y^r were sold allmost xx vncs of oú plate for ye relief of the poore.

Allhalowes Goldsmyth Strete. Geffray Arundel and Richard Prestwood Churchwardens ... saie y^t at ye comocion tyme there was in ye church another chalice but ye same was sold to Thomas Richardson Apotecary to paye souldyers waiges when the citie was besieged.

St. Sidwell. Richard Hutchins and William Harrys ... depose y^t thei have no vestiments left and y^t all were stollen awaye in ye comocon tyme and that ye Cath. Church geven them an old payre of vestiments.

.. thei depose y^t thei have but one bell and that thre bells were taken awaye by Bernharth Duffelde. .... one William Slocum of ye same parishe ... confesseth y^t he had in keping the foote of a crosse a fayre foote of sylver weyeing by estimacon xl unces which foote this deponent delivered to Thomas Chapel and the saide chalice to Richard Lake servaunt to Mr. Anthony Harvy. This deponent affirmeth also y^t ye saide foote was taken awaie afterwards by Mr. Jhon Buller and Richard Wallys sometyme porter of Eastgate. And as farre as this deponent doth know Sir Roger Blewet Knight had it ffor so the said Sir Roger Blewet himself confessed to Mr. Blackaller and others. Which thing Thomas Chapel of St. Stevens parishe also witnessed before ye aforesaide commissioners when he was deposed.[1]

---

[1] In another copy of the certificate preserved at the Guildhall we read: A challis whiche Willm̄ Slocū delyūd for the kinges vse to be kepte to one Richard Lake at the Commotion tyme seruant to Mr Anthony Hervey: wch he doth kepe vntill y^s tyme. Itm̄ A fote of a Crosse whiche the foresaid Willm̄ Slocū delyūed to thomas chappell the same daye that my lorde came in to exeter at the comōtion tyme: whiche was taken frome the said thomas by the hands of master buller then Capten of the estgate: and Richard Wallys wch the same goods doth remayne in the hands of Syr Roger bluet knight vntill this tyme.

Alyce Rogers of ye aforesaide parishe of St. Sidwells . .
deposeth y^t a crosse of sylver a chalice a shippe a censor
and a sylver spoone as her husband sayed was taken out
of her house by Mr. Walter Rawley Jhon Stowell and
Edward Senbarbe upon the entrie of the Lord Lieutenant
in to ye Citie of Exeter at ye comocion when ye rebells
were fled from the Citie. Jhon Rydge of St. Sidwells . .
testifieth that he was willed by Mr. Rawley and Jhon
Stowell to cary ye saide plate downe to the said Stowells
house and y^t he this deponent saw ye saide crosse y^e
chalice and ye censor ye same time and y^t y^r were caried
twoo burthens of stuff whereof y^r deponent can not tell
what ye rest was . . . . .[1]
As for ye vestiments of the saide parish William Worth . .
doth testifie y^t when the deponent came to Mr. Rawley
in St. Peters Church desyring him y^t ye parishe of S.
Sidwells might have ye best cope of cloth of Tyssue worth
xx (shillings ?) the saide Mr. Rawley answered y^t yf it were
not cut allready for the sparver of a bed thei shulde have
it. . . . Thomas Coliforde of Colompton witnesseth y^t when
Mr. Rawley and he w^t ye o^r soferers being delivered dyd
entre in to ye citie y^r came in on Stoyle of St. Sidwells
parish.
Mem. Y^t 7 November Ric. Lake appearing before us for
ye said chalys deposeth and we have good recorde of the
same y^t ye said Ric. serving the Kings ma^{tie} w^{t}in ye citie
of Exeter at ye tyme of ye late comocon and being destitute
at ye orderyn of ye citie went out among ye Rebells and
by virtue of y^e ꝓclamacen toke ye chalys wch he found
among them and so wold he have done (illegible) he might
have gotten it.
Mem. At ye comocon tyme ye church was spoyled
of all things movable in a man^r save onelie a pix
a paten and two cruetts and four bells whereof one
Bernhard Duffield toke thre awai wch he hath not restored
neyth^r can we tell where to have them. . . . . As for y^e
fote of ye crosse y^t S. Rog^r Blewet had for asmuch as we
can not come by him o^r humble desyre is y^t he may be

---

[1] The certificate gives a long list of goods taken by Mr. Rawley, Edward
Senbarbe, and John Stowell.

charged w^{t}all and y^t it maye be required of him for we are
sure y^t he had it.

St. Pancras. Harry Harrys Churchwarden . . saieth . . y^t y^r
was (a censer) and shipp wayeng xxix vncs and y^e (w^{ch}
was sold in) the cõmocion tyme for ye reteyning of y^e
(soldiers ?) . . y^r was likewise another chalice, weyeng
xvj vnces and y^t the same was in ye custody of one Richard
Lymbeare, on of the saide parishe, who saith y^t was stollen,
where he bestowed it at the last comocion, as he the said
Richard will make furth^r informacon therof. And y^t y^r
is gone in like mañ a pix of silū whyte weyeng xiiij vncs,
at ye same tyme and likewise a pax weyeng fyve vncs
stollen out of the custodie of the saide Richard. The said
Richard Lymbeer . . deposed y^t ye said plate namelie a
chalice, a pyx and a pax were stollen frō him at ye late
cõmocion. And . . . . Mr Jhon Blackaller (and others
deposed that they believed Lymbeare) and y^t the said
plate was stollen frō ye said Richard at ye cõmociõn tyme,
being hyd in a garden, where more was stollen then yt.

Inventory . . A ship and a sencer white wayeng oncs
xxix the whyche was sold at the last Comocyon for the
defence of the rebelles and ayde for ou^r Soldears at that
tyme bestowed.

St. John's Bow. Robert Chaffe and Richard Taylor Churchwardens . . saye y^t their plate weyeth an hundreth
fiftie and sixe vnces, besides a pyx of ix vnces which was
sold in ye comocion tyme for relyef of ye poore whē the
citie was besieged, & for mendyng the Clock.

Inventory . . a pyx of syllver and gyllte, wayenge six
vnces the wch lyeth in gage for xls, whereof xxxiiij^s iiij^d
was geven to poore people in the tyme of comocion when
the gates were shutte and v^s viij^d was payd for mendyng
of the clock.

St. Stephen.

a chales weyng by estimacon xv oncs or ther abowt was
taken from s^d clarke in the comoscion tyme after mi lorde
of bedford came in to the Cettie by a Welchman who
went in to the church & lockyd the clark in the church
. . . . & went away w^t the chales.

Inventory . . a Chalice waying by estymacon xv vnces was

taken from the Clarke of the saide ₚysshe yn the comocion tyme after the intryng of the ryght honorable John Erle of Bedford leiutenute of the kyngs ma^ties armye yn the Weste ₚte by a Walsheman, who came yn to the Churche and loked the saide clarke yn the same Churche the same tyme.[1]

The following references are to be found in the return of Church Goods for other parishes in Devon.[2]

Tavistock . . . . for certen plate & vestyments the value of xl^l xvij^s j^d ẘof they paid for the charge of xx men to serue the Kyngs maj^tie in the cõmocyon tyme xiij^li vj^s viij^d. and they bestowed towards the repraccon of a certen bridge called Neubridge xiij^li vj^s viij^d. . .

Dawlish. Ǫne Crosse of sylũ one sence of Sylũ one Shippe of Sylũ ij cruettes of sylũ one cope of grene vellett specified in the last certificath which was taken away from the seid ₚisshens yn the cõmocyon tyme by one John Stowell of Exeter now deceased. His wief a very poure woman which maᵗ is also reserved to the Kyngs ma^ti Councell.

East Budleigh . . one Crosse of Sylũ was sold by the said ₚisshens . . . . for xlv^li whereof they gave to Mr Duke xxv^li towards the makyng of the seid haven of Ottermouth and with the rest they bought a pece of ordyn^ance called a Slyng̃ for the defence of the Country their, which cost xx^li and the same pece of ordyn^ance is nowe in the Custody of the maire of exeter.

Modbury . . . iij Chalices of Sylũ one sence of Sylũ one spone of Sylũ too Candelsticks of sylũ which Juells were sold by Sr Arthur Champnon knyght for his necessitie in the Comocyon tyme to serue the kyngs ma^tie.

Heavitree. One Crosse of Sylũ the value of xvij^li which Crosse was delyũyd to one John Coker of Exeter savely

---

[1] The above are copied from the originals in the Guildhall, Press HH 8. Several of them have been printed in the third, fourth, and fifth volumes of " Notes and Gleanings," but not quite correctly.

[2] These are preserved at the P. R. O. Church Goods, Devon, ²⁄₇ et seq. They were transcribed by Mackenzie Walcott and printed in the Transactions of the Exeter Diocesan Architectural Society, 2nd Series, II. 270 et seq., but the originals are copied here.

to be kept to the vse of the seid ꝑisshens & one Barnard
Dovell yn the Comocyn tyme toke by force the seid Crosse
from the seid John Coker and doth reteyn the same & the
seid Dovell nowe remayneth in Ward yn the kynges ma^{tie}
bynch for dett.

Ashburton. . Too Chalices one pixe of Sylu̇ omitted in the
last certificath was sold by the ꝑishens att the Cõmocyon
tyme for x^{li} with the which mony they seruyd the kyngs
ma^{tie} ayenst the rebells for the preseruacon of the Townnys
of Tottenes & Plymmouth by the cõmonndment of the lord
of Bedford. . .

INDEX

ABEVAN, Gulphinus, 23
A Leigh, Thomas, 355, 380, 497
Alley, Roger, 416, 420
Alley, William, Bishop of Exeter, 382, 420
Alsa, William, 104, 497
Amadas, John, 85n.
Amadas, Mistress, 181n.
Amys, William, 85, 88, 424
Andover, 238n.
Answers to Western Rebels, Cranmer's, 222; King's, 214; Somerset's, 218, 433
Answer by Western Rebels, 215, 406, 441
Apowon, —, 299, 408
Aphowell, Fulk, 58, 59
Article of Baptism, 163, 434
Articles of Norfolk Rebels, 224; of Pilgrimage of Grace, 6, 11, 13, 18, 224; of Western Rebels, 126, 185, 211–231, 473, 492
Arundell, Humphrey, 18; his wife and family, 98–100; leads rebels, 139; advances to Crediton 184; besieges Exeter, 208; signs articles, 219; attacks Russell at Sampford Courtenay, 298; escapes to Launceston, 299; captured, 301; sent to London, 340; tried, 347; executed, 349; property granted to Carew, 380
Arundel, Sir John, 155n., 432, 497; accused, 237; imprisoned, 351; released, 355
Arundell, Sir Thomas, 26, 41, 155n., 343n.; accused, 351; executed, 354
Arundell, Thomas, 83
Ashe, John, 102
Ashridge, —, 186, 497
Ashridge, North Tawton, 134
Aske, Robert, leads Northern Rebellion, 9; goes to London, 14; returns to Doncaster, 14; tried, 15; executed, 17

Audeley, Thomas, Lord Chancellor 4, 67
Aylesbeare Common, 264n., 265n.

BALLADS on Rebellion, 335
Ballamey, Peter, 497
Bampton, 304
Barclay, Alexander, 26n.
Baret, Nicholas, 101, 497
Baret, Roger, 101n., 185, 222, 355n., 473, 475, 494, 497
Barnstaple, 376
Barnstaple, Archdeaconry of, 60, 68n., 72, 415
Barrow, John, 104, 497
Barteville, John, 354
Basset, Gregory, friar, 175n., 178n., 179
Bath, 318
Battles or affrays, at Carey's Windmill, 266; Clyst St. Mary, 268; Crediton, 143; Fenny Bridges, 255; Kings Weston, 305; Launceston, 299; Sampford Courtenay, 297
Bechamp, John, 85n., 151
Becket Gilbert, 24n, 25, 101n.
Becket, Roger, 24, 101n.
Beckington, 318
Bedyll, Thomas, 172, 415, 416
Bells confiscated, 372
Benet, Richard, 104, 497; Thomas, 108
Bennet, alias Dusgate, Thomas, 178
Bere, William, 84n.
Berkshire, 97n., 139, 234, 262
Berrynarbor, 102n.
Berry Pomeroy, 103
Berthelet, Thomas, 429
Bickleigh, 304
Bicton, 148
Bishop's Clyst, 271n.

2 L

518

INDEX

THE END

/ 𝒍 𝒍

PRINTED BY WILLIAM CLOWES AND SONS, LIMITED, LONDON AND BECCLES.

WS - #0033 - 220822 - C0 - 229/152/29 - PB - 9780282764562 - Gloss Lamination